PC
MAGAZINE

Webmaster's
Ultimate
Resource
Guide

Webmaster's Ultimate Resource Guide

Ziff-Davis Press
An imprint of Macmillan
Computer Publishing USA
Emeryville, California

Jason Wehling, Robert McDaniel,
Mark Hall, Wayne Ause, David Pearce,
Phyllis A. Huster, and Shel Kimen

Publisher	Stacy Hiquet
Acquisitions Editor	Kelly Green
Development Editor	Kimberly Ann Haglund
Copy Editor	Kimberly Ann Haglund and Aidan Wylde
Technical Reviewer	Judy Berck and Mark Brownstein
Project Coordinator	Ami Knox
Proofreaders	Jeff Barrash, Joe Sadusky, Vanessa Miller
Cover Illustration and Design	Megan Gandt
Book Design	Laura Lamar/MAX, San Francisco
Word Processing	Howard Blechman
Page Layout	Janet Piercy
Indexer	Valerie Robbins

Ziff-Davis Press imprint books are produced on a Macintosh computer system with the following applications: FrameMaker®, Microsoft® Word, QuarkXPress®, Adobe Illustrator®, Adobe Photoshop®, Adobe Streamline™, MacLink® *Plus*, Aldus® FreeHand™, Collage Plus™.

Ziff-Davis Press, an imprint of
Macmillan Computer Publishing USA
5903 Christie Avenue
Emeryville, CA 94608

ISBN 1-56276-435-7

Manufactured in the United States of America
10 9 8 7 6 5 4 3 2 1

ABOUT THE AUTHORS

Jason Wehling is a freelance writer from Portland, Oregon. He creates and maintains Web pages through Midnight Madness, a Web page design company. He has also written articles on Internet-related subjects for a variety of newspapers and magazines around the world. Jason is author of *Late Night Advanced Java Programming*, published by Ziff-Davis Press in Fall 1996.

Robert McDaniel is Manager of Technical Operations for The Palace, a company that makes software for visiting and creating virtual worlds on the Internet.

Mark Hall has been in the computer consulting business for the past 13 years, and is presently a computer consultant supervisor for the Community Colleges of Spokane. He has a BA and Masters degree in Computer Science Education, and teaches part-time at Eastern Washington University. Mark has also worked as a technical editor on 47 book titles.

Wayne Ause is a writer, Web page creator, graphic artist, father, gardener, and Internet surfer in Portland, Oregon. Wayne is the sole proprietor of a Web consulting agency, Koala Web Design. Wayne's most recent book is *How to Use the World Wide Web*, co-authored with Scott Arpajian (Ziff-Davis Press, 1996), and he is also the author of *Instant Web Pages* (Ziff-Davis Press, 1995). Wayne can be reached via e-mail at wause@koalaweb.com, or you can visit Wayne's Koala Web Design Web site at http://www.koalaweb.com/.

David Pearce works at *HotWired* and is also a freelance writer for various Internet-related publications. Past Projects include articles for *The Net* magazine, the 24 Hours in Cyberspace project, and Microsoft's "Where Do You Want To Go Today" TV ad campaign.

Phyllis Huster has been working with Internet technology for over 10 years. She studied Computer Science at Georgia Institute of Technology. In 1995 she began an Internet company that patented sending and receiving faxes and voice mail via the Internet. Currently Phyllis is President of IntraNet Solutions in Atlanta, and is working with large bell operating companies and several fortune 500 companies to incorporate Internet computer telephony and unified messaging into enterprise-wide Intranets. She can be reached via e-mail at phyllis@intranetsolutions.com.

Shel Kimen is an independent 3-D projects consultant and professional writer in Northern California. She wrote her first computer program in 1980 at age 9, when she brilliantly flashed the word *go* on the screen 25 times. She is also a contributing editor and columnist for several technology magazines, and spends too much of her time trying to convince the world that VRML is good, closed architecture systems are bad, and information should be free. Read her words in *The Net* magazine, *Boot, MacAddict*, and on several Web sites. Send thought provoking e-mail to kimen@well.com.

CONTENTS AT A GLANCE

CONTENTS AT A GLANCE

TABLE OF CONTENTS

CONTENTS AT A GLANCE

TABLE OF CONTENTS

TABLE OF CONTENTS

TABLE OF CONTENTS

TABLE OF CONTENTS

TABLE OF CONTENTS

TABLE OF CONTENTS

TABLE OF CONTENTS

TABLE OF CONTENTS

TABLE OF CONTENTS

TABLE OF CONTENTS

TABLE OF CONTENTS

ACKNOWLEDGMENTS

Jason Wehling: As with any project, more people made a valuable contribution than those whose names appear on the front cover; this book is no exception. Unfortunately, there are a battery of these people will have to remain nameless because their names are unknown to me. These include computer system folks that solved many of the software compatibility problems that are inherent to projects such as this. The production people that made the book look attractive also deserve mention.

Technical editors are people that make sure that the facts and figures that are presented to you the reader are actually true. The responsibility for this important task was carried by Judy Berck and Mark Brownstein. As much as you might know a subject, when you write large portions of a book, you end up saying the darnest things. Often chapters come back to the authors and you wonder how you could have wrote what you did. It was Judy and Mark that helped to catch the silly mistakes that are inevitable.

Special praise must be given to the person that brought continuity and style to this project: Development Editor Kimberley Haglund. She is really responsible for making this book as readable as it is. Most computer-related books read more like math manuals; Kim pushed the authors to add a little humor and finesse to our writing. If you find yourself smiling at any point during your journey through this book, think of Kim's hard work.

The idea for this project was brought to life by the Acquisitions Editor, Kelly Green. She built the outline for this book and spent the time to find the contributing authors, which is no easy task. Kelly was a pleasure to work with and was always supportive and helpful throughout.

Having experienced the writing process myself — as clichéd as this sounds — I have to say that the support of friends and family was extremely important. Writing anything, especially a full-length book, isn't like a regular job where you work 9 to 5. Writing is a battle wrought with fits and spurts of inspiration, often followed by unexpectedly long periods of unproductive paralysis. The stress inherent in this type of situation unfortunately is borne by those closest to you and they deserve appreciation.

Robert McDaniel: As always, I would like to thank my wife Vonda for supporting me in this project. I would also like to thank Kelly Green and Kim Haglund for their help and guidance. Finally, a big thanks to all the software companies who provided their information and answered my questions in a most timely manner.

ACKNOWLEDGMENTS

Mark Hall: Thanks goes to Kelly Green for having the confidence in my abilities and encouraging me when my light was dim. Kim Haglund deserves a gold metal for patience, insight, and thoroughness. I would also like to thank my family Lori, Ashton, and Tony for putting up with me when I copped an attitude. Kudos goes to the Briley Bed and Breakfest for providing a private room in which to bang my head against the wall. And the most important aspect of all is that my daughter, Ashton, can now proudly say "My daddy's an author".

Wayne Ause: First, I would like to thank Kimberly Ann Haglund for her insights, careful editing, and tireless efforts in bringing this book to completion. I would also like to thank everyone at Ziff-Davis Press who contributed to this effort, as well as for inviting me to the party. It's an honor to be included with this project's impressive list of contributing authors.

I would also like to acknowledge the help of my friends and associates in this effort, especially assistance from Lenny Charnoff, Geoffrey Kleinman, Thomas Young, Kristina Olson, and Michael Corning. I would also like to thank the thousands of people who helped me without even knowing it just by contributing helpful information and resources to the Internet. And, of course, I wish to thank my wife Kendra Hogue for her limitless faith and love, and my son Carter for drawing crayon squigglys all over my manuscript copies.

Shel Kimen: Shel wishes to thank Mark Pesce, Tony Parisi, Scott Fraize, Megan McFeely, David Frerichs, Kevin Hartz, and Tom Meyer.

David Pearce: David would like to thank Kim Haglund for her patience and discerning knife as an editor, Kelly Green at Ziff-Davis Press, Priti Khare of NetObjects, and Rebecca Michals of Adobe Systems, Inc.

INTRODUCTION

THE INTERNET is an ever-evolving and exciting environment. People from all over the world interact in ways not thought possible even a decade ago. A computer network has now become a rival to the old-guard mass media—it is now possible to communicate with and provide information to millions of people without owning your own TV network, magazine, or newspaper. All it takes is a little know-how, a computer, and a connection to the Internet.

The Internet has been around since the 1960s and has been evolving ever since. Up until fairly recently, cyberspace has remained inaccessible to most people because of the technical knowledge curve that was necessary to use it. As popular as e-mail and Usenet were (and still are), it was the advent of a hypertext medium—namely the World Wide Web—that brought the power of the Internet to anyone that could point and click a mouse.

This book is for those who want to harness this incredible technology. Providing information on the Web is not difficult, but it does take some skill and knowledge. The following chapters provide you with a road map to what you'll need to create and maintain the best, most up-to-date Internet presence around. This book spells out plainly what kinds of things you'll need to start or improve your own Web site, from hardware to software to services.

Every topic — from servers to Java tools — is discussed at length in the chapters that make up the first half of the book; the corresponding appendixes provide in-depth comparisons of individual products. Interested in e-mail applications? The chapter explores the standard protocols and various features available; the appendix lists e-mail applications and their accompanying features. There's no need to read through thousands of pages of company hype: This book offers straightforward, unbiased, and useful information for Webmasters, developers, and programmers. This information is vital to anyone currently working on the Web, or those that are interested in starting.

For those that are new to the Web, this book provides a valuable introduction to the mountains of cyber-jargon. What on earth is Java all about, and do I need to know about it? What is VRML and where do I find out more about it? What's the difference between serial, PPP, and ISDN connections? What will a video card do for me? What on earth does WYSIWYG mean? The answers to these questions (and many more) await inside.

The chapters within also provide important information for Web veterans. Who has the time to research 30 different products — we've done it all for you. I know the difference between POP and MAPI e-mail service, but which e-mail application is best? How does PageMill rate against other HTML authoring tools? I know what plug-ins are, but where can I get information on how to build my own? Turn the page to find all the answers.

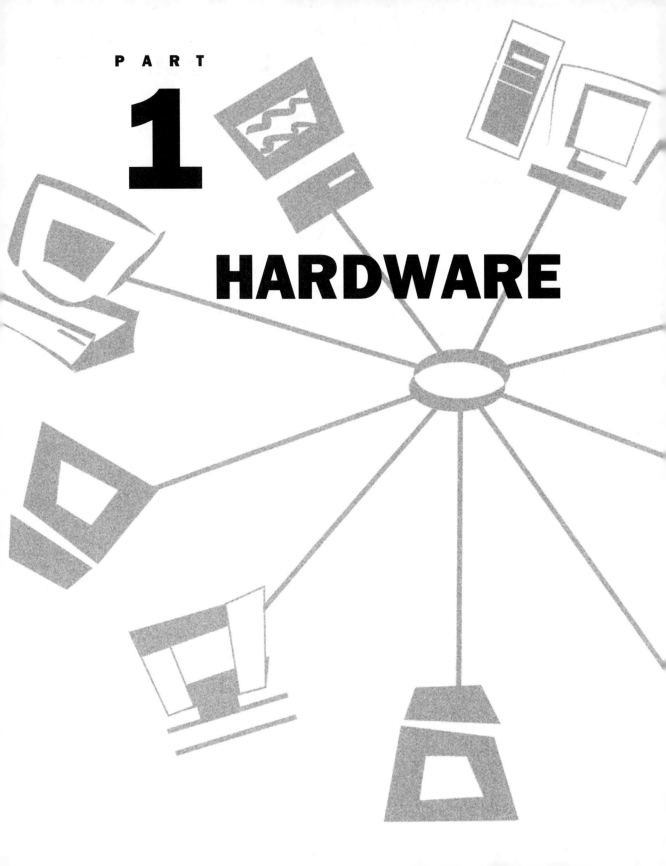

P A R T

1

HARDWARE

Choosing the Right Server Platform

Access Technologies

Graphics Hardware

Sound Cards

CHAPTER

1

CHOOSING THE RIGHT SERVER PLATFORM

AS THE INTERNET rapidly evolves into the next publishing frontier, hundreds of thousands of businesses with something to say to the world are seeking affordable ways to enter this new electronic medium—above all, by publishing on the World Wide Web. Launching a Web site is one of the most popular things to do on the Internet today. The Web can be many things to you or your organization, including an inexpensive worldwide marketing vehicle, a means of distributing software, or even a database front-end to your personal or corporate mainframes.

CHOOSING THE RIGHT SERVER PLATFORM

MORE BUSINESSES ARE finding the Web's productivity implications so attractive that they're buying servers solely for internal information delivery, rather that making them available to the rest of the public. These types of servers are referred to as Intranets and they allow businesses to share confidential information, without the threat of the entire World Wide Web having access.

Whatever your plans are for getting on the Web, your first step in making your Web plan work is to buy the right hardware and software. Since your server platform interprets incoming requests and delivers the requested services to your users your full attention should be given to selecting a hardware and software combination which will provide fast and reliable service to your users. A successful Web site is one which is capable of storing your content and performing your services without slowing down other processes necessary to other users or services on your server. Your deployment plan should include provisions for worst-case scenarios in both performance and capacity planning.

In this chapter, we will present you with information about turnkey Web servers and build-your-own solutions. After you have analyzed your needs for service and user customization, your decision to either purchase a turnkey system or build your own should be very clear. For more information about the pros and cons of each solution, read on!

What a Server Does

A server platform consists of two essential elements: the hardware (processor, RAM memory, hard drive, network card, tape backup, monitor, keyboard, and video card) and an operating system (Macintosh, Microsoft NT, Novell, or Unix). There are, of course, many other components of a server platform, such as Web management software and home page development tools, but our focus in the first section of this chapter will be to describe and analyze hardware topics which will help you decide whether to purchase a turnkey system or build your own.

Since the most important decision you will make in your quest for Webmaster longevity is your Web server platform, your full attention should be given to this topic right now, although there are many other things you will eventually worry about. Your server hardware decision will dictate future choices about Web management software, Web creation tools, browser compatibility, hardware support, and future upgrade paths in both hardware and software.

What to Look for in a Server

There's a wide spectrum of options for establishing a Web site, from farming the whole process out to consultants and service providers to buying a turnkey server setup to assembling the necessary hardware and software and building a site yourself. But is the do-it-yourself approach feasible for

CHOOSING THE RIGHT SERVER PLATFORM

non-experts? And if it is feasible, what's the most advantageous platform to do it on? These questions and more will be covered in the section "Building Your Own Platform."

A couple of years ago, building and maintaining a Web presence required a lot of technical expertise. The only servers available ran on Unix; if your business was not already Unix-savvy, you had to make a major investment in time and resources just to get into the game.

Today, servers are available for many platforms, and hardware/software vendor solutions put server setup and management well within the reach of those with only modest technical knowledge. You'll still have to do it yourself as far as building appealing content goes, but today's turnkey server solutions help you focus on that task by hiding the intricacies of server management behind clever setups and intuitive configuration interfaces.

As part of your decision you must also evaluate your access needs carefully. If you plan on only supporting five concurrent users for the duration of your service, your hardware decision will be much different than a person who plans on supporting 100 concurrent users. The underlying message here is that you must plan your decision based on the maximum number of users you intend to service. A platform decision that is underpowered will leave you wishing for more. The best plan of attack here is to project your needs for the long term, since it is less expensive to buy more horsepower up front, not to mention the time and hair-pulling you can avoid by not having to bring down your service to upgrade your platform later.

The following sections discuss things to consider when choosing a server platform, be it a turnkey solution or something of your own creation. Our goal in this overview of features is to make you aware of major areas you should focus on. Specific comparison of features of the various systems can be found in the charts in Appendix A.

Usability

Ease of use should be by far the most important factor in your buying decision, surpassing even performance. The less trouble you have with the interface, the more successful you'll be at implementing new ideas and content down the road. NT solutions are obviously the cleanest fit for most offices familiar with the Windows environment, and Macintosh solutions are the obvious choice for Macintosh users. But don't judge a server based only on the operating system. Rather, the server configuration and management tools often make or break a turnkey server.

To install a Web server, you need to supply information such as the name of the server, IP address, the server's network port, and the top-level or "root" directory where the HTML files will reside. While this information is generally stored in text configuration files, most servers provide

CHOOSING THE RIGHT SERVER PLATFORM

graphical tools to let you fill in the blanks where appropriate. Some Internet servers arrive preconfigured from the factory to shield users from the bare Unix command lines that make this level of server management difficult to administer.

Authoring Tools   Your Webmaster's work doesn't stop with user accounts and IP addresses. Administrators face the sometimes awesome task of authoring and maintaining content which may involve posting new HTML documents and modifying them as links change. As time passes, duties may include adding pages rich with graphics, audio, and video, or writing Common Gateway Interface (CGI) scripts and Java applets to give the site more attractive features. Evaluate your Web solution to ensure that these programming interfaces are available to you. If your decision leans towards more of a turnkey system, then programming interfaces might be too complex for your needs. However, if your goal is to give yourself programming access and flexibility to customized interfaces, then the use of tools such as CGI scripts will be a necessity.

CGI scripts are especially handy because they enable your Web server software to access other applications, such as databases, and generate HTML pages on the fly based on user queries. If you're calling on external applications, however, you'll need a sound working knowledge of the operating system. On top of that, database vendors charge by the license, and costs can vary somewhat based on the operating system.

Besides the amount of traffic, probably the biggest factor in determining how much maintenance your site will need is its size. A basic "store front" scenario with a few pages of information and links limited to other pages on your site can get by with almost no attention. On the other hand, sites with 75 to 100 HTML pages and 25 to 50 images require 10 to 20 hours per week of the typical administrator's attention. Of course, the more frequently you update content—a good idea if you're trying to generate attention on the Internet—the more maintenance you'll need to do. Even if your initial needs are modest, effective authoring tools help make your job easier.

Horsepower Considerations

As you might expect, your performance needs depend greatly on how many users you anticipate. Obviously, if you have a large company with a certain level of guaranteed traffic from established customers, your performance standards may be higher than those of someone buying a Web server for internal use in a small department. If you attach the server to the public Internet, the bandwidth of your connection plays a big role, but equally important is your success at garnering attention for your new site. It's difficult to predict your performance needs without knowing how many users you'll have, and without good performance, it's hard to gain

CHOOSING THE RIGHT SERVER PLATFORM

new users once your Web site is in place. Understanding which aspects of Web server hardware and software affect performance can help you make an informed buying decision in the face of this dilemma.

In a nutshell, Web server performance consists of providing a Web server connection to many remote clients, efficiently sending HTML documents and any related graphics to them, and disconnecting quickly when the clients no longer need the server. Many issues come into play in analyzing the performance of Web servers, including the performance of the hardware and the operating system; the speed of network or your Internet service provider's connections; and the efficiency of the Web server software in meeting multiple requests from clients.

Unfortunately, there are currently no industry-accepted standards or benchmarks to measure Web server performance. One way to examine performance, however, is in terms of pages served per hour. To that end, some tests used to measure server performance have been set up and run on NetWare LANs that are not connected to the Internet. Each system is configured to run on the LAN. Tests are then performed which continuously access HTML pages from each server, gradually increasing the number of test clients; this allows you to measure how many HTML pages the server could deliver per hour.

Since requests can be made much faster over the test network than through slower Internet connections, the test does not reflect the bandwidth constraints you'll face with a service provider. Furthermore, in the real world, requests generally come in bursts rather than the high constant levels of the tests referenced here. Therefore, rather than simulating typical usage, these tests give a sense of each server's performance potential in a worst-case scenario. Note that these specific results apply only to the specific LAN-based intranet configuration designed for the purposes of this discussion.

In determining Web performance, throughput is what counts. Your system's CPU is a less important factor than the amount of memory, the operating system, the disk subsystem, and the bus. While the processor does little more than pass the documents to clients, every connection requires a certain amount of memory. Therefore, there's a direct relationship between the amount of RAM in your system and the number of simultaneous users you can support. The more simultaneous users you can support, the more pages you can serve per hour.

If you're about to purchase your first Web server, you can get by with 16MB of RAM, but 32MB is a good rule of thumb. In fact, it's not uncommon for high-volume sites to provide as much as 128MB of RAM. Note that CPU horsepower begins to play a larger role as you add back-end applications that the server needs to execute on the fly. Applications launched through CGI or proprietary APIs such as Netscape's NSAPI

CHOOSING THE RIGHT SERVER PLATFORM

and Silicon Graphics's Open Inventor all require processor resources on the server itself.

System Documentation

Whether printed or electronic, there is wide diversity in documentation ranging from meager to confusing to good—no one's documentation right now is considered great or outstanding. Fortunately, unless you manage to lose the entire contents of your system and need to rebuild it from scratch, you should be able to configure and run your system with whatever documentation is provided. Also, don't be alarmed to find very little hard printed documentation for your Web server software. It is a de facto standard that Web server vendors provide their documentation on the Web. While this makes economical sense to the vendor, it can be a nightmare if your Web server is down and you cannot get access to your vendor's Web site. For this reason alone it is generally a good idea to print out as much hard printed documentation as you can for future reference.

A good reference book to supplement your system documentation is O'Reilly & Associates' *Managing Internet Information Services.* This noteworthy book is an excellent resource for gaining a deeper understanding of the inner workings of servers and their underlying technologies; it's also helpful if you want to add functionality.

Installation Variations

Since all out-of-the-box solutions have their own installation interfaces, you should evaluate each product to make sure the process is understandable to you. Very few systems today include a clear and easy-to-follow road map or checklist for setting up the system. Vendors typically expect you to purchase their solutions through a value-added reseller (VAR), who is normally responsible for helping you install and configure the system. Overall, today's solutions are easy enough to install that, with a few possible exceptions, most purchasers can probably get them set up, even without the assistance of a VAR, in an hour or less.

Your own solutions are hard to predict in the area of installation guidelines. Since you are responsible for determining the best hardware and software fit, you are also responsible for installing these systems independently from each other. In the area of hardware, typically there are very few guidelines in the box that address the area of customizing your installation. You will need to pick up a "how-to" textbook or consult a VAR for detailed hardware solutions. Software installation guides are usually a little more helpful because the financial success of the product relies on the hardware running it. Software support is also a little easier to obtain since there are definite standards for hardware platforms which can assist support personnel in diagnosing problems relating to hardware and software inconsistencies.

CHOOSING THE RIGHT SERVER PLATFORM

Security

System security (as opposed to transaction security, which covers the handling of credit card purchases and the like over the Internet) is of great interest to any Webmaster. The perils of security breaches are real: Anyone penetrating your networks may be able to access sensitive data. Or, if someone breaks into your system and modifies your content, you could be held liable for what goes out on the Web under your name.

You should be concerned about security on the Internet. It will be well worth the effort required to become thoroughly familiar with Internet security issues before you "go live" with your new system. For the vendors that work with them, VARs should be good resources for developing adequate security provisions for Web publishing operations.

Service and Support

Service and support is a crucial consideration for any PC purchase, but it's especially important with servers. You have to minimize downtime; regardless of your skill level, you should ensure that you have parts replacement and toll-free tech support for both software and hardware. In the case of turnkey systems, support will cover both the hardware and software. Vendors who offer turnkey systems have evaluated and installed what they determine to be the best combination of hardware and software. Since they have installed and recommended these combinations, they will know all of the problems and solutions to assist you in a timely fashion. These vendors will fully cover any technical questions concerning the interoperability of these systems, as long as you have not installed any additional hardware or software that they have not recommended. This is a large plus for users who are not technically capable of or interested in diagnosing hardware and software issues.

Users who choose to build their own solutions will have to diagnose interoperability issues with both hardware and software vendors. This process can be very frustrating and time-consuming since support technicians have no responsibility to ensure that other vendors' products work on their platform. In the support game, dissimilar vendors usually like to blame each other, so your role is to sometimes be a facilitator between the two parties. Our advice to you is to make sure when analyzing your purchases for a build-it-yourself system that the products you are assembling are supported by each other.

Other Technical Concerns

Several practical issues not directly related to the makeup of the vendors' product offerings will also have their impact on the success of your online publishing activities. First, make sure you have adequate bandwidth in your Internet connection to support the kind and volume of Web traffic you anticipate. A slow or unresponsive site can give you a bad reputation

CHOOSING THE RIGHT SERVER PLATFORM

on the Web, as users get exasperated while waiting for your pages to come up. If you ignore slow connectivity problems, your Web presence could hurt you more than help you.

Second, equip your server with as much memory as you can afford; this can make for a big performance improvement. Maximizing system RAM helps cache as many pages as possible, which in turn reduces dependency on the I/O subsystem's ability to handle high throughput.

If you're planning to run a search engine on your server, consider a computer system that supports multiple microprocessors—search engines gobble processor power. Finally, make sure to ask your VAR about upgrade costs and options. Can you add as many disks, as much memory, and as many CPUs as you want, or will you need more servers to expand and support your Web publishing presence?

Turnkey Solutions

Until recently, if you wanted a Web server, you had to put all the pieces together yourself. This process required you to become an expert with unfamiliar equipment and operating systems. While many of the first Web server software packages, such as versions of CERN and NCSA, were free, the hardware that ran them was expensive and cumbersome; furthermore, installing and managing a site required an in-depth understanding of Unix and its syntax. Since few companies supported any Web-related software, you had little choice but to hire a specialist. If the development of your server became too overwhelming for your specialist, you then had to call in big-gun Unix gurus who then gobbled up half of your profits with their exorbitant consulting fees.

As the Web rapidly becomes a necessity in today's business environments, administrators accustomed to the plug-and-play experience have demanded an alternative to the old system of outside programmers interpreting a business's needs and providing a hard-coded solution. A host of hardware and software vendors have gotten the message and have integrated all the pieces into turnkey solutions. These new, all-in-one servers include all the hardware and software you need right out of the box and are designed to let even non-Unix-savvy administrators get a site up and running in one day or even one hour without outside help.

To the rescue comes server software from almost every vendor imaginable. Your challenge is to sift through the hype and select a packaged system which best meets your needs and budget. Caution should be exercised to make sure that the systems you review are measured for ease of use, features, and performance. Thank goodness today's Unix servers mask arcane command lines, allowing you to benefit from the operating system's stability and performance without having to face its complexity daily. Along with better management tools and a trend away from Unix

CHOOSING THE RIGHT SERVER PLATFORM

command lines comes a shift from expensive RISC boxes to lower-cost hardware, including Pentiums and Macs.

Out-of-the-box Web servers today include all the hardware and software required to launch a Web site. These solutions include products from Apple Computer Corp., BBN Solutions & Technologies, Digital Equipment Corp., Intergraph Computer Systems, and Silicon Graphics.

These packages run the configuration gamut. The Digital and Intergraph units are NT servers running on Alpha and Pentium systems, respectively. The BBN server consists of a PC-compatible version of Unix running on a Pentium, and the server from Silicon Graphics is a full-fledged RISC box. The Mac server from Apple runs System 7. Three of the packages (Digital's, Intergraph's, and Silicon Graphics's) rely on Netscape server software, making site management fairly consistent within the group, especially given the number of new server solutions coming out every day. But all the systems take different approaches to network configuration, bundled software tools, and service and support.

The good news here is that you can pay, then plug and play, as little as $3,000 to $7,000. Of course, you can just as easily drop more than $17,000 on a higher-end system like Silicon Graphics's server.

Regardless of the platform, Netscape's Communications server software uses the same HTML forms for configuration and management; most of the time, you won't know whether you are managing a Unix or an NT server. This Web browser–based approach also means that you can manage your site over the Internet without even logging on to your LAN. Other remote-management clients are proprietary, such as the Mac-based versions for the Apple and BBN servers. The Apple tool makes it easy to monitor multiple servers, shut them down, and restrict access to specific users through passwords and IP addresses. The BBN client, on the other hand, is unable to monitor performance remotely or even start and stop the server using the management client.

Most of these turnkey servers provide little in the way of authoring tools, though most of them bundle at least one HTML editor. Some solutions are little more than bare-bones shareware while other tools are more graphical. There are some vendors who offer full-fledged authoring suites, which stand out as a combination authoring/serving platform.

Of course, thousands of tools are at your disposal on the Internet, and like word processors, choosing one is often due more to taste than to qualitative differences. Be advised, though, that the platform you choose defines, to a great extent, the available toolset. For example, if you go with Digital's Alpha-based server, you have only a small selection of native Alpha applications available to you; x86 applications must be run under NT's 286-emulation mode. You can always author content on another workstation if you don't want to work directly on the server. If you go that route, note that operating-system consistency can be beneficial. For example, NT's drive-sharing

CHOOSING THE RIGHT SERVER PLATFORM

capability with other NT and Windows for Workgroups systems is one easy method for posting new content from a remote machine.

These turnkey solutions also differ in the level of performance they offer. Since throughput is what counts, operating-system efficiency, bus architecture, and disk subsystem performance help explain the group's wide gaps in performance. For example, Apple's Internet Server 6150, which uses Macintosh's System 7 and NuBus, is simple to set up and attractively priced but is no match in performance for the NT and Unix systems.

Configuration Menus

The de facto standard for configuration menus within packaged systems is to use HTML forms to configure and manage the systems. This use of HTML forms to perform all system and server software configuration and management functions results in a tremendous reduction in the Unix proficiency required to manage and maintain these systems.

These graphical user interfaces guide Webmasters to system requirements, with lots of online help at their fingertips. Operating systems such as Windows NT provide graphical interfaces that make server management inherently easy. These Windows-based applications perform Unix system tasks—a definite improvement over the bare system prompt and command line which used to take a skilled, highly paid Unix programmer hours to program on a system.

These HTML forms are also designed to double-check your entries before implementing them. This is a major advantage over direct Unix data entry. Since Unix is very unforgiving, the simple addition of an extra space or the omission of a period can effectively bring down your service. And if having your service down is not enough, you then have to debug the system to find the syntax mistake. This needle-in-the-haystack search could take from five minutes to days to evaluate.

Security

The weakest aspect of all turnkey solutions is system security. Today's vendor approaches to security range from not visibly dealing with it to giving bad advice on how to manage your system. While all of the vendors make an effort to address security issues, none has created a solution that is a clear result of solid experience in dealing with Internet security.

Features

Vendors are putting an impressive range of functionality into their server solutions. While some vendors provide little beyond the HTTP server software and some server-management tools, others are true multipurpose Internet servers, offering FTP, Usenet news, and e-mail in addition to the Web. But attractive as this may seem, you should be cautious about loading too many functions on a single system, especially your Web server.

CHOOSING THE RIGHT SERVER PLATFORM

Some Internet services (particularly Usenet news and FTP) can be huge drains on system resources; this can affect your Web server performance and, through it, your accessibility on the Web. However much these "free goodies" may tempt you, try not to get carried away; use only the services you need and be prepared to move the resource hogs to another system.

Support for Hire

Although all of the vendors provide some level of support, most of the plans are anything but turnkey. Most companies offer an array of a la carte service options that you need to factor into your budget. These additional charges can jack up the cost of your server from a few hundred dollars to more than a thousand dollars per year. Considering that many users will also need to pay Internet service provider fees, these additional charges shouldn't be taken lightly. For example, some vendors provide a one-year warranty on the hardware, but software support costs may run an additional $750 to $1,120 per year. These support contracts are necessary if you intend on updating your software and having a lifeline in your times of crisis management. What you will find if you elect not to carry a service contract is that your requests for help are sometimes put on a hold queue where registered uses have priority over you. This delay in service will lead you to an early grave if your other phone lines are busy with disgruntled users wondering when the service will be restored. Our best advice here is to budget this yearly maintenance amount as part of your operating expenses.

Perhaps more than any other purchase you make this year, buying a Web server demands that you strike a delicate balance. In this case, it's between the features you can afford and your working knowledge of running a Web site—knowledge that you'll attain only after you buy.

Future Directions

Turnkey Web servers are hardly interchangeable. In fact, each emphasizes different aspects of launching a Web site, so deciding which server is right for you depends a lot on your operation's scope. You should look at your in-house personnel resources, the environment where you're planning to install the server, and your best usage estimate. And you need to decide whether you want your server to double as an authoring platform.

These servers mark the beginning of a trend toward usable, integrated solutions. More Windows server software is appearing every day, including Windows 95-compatible solutions, such as O'Reilly & Associates's WebSite, and forthcoming NT servers from the CompuServe Internet Division. CompuServe says it already has an agreement with Advanced Logic Research to bundle its Spry Web Server into a turnkey server, which is due out by now; the provider is in discussion with other system vendors. Meanwhile, Bill Gates recently announced that Microsoft's own

CHOOSING THE RIGHT SERVER PLATFORM

nascent Internet server technology will be integrated into a future version of NT itself.

Buying a Web server won't soon become as routine as buying a new set of workstations, but it's certainly no longer a mystery. The bottom line here is that vendors are putting in a real effort to build turnkey solutions that provide functional, reliable, easy-to-use Web servers. Since these products have not been simplified to be interchangeable and they differ in quality, you need to make a sound, educated purchase decision to make best use of your time, energy, and money for building your presence on the World Wide Web.

A ready-to-run hardware/software solution can get your Web publishing operation off the ground in no time. Your key to future success will be to ensure you have analyzed your needs and acquired the necessary products to support your ideal operating environment.

Building Your Own Platform

All of the ideas and concepts discussed in the previous sections apply here. What makes your decision to become a do-it-yourselfer tougher is that you are responsible for ensuring that all your decisions for hardware and software are compatible. While building your own platform solution offers lots of benefits such as complete control over customization and implementation, it does present issues involving multiproduct, multivendor coordination. Our most important recommendation on building your own platform is to make sure you have the technical experience to integrate the hardware and software. If you are a novice at software and hardware integration, don't make this project your first attempt.

Server Issues

After you have made the decision to build your own solution, your primary concern is what hardware server to purchase. Your Web management software and operating systems are also of primary concern so make sure your hardware platform (server) supports these options. Our goal in this section is to give you some guidance on selecting a hardware solution (server) and operating system. Charts are provided in Appendix A which compare Pentium- and Macintosh-based servers. While these charts do not include every conceivable vendor, they do compare most of the well known manufacturers. Use these charts as a guide when comparing features.

Keep in mind that your server is the foundation of your Web service. With this in mind, put a lot of thought and consideration into your choice and build the best, most reliable foundation you can. A server that will be an asset—not a liability—to your company must not only be a top-notch performer with enough bandwidth to service all of your clients efficiently,

CHOOSING THE RIGHT SERVER PLATFORM

it must also be secure, expandable, manageable, and fault-tolerant. File servers are no longer inconsequential boxes sitting in the back of your server room, cranking out files: They're mission-critical pieces of machinery that must service increasingly demanding clients 24 hours a day, seven days a week.

Most servers today are built to cater to specific environments. Server systems are available and well suited for handling from five to 1,000 demanding users. Your mission is to evaluate this hardware with your eyes open, and buy a system which will support your Web presence for a long period of time. With budgetary items always a determining factor you should get a total solution, not just a big, fast piece of hardware.

When evaluating your server options, features such as hot-swappable hard disks, fault tolerance, robust management software, ECC (error-correction code) memory, and a cutting-edge design that will grow with your network are indispensable elements.

The essential elements to look for are:

- *UPS (uninterruptible power supply)*. Look for a UPS that can support the server's power consumption for 20 minutes.

- *VGA display*. A 14- or 15-inch monitor is more than adequate for a file server.

- *4-mm DAT (digital audio tape) backup*. Capacity should meet or exceed disk subsystem capacity.

- *Quad-speed CD-ROM drive*. Install multiple drives for sharing data.

- *Lockable front panel*. You need this to protect your server against unauthorized access.

- *Hot-swappable hard disks*. These are essential for configuring the disk subsystem in a RAID array.

- *ECC RAM (error-correction code)*. To preserve data integrity, purchase error-correction code memory.

- *Power supply*. Make sure your wattage can handle a fully loaded configuration.

- *Minimum 100-MHz Pentium*. Your CPU should support a 66-MHz system bus.

- *PCI/EISA bus*. The server must have enough slots to handle all add-in devices.

CHOOSING THE RIGHT SERVER PLATFORM

Fault Tolerance

Here's a prediction: Your hard disk will fail. Following Murphy's Law, it will be exquisitely timed to go down at the worst possible moment. Your boss will not be interested in why it happened, nor in the four hours you'll need for restoration from backup tape. Fortunately, there are fault-tolerance options that you can build into your server purchase that will be able to minimize downtime and keep this scenario from playing out.

Hot-swappable disk subsystems, which allow you to remove and replace a failed disk without downing the server, are an appealing feature for your Web server. When coupled with some form of drive redundancy such as RAID (or Redundant Array of Inexpensive Disks), hot-swappable drives increase server up-time. Although this capability is a critical component, some vendors' implementations are better than others. For example, one vendor's solution features eight hot-swappable drive bays, and although this number is impressive, you must remove the server's casing to access the drives. This hampers access and can slow down disk replacement (a major problem for time-sensitive, mission-critical operations). Another vendor's implementation of hot-swappable drives are fully accessed in the front panel. Simply replace a drive and run a software utility to initialize the drive. This method of replacement is preferable. If you have to remove any casing or move the server, you always run the risk of bringing down your server. The whole point of hot-swappability is to prevent interruption of services to you or your users. The less fuss the better here.

In shopping for a mission-critical server with a large storage capacity, you should get to know RAID—a technique for combining several small disks into a single volume. You may be using a form of RAID, such as duplexing or mirroring, right now, but it may not be sufficient for your needs. RAID is categorized into different levels, each providing a different method of combining multiple disks and providing fault tolerance.

RAID Levels   RAID 0, otherwise known as *striping,* combines multiple disks into a single volume. Striping distributes data evenly across all hard disks, removing physical boundaries. Novell's NetWare provides software striping, but hardware striping with a RAID controller will provide faster performance. Striping can be done at either the bit or the byte level (RAID 2 and RAID 3, respectively). Most RAID systems, however, use block-level striping to complement the use of data blocks in a LAN environment (RAID 0, 1, 4, and 5). Striping disk arrays also has the advantage of creating a very fast volume, especially for continuous streams of data in multimedia applications.

RAID 5 provides the best protection for large volumes of critical data. Unlike duplexing, it uses parity information to provide data redundancy.

CHOOSING THE RIGHT SERVER PLATFORM

Parity is a method of providing the data protection of mirroring without the cost of mirroring each disk. No matter how many disks you stripe, you only need to keep one disk's worth of parity information to recreate lost data. RAID 5 distributes parity data across all hard disks, so in the event of a disk failure, the disk can be hot-swapped with no downtime.

External RAID Subsystems   If you need a large-capacity storage system, you will need more drive units—which will lower your subsystem's overall MTBF (mean time between failure) rating. In this scenario, an external-storage subsystem makes sense, because it is much easier to replace components that are sure to break. The most likely items to fail are the power supply, the cooling fan, and, of course, the hard disks themselves.

Many external RAID 5 subsystems offer redundant, hot-swappable components to keep everything up and running all the time. Look for a subsystem with front-accessible hard-disk modules that connect to the SCSI chain via a common SCSI backplane. These modular subsystems will allow easy hot-swapping without opening the subsystem's case.

A new SCSI specification, SCSI Accessed Fault-Tolerant Enclosures (SAF-TE), is currently under joint development by Intel and Conner (with endorsements from others including DPT, Mylex Corp., and Tricord Systems). The goal of this specification is to provide a standard way to monitor and report on the status of cooling systems, power supplies, and hard disks in servers and RAID arrays.

It is certainly a buyer's market in the RAID arena, with many vendors offering excellent external RAID systems. Conner, Cubix Corp., Micropolis Corp., and Storage Dimensions are just a few of the vendors of RAID subsystems. Since most RAID subsystems offer similar levels of performance, look for other features such as hot-swappability, security, scalability, and redundant power supplies.

RAID's Future   On the horizon are new RAID levels such as Micropolis's Level 5+ to improve the caching capabilities of RAID 5. On the hardware side, be on the lookout for Ultra SCSI RAID adapters from Adaptec and others. Ultra SCSI promises peak transfer rates up to 40 MBps. In the future, we can also expect Serial Storage Architecture (SSA) and Fibre Channel adapters to hit the market, allowing transfer rates of 80 MBps and 100 MBps, respectively.

Most of today's systems also support hardware-level RAID, whether preconfigured or through an upgrade. There's no doubt that RAID—especially RAID 5—provides an additional level of data security; depending on the RAID level you use, it may also boost performance. But RAID can also be expensive to implement: To add a hardware RAID controller to a Compaq or HP would cost about $2,000.

CHOOSING THE RIGHT SERVER PLATFORM

An alternative to RAID is duplexing, which is very popular in server environments because it can provide data security through mirroring and is relatively easy to implement through the operating system. Some systems provide an easy route to duplexing through dual integrated SCSI controllers, a setup that allows you to duplex the server's disk subsystem right out of the box. Duplexing does offer potentially better performance, as well as a redundant controller, although it doesn't support hot-swapping.

ECC Memory   Another fault-tolerance feature that you'll find in these machines is ECC (error-correction code) memory. ECC memory has the ability to detect and correct single-bit errors in memory. The majority of the vendors offer ECC memory with their servers as a standard feature. Although the maximum installable amount of ECC RAM varies from server to server, typically a maximum of 256MB is allowed. ECC memory is definitely more expensive to implement than standard DRAM (both at the design level and in the price of the memory modules), but the added level of data integrity is well worth the cost.

Hard Disk Considerations

Two different SCSI-2 technologies, Fast/Narrow and Fast/Wide, are the most widely used technologies today. Conventional Fast/Narrow technology supports an 8-bit data path and transfer rates of up to 10 Mbps; Fast/Wide doubles Fast/Narrow on both counts, supporting a 16-bit data path and throughput up to 20 Mbps. Fast/Wide technology may give an extra boost to your server's performance, especially in a disk-intensive environment. While all of this may seem like techno-babble, these are issues you will want to monitor. Since your hard drive contains all of your data (HTML pages) you will be very interested in how fast the data is retrieved from the disk and delivered to your users. It would be foolish to invest in a powerful processor if your I/O (input and output) bottleneck is your hard drive or hard-drive controller. It is advisable to put some of your investment in this fast speed technology.

Server Management

Server management is also a key ingredient in a well-rounded server solution. Functions of the server management software packages should range from basic system-monitoring capabilities such as temperature and voltage tracking to comprehensive out-of-band management features including remote dial-in and reboot.

A well-rounded and useful server management solution is a critical feature for any machine of this class. Once your new server is in place and operational, you must be able to keep a finger on its pulse at all times in order to ensure maximum uptime. Events should be monitored through user-defined thresholds that alert the network manager when an error

CHOOSING THE RIGHT SERVER PLATFORM

occurs. Notification in the event of an alert or a failure is delivered in many different ways: on-screen messages, pager, e-mail, fax, and SNMP are among the most widely used.

Most vendors supply their own server management software package, although some are more feature-rich than others. Some vendors provide add-in boards with their servers to manage system assets—including overall system status, voltage, and temperature—and to send remote notification via modem or pager in the event of a failure. Typically these solutions are usable only for in-band management (internal access within network), but there are a few vendors whose adapters operate with extensive out-of-band management (external access outside network) support. Because these services are connected to their own power supplies, you can access the server over a dial-up line whether the server is operational or not.

Operating Systems

The most powerful and feature-rich operating system for implementing and maintaining your Web service is Unix. Unix is the original language of the Internet, so all services created and accessed on the Web are Unix based. Other operating systems such as Novell, Macintosh, and NT are simply graphical front ends to Unix.

As reviewed in previous sections, the only drawback in a Unix operating system is that you must be Unix literate. While this might not seem like a large task, you must be willing to learn a different language and totally immerse yourself in the Unix world. Unix programming syntax is at a very low level, so you must be willing to learn cryptic operating commands. You should also be aware that Unix programmers usually have long hair and beards: While it is not absolutely necessary for *you* to adopt this look, it will help you in getting customer support!

Unix is traditionally unforgiving in entering commands. A simple extra space or period in the wrong place can take your server or service down. The challenge is then to diagnose where the problem lies. This type of diagnosis is time-consuming and better left to someone who fully understands the implications of making changes to a Unix operating system.

There are of course other operating systems which perform Unix operating commands using graphical (user-friendly) menu systems. The three most popular of these are Novell NetWare, Macintosh, and Microsoft NT. These operating systems each offer unique ways to manage services and user accounts. All of these operating systems also vary in the way they provide graphical user interfaces to disguise complex Unix command code syntax. However, even though Novell, Macintosh, and NT include graphical interfaces, you must have a good understanding of networking and specifically IP protocols to be successful in bringing your system on line.

CHOOSING THE RIGHT SERVER PLATFORM

The hidden message here is that you must still understand operating systems and networking to successfully install and implement your system. While the Novell, Macintosh, and Microsoft NT operating systems offer graphical menus to administer services and user account information, Unix is totally command line–driven which means you must have a solid understanding of the its command set and the structure of the operating system to use it successfully.

Another point to keep in mind is that after you get your system on line the real work of a system administrator starts to kick in. You'll have to be worrying about managing such things as user accounts, processor utilization, networking protocols, and service provider connection issues such as the diagnosis of potential bandwidth problems, backup policies in the areas of system management, data recovery, telephone support, redundant connections to service providers, and so on. This list goes on and on. These issues demonstrate typical concerns of Web system administrators. Not only do you have to be proficient on operating system issues as described above, you must also be a manager of connectivity related issues.

With these areas of responsibility in mind, you must also plan for technical support. You'd better plan on $100 to $250 per hour for on site support for all types of operating system support (Unix, Novell, Macintosh, or NT). Phone support can also be acquired for an average cost of $120 per call or incident. As you can see, the prices for this type of support can get very high. An alternative is to obtain training for yourself or another staff member. Training classes for operating systems range from $2,000 per week to $4,000. Also take into account that these training classes are generally only offered in larger cities so costs for room and board may also need to be taken into account.

Just as Ford and Dodge enthusiasts have strong feelings about Chevy enthusiasts, NetWare, Macintosh, and NT have their rabid fans. While it is obvious that users who currently use Macintosh software and equipment will be most comfortable using the same interface to manage their servers, it is currently unclear which of the other two operating systems is best in all aspects of performance and user maintainability. While NT seems to be winning market share for its price and Web functionality, Novell has been receiving high marks for its reliability and throughput.

Macintosh   People who currently use Macintosh computers on a daily basis will usually opt for the same operating system to manage their Web service. The menu interface and programming options will be the same. Macintosh has traditionally had an operating system which is closed to the normal user, and as a result the operating system is pretty bulletproof. Software designers who develop applications for a Macintosh have to write specifically to the closed operating system, so memory conflicts

CHOOSING THE RIGHT SERVER PLATFORM

normally encountered by an open architecture operating system such as Windows or NT are avoided.

If you have never used a Macintosh then choosing this operating system (which requires a Macintosh computer) would not be a wise move. You will have lots of other management issues to deal with without the introduction of additional hurdles.

Since the Macintosh has traditionally been heavily favored in the graphical design market, a lot of Mac users are developing graphical content for home pages. Such graphical interfaces will be consistent in the operating system management portion of your Web services. The message here is if you use a Macintosh currently, use the Macintosh operating system to manage your Web services—this will save you the time of learning a new operating system and graphical interface when you will have plenty of other things to keep you busy.

Novell NetWare   Traditionally NetWare has been managed by highly skilled system operators in locked computer rooms. These people usually have had a fair amount of training in networking and specific NetWare functions. NetWare is nothing like DOS or Windows: It is a proprietary operating system which requires the user to understand and implement functions in NetWare's proprietary menu interface. NetWare, an operating system designed to serve applications and share resources, has had the largest market share for network operating systems for approximately eight years. Therefore, their operating system is solid and highly reliable.

While NetWare is the most reliable OS in our opinion, its downfall is that you must first fully understand NetWare's proprietary menu interface and how to configure access to user accounts before you can get up and running. Realistically in today's business world, either VARs (value-added resellers) are called in to install and manage Novell systems or in-house technical staff are assigned the responsibility of setting up and managing the day to day operations of a Novell operating system.

It has only been recently (within the past nine months) that Novell has actively pursued the Web server market. (Traditionally Novell has been used for corporate file and print sharing.) Keeping this in mind, with the explosion of the Internet and related services, Novell will be introducing and implementing more and more Internet services to run on their operating system.

Microsoft NT   The same can be said here about NT as was previously stated about NetWare: Setting up an operating system should not be taken lightly. You must be prepared to take on additional job duties in conjunction with being a Webmaster who is only responsible for content.

What makes NT a little more appealing to the average user is that the network operating system's interface is based on Windows. Therefore

CHOOSING THE RIGHT SERVER PLATFORM

management concepts such as the Program Manager and groups are still present. Utilities such as File Manager and Print Manager are also still incorporated. While these interfaces are still used, there is an additional set of utilities which manage the network. So, as with Novell, an NT system manager must now take on the role of implementing user accounts and assigning rights to resources. Also like Novell, VARs are usually called in to initially install and manage NT systems or in-house technical staff are assigned the responsibility of setting up and managing the day to day operations of an NT operating system.

Currently NT also has pricing edge. In some markets you can purchase NT for approximately four times less that a comparable Novell operating system (user for user license).

Our only major concern with NT is its reliability. While NT provides a utility or program for almost every technical question, the stability of the operating system is sometimes jeopardized. Microsoft is now claiming that with the release of their updated operating system, NT 4.0, operating system stability and reliability have been modified and improved. NT has also been hammered in the trade rags for throughput problems; again, with NT 4.0 these issues are supposed to be addressed.

Conclusion   While it is not the intent of this text to specifically recommend or promote certain products, we have tried to give examples of features to look out for when evaluating operating systems. The topic of operating systems can be written about for thousands of pages and then some. The OS is a very complex and costly component of your self-built Web server, so care should be taken to ensure you have analyzed your budget in reference to your anticipated services. Money should also be set aside to anticipate costly services for technical support or training.

Implementing Your Solution

After you have chosen your hardware platform you will then have to arrange for TCP/IP connectivity for your server. This means that your machine must be connected to the network with a network interface card and the appropriate low-level network drivers. In addition, a TCP/IP protocol software stack must be installed on your machine. The TCP/IP software must be configured with your machine's IP number and the IP number of your network gateway machines and DNS (domain name service) servers. Any routers on your network may need to have their filtering tables updated so that TCP/IP traffic from your machine will pass through the routers and ultimately to the Internet. Finally, you must update the DNS servers for your network domain with the name, Ethernet ID, and IP number of your machine.

CHOOSING THE RIGHT SERVER PLATFORM

Installing and procuring the TCP/IP stack are quite different for each platform. Unix workstations include TCP/IP support as a matter of course—it's part of the definition of the workstation. The TCP/IP stack on Unix systems is configured by cryptic text files that are scattered all over the boot volume, but the default configuration usually works fine. Microsoft Windows NT and Novell operating systems include a TCP/IP protocol stack, but the setup programs do not install it automatically; you must refer to the online help to install and configure TCP/IP as a separate step after the system is running. Configuration for NT is carried out by a standard Windows NT Control Panel applet and is quite straightforward if you understand the terminology. Novell's IP configuration feature is menu driven, but as with the NT server you must understand the terminology.

Macintosh System 7.5 includes the Apple TCP/IP protocol stack (called MacTCP), but the configuration process is uncharacteristically obscure. Earlier versions of Macintosh systems do not include MacTCP, but a licensed copy is bundled with virtually every Macintosh communications or TCP/IP utility product, and it can be also be purchased separately for a nominal fee. Microsoft Windows 3.1 users must resort to public-domain implementations or purchase one of the several expensive third-party Windows TCP/IP packages.

The network connectivity and TCP/IP issues are pretty exotic from a software developer's point of view, so you will need to work closely with your company's network support staff and/or your Internet service provider to get everything properly set up. The provider must allocate an IP number and machine name for your machine and update their equipment to advertise you as a service to the Internet.

2 ACCESS TECHNOLOGIES

AS THE INTERNET BRINGS the global marketplace to yours and millions of other desktops, you will want to consider the implications of this interconnectedness for the services you provide. To best understand how to use the Internet to meet your goals, you need to understand not only the software and hardware that serve applications but also the methods of connectivity used to interconnect all of the resources on the Internet. In this chapter we will present you with information that will help you determine the best methods for you to connect your services. Our discussion of access

ACCESS TECHNOLOGIES

technologies will address the connectivity issues involved with using normal external modems and specialized cable access modems. We will also review network connectivity methods such as T1, ISDN, and ATM networking technologies.

We will not cover local area network access (direct connect) in depth but we will briefly describe direct connect issues related to the TCP/IP stack. Internet connectivity through a direct connection requires a network interface card installed into your PC. This card is then initialized with a TCP/IP software protocol stack to enable the card, which is connected to a local area network via twisted-pair cabling, to exchange information with the Internet. In this configuration your PC is theoretically directly connected to the Internet. This type of direct connect communication to the Internet passes via your local area network to a service provider who pays for a connection to the Internet. Your local area network is connected to each of the other service providers through hardware interfaces known as *routers*. Although connection via local area networks and remote access computers both involve the use of TCP/IP as a transport protocol, the connectivity issues are somewhat different.

Direct connect PCs that require access to the Internet need a TCP/IP stack loaded with the appropriate network interface card configured to work on the specific local area network. Other high-level connectivity issues dealing with routers, IP addressing, domain name registration, and bandwith are usually left up to highly skilled in-house technical support staff who monitor bandwith and acquire more when needed. If you choose to get involved with networking at this level you should do your homework and expect not to get much sleep at night due to the added responsibility your taking on.

In the case of remote Internet access, a computer will need to be configured with a TCP/IP stack. Another piece of protocol software then needs to be configured to allow the remotely connected PC to act as if it were locally connected to the service provider's network. The most popular communications protocol used for this purpose is PPP (Point to Point Protocol), although SLIP (Serial Line Input Protocol) is also popular. All remotely connected PCs will need to be configured with both TCP/IP and PPP (or SLIP). If this is the type of connectivity you use, you as the service provider need to be concerned about bandwith demands, since slow performance will cause users to seek other providers who can offer a faster pipe for their needs. Therefore your primary responsibility is to monitor and adjust your bandwidth to satisfy your clientele.

After you have successfully configured your computer to run these protocols you will need to use a communications package to dial your service provider. This method also assumes you have some type of modem installed and configured for your PC. Since there are literally hundreds of

ACCESS TECHNOLOGIES

communications packages and TCP/IP stack solutions, we can only say that if you need help configuring your particular workstation with these protocols, turn first to your service provider or call the manufacturer of the software. If these protocols aren't correctly configured, access to a remote Internet connection is impossible.

After configuring your PC and hardware, you will then have to acquire an account on an Internet service provider's network (ISP). For references on Internet service providers refer to Chapter 21. If you intend on becoming a service provider yourself, you will have to live, eat, and breathe all of the issues mentioned above. If your intention is to use an established service provider, then your task of either managing a Web site or simply surfing the Net becomes a little easier.

The following sections will describe access technologies for both hardware and leased lines. These technologies can be used to complete your connection as described above. Our purpose here is to give overviews of each of the technologies. While some have stood the test of time, others are emerging technologies, many of which show major growth potential and give tantalizing glimpses into the future of Internet access. You will also need to keep in mind that these technologies require some do-it-yourself work in the areas of installation and implementation. While this may seem like a small challenge, experience has proven that patience and persistence is the best recipe for success.

Modems

The early days of text-based transfers and non-GUI screen retrieval from the Internet to your PC are gone forever. We are now living in an Internet world full of colorful graphical screens and movable images. With this graphic-intensive change, older modem speeds of 2,400 bps and 9,600 bps are not able to provide transfer rates adequate to satisfy users' demand for speed. This need for speed and the current scramble by small businesses, personal computer users, and entrepreneurs to set up Web sites has pushed vendors to produce higher speed modems. With all of these factors in place there's never been a more compelling time to get an up-to-date modem.

Almost ten years ago, Rockwell International Corporation and other manufacturers made chip sets available for modems following the international V.22bis standards. At that time the maximum transfer rate was 2,400 bps. With the implementation of international standards in communications, proprietary protocols fell by the wayside. Manufacturers changed to the international standards, and modems became truly high speed. This means you can send larger files faster, saving on connect charges and your time.

ACCESS TECHNOLOGIES

The ITU (International Telecommunications Union) formerly known as the CCITT (Consultative Committee for International Telephone and Telegraph) was established in the early 1970s to address the question of worldwide modem compatibility and to create coordinated standards. The ITU has accomplished its work quite well, producing so far five important standards applicable for today's modems. Listed below are definitions of the standards. (When a second, improved version of a standard is released, it is dubbed *bis*. If a third version of a standard is released, it has the suffix *ter,* for third.)

- **V.32**. The V.32 standard is the mother of all standards. Introduced in 1985 to avert the chaos that would have ensued if manufacturers had implemented incompatible proprietary standards, the V.32 standard was conceived and implemented to enable transmissions up to 14,400 bps. This V.32 standard is also necessary for higher speed modems (faster than 300 bps) to communicate. This standard describes how modems should talk to each other using two-way signaling at 4,800 and 9,600 bps over dial-up telephone lines.

- **MNP 4 and MNP 5** MNP (Microcom Networking Protocol) is an independent standard created by Microcom, a modem manufacturer, to improve data transfer. Versions of MNP are now available in a variety of modems and communications software packages. MNP 4 (an error-correction scheme) and MNP 5 (a compression method) are compatible with, but not supported by the ITU. However, many modem manufacturers use both MNP 4 and V.42 standards for the best possible combination of error detection and correction.

- **V.42 and V.42bis** In 1989, the ITU issued a hardware-implemented error-correction standard called V.42 that describes two error-correction schemes. The primary protocol is named *link access procedure for modems* (LAPM). The secondary (or support) protocol is functionally the same as MNP 4. If you want to communicate between two modems that are V.42 compliant, you should connect them with the LAPM protocol. LAPM offers slightly better error recovery and reliability than MNP 4.

   In late 1989, the ITU issued the V.42bis standard, which describes how to implement data compression in hardware. Using the Lempel-Ziv compression algorithm, the new V.42bis protocol offers much greater data compression than MNP 5. For a 9,600-bps modem, there is a potential transfer rate of 38,400 bps for compressable files. For most file transfers, however, you can expect transfers of around 19,200 bps for files not previously compressed through other means.

- **V.32bis** In early 1991, the ITU approved a revision of the V.32 standard. V.32bis adds 7,200-, 12,000-, and 14,400-bps transfer rates and a faster

ACCESS TECHNOLOGIES

renegotiating protocol. V.32bis is able to renegotiate the protocol in less than 100 milliseconds.

■ **V.34/V.Fast** In the last few years, a new high-speed standard loosely call V.Fast or V.Fast Class has been in development. The standard has now been finalized as V.34 and allows a 28,800-bps data transfer rate.

Most modem vendors today base their products on a two-chip package including a hard-coded processor chip or *data engine,* which contains the algorithms necessary to use the full bandwidth of the telephone lines, and a *digital signal processor* (DSP) chip programmed to perform the computations required by the data engine. Complex, high-speed protocols such as V.34 would be limited to complex, high-cost modems if not for the advent of increasingly powerful, programmable DSPs.

Several manufacturers are taking DSP-based products to a new level of functionality by eliminating the traditional two-chip modem package. Some vendors today use a technology that works by storing the instructions traditionally carried out by a modem's hard-wired data engine on your PC's hard drive and feeding them to the DSP when needed. This makes implementing modem enhancements even easier than flash ROM does.

Besides its easy upgradability, the beauty of DSP technology is that there's no reason to limit the DSP to processing only traditional modem instructions. Applications such as 16-bit digital audio, voice mail, speech recognition, and fax on demand are all available from DSP-driven multi-function modems from a multitude of vendors. These products offer a cost-effective way to add multiple functions to your system.

For now, separate communications and multimedia hardware is still a must for users concerned about CPU performance degradation. But as processors grow in power, their ability to help out with signal-processing tasks will grow as well.

While modems that conform to V.32bis (14.4 kbps) and older standards establish transfer rates by trial and error, when two V.34 modems connect, they exchange a tone to test the capabilities of the line. The condition of the tone received at either end of the connection lets the modems determine which of 60 possible modulation methods and line speeds to use. In contrast, V.32bis has only five possible permutations of these variables. Once connected, V.34 modems can equalize their signals depending on the line impairments. V.34 also offers some additional features over V.32. For example, a pair of V.34 modems can connect at different speeds if the line quality is better in one direction than the other. In short, while V.34 modems still have trouble connecting at 28.8 kbps on a given line, they have the greatest latitude of any modem to date in selecting the highest practical transmission rate.

ACCESS TECHNOLOGIES

There's always a lag between the introduction of a new modem technology and its adoption. But thanks to extensive beta testing with V.34, national online services are ready to roll out 28.8-kbps lines. America Online (AOL) says it will have 28.8-kbps connections available by the time you read this. CompuServe and Prodigy claim that they will also be up and running.

Even when all of the online services move to the new standard, as long as they use Rockwell-based V.34 modems or other manufacturers like U.S. Robotics, who have chosen to remain compatible with the interim spec, you'll be able to connect at 28.8 kbps if you have a V.34 modem. CompuServe, which will use U.S. Robotics Courier modems for its 28.8-kbps lines, and Prodigy both affirmed that they will offer V.32 backward compatibility. Prices for V.32bis and base-model V.34 modems have about hit rock bottom, so even the budget-conscious can communicate in style. If you can afford a flash ROM, you'll get a longer, more trouble-free lifespan from your purchase and put yourself in a position to benefit from enhancements such as the new 33.6-kbps step up from standard V.34.

Knowing your current and future communications plans is the most important part of comparison shopping. Two-way (also known as *full-duplex*) transfers put the most stress on the modems' controllers, yet this type of transfer is becoming increasingly important as distributed computing, remote networking, and new online applications and services perform more complex interactions. Even as dial-up Internet packages have rapidly expanded the use of more complex network protocols like PPP and SLIP in the past year, the most popular bandwidth-hungry tool for the Net is still the World Wide Web browser (Explorer and Netscape Navigator), primarily a request/wait application. While there is a multitude of options available in today's modem market, you should research your current and future needs to make your hard earned investment in your hardware last a little longer.

Cable Modems

A *cable modem* is a communications device that allows high-speed data transfers via a cable TV (CATV) network. A cable modem will typically have two connections, one to the cable wall outlet and the other to a computer. Cable modem speeds vary widely. In the downstream direction (from the network to the computer), speeds can be up to 36 Mbps. Only a few of these high-speed modems are currently on the market; more are expected to be introduced this year. Since today's computers are unable to connect at such high speeds, a more realistic rate is 3–10 Mbps. In the upstream direction (from computer to network), speeds can be up to 10 Mbps. Since most modem producers will probably select an optimal

ACCESS TECHNOLOGIES

speed of between 200 kbps and 2 Mbps, this bandwidth will be more than adequate to handle all of your home access needs.

The fact that the word *modem* is used in the name "cable modem" can be a little misleading because it tends to conjure up images of a typical telephone dial-up modem. A cable modem *is* a modem in the true sense of the word—it *mo*dulates and *dem*odulates signals. But the similarity ends there because cable modems are practically an order of magnitude more complicated than their telephone counterparts. Cable modems can be part modem, part tuner, part encryption/decryption device, part bridge, part router, part NIC card, part SNMP agent, and part Ethernet hub.

There are several methods for computer connection to a cable modem but it appears that Ethernet 10BASE-T is emerging as the most predominant method. Although it probably would be cheaper to produce the cable modem as an internal card for the computer, this would require different printed-circuit cards for different kinds of computers, and additionally would make the demarcation between cable network and the subscriber's computer too fuzzy. Listed below is a typical shopping list for cable modem requirements:

Customer-Supplied Components	Cable Company–Supplied Components
10BASE-T network interface card (NIC) with RJ-45 network cable connector	Cable modem
TCP protocol stack (included in Windows 95 or Windows NT; the Macintosh uses a shareware protocol stack called MacTCP)	Cable from wall outlet to cable modem
Web browser (Netscape, MS Explorer, or Mosaic network browser)	
Mail program that supports POP-3 mail	
A hub may be required for the some units if more than one IP address is requested	

The most popular service on cable modems will undoubtedly be high-speed Internet access. This will enable the typical array of Internet services at speeds of 100 to 1,000 times as fast as a telephone modem. Other services may include access to streaming audio and video servers, local content (community information and services), access to CD-ROM servers, and a wide variety of other service offerings. New service ideas are emerging daily.

It is estimated that when cable modem service starts to become widespread that the per-month cost of these connections will range from $15 to $25 per month. Add these additional costs per household together with the current average bill of $30 a month for cable service, and you can

ACCESS TECHNOLOGIES

■ Market Economics 101

Here are some numbers that will give you an idea why cable companies are licking their chops at the chance to get into the Internet service market:

- In the U.S., there are 63.2 million cable subscribers.

- Cable passes through or by 96.6 million U.S. households.

- There are 11,606 U.S. cable systems.

- The average monthly cable bill in the U.S. is $30.59.

- In the U.S., 46 percent of subscribers get 54 or more channels.

- In Belgium, 97.4 percent of homes subscribe to cable.

- Cable companies have more than 1.77 million miles of fiber laid in the U.S.

- 13 percent of all Americans have an Internet account (or think they do). ■

---

start to see that these cable operators are looking to double their money using their existing cabling infrastructure. Clearly, cable companies have good reason to be eager to become Internet providers.

Cable modem pilot tests are already underway in many cable networks. But testing is still in an early phase, and large scale testing won't take place until the fall of 1996. Many of the cable modems will first appear on the market in November of 1996. Wide-scale deployments probably won't start until some time in 1997. So, while this technology is not yet ready for prime time, it's a technology that you want to keep an eye on. With the potential for financial windfalls for cable providers, we know this technology will be pushed on consumers just like Mike Tyson's "last" fight.

On-Demand Access: ISDN

In most parts of the U.S., you can connect your computer to the world with a super-fast technology called ISDN (Integrated Services Digital Network). It lets you work with more information faster and more efficiently than you'd ever dream a traditional phone line and modem connection could. ISDN opens a whole array of possibilities, including video conferencing, the ability to let two people in remote locations work on the same project, digital audio transmission, and a multitude of other opportunities—as well as providing traditional voice phone service.

ISDN is a completely digital connection—all the way from the phone company to you. This is a big improvement over traditional analog phone signals, which can be difficult to transmit clearly over long distances and which take more time to deliver information than digital signals. The

ACCESS TECHNOLOGIES

phone companies once used only analog equipment to transmit sound. After a while, they discovered that if they converted sound to a digital format at the central office, they could then transfer that audio information from place to place faster and more efficiently.

Most phone services today use a hybrid of analog and digital technologies. Your phones and modems send out an analog signal which the phone company converts into digital form once it reaches the switching equipment at the central office. The phone service converts the signal back to analog before the connection reaches the destination phone or modem.

An advantage to this analog-to-digital-to-analog conversion is that it's cheap to implement and easy to maintain. The downside, however, is mediocre sound quality. Although the audio doesn't need to be perfect, modems are severely limited by poor sound quality as they transmit data. Computers just can't process information like humans can—even the slightest noise or a momentary interruption can create critical errors in a computer signal that will cause your modem to disconnect. That's one of the problems with using modems in conjunction with analog phone lines. ISDN completely eliminates the analog-to-digital and digital-to-analog (AD/DA) conversions, allowing your computer to push more data through the phone lines than a standard modem would allow. ISDN's signal isn't limited to the narrow constraints of an analog phone line's "last mile" from the central office to your home or business. Also, your connection doesn't lag as a result of the analog/digital conversions, which impose their own sets of costs and inefficiencies. For your Internet surf sessions, ISDN's digital connection means more dependable Internet connections at much higher speeds.

Since ISDN provides a completely digital connection from one point to another, your connection is very fast. As a matter of fact, a *basic-rate ISDN,* or *BRI* (basic-rate interface), line provides a multichannel digital connection that consists of three separate channels: two 64-kbps B (bearer) channels and one 16-kbps D (delta) channel, commonly referred to as 2B+D.

The B channels in an ISDN line move data at transmission rates of up to 64,000 bps per channel—before any sort of data compression. ISDN's smaller D channel manages the B channel connections and handles control and connection information, such as busy signals. Since the D channel demands only 16 kbps to check to see if a line is busy, the connection is much more efficient for the phone companies to handle and thus is faster. As a result, ISDN's digital communication lets your computer create nearly instantaneous connections to other ISDN services, such as your Internet provider.

ACCESS TECHNOLOGIES

■ Glossary of ISDN Terms

BRI (basic-rate interface)
An ISDN service that provides up to two bearer (or B) channels of 64 kbps each, plus one 9.6-kbps delta (or D) channel for signaling and control. Individuals usually choose this type of ISDN service.

ISDN adapter
An internal card that connects the computer to the ISDN line. It runs at the speed of the system bus.

ISDN modem
An external or internal device that connects the computer's serial port with the ISDN line. It's limited to the speed of the serial port.

Multilink PPP
A standard way to automatically combine both ISDN B channels into one 128-kbps channel for faster transmission. Previously called *bonding* or *bandwidth on demand.*

POP (point of presence)
The physical site where an ISP has its modems and other networking gear. You dial into the POP for Internet access.

PRI (primary-rate interface)
A high-volume ISDN configuration with 23 or 30 digital channels. Each channel is 64 kbps, for a total of 1.544 Mbps and 2.048 Mbps, respectively. Often used by ISPs to connect their network backbones.

Router
A device that connects multiple network topologies, such as dial-in and Ethernet.   ■

ISDN's multichannel lines also provide the ability to make more than one connection at a time. For example, with ISDN, you can talk on the phone with one of the B channels while simultaneously looking up information on the Internet with another. By using equipment designed to do so, you could also bond both B channels to produce a 128-kbps signal, thus creating a very fast Internet connection.

Since ISDN uses technology that is different from standard modems to transmit information, you'll need some new hardware to take advantage of this digital technology. Your Internet service provider must also have the hardware to support ISDN. In addition, you'll need to ask your local phone company to install an ISDN line in your home or office. When your phone company installs the ISDN line, you'll need a network termination device—called an *NT* or an *NT-1*—to convert the ISDN signal into something your computer can use. An NT-1 will also let you attach other devices to the ISDN line.

To make the connection from your computer to the NT-1, you need an ISDN *terminal adapter* (TA)—the digital equivalent of a modem. This TA will connect to the NT-1. Many of the newer TAs include a built-in NT-1. This is a good feature to look for in a TA—especially if you plan to use ISDN for digital communication between computers and the Internet.

ACCESS TECHNOLOGIES

There are several configurations you can choose from when you look for ISDN equipment. For a single user, you can connect your computer directly to a TA with a built-in NT-1 for the easiest and least-expensive solution. Selecting a TA with an Ethernet connection may provide the best way for more than one computer to connect to the Internet.

ISDN equipment needs to interact closely with your local phone company's and Internet provider's hardware. Although most newer ISDN equipment should support a wide variety of standard phone equipment, you should consult your Internet provider before making your final purchase. An Internet provider will most likely have experience with a variety of ISDN options and can guide you to those vendors whose products the provider can support. Your Internet service provider can also give you an idea of how much your ISDN hardware and connection should cost. All this technology does come at some price. However, that cost isn't as high as you might think. An ISDN line costs a little bit more than traditional analog phone lines do, but the extra advantages over basic analog phone service far outweigh the costs. Currently, an ISDN line can cost anywhere from $40 to $200 for installation if your local phone company provides the service in your area. Connection fees can run anywhere from $25 to $100 per month for a single BRI 2B+D line. Your Internet service provider may also charge an increased rate for ISDN access. Finally, expect to pay prices that start around $495 and up for a TA with a built-in NT-1. The following list of currently available products will give you some places to start looking for ISDN equipment:

Pipeline 25 and Pipeline 50
Company: Ascend Communications
Price: Pipeline 25, $895; Pipeline 50, $1,295
OS Support: Windows 95, Windows NT, Windows 3.1
Phone: 800-272-3634; 510-769-6001

Supra NetCommander ISDN
Company: Diamond Multimedia Systems
Price: $299
OS Support: Windows 95, Windows NT
Phone: 800-468-5846; 408-325-7100

PC IMAC
Company: Digi International, Inc.
Price: $795
OS Support: Windows 95, Windows NT, Windows 3.1
Phone: 800-344-4273; 612-912-3444

ACCESS TECHNOLOGIES

Netopia ISDN Modem
Company: Farallon Computing, Inc.
Price: $399
OS Support: Windows 95, Windows NT, Windows 3.1
Phone: 800-995-7761; 510-814-5000

XpressConnect LANLine 5242i
Company: Gandalf Technologies, Inc.
Price: Bridge, $1,145; router, $1,550
OS Support: Not applicable
Phone: 800-426-3253; 609-461-8100

BitSURFR Pro
Company: Motorola
Price: $380
OS Support: Not applicable
Phone: 800-221-4380; 205-430-8000

ATM

ATM (asynchronous transfer mode) derives its strengths from three fundamental features—it is switch-based, it segments information into same-size cells or packets, and it can negotiate quality of service. Rather than depend on a shared network medium (as does Ethernet, for example), ATM utilizes high-speed switching to provide connections between clients. This connection-oriented approach allows ATM to provide dedicated bandwidth for each connection, flexible access speeds, and a higher aggregate bandwidth.

In addition, ATM's use of same-size cells simplifies the traffic manipulation requirements for connections and also accommodates different types of traffic, such as voice and data, on the same network. ATM is unique in that it provides built-in support for negotiating the type and speed of a connection, determining the end-to-end quality of service. Simply comparing ATM speeds to those of other networks is insufficient because shared-media networks cannot offer users a quality-of-service guarantee for connections, as ATM can.

It's become easier for companies to enjoy ATM's performance benefits because many of the standards required for robust end-to-end ATM networks have been approved in the past year. Other important standards currently nearing approval include PNNI-1 (Private Network Node Interface), explicit-rate ABR (Available Bit Rate), and UNI 4.0 (User Network Interface). PNNI-1 is an important routing protocol enabling better interoperability of multivendor switches, while ABR helps with traffic management. UNI determines how users get access to the ATM

ACCESS TECHNOLOGIES

network and what requirements they specify to the network at connection setup time.

Although more networks are using ATM as a backbone protocol, employing ATM at the workgroup and desktop level has not been an equally straightforward decision. But network managers now have two choices for connecting their workgroups to ATM—LANE (LAN emulation) and ATM 25. One solution is to maintain current Ethernet and Token-Ring LANs and use "edge devices" that support LANE to tie these LANs to ATM switches. LANE 1.0 was approved in mid-1995, and vendors are beginning to offer switches and routers with LANE support. This integration method provides a simple means of maintaining connectivity to ATM nets with minimal disruption—you don't have to replace the workstation interface cards, for example—but does not offer the real-time capabilities and QoS (quality of service) guarantees of ATM at the workstations. However, LAN emulation still has to prove itself since no one currently knows how well LAN will scale on large networks.

A second approach links workstations to ATM by installing 25.6-Mbps ATM network adapters in each one. This offers real-time access and QoS to the user. Both LANE and 25.6-Mbps ATM workgroups cost about $1,000 per workstation, with LANE currently slightly less expensive. Because the price difference between the two alternatives is only $200 to $300, network managers looking to support real-time applications or guarantee a specified QoS to workstations should consider 25.6-Mbps ATM as their solution. LANE will be merely a stopgap or transitional measure for many.

To allow ATM users to negotiate QoS for a connection, ATM offers a set of service classes that are assigned on a connection-by-connection basis. The four classes are CBR (Constant Bit Rate), VBR (Variable Bit Rate), ABR, and UBR (Unspecified Bit Rate). VBR may well be split into two classes—VBR (RT), or VBR Real Time, and VBR (NRT), or VBR Non-Real Time.

ABR and VBR (NRT) were not defined in the UNI 3.1 standard, and revised definitions of the other service classes will be included in UNI 4.0. While UNI 4.0 is expected to be ratified later this year, the ABR standard has almost completed the ratification process. This will be good news for vendors and users planning to support the "bursty" traffic associated with LANs.

ABR systematically and dynamically allocates available bandwidth to users by using feedback to control the rate of traffic. It is basically a mechanism to allow bursty LAN-style traffic to run well on busy ATM networks. Implementation of this standard will replace a number of vendors' proprietary mechanisms for congestion control.

ACCESS TECHNOLOGIES

Because ABR depends on rapid response to traffic conditions, it needs to be implemented in hardware near the place where ATM cells are sent and received in the switch. If ABR isn't already supported on your switch, it's likely that you'll have to purchase a new ATM switch whenever you decide to build a network that supports ABR. Using switches upgradable at the microcode level, such as those becoming available this year, is the best way to go.

Prior to the approval of many of the ATM standards late last year and early this year, proprietary implementations often forced network managers to go with single-vendor solutions for their ATM networks. Now that more vendors employ the ATM standards, more ATM devices interoperate, affording a wider range of choices for network design. One of the biggest problems facing early users of ATM was the incompatibility of switches and other ATM devices as the standards were being developed. But many vendors are now using more powerful processors in their switches, enabling software upgrades for the ATM protocols as the standards are approved. Although it's at least a year away, support for ATM APIs within Winsock 2.0 should make developing applications, especially those with QoS requirements, easier. This, in turn, should drive up demand for ATM networks.

ADSL

The Asymmetric Digital Subscriber Line (ADSL) is the current darling of the phone companies for delivering advanced digital services. It offers the promise of high-speed transmissions, yet allows the phone companies to use the copper wiring that already connects to each home. Someday, ADSL could be the darling of consumers as well: Because ADSL works over a pair of ordinary phone wires, you can use your existing analog phones and maintain a high-speed data connection at the same time.

To use ADSL—once it's commercially available—you'll need an external ADSL modem; there will another such modem in the phone company's central office. While ADSL modems are still being developed, one prototype has three connectors on the back of the unit: One goes to the wall jack and then out to the phone company; one is for a standard RJ-11 phone jack for analog phone service; and one is an Ethernet twisted-pair RJ-45 connector that hooks the ADSL modem to your computer equipment. This means that once you install an ADSL modem, you won't need special interface electronics to run your analog phones. That's a big plus, one that could speed ADSL's adoption as a single solution for home PC users and small businesses that don't want to install and pay for an extra data line. Also, most home PCs are located near phone wall jacks, which will make ADSL easier to install than, say, cable modems.

ACCESS TECHNOLOGIES

While ADSL is attractive, theoretically, the marriage between the Internet and ADSL has not yet been consummated. Barely a year ago, ADSL was still viewed as a way for the phone company to deliver video movies and better compete with cable TV companies. Now, ADSL is newly incarnated as a means to high-speed Internet access, although companies are just starting to test the technology. Most ADSL Internet products are still on the drawing board, and only a few field trials comprising several dozen users have taken place. As an Internet pipeline, ADSL is too untested to count on. No ISPs have announced any ADSL service yet, making it even more difficult to make sweeping predictions.

Continuous Access: Leased Lines

If you need continuous, high-speed Internet access and are willing to pay several thousand dollars a month for it, then leased lines are the ticket for you. If you have the budget and want all possible bandwidth, all the time, then consider using a leased line to access the Internet; this technology offers the highest quality and the fastest connection. And since you or your company probably leases lines for voice calls among branch offices already, you may have most of the infrastructure you need to make the connection. You'll just need to purchase a separate line to run between your headquarters and a local ISP.

Leased lines are dedicated, 24-hour-a-day circuits that the phone company runs directly from your door to your ISP's point of presence (POP); you can use them to send voice or data between two points. There are several flavors of leased lines, and they handle data rates from 56 kbps up to 45 Mbps. Often, leased lines consist of fiber-optic cabling, though they can be copper if the distance between you and the ISP's POP is under (roughly) 3.5 miles.

If you want to run Web and mail servers that outsiders can access, have a large network with dozens of active Internet users, or upload and download multimegabyte files frequently, leased lines may be the most cost-effective Internet access solution for you. Unlike ISDN, your connection is active full-time—perfect for delivering surfers to your Web site. Unlike satellites and cable modems, you get the same bandwidth in both directions. Another advantage of leased lines is that you don't have to install anything other than the TCP/IP protocols and Internet applications on each desktop. As far as each client computer is concerned, the Internet is a local-area resource. Once connected via a leased line, you don't have to worry about "dialing" into the Internet; it becomes a natural extension of the local-area network.

Typically, your choice of which leased line to buy is somewhat limited. The local phone company is pretty much the only game in town, although AT&T, Sprint, and MCI are other options, particularly if you need to go

ACCESS TECHNOLOGIES

■ Glossary of Leased-Line Terms

DSU/CSU (data service unit/channel service unit)
A device that terminates the digital line at the customer premises; the phone company uses it to diagnose the line and assess other technical aspects of the data service.

DDS (digital data service)
A broad term that refers to digital connections available from the phone company, including Switched 56, and T1, and T3 lines.

Switched 56
Often the least expensive high-speed digital service, it operates at 56 kbps and is used for point-to-point connections.

T1
A line made up of 24 separate channels of 64 kbps each, plus one 8-kbps channel for signaling and control. Its total bandwidth is 1.5 Mbps. T1 is used mainly for bulk connections, typically among ISPs.

T3
A line equivalent to 30 T1 lines that provides an overall bandwidth of 45 Mbps.

V.35
The interface digital data lines use to connect to computers and routers.   ■

longer distances. To establish a leased line connection to your ISP's point of presence, you'll need several pieces of gear, including a Data Service Unit/Channel Service Unit (DSU/CSU) and a router. These terminate the line and also provide signaling for the phone company. Phone companies often refer to leased lines as *digital data service* (DDS). You can connect a single computer or your entire corporation to a leased line. Typically, you'll still want to make use of an Ethernet connection from the PCs to a combined router and DSU/CSU.

Before you buy any equipment, however, find out if your ISP offers leased line services at the POP nearest your home or office. When it comes to leased lines, you pay by the mile for the line the phone company runs between the two points. This can be costly even for a few miles of line, especially if you're in a rural area or if there's no spare capacity in your building (if it's a large building complex, for example). Whenever phone company installers have to be on the premises, pulling wire from the street into your building, it will cost you.

There are other cost variables, including your ISP's pricing structure. Some ISPs have limited offerings of just a few different data rates, while others have more flexible plans. The price depends on the type of phone service you want. Obviously, the higher the data rate, the more expensive the line will be to rent from the phone company. A good rule of thumb: Figure on about a thousand dollars a month for short distances within major urban areas, with higher costs for longer lines in rural or suburban areas. Of course, if you have an ISP in your own backyard, leased lines could be relatively cost-effective, especially if you need full-time connections.

Table 2.1 lists Internet access methods.

ACCESS TECHNOLOGIES

■ Table 2.1   Internet Access Methods

Type of Line	Capacity	Initial/Monthly Fees	Pros	Cons
Switched 56	56 kbps	$1,200/$500	Available in dedicated and nondedicated versions; the latter is more flexible for connecting multiple sites; dedicated can be more cost-effective than ISDN for continuous use	Not upgradable, so if you need more bandwidth, you have to move to a different technology (such as T1)
Frame relay	56-512 kbps	$1,000/$300	Good price/performance combination for occasional connections; as prices drop, its 56-kbps links will compete with ISDN in the under-$250 range	Few ISPs support it; up to 128 kbps, it's more expensive than ISDN; not a dedicated line, and long latencies can occur
Fractional T1	One or more 64-kbps T1 channels	$1,000/$800	Expandable, because you can grow it to a full T1 line if needed	Expensive compared to technologies with comparable bandwidth, such as ISDN and Switched 56
T1	1.544 Mbps	$2,500/$1,000	Every ISP supports it; it's an established and well-understood technology	Expensive; large T1 networks are complex to manage
T3	45 Mbps	$50,000/$7,500	Fastest leased line method available today	Incredibly expensive; for use primarily by ISPs and enterprises

In deciding which leased service best fits your needs, you must first decide how much bandwidth you can afford. The least expensive lines run a service called Switched 56 from the phone company. Because these 56-kbps digital data lines are switched, they can connect to various endpoints or to network topologies. You pay only for the data (monthly or hourly rates).

Frame Relay

Frame relay service is a popular alternative to Switched 56 that delivers from 56- to 512-kbps bandwidth. It's a packet-switching service designed to serve multiple locations, and it lets you purchase bandwidth when you need it. To understand frame relay, think of many users connecting to a shared virtual pool of connections, in which everyone's packets are individually labeled and mixed, then sorted out by their destinations. This is a very different technology than T1 service: You don't have a dedicated route from point A to point B. The route between the two points is never really known and changes from moment to moment.

Frame relay can be very cost-effective in situations in which you don't need a continuous connection but still want a fast link when you do need it. However, ISPs that offer frame-relay access are still relatively rare, although this could become a growing field and compete with ISDN in the under-$250-per-month category for 56-kbps links to the Internet.

ACCESS TECHNOLOGIES

Fractional T1

Fractional T1 service is an alternative to Switched 56 and frame relay. As the name implies, you buy a fraction or a fixed number of 64-kbps T1 channels. Some phone companies and ISPs offer this service and will sell you increments (from a half down as small as an eighth) of a full T1 line usually at proportionally cheaper rates. You don't share the line with anyone else; you just use it at slower than its maximum rate, typically for cost-saving reasons. Unlike frame relay services where you pay for the lines only when you use them, with fractional T1 service, you pay a fixed monthly rate since the line is up and running constantly.

Full T1

The best and most expensive services—T1 and T3 lines—are services which give you 24-hour service running at 1.544 Mbps and 45 Mbps, respectively. A T1 line is made up of 24 separate channels, each of which can transmit data at a rate of 64 kbps; there's another 8-kbps channel for signaling and control, which lets you identify the calling party's number and track the amount of bandwidth a line is using, among other things. In most parts of the country, the cost of 8 to 12 slower lines (either Switched 56 or frame relay) equals the cost of a full T1 line. Typically if a Switched 56 line costs $100 per month, a full T1 connection will run $1,200 per month. If you have large-scale data-transmission needs like video conferencing over the Internet, a T1 line might be more effective than multiple separate Switched 56 lines.

As with ISDN, pricing varies. Typically ISPs charge $1,000 (for 56-64 kbps) or $2,500 (for T1 service) to set up a leased line account, with monthly charges ranging from $300 on up to $1,000, depending on the throughput you request. This doesn't include the costs for the DSU/CSUs, routers, or other computers at your end of the connection, which can run from $1,500 on up, depending on line speeds and how many networks and nodes you need to connect.

However, not every ISP offers these advanced digital connections. To find a list of ISPs in your area that have these types of services, search on "T1" through Yahoo! or AltaVista. It is common practive for many ISPs of leased lines to provide wholesale Internet service to other, smaller ISPs down the line. In other words, the larger guys often rent a fraction of their leased lines to other ISPs.

Once you've found a local POP that supports leased lines, you'll need to purchase a DSU/CSU. A DSU/CSU is actually two separate hardware components: One unit terminates the digital line at your office or home, the other terminates the line at your ISP. Kentrox, Adtran, and Bat make popular models. Phone companies also use the DSU/CSU to diagnose the condition of the line, provide the correct power to the circuit, and perform

ACCESS TECHNOLOGIES

other technical chores. Think of the DSU/CSU as an equivalent to a high-speed modem, although it doesn't modulate or demodulate the signal since the circuit is already a digital connection. Without a DSU/CSU, the phone company has no way of knowing whether a line problem is on its side of the line or yours; with it, this still may be an issue, but at least the company has the tools to diagnose the problem.

DSU/CSUs typically have two ports. The unit takes the digital signal coming from the phone jack's four wires (two for transmitting, two for receiving) into a V.35 interface, which is a high-speed serial communications connection between the DSU/CSU and your own networking gear, typically a router. It is a huge interface plug, about an inch square. Routers have similar plugs to accept the V.35 cable from the DSU/CSU. Your PC connects to the router via an Ethernet cable. On the other side of the router is your LAN.

You choose a DSU/CSU according to the speed of the digital connection and the kind of digital circuit you're buying; the faster the circuit, the more expensive the DSU/CSU. For example, those that handle 56-kbps circuits cost about $250, while those designed for T1 speeds run approximately $1,500. You generally don't have a great deal of choice here; you buy whatever brand the ISP is using. In some cases, the ISP will sell you the unit as part of its service package. While both ends of the connection are not required to use the same brand, it is good practice to do so to make it easier to debug problems.

There are some combination DSU/CSU and router devices, which are useful for small networks because they're easier to configure than two separate devices. But for the most part, purchase separate DSU/CSUs and routers; they're more flexible and easier to manage. If you upgrade your line speed from 56 kbps to 256 kbps, for instance, replacing a DSU/CSU is a simple operation compared with replacing a combo unit.

Although leased lines are the fastest way to access the Internet, they're not among the most innovative technologies, especially compared with ISDN and cable modems. Leased lines have been around for years. What is changing, though, and fast, is the price of DSU/CSUs. Having the Internet as a high-speed communications medium has made for more of a market for this equipment, which used to be available only from telecommunications wholesalers.

While you can't buy a DSU/CSU at your local computer superstore, they are becoming more readily available through ISPs. And as more users seek faster and more-continuous Internet access, leased line prices will drop, particularly as the telecommunications deregulation fever motivates cable companies to offer competitive service at cheaper rates. This has already begun in areas where cable companies are allowed to offer bypass service, meaning they can circumvent the local telephone companies and

ACCESS TECHNOLOGIES

offer Internet access (or other wide-area networking). Local phone companies, too, will get into the Internet access game. Given that leased lines are one of the phone companies' more profitable businesses, expect it to be a hotly contested corner of the market in this new era of deregulation.

3 GRAPHICS HARDWARE

IN THE FAST-PACED ARENA of Web design and development you must be familiar with graphical hardware components to customize and glorify your presence on the Web. The old days when merely listing a URL at the bottom of your advertisement was enough to lend your business an air of cutting-edge mystique are gone for good. The Web community, faced with the choice of over 11 million different home pages, has become very picky. If your page is boring, cluttered, or uninformative, users will move on to other sites that are more captivating. Capturing the interest of the Web community is an ever changing challenge. With the development

GRAPHICS HARDWARE

and implementation of new Web browsers come additional capabilities to spice up your page. Those services which keep up with this technology will be able to promote themselves successfully and to reap financial rewards by becoming billboard sites for others' services or products as well.

As you'd expect, standards for what you see on screen aren't standing still, either. Manufacturers are coming out with graphics and dedicated video cards that provide the best-looking animation and the most lifelike video playback you've ever seen on a computer. A graphics card with a 16- or 32-bit graphics controller chip translates most digital data into screen images. An accelerated graphics card includes functions that speed up certain activities, such as resizing windows or moving an icon from one place to another.

However, to manage the increased color and graphics information of even everyday software efficiently, you most often need a 64-bit accelerated graphics card. To view your programs at a fairly sharp resolution (800 by 600 pixels on a PC or 832 by 624 pixels on a Mac) and with a minimum of 256 colors, you'll need to buy a card that contains at least 2MB of RAM. To take full advantage of the latest 3-D animation technology used in games, you'll need to get one of the new graphics cards that has built-in 3-D animation acceleration. These cards will allow animated characters in multimedia programs to move more smoothly, and you'll get more realistic-looking landscapes and buildings in flight-simulator games without sacrificing any high-speed action.

If you have a PC, Windows 95 is a must to make the most of 3-D animation, since it includes a set of animation commands called WinG that these graphics cards and games support. Graphics cards and games for the Mac rely on a built-in animation-command set called QuickDraw that's in Apple System 7.2.1 and later versions.

Along with these new capabilities comes the task of creatively implementing these technologies into existing Web sites. While this all seems like fun, it is a constant challenge. If you are to succeed in implementing new technology, you must understand the basics of how it is going to be utilized and implemented on users' workstations and in your Web development. In this chapter, we'll lay the groundwork in the basics of graphical display methodologies and the methods of collecting this visual data. Armed with the information presented in this chapter you will be able to implement new technologies in your home page in ways that are both informative and accessible to those in the ever expanding Web community.

Video Display

Conceptually, understanding how a graphics card and monitor work together to display text or graphical images isn't that difficult. On any monitor, the video card commands a cathode-ray tube or CRT (just like the one you use to watch *Gilligan's Island* on your TV) to paint an electron

GRAPHICS HARDWARE

beam across the inside of the tube. Coating the inside of the tube is a phosphorescent material that glows for a fraction of a second when hit by the electron beam. If the beam only played over the screen once, the image wouldn't remain there for long. That's why the image must be refreshed by repainting the image many times per second. If this refresh rate is too slow, then the image won't appear to be steady and it will flicker.

There are two methods of screen painting used to refresh the image which differ in the way the video card and monitor draw the image onto the screen of the monitor. In a *noninterlaced display,* the image is created by painting every line in sequence, from top to bottom, on the display. Since the screen is repainted many times per second, you can't see the computer actually painting the screen. On the other hand, an *interlaced display* creates the image on the monitor screen by first painting the odd lines (in other words, every other line) and then starting over at the top painting the even lines. Even though the process is happening very quickly, some people can see a flicker effect because the same image is being painted in two passes. Most video cards today are noninterlaced, because users demand the sharpest and most flicker-free picture on their computer monitors. Noninterlaced graphics cards also reproduce sharper moving images with less distortion.

Each of today's graphics adapters includes the same integral parts. The graphics controller, for example, accelerates the GDI calls (graphics device interface) that your application generates as you work. Otherwise, GDI calls would have to be processed by your CPU and the Windows 95 DIB (Device Independent Bitmap) software accelerator, or the Windows NT GDI, or the OS/2 Presentation Device Driver. The board's driver, which provides the interface to the operating system, hands these calls to the graphics controller, which transforms the binary fonts, lines, pictures, fill colors, and whatever else needs to be presented to the screen into *pixels,* or picture elements.

The controller then sends the pixel information to the card's onboard RAM, the *frame buffer,* which stores the new screen image according to an x-y grid representing the screen resolution. Next the controller is accessed, many times a second, by the RAMDAC, which converts the computer-generated digital pixels to the RGB (red-green-blue) analog signal that the monitor requires.

The most popular business resolutions today are 800×600 (SVGA) or even 1,024×768 for those with a 17-inch monitor. A little math quickly tells us that the perfect graphics board would need at least 2MB of RAM for the frame buffer to deliver 16-bit color at 1,024×768. If you want to run at 24-bit color or if you plan to move to a higher resolution down the road, you're best off looking for a board that lets you upgrade memory beyond 2MB later on. Graphics professionals who work with image-

GRAPHICS HARDWARE

editing packages at even higher resolutions—up to 1,600 by 1,280 pixels— should choose a board with 6MB of RAM or more.

Graphics Cards

Now that you understand the graphical display methodology your computer uses, we should discuss the types of graphics cards available for you today. Add-in graphics cards come in four basic flavors: 8-bit, 16-bit, 32-bit, and the up-and-coming 64 bit. These terms refer to the number of data bits the card sends out at one time. Ideally, a 16-bit video card would send an image to the monitor in half the time it takes for an 8-bit version to do so. It's important to know what kind of card your machine accepts. The older PCs and XTs usually have an 8-bit or PC bus, which accepts only the 8-bit cards. The newer machines use a PCI bus combined with ISA (Industry Standard Architecture).

The dominant internal bus in PCs today is PCI (Peripheral Component Interconnect). With its 133-MBps maximum throughput and Plug-and-Play compatibility, PCI has proved ideal for high-performance devices such as hard disks, graphics accelerators, and network cards. Since its introduction in late 1993, PCI has steadily taken the reins from the competing high-performance technology, VL-Bus—which should be all but extinct by the end of this year. Another competing architecture, EISA (Enhanced ISA), will also fall by the wayside as PCI continues to improve.

Display Resolution

Display resolution is measured in picture elements, or pixels. The display resolution is the number of pixels across the top of the screen by the number down the side of the screen. Therefore, a standard VGA screen is capable of displaying 640 pixels across the top and 480 pixels down the side. If you multiply the two numbers, you see that your CPU has to actively manage 307,200 discrete pixels just to display one image on the monitor. Today most Windows users have switched to resolutions of at least 800 by 600 or higher.

At 640 by 480 pixels of resolution, your computer is moving about 300KB of data around. At 800×600, that number jumps to 468KB. At the current top-of-the-line resolution, 1,024×1,024, your system is moving just over 1.3MB around just to display a single screen of information.

In our current GUI (graphical user interface) operating environment the term *WYSIWYG* (what you see is what you get) is pushing the resolution factor even more. The users' demand for sharper images, redrawn at faster rates, will continually motivate manufacturers to produce cards and monitors that operate at higher resolutions.

GRAPHICS HARDWARE

Frame Buffer Graphics Cards

The simplest kind of video card, and the one that has been around the longest, is the *frame buffer*. This kind of card has no intelligence built into it so it must be told exactly what to do. A frame buffer does one simple job: It displays what the CPU tells it to display. If the CPU has to create complex graphics it gets bogged down. Images take longer to display, leading you to perceive your system as slow.

Because these boards don't have intrinsic intelligence, they are often known, less than affectionately, as dumb frame buffers. They rely on the CPU to perform all the calculations necessary to position each pixel on the monitor. Once the position of each pixel has been calculated, the CPU simply sends this information to the memory on the card. The card's memory buffers the image of the frame; thus, the name frame buffer. This type of card works great in DOS-based machines but it just can't produce the kind of images users are looking for in today's graphical environments, which demand a faster screen draw.

Fixed-Function Accelerators

The next level up in complexity, price, and performance from a frame buffer is a *fixed-function accelerator card*. Fixed-function accelerators can speed things up to ten times faster than a similar frame-buffer card.

Fixed-function accelerators attempt to take some of the load off the CPU chip by building specific graphics functions into hardware on the chip. So instead of the CPU chip having to calculate where an image should be placed, the CPU can tell the graphics card to figure out where to place the image. This allows the CPU to move on to other tasks. These types of cards are well suited for today's graphical demands.

Fixed-function cards, as their name implies, are programmed to do only certain graphical functions. These functions are typically the most time-intensive operations of a graphical interface. The greatest gain in speed comes if you can accelerate those tasks that normally take the most time to do and occur most often in an application.

In both fixed-function cards and programmable accelerators (discussed in the next section), your speed increase comes in two ways. First, since the CPU can just send a command to the accelerator card, the CPU can then go on to other tasks and know that the image will be drawn correctly. Second, transmitting a command to draw a line to the accelerator card is much more efficient and uses fewer resources than actually creating the entire image in memory and then transferring the entire image to the graphics card, as is the case with frame-buffer cards.

GRAPHICS HARDWARE

Programmable Accelerators

Programmable accelerators, also called graphics coprocessors, can be programmed to do any kind of task, unlike fixed-function cards, which are programmed specifically to carry out graphics commands. Programmable accelerators are very popular in the professional graphics arena, speeding things up for artists, layout professionals, and computer-aided drafting shops. For general business applications such as Windows, choose a fixed-function accelerator. In general, fixed-function products cost less than comparable ones based on programmable accelerator chips.

A downside to many boards based on a programmable accelerator is that they don't generally provide VGA support. If all you ever do is boot Windows or OS/2 and run in high resolution all day, you'd never have a problem. But if you ever run DOS-based VGA programs (such as Word-Perfect 5.1 for DOS), you'll need to purchase a VGA card and connect the two boards internally. Although the VGA card won't be that expensive, it's still an added cost and takes up a precious expansion slot inside your PC.

Graphics accelerators help speed things up by efficiently and quickly performing graphical tasks that software programs often perform. Two of the most common graphical tasks are line-drawing and *bit-block transfers*. In the case of line-drawing, a simple frame-buffer graphics card requires the CPU to calculate the position and color of every pixel between the end points of the line. With a graphics accelerator, the CPU just has to tell the graphics board to draw a line between two end points and to give the line a certain color.

Bit-block transfers are what happens when software operating systems want to move a block of bits from one place on the screen to another. A frame-buffer graphics card lets the CPU calculate the position and color of the new position, along with what to display at the old position. On the other hand, if a graphics accelerator is installed, the CPU can just tell the accelerator where to move the bits and the fixed-function or programmable chips on the accelerator will take care of the move. In both cases, performance improves because as soon as the CPU is done giving instructions to the graphics accelerator, it can return to doing something else, confident that the task will be carried out by the accelerator card.

Choosing the perfect graphics accelerator for the type of work you do can increase the overall performance of your system. These internal peripherals come in many flavors, so choosing the right one will require a little homework. One rule of thumb to keep in mind is that the majority of users on the Internet today have VGA graphics cards and monitors. Therefore, when you are creating graphics-intensive Web page material you should always check your work out on a typical 640×480, 14-inch VGA monitor. While it's fine to create your graphical images on your high resolution monitor, make sure your end product looks good on a standard workstation as described above.

GRAPHICS HARDWARE

Video Capture Cards

With the proliferation of faster processors and new add-in boards, video clips are practically everywhere: You'll find them scattered across the Internet's World Wide Web and embedded in programs ranging from basic tax-return software to CD-ROM edutainment packages. With video playback going mainstream, video capture is becoming an increasingly practical means to digitize raw material for editing and subsequent redistribution as stand-alone files or as part of your own presentations. Chances are you'll be working with video in some form if you have a CD drive, or are developing Web pages for use on the Internet. Therefore, the perfect graphics board should handle video. In its simplest form, processing motion video means processing a succession of bitmap data at 15 to 30 frames per second (which gives the video realistic animation). This is a daunting task even for a graphics board with a dual-ported memory design. Video capture is one of the most demanding functions a desktop PC can perform. The challenge is to digitize and store a data stream of up to 30MB per second in real time, without dropping frames and thereby ruining the smoothness of the display. Look for a board that offers motion video acceleration and scaling, preferably with video-acceleration functions rolled into the controller.

In analyzing video-capture performance, it's important to note that most basic functionality comes from your capture board, not the software. The latter simply accesses onboard options like capture format, resolution, and adjustment of incoming color and brightness. However, this doesn't mean that each program produces identical results, even when using identical hardware. Though they exercise the same hardware functions, different editing programs do so with different amounts of overhead. The more efficient the program, the fewer dropped frames.

3-D processing is the newest challenge for mainstream graphics boards. Like video processing, it will be rolled into many of the new boards. A 3-D processor will be responsible for applying the shading on the wireframe geometry that represents the 3-D image. The mainstream boards won't rival the $2,000 cards aimed at CAD and animation pros, but they should prove fine for games and business applications with 3-D features.

Any time you transfer video from one format to another, you risk lowering video quality. Therefore, the less you do to alter the incoming video, the better your resulting digital image. However, in its raw state, full-motion video can take up to 30MB per second. This typically results in lost frames, which can severely dampen the effect of your captured video. Video capture, then, is inherently a compromise, getting the most video information into the PC without dropping frames.

Generally, video-capture boards let you digitize video in two formats, RGB and YUV. RGB, the highest quality, is the format your monitor displays, while YUV, made up of luminance (brightness) and chrominance

GRAPHICS HARDWARE

(color information), is a more compact form of video that relies on the fact that your eyes are more sensitive to changes in brightness than to individual color variations.

Real-time compression is also becoming a standard feature on video-capture boards. Don't misinterpret this as just a method of saving hard disk space. Rather, the function of on-the-fly compression is to help you capture the highest quality of video possible without dropping frames. With the latest compression chips, capturing 30 frames per second (fps) at window sizes of up to 320×240 is now a reality. With this increased functionality and marketability the price drops have ensured that you can buy a high-quality board for around $400 or even less.

Evaluate Your Needs

Before you capture a single frame of video, it's important to characterize your intended use. Video capture typically falls into two general categories: capture for compression and distribution, and capture for hardware-assisted playback on a single PC or small group of computers.

For most people, capturing video for distribution and playback on any number of PCs is the compelling reason to own a video-capture card. In this scenario, the board is simply a vehicle to bring video to disk, where you edit it and compress it again with a software codec (*co*der/*dec*oder) for the optimum file size and transfer rate, particularly important if it's going to end up on CD-ROM.

For this type of application, you want a capture board that achieves the ultimate image quality. Frame rate is a secondary consideration since software playback performance ultimately is determined by the target PC's speed and video acceleration features. However, if you are setting up a dedicated video-playback station for an ongoing presentation or a kiosk, you'll want a board that will maximize your playback frame rate as well as your image quality. Whatever you do, don't get too hung up on the type of codec the boards use; focus instead on how the results come out.

Motion JPEG boards feature hardware-assisted playback as well as *video overlay,* a method of placing video windows on top of your graphics display. In contrast, cards designed for video distribution applications are typically capture-only since it is assumed that the edited video will be played back on other PCs. Of course, nothing stops you from buying a board with playback features, then recompressing some video files for distribution, while playing the rest with the card installed. But electing not to get the playback features generally means that you won't have to deal with the complexities of common overlay features like the 8-bit VESA feature connector.

Other functions you might want, especially if you're just using the PC for editing purposes, include VGA-to-NTSC encoding. This will let you

GRAPHICS HARDWARE

output your newly created video to VHS or similar tape for distribution in analog form.

Finally, if there's one peripheral dying for plug-and-play capability, it's video capture boards. As in the playback world, video capture is going to have to move away from outdated feature connectors to make way for integrated products and affordable capture-only cards before it becomes standard fare for the average user to implement in their environment.

Besides the combination video capture/graphics accelerators, there are accelerated playback models composed of add-in cards that connect to your graphics card through the VESA feature connector. Accelerated play-back cards present several problems, from installation snags to limitations on display modes. For example, almost all the boards that require feature connectors limit the graphics color depth to some degree, often to a mere 256 colors. This negates the usefulness of any fast 24-bit graphics cards you may have. In a kiosk, where you might use a lower-end graphics card, this is less of an issue than it would be on your everyday system. Note that the video overlay itself is always in true color despite the graphics mode.

Installing video capture cards is notoriously difficult, and for the most part, this reputation still holds true today. These conflicts are not only with particular graphics cards, but with certain systems. As the need for captured video increases there will be a greater push to make these cards plug-and-play.

No matter what you do with a file after capture, you can't surpass its original frame rate. Therefore, if 30-fps capture at 320×240 is a must-have for you, you must choose a board that can capture at that rate. Even if you think 30 fps is a must, it makes sense to look at the top runners among the 15-fps contenders as well since some of them function equally well. Furthermore, even for kiosk applications, cheaper capture-only boards often equal or surpass overlay cards with the same native files.

Before deciding on which video capture board is right for you, you should make several inquiries to the technical support department of all the companies you're considering and make sure the board will end up giving you what you want. There are many standards out there. Although it looks like the Microsoft AVI standard will survive as the main con-sumer standard for video on the PC, your application may require MPEG or something else. The two are compatible in some ways and not in oth-ers, so we urge you to be aware of all the potential problems in mixing and matching software.

Make sure that your video capture board will copy your edited video down to your VCR. Most of the boards on the market today don't pro-vide output, allowing only input from a VCR, tape recorder, camcorder, and other such equipment. While these video capture boards and the asso-ciated software offer a huge improvement over conventional methods of editing video, you still need to get your edited video copied back down to

GRAPHICS HARDWARE

your VCR. There are cards on the market which perform this transfer, but the cost is somewhat restrictive—unless you have three to four thousand to burn.

In conclusion, the more you know about what you want to do with video, the easier your buying decision will be. As video capture moves toward simpler installation procedures and lower cost, these choices are only going to get better. Another rule of thumb to keep in mind is that if you are incorporating video into your home page development make sure that the content of the presentation is skillfully designed and implemented. Nothing is more aggravating to a user who waits several minutes to download your video only to find the presentation uninteresting and useless.

Scanners

Just as keyboards are most suited for entering and editing text, and mice and graphics tablets are best used for pointing, scanners are the best choice for getting existing graphical images into your PC. A scanner is not just another input device—it's a pair of eyes for your PC, letting your computer digitally read text-based information, photographs, or complicated diagrams. Just as human eyes interpret information to the brain, a scanner simply converts text and images to digital data for your computer, relaying the patterns or shades it sees to your CPU and software for analysis. The combination turns an illustration or photo into a digital image usable by graphics, presentation, or electronic publishing applications.

You have full control over manipulation of these digital images once you have them scanned, which makes it easy to incorporate all sorts of hard-copy images—a photo of your product, a sketch by your three-year-old, or an illustration from a book or magazine—into your Web pages. These images can be brightened up with sharper colors, rotated to different angles, and stretched to distort their appearance—it's totally up to you as the owner of the digital data how you want these images to appear. (For once in your life you can distort the truth and get away with it!)

Scanners come in many shapes, sizes, and costs. Just as you wouldn't use a flamethrower to hunt for rabbits, you wouldn't necessarily spend a couple of thousand dollars on a flatbed scanner that is only going to be used to scan simple images for your daughter's Girl Scout newsletter. On the other hand, a professional artist would be foolish not to use a top-of-the-line flatbed scanner with high-quality color reproduction capabilities.

Scanners come in two primary flavors: *handheld* and *flatbed*. With a handheld scanner, you scan an image by rolling the scanner over it. A flatbed scanner looks and works like a copier: You put the image you want to scan on a glass plate and close the lid while the scanner reads the image.

If you need to convert existing text documents into a format that your computer can understand, use a scanner to get the document image into your computer. With optical character recognition (OCR) software, a

GRAPHICS HARDWARE

scanner turns faxed or printed pages into editable word processing files. When teamed with a document management program, these scanned images let your PC absorb volumes of information, index everything, and retrieve the data you want at a moment's notice. This ability to scan existing documents also gives you the ability to save and manipulate the converted images as text files that you can edit, print, and store for future use.

Color Scanners

In today's world, demand for thrilling color graphical images is overwhelming. Fortunately, color is cheaper than it's ever been. If there's even a chance you'll want to digitize and then display or print color images, get a color scanner.

A scanner's color capability, like a graphics card's, is measured by bit depth. Twenty-four-bit color provides 8 bits of data or 256 different possibilities for each pixel in each of the three color channels: red, green, and blue. That multiplies out to 16.7 million possible colors. Many scanners aimed at graphics professionals are 30-bit devices capable of more than 1 billion possible colors. Some manufacturers support a still greater palette—36-bit color.

More isn't always better when it comes to color depth. A 24-bit or 30-bit color image will be wasted when displayed in a presentation using 256 colors. And as you'd expect, the more bits per pixel, the larger the image file. High-resolution, high-color images can fill a hard drive in a hurry.

As far as text is concerned, the most accurate OCR involves not 24-bit color or even 8-bit monochrome (256 gray scales), but 1-bit, black-and-white scanning. On the other hand, the richer its palette, the more accurately a scanner can capture an image's shadows and color subtleties. Though a 30- or 36-bit scanner can be overkill when you're printing digitized images on an inkjet, it can work wonders with transparencies. Color slides have a much greater range of color qualities than images on paper. When fed through a high-quality scanner with a transparency adapter, they can produce stunning images. For most work, though, 24-bit color is sufficient. Don't settle for anything less. You really don't have to settle, since 24-bit color is the current de facto standard. However, don't pay for more unless you're sure you'll use it.

Resolution

In contrast to your 20/20 vision, a scanner typically has 400×800 vision. Its optical resolution, measured in dots per inch, defines the sharpness of detail it sees. A flatbed scanner's optical resolution, also called *true resolution,* is listed as horizontal times vertical dots per inch. A 400×800-dpi scanner, for example, divides each horizontal inch of an image into 400 pixels and reads 800 lines of data from each vertical inch. In other words, its motor takes 800 steps to move the CCD (charge-coupled device) one

GRAPHICS HARDWARE

inch, while the CCD itself contains 400 light-sensitive elements across each inch of its width.

Some 300×300-dpi flatbed scanners are available, but current low-end color models start at 300×600 dpi. The norm today is even higher—600×600-, 400×800-, and 800×400-dpi devices can be readily found for less than $1,000 direct.

Although higher-resolution scanners produce more-accurate digital images, they're generally slower at scanning. And the image files they produce are much larger: An image scanned at 600×1,200 dpi contains four times as much data as one scanned at 300×600 dpi, so you'll need plenty of RAM and hard drive space to edit and store such fine scans. Nevertheless, a high-resolution scanner can be a good match for a high-resolution output device. If you're converting grayscale images for printing on a 1,200-dpi laser printer, for instance, a scanner in the 1,200-dpi range makes sense.

Handheld Scanners

Handheld scanners are less expensive than flatbeds and take up a lot less room. Their only drawback is that they can only scan a 4-inch-wide photo or part of a document in a single pass. While you can electronically "stitch" these pieces together with software to create larger images, it is time consuming and tedious, requiring many passes to stitch together a large image. Handhelds are slower than flatbeds, and you have to roll them steadily to get good quality results. Once the only choice for scanning on a budget, handheld scanners have been pushed into the bargain basement by the declining price of their full-page, flatbed cousins. Even so, they still fill a useful niche.

Like their flatbed cousins, handhelds combine a light source with a charge-coupled device (CCD) that reads the reflected light intensity and converts it to digital information. Rather than use a motor to move the scanning hardware past the image, however, a handheld scanner depends on your muscle power. That's a disadvantage, since few of us can drag a peripheral across a page as smoothly as a machine can.

Because handhelds scan such narrow three- to four-inch strips, you're either limited to small images or skinny columns of text, or you're at the mercy of the software used to stitch together multiple scans. Make sure a handheld scanner comes with stitching software before you buy. Ask, too, if the scanner/software combination can warn you when you're moving the scanner too quickly, causing it to skip part of the page or image.

On the positive side, handheld scanners are easy to install—most plug into a PC's parallel port, making it easy to move the scanner from one system to another or to carry one with a laptop PC. For real portability, there are portable grayscale plug-and-scan handheld scanners that connect to a notebook's PC Card slot and even draw their power from there.

GRAPHICS HARDWARE

You'll find grayscale and color-capable handheld scanners with resolutions as high as 400 dpi. It's difficult, however, to perform accurate hand scans at resolutions above 200 dpi, since the higher the device's resolution, the slower and steadier your hand-dragged path must be across the image. At the high end of the handheld market are products that produce 24-bit color images, which sell for about $200 direct. At the low end are grayscale scanners available for about $80. There are of course lots of other products between the low and high models.

Flatbed Scanners

Flatbed scanners tend to provide high resolution and more options such as automatic document feeders or transparency adapters, and can handle larger-format material in a single pass. They also enable you to readily scan books or other three-dimensional objects (coins, keys, hands, and so on), and they offer greater OCR (optical character recognition) accuracy.

While flatbed scanners tend to be a lot more versatile, they can cost as much as $300 more than a handheld model. If you're incorporating a scanner primarily to import photos and other artwork for publishing purposes, you'll want a flatbed model. Don't overbuy, however—match the scanner's resolution with that of your intended output device. If you'll be digitizing photos for later printing on a 600-dpi monochrome laser printer you'll be satisfied with a 600-dpi grayscale scanner. A higher-resolution color scanner makes sense for prepress color separations, or enlarging scanned images such as small photos or 35mm slides.

The advantage of flatbed scanning is crystal clear as soon as you start scanning even a short stack of documents or images. Slap down the paper, close the lid, click on your software's Scan icon or press a key, and the CCD moves down the length of the sheet. You get a full-page scan in one shot—most of the time, anyway.

Grayscale scanners need just one pass of the CCD to finish the job, but when scanning in color, many low- to mid-priced flatbeds make three passes to gather red, green, and blue (RGB) information. A more accurate method—and a more expensive one, although its price has fallen over the past year—is single-pass scanning. A single-pass color scanner either uses three light sources almost simultaneously, or separates a single white light source into the RGB components with a filter.

If speed is important and you make more than a few scans each day, look for a single-pass scanner and ask the vendor or reseller about different models' scanning speeds. Even at the same resolution and color depth, some scanners are quicker than others. No matter what speed you seek, ask if the scanner's light source remains on constantly. Some units don't turn off their lamps between scans, which makes for more frequent replacement of burned-out bulbs.

GRAPHICS HARDWARE

Check, too, on the availability of add-ons such as automatic sheet feeders for high-volume OCR work and transparency adapters for turning slides into digital images. Most of these add-ons can be installed in a few minutes without any outside help. By contrast, most flatbed scanners themselves connect to your PC through an included 8-bit SCSI interface card, so you may have to wrestle with IRQs and address conflicts during installation and configuration. Some scanners, such as HP's ScanJet series, come with documentation and software that make installation as painless as possible.

If your computer already has a SCSI interface, perhaps for its hard drive or CD-ROM drive, find out if the scanner uses standard SCSI or some more exotic variant, then make sure the vendor provides a suitable Advanced SCSI Programming Interface (ASPI) driver. Some models even include drivers for use over a network, letting you share a scanner throughout a small workgroup.

The price for this flexibility has fallen dramatically. Three years ago, a 24-bit, true-color flatbed scanner easily could have cost a cool $2,000. Today, you can find one for as little as $400. Scanners under $1,000 abound, many capable of scanning at ultra-sharp resolutions that not long ago were out of reach of anyone but well-heeled graphics professionals. Almost all units come with capable image-editing and OCR programs. Many can be equipped with optional sheet feeders and slide adapters.

Shopping Tips

- Although a scanner's resolution is properly measured in horizontal by vertical dots per inch, as in 600×1,200 dpi, vendors sometimes list only the higher of the two values, or the scanner's *interpolated* (software-enhanced) *resolution* instead of its optical or true resolution.

- Compare scanning speed in terms of pages per minute for OCR, or identical resolution and image size for graphics.

- Some grayscale flatbed scanners can be upgraded later to color. But if you think there's a good chance you'll want to scan color images someday, you'll save money by buying a 24-bit, 16.7-million-color flatbed right away.

- A one-pass color scanner costs slightly more, but produces sharper and quicker scans than a unit that takes three passes for red, green, and blue.

- If you're shopping for a cost-cutting small-office solution, you may be tempted by a multifunction scanner/printer/fax/copier. Just remember that these all-in-one peripherals' scanning capabilities are currently limited to grayscale, not color, and scan at optical resolutions no higher than 400 dpi.

GRAPHICS HARDWARE

- On the hardware side, make sure the scanner you buy supports standard SCSI so you can daisy-chain it to other SCSI devices connected to your PC, rather than being restricted to a proprietary adapter.

- The quality of the software bundled with your scanner can determine the quality of the images you produce. Many scanners come with unimpressive "lite" versions of popular programs. Look for OCR software with at least a 99-percent accuracy rate and an image editor that includes a complete set of editing tools and supports standard graphics file formats.

- Look for at least a 30-day money-back guarantee and a one-year parts-and-labor warranty, and make sure to get an extra bulb you can replace yourself without having to return the scanner to the factory. The bulb will last longer if the scanner switches it off between scans.

4 SOUND TECHNOLOGIES

AS STATED IN PREVIOUS CHAPTERS, progressively designed Web sites with the last word in video clips, animated graphics, Java scripts, and sound technology are the "hot sites" on the Internet. The creative implementation of these technologies is what draws attention to the service being provided. As the Web community becomes used to these new implementations, it is your goal as a successful Webmaster to keep up with the technology used to develop and implement these multimedia presentations.

SOUND TECHNOLOGIES

If your current Web experience is limited to text and graphics, you're missing out on the Web's true multimedia power. Until recently, bandwidth limitations and the large size of audio files made it impossible to use the Web to efficiently and reliably access large volumes of archived audio content. Live audio across the Web was simply out of the question. The most you could expect was a quick greeting or a simple message, usually no more than a few seconds of sound.

The silent Web is changing fast. Newer technologies make efficient use of the bandwidth available, which in turn makes it possible for you to enjoy the sounds of the Web. In order for you to experience this sound you will need to have a sound card and speakers. Since most PCs come bundled with both speakers and sound cards, we will limit our discussion of sound card features and instead focus our attention in this section so as to give you a strong understanding of the technologies currently used to produce and transport sound. As with any technology there are low, medium, and high budget options for sound cards, so we have included a comparison chart in Appendix D for a quick review. At a minimum, you'll need a 14.4-kbps modem connection to have a good experience with sound, although you really should use 28.8 kbps for improved audio quality and playback.

Until recently, one of the most annoying facts of Internet life was the periodic delays involved in downloading large audio files. Audio files have an average 5:1 transfer ratio over dial-up connections; that is, for every minute of audio playback time, you have to wait five minutes in download time. Therefore, if you wanted to download a 30-minute radio program, you would have to wait two and a half hours before you could start listening to it! If you pay to access the Internet in hourly increments, imagine the cost—and your frustration when you find out a few minutes into the program that you aren't really interested in hearing it. And don't forget about the disk space required to store 30 minutes of audio. What's more, should any problems occur at any point during the download, the entire file will be lost. In short, using conventional technologies (like FTP followed by an audio player) to download audio files and access them off line is not an option.

To address these issues, companies have finally designed and implemented audio technologies that allow you to listen to audio files while you download them. Furthermore, you no longer need to store the file on your local drive, so you can listen to that 30 minutes of audio no matter how limited your hard disk space. Usually, after only several seconds' delay, you can start listening to the audio file you want. Skipping to any point in the audio file is also possible, so you can get past the introduction sections and jump right to the meat of the presentation section in no time.

Although you can use these new technologies at any connection speed greater than 9.6 kbps, your connection speed will determine the maximum possible quality you can attain. Also, the connection quality makes a difference, particularly at the lower connection speeds, which are

SOUND TECHNOLOGIES

more susceptible to packet loss. Some technologies deliver superb audio with packet loss rates of up to ten percent. Their algorithms deal with packet loss rates between four and ten percent. When these loss rates are detected the algorithms attempt to predict what the lost packet information was, producing audio similar to that from faint short-wave radio signals. In some cases, this can add a strange undertone to the audio you receive. Still, this fill-in-the-gaps technology can avoid choppy audio, making it easier to listen to audio files even at high packet-loss rates.

There are also less forgiving technologies where packet loss is more noticeable, resulting in choppy audio at packet-loss rates greater than five percent. Given a good-quality connection, however, all these technologies deliver crisp audio to your desktop via the Internet.

With the introduction of these new technologies you can now fast-forward, rewind, seek, and pause audio files in real time. We'll look at how these current audio technologies work and examine their strengths and drawbacks. We will also present an overview of issues relating to the integration of embedded streaming audio into your home page development.

Streaming Audio Technologies

Streaming (continuous-delivery) audio technologies provide an answer to the long delays previously experienced when downloading sound files. This instant audio gratification is what most surfers expect nowadays. Streaming technologies start playback after a short buffering period and continue to play until the message is finished. Some provide VCR-style features such as seek, fast-forward, and rewind. Much more responsive than older download-and-play technologies, streaming technologies give end users a sense of immediacy and offer Web authors a powerful hook for attracting and keeping an audience that's always just a click away from the next person's site.

Streaming audio technologies are designed to overcome the fundamental problem of multimedia elements distributed over the Web: limited bandwidth. While your 28.8-kbps modem or 128-kbps ISDN connection may seem screamingly fast, it pales in comparison to even an ancient single-spin CD-ROM drive, which can transfer 150K of data each second.

Where most of us think in bytes (or kilobytes) per second, the communications world thinks in bits, which come eight to a byte. Your 28.8-Kbps modem passes 28.8 kilo*bits* per second; that works out to a throughput capacity of only about 3.6 kilobytes (3.6K) per second, or approximately 1/40 the speed of the single-spin CD-ROM drive you replaced last year because your response was too slow. CD-quality audio requires about 176K of raw data per second, close to 50 times the capacity of your 28.8-kbps modem. For this reason, all streaming audio technologies compress the audio data stream drastically to match the throughput of your Internet connection, which may be as low as 9,600 bps.

SOUND TECHNOLOGIES

All streaming audio products are *codecs* (coder/decoders) with at least two components: a compressor (or encoder) which compresses the audio stream, and a decompressor (or player) which decompresses and plays the compressed audio stream. A third component is dedicated server software which either delivers the audio streams to the clients or provides advanced functionality to the player, or both.

Encoders tend to be standalone products charged with one simple task: shrinking the audio bitstream to match the capacity of the low-bandwidth connections we use for Internet access. All streaming products use *lossy* techniques to achieve the high compression rates needed; this means that the original file is not reproduced exactly during playback—something is lost. During compression, the codec discards the original data, replacing it with a more compact representation. During playback, the codec reassembles the information into a file that approximates the basic structure of the original but isn't exactly the same.

All lossy compression technologies, whether for audio, still images, or video, share one characteristic: The more you squeeze, the more you distort. When comparing streaming audio encoders, one obvious measure is to see which technology produces the least distortion at a common compression ratio; that is, which technology sounds best during playback.

Buffering

As mentioned earlier, the predominant audio technology used on the Web relies on use of buffering, codecs, and audio streams. These audio technologies differ mainly in the algorithms they use to deliver the audio data (that is, via UDP, TCP, or IP multicasting). Buffering is responsible for the 1- to 2-second delay that occurs between starting or repositioning playback (by fast-forwarding or rewinding, for example) and hearing sound. By allocating portions of memory to store a few packets of audio information (usually a dozen or so), the audio player can achieve very smooth playback. As each audio buffer is played, it is refilled with new data received from the server; the player always takes its data from the buffer rather than waiting for the server. The assumption is that the buffer will make up for transmission delays, which could result in audio gaps until new data is delivered to the player.

Compression

Like modem technologies, codec technologies do something to the data, transmit it, and then undo what was done before transfer. In this case, codec technologies compress the data in the most efficient way possible using the vendors' compression algorithms. Some compression algorithms are better than others, so while the underlying technologies used by all vendors are similar, each can achieve dramatically different performance depending on its codec technology.

SOUND TECHNOLOGIES

Repositioning within a Sound File

Audio stream technology allows for real-time repositioning within a file as well as playing audio files as they are downloaded. Previously, an entire audio file had to be completely downloaded before the audio player could recognize and play it. In audio stream technology, the minimum unit of audio is a single packet of data. The audio stream player can therefore play an audio packet as soon as it is received. Furthermore, the player can request a specific audio packet from the server, because in audio stream technology, the transfer communication is bidirectional (that is, the server not only transmits data to the player, but the player can transmit data to the server). This request capability enables the fast-forward, rewind, and seek features of audio stream players.

Digital Audio Formats

There are numerous formats for digital audio in the marketplace. There are Macintosh-only formats such as 8- and 16-bit AIFF, and Windows/Mac formats such as RealAudio, u-Law, and MPEG audio. (For a list of available audio formats refer to Table 4.1 below.) The most popular Windows/Mac formats available today are MIDI (Musical Instrument Digital Interface) and WAV files. These formats provide a digital representation of analog sound, much the way a graphics bitmap gives a digital representation of a real-world image. In fact, WAV files are similar to the digital audio stored on audio CDs. In the next two sections we will define and describe these two predominant digital audio formats.

MIDI Audio Format

MIDI is the acronym for Musical Instrument Digital Interface. This protocol was developed in 1983 in an unprecedented display of cooperation be-

■ Table 4.1 Sound Formats

Sound Format	Platform	Advantages	Disadvantages
Real Audio	Win/Mac	Real-time playability	Inferior sound quality
16-bit AIFF	Mac	Best sound quality	Large file sizes
8-bit AIFF	Mac	Medium file sizes	Grainy sound quality
16-bit Quicktime	Win/Mac	Best sound quality	Large file sizes
8-bit Quicktime	Win/Mac	Medium file sizes	Grainy sound quality
16-bit WAV	Win/Mac	Good sound quality	Large file sizes
8-bit WAV	Win/Mac	Medium file sizes	Grainy sound quality
MIDI	Win/Mac	Very small files; sound quality is only as good as MIDI device	Not strictly audio, can only utilize MIDI sounds

SOUND TECHNOLOGIES

tween the music industry's major electronic instrument manufacturers including Roland, Sequential Circuits (now absorbed into Yamaha), Yamaha, Korg, and others. MIDI allows electronic devices such as synthesizers, computers, light show controllers, VCRs, and multi-track recorders to interact and work in synchronization with other MIDI-compatible devices. This format allows professional musicians to create music much faster and also allows a single musician to be a one-person orchestra. In addition, MIDI devices have opened the world of electronic music to amateur musicians, allowing them access to the same sounds used in the professional music industry.

The original purpose of MIDI was to allow a *master controller,* usually in the form of a keyboard, to play or *trigger* many other keyboards remotely, including those manufactured by other companies. Before the development of MIDI, most keyboard manufacturers had a proprietary protocol that allowed their instruments to interact with others produced by the same company. For example, a Yamaha keyboard could trigger other Yamaha keyboards, but it couldn't act as master to a Roland device. Musicians who used overdubbing techniques in the recording studio to "thicken" sounds wanted a convenient way to achieve the same effect in live performances without being restricted to the use of only one manufacturer's products. For such musicians, MIDI was a dream come true.

MIDI is a series of two- to three-byte messages transmitted at 31.25 kbps which define "performance gestures" only—MIDI does not transmit sound. Instead of transmitting the actual sound of a note, MIDI transmits the information that a particular key was depressed and how fast the key went down (known as *attack velocity*). As long as a connected instrument or *slave* is assigned to a corresponding channel (MIDI has 16 channels) the slave will respond by playing whatever sound is assigned to that key. When a key is released a new message is sent telling the receiving device to stop playing the sound. If a MIDI musician connects many instruments together and assigns them all to the same MIDI channel, a thick layer of all their combined sounds will be heard whenever the master keyboard is played. MIDI master controllers come in many shapes—ones resembling woodwind instruments, drums, and guitars being very popular. Other MIDI messages include pitchbend, aftertouch (a special effect created by applying pressure after a key has been depressed), program change, and a catchall category called controllers which include parameters such as volume, sustain, panning, and others.

Manufacturers soon recognized that slaves didn't need to have keyboards since they are not actually touched in performance. *Sound modules,* or synthesizers without keyboards, have all the sound synthesis potential as a regular synthesizer. Most new instruments are available with or without a keyboard. Sound modules usually cost about 70 percent of the price of the full keyboard version. After buying one or two

SOUND TECHNOLOGIES

keyboards, most MIDI musicians opt for sound modules to complete their MIDI systems.

Drum machines are sound modules loaded predominantly with percussion timbres. These can be played from external controllers but are most commonly played by pads built into the device. The drum pattern is created by putting the machine into record or *sequence* mode. Sequencers allow the musician to record, edit, and play back MIDI information. Dedicated hardware sequencers were very popular in the mid-1980s but have since declined in popularity in comparison to the software sequencers created for the Macintosh, IBM, Atari, Next, and Commodore computers. Software sequencers allow the musician to edit using a large screen, take advantage of the powerful processors available in the home PC, and create files much larger than those possible with the limited RAM found in hardware sequencers. Hardware sequencers, usually light and compact, are now used most commonly for performances where transporting a personal computer is not practical.

MIDI has been continually expanded to add other features, including MIDI Time Code (to allow synchronization of video and audio tape), Sample Dump Standard (to allow transfer of digital audio files), and MIDI Show Control (to allow control of devices used in the theater). One new feature created with the hobbyist in mind is General MIDI, which allows sequenced song files to be effortlessly shared among all musicians owning GM devices. The protocol requires that everyone use the same set of sounds to ensure compatibility.

There are some products that also feature software-based wave-table MIDI, which uses your system's CPU to handle the processing of sampled MIDI sounds. This allows less expensive PCs to produce rich, wave-table MIDI playback under Windows. Processing wave-table MIDI sounds can consume a good deal of CPU time, impairing performance. If you want wave-table MIDI for games or video presentations, you should use a sound board that offers wave-table processing in hardware. Otherwise, you may be able to save a buck with a software-based wave-table MIDI.

While most sound cards have a built-in amplifier, the signal is generally weak (only 4 watts per channel, with high distortion), even on high-quality cards. This means that the perfect sound system requires a set of speakers with their own power source and amplifier built in. Most of the speakers that come bundled with multimedia PCs produce noise and distortion; a power amplifier will alleviate this problem.

MIDI is not without problems. The range of parameters is limited to only 7-bit resolution (128 steps) and many people would like to see more than 16 channels. The relatively slow transfer rate of 31.25 kbps becomes a problem when transferring large samples between devices, and it is generally agreed that the interface is too difficult to use. The recently proposed XMIDI is intended to solve many of the limitations addressed here

SOUND TECHNOLOGIES

and to be backward compatible. Whether or not XMIDI succeeds, we are sure that in one form or another musicians will be using MIDI to create music well into the next century.

WAV Audio Format

WAV audio format is a digital format that was created and implemented by Microsoft. This audio capture format differs from MIDI in that WAV files are actual recordings of digital audio, while MIDI merely controls prerecorded digitized instruments. When using WAV files you must also configure and use an audio player. There are many audio players on the market, some freeware or shareware. The most popular of these players are included with today's popular Web browsers, as Netscape's NA Player is, for example.

When your system records a WAV file, the incoming signal is converted to a series of bits representing the curve of the original analog signal. The quality—and size—of a digital audio file is related to its resolution and frequency. For example, CD-quality audio has a resolution of 16 bits and a frequency of 44.1KHz, while the audio found in most AVI video clips is about 8 bits and 22KHz.

The following terms relate to the components of a WAV file and are essential to understanding how these files work:

- *Sample rate*—The number of times each second that the system takes a snapshot of the analog signal. Sample rate is measured in kilohertz (KHz), which represents thousands of samples each second. Audio CDs store sound at 44.1KHz

- *Bit Depth*—The number of bits that are dedicated to each sample. 16-bit audio, which is what audio CDs use, uses two bytes of data for each sample.

- *Stereo/mono*—Stereo means you are storing two channels of sound, which can vary to provide spatial quality to the audio playback. Mono uses a single channel.

The audio format determines the digital quality of the sound, but sound hardware is important, too. Interference inside the PC and the quality of audio components affect sound output. Many sound boards have inferior frequency response, which means they do not accurately reproduce sounds at the high and low end of the human hearing range. Most boards also produce poor *signal-to-noise ratios*—a measure of how much noise is mixed in with the output—with performance generally below that of CD players.

File Size   As mentioned above, audio files can be quite large. Table 4.2 below gives you an idea of how large uncompressed digital audio can get.

SOUND TECHNOLOGIES

To conserve disk space, you can reduce the number of bits dedicated to modeling the curve of analog audio. For example, by capturing to mono format instead of stereo, you can cut the size of the file in half, because only one channel of information is being stored. In addition, you can reduce the number of times each second you sample the incoming analog signal. By going from 44.1KHz (or 44,100 samples per second) to 22.05KHz (22,050 samples per second), you can cut the file size by half again. Dropping to 11.025KHz provides further economies. Finally, you can lower the number of bits dedicated to each audio sample. Dropping from 16-bit to 8-bit resolution again cuts the file size in half.

Unfortunately, the less information you store, the less realistic the audio playback. Losing the stereo data can render audio playback flat and leave out spatial cues that result from instruments or sounds coming from one speaker or another. Dropping the bit depth can add an audible hiss to sound files and lessen the precision of reproduction. Lowering the frequency means that the audio is being sampled less often, so the card is unable to smoothly recreate changes in sound.

Another way to conserve space is through compression. As with video files, audio compression techniques reduce file size by coding redundant information in compact format and even by throwing out some information. The only pitfall when using compression is that the speed at which the file can be played is delayed due to the time it takes to uncompress the file.

WAV files are being used more and more on the Internet. If you want to have sound welcome users to your home page, all you have to do is either digitize the file yourself or visit the Bart Simpson home page on the Internet to download the WAV file.

Sound Transport Methods

Each vendor usually has its own philosophy about which transport mechanism uses available bandwidth most efficiently. Because of the architectural design of the protocols used on the Internet (based on TCP/IP), the Internet is not an efficient medium for handling continuous, time-based

■ **Table 4.2   Size of One Minute of Uncompressed Stereo Wave Audio**

Frequency	8-bit	16-bit
11KHz	1.2MB	2.6MB
22KHz	2.6MB	5.2MB
44.1KHz	5.1MB	10.4MB

SOUND TECHNOLOGIES

information. Therefore, the way data is transmitted across the Internet and the protocols used have a direct impact on overall efficiency, reliability, and performance.

One of the most popular transport methods is the *User Datagram Protocol* (UDP). A *datagram* is the information being transported and is contained between the header and trailer of the packet. UDP is a maintenance protocol that transmits small packets very quickly (at a high priority) but does not guarantee packet delivery. Therefore, while UDP is perhaps the most efficient way to transmit audio streams, it introduces packet loss, which must be dealt with by the application that uses it. However, UDP was never intended to transmit large volumes of data; whenever it is used for that purpose, it tends to saturate communication lines. For example, NFS (which also uses UDP) usually calls for a dedicated link between the NFS server and client to avoid saturating the network with NFS traffic. UDP is efficient and fast for single point-to-point communications, but it should never be used without some flow-control mechanism to limit its use of available bandwidth.

Another transport protocol is Transmission Control Protocol (TCP). TCP is the most common protocol on the Internet and is used to transmit large volumes of data with guaranteed packet delivery; it also incorporates flow-control mechanisms that help ensure fair resource utilization for all users on the Internet. Packet size is usually larger than with UDP packets to accommodate the transmission of large volumes of data.

A major drawback of TCP in dealing with audio streams, however, is that if a packet is lost, the server must retransmit it. And because the packet is significantly larger than a UDP packet, it takes longer to retransmit. Therefore, while a lost UDP packet results in a tiny gap in the audio transmission, a lost TCP packet knocks out a huge hole, probably causing audio playback to stop until the packet is retransmitted and successfully delivered. This packet retransmission also results in higher overhead on the server than UDP-based solutions.

Still another transport protocol is IP multicasting: A host group is created, and every IP datagram sent by the server is received by all members of the host group. Membership in a host group is dynamic; your desktop computer becomes a member of the host group while you are accessing an audio stream server. In IP multicasting, all IP datagrams are delivered using the same "best-effort" reliability used with regular unicast IP datagrams (those sent to a single host).

Because of the properties of IP multicasting, the server overhead required to manage point-to-point communications with single hosts is reduced. This information-delivery mechanism is particularly useful when dealing with scheduled programming or live audio; in either case, the expectation is that many people will listen to the same audio at the same

SOUND TECHNOLOGIES

time. Under IP multicasting, the server needs to send the audio stream only once to all computers.

In general, UDP is best used in momentary audio-delivery applications such as Internet phone products. TCP strikes a happy medium, perhaps the best all-purpose solution despite its inherent limitations due to packet size and retransmission factors. IP multicasting is ideal in situations where the same audio stream will be delivered to many people simultaneously. While there's no outright clear winner at this time, your goal is to evaluate your specific needs and seek the product that delivers for you. You should also consult your service provider to check on their recommendations for access to your sound files.

Cutting-Edge Sound: 3-D Audio

The hottest ticket in sound these days is *3-D sound*. Sound card and speaker vendors have teamed up with companies such as Binaura, Dolby, Q-Sound, Spatializer, and SRS to add dimensional effects to the sound being generated. These effects serve to widen the stereo field to give more depth to the inherently shallow listening field of most small, closely spaced PC speakers.

Most 3-D effects are caused by mixing specifically delayed versions of the left and right channel outputs with the original signal, simulating reflections off walls, or adding spaciousness and directionality to the sound. This approach is used by Binaura, Spatializer, and SRS. Even better are the sound effects of Q-Sound and Dolby's Pro Logic, which let multimedia developers pinpoint sounds in space and move them around the listener. These effects must be programmed into the multimedia presentation, however, and you must have a sound card or speakers designed to deliver the desired effect. While this technology is just starting to be developed, it is always a good idea to keep your eye on such advances. Three-dimensional audio motherboards, chip sets, sound cards, and speakers are starting to show up on the sound horizon. Multimedia PC vendors ranging from Compaq to Packard Bell have announced dozens of 3-D–enabled systems, and many more are expected by year's end. Even Microsoft has blessed the technology by previewng a 3-D extension to its Windows 95 DirectSound API.

There are two general approaches to 3-D sound enhancement. Some technologies are *single-ended*—that is, they don't require a preprocessed audio-input signal. Instead, they modify audio's harmonic structure or phase characteristics on the fly, widening the stereo image so that it seems as if you're listening to larger speakers spaced farther apart.

Systems using the second approach require specially processed source material. They use encoded positional information to give developers—and sometimes listeners—precise control over the placement of each

SOUND TECHNOLOGIES

sound in three-dimensional space. While all 3-D enhancers create a dramatically broadened sound stage, this second kind of system can produce panoramic sound effects that swoop across the room or speech that follows onscreen characters.

In most cases, the best 3-D sound requires preprocessed source material, but there remain relatively few 3-D–encoded titles on the market. For now, your best bet may be with an inexpensive single-ended solution such as Labtec Enterprises' $40 Imager LCS-9210 add-on module. With developers still vying to enlist content providers, it's too soon to tell which 3-D technology will win the broadest support.

Conclusion

When using audio-based applications on the Web, you will run into problems at some point or another. The most common is choppy audio, caused by packet loss. Make sure you are using the fastest modem connection you can get; even if your phone line quality is not particularly good, the higher speed can help make up for it (assuming you are not using a UDP-based product, where packet loss cannot be corrected beyond a certain point). Also, a fast CPU will help process the audio signal faster, leaving more time for the CPU to handle incoming data.

Expect to get lower quality out of live audio applications such as video-conferencing products. Particularly with video conferencing, you have very limited bandwidth to handle both video and audio, so choppy sound due to audio packet loss is more noticeable. Another contributing factor is that it is more difficult to handle live audio than recorded audio, which can be precompressed. Although codec technologies are getting better by the hour, the time it takes to compress live audio represents a significant delay, which can result in lost packets. Because of the high demands of compression on-the-fly, live audio (as well as video) is one of the toughest challenges to resolve on the Internet.

Although you will run into some problems in the short term, audio on the Internet is a reality you can enjoy today. Many sites already offer audio on demand, including news, special programming (such as interviews, concerts, and documentaries), and music. Be aware of the limitations of the technologies available; for the short term, you will probably want to use a couple of different products to access all the Internet has to offer. As improved versions of today's products are released, however, expect better performance, reliability, and quality.

P A R T

2

SOFTWARE

Browsers

Plug-ins

E-mail Applications

Graphics Software

What Is a Web Server?

Web Management Tools

E-mail Servers

FTP Servers

News Servers

Web Administration Tools

5 BROWSERS

WEB BROWSERS ARE PERHAPS the most basic and necessary tool of a Web master. A Web master without a browser is like a couch potato without a remote. Like any thing else, not all browsers are created equal. The features and capabilities can vary greatly from browser to browser.

BROWSERS

The Many Forms of a Universal Language: HTML

The fundamental task of any Web browser is an ability to display text and images based on universally accepted HTML (Hypertext Markup Language) standards. This isn't totally accurate, but we'll get to the specific variants later on in this chapter.

HTML is ultimately derived from SGML (Standard Generalized Markup Language). SGML is an international standard for a device- and system-independent method of representing text in electronic form. HTML merely extends this universal way of presenting electronic information into a *hyper-text* medium where these universally readable documents are also linked together in some fashion. The idea behind HTML and the Web is to design a system that allows a client, using any type of system, to access hyper-linked documents. This universality is the core reasoning behind the creation and standardization of HTML and the Web.

HTML is a language like any other. It has to be uniform in order to provide a means of communication. Similar to a language like English, there must be some common assumptions between the people who speak it. Not unlike English, there are variations of HTML: HTML 1.0, HTML 2.0, HTML 3.0, HTML 3.2 HTML+, and NHTML. These "dialects" are all related, but different browsers have differing abilities to understand one or more of these variations. It is important to understand both the various forms of HTML and which browsers support these variations, in order to pick the best browser for the job.

HTML 1.0 is the most basic of these variants. All Web browsers can read, understand, and render HTML 1.0 documents. HTML 1.0 includes many tags also found in the later versions, but each new version tends to build upon the earlier versions by adding some new tags. HTML meets the universality test, but problems with 1.0 rose out of its limitations. HTML 1.0 is very static, in that it provides very limited interactivity.

The first movement away from a static Web toward greater interactivity was the use of other languages in conjunction with CGI (Common Gateway Interface). This maintained the universal nature of the hypertext medium by interfacing a given document with another programming language to achieve the desired results. The problem with HTML 1.0 was that there was no built-in, interactive way to communicate with other programs. Commands for calling other programs could be codified within HTML documents, but Web servers had no good way to allow Web clients to select which documents were retrieved or what information they contained.

HTML 2.0 sought to remedy this situation with the introduction and standardization of form tags within HTML. Forms are a way of retrieving information directly from Web clients from within HTML documents. Nearly all newly developed Web browsers can understand HTML version 2.0.

BROWSERS

Content versus Presentation

The next changes in HTML arose in response to still-debated goals of the Web. What is more important, content or presentation? Should the Web still maintain the goal of universal access regardless of platform and system? The Web was largely popularized due both to its ease of access even for computer novices, and to the fact that the information looked pleasing. Instead of hours upon hours of staring at nothing but text, the Web provided the rich information available on the Internet in a nice eye-catching package: pictures, headers, and different sizes of text. This was a much better way—certainly more pleasing to the eye—of presenting material.

Now if there is only one way of viewing this information, say with only one browser, then there is no contradiction between universal content access and improved presentation. Unfortunately, this is not the case. Even though there are now a large number of different Web browsers available, many of them still uphold the universal nature of HTML. Browsers like NCSA's Mosaic (see Figure 5.1), Viola, Arena, and Lynx all conform rigorously to the HTML standard.

This began to change in March of 1994, when a group of colleagues left NCSA to form Mosaic Communication Corporation—later known as Netscape. Netscape, in its now successful drive to dominate the browser market, created what is known as NHTML, or Netscape-enhanced HTML. NHTML includes a number of HTML-style tags that greatly improve a Web page designer's ability to render text and pictures in new and innovative ways. Probably one of the most popular of these is the <TABLE> tag.

This is how the debate started. In order to see these Netscape-enhanced pages, a given Web client needs a copy of Netscape's Web browser. Using another browser often results in missing or misplaced elements, or worse still, loss of hyperlinks to certain elements contained within NHTML. A good example of this is the use of tables with an older version of Mosaic. The linking text is seen, but is not linkable.

A real contradiction has developed between the goal of universal content access and the improved presentation abilities of NHTML. To widen this problem, NHTML is not the only deviation from the HTML standard. In fact, HTML+ has been deemed as the meta-category of HTML deviations and includes NHTML. The problem or advantage—depending on your own personal position on the matter—has been enhanced by the emergence of rivals to Netscape's browser market dominance. The biggest rival is Microsoft and the introduction of its Internet Explorer. In order to compete with Netscape, Microsoft has created some of its own additions to HTML+, such as the Marquee tag, control over displayed fonts, and fixed body background properties. The number of these new HTML+ gizmos has exploded in recent months. Probably the best known

BROWSERS

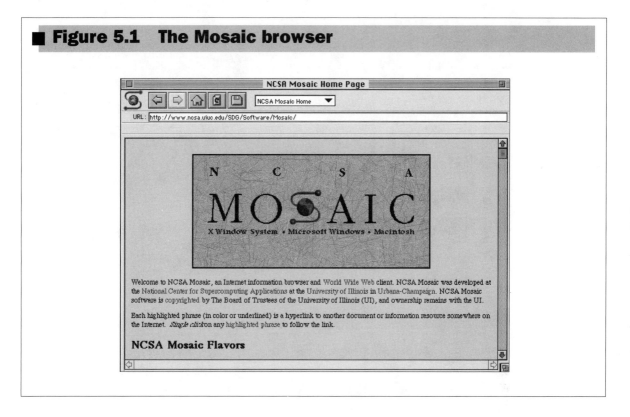

■ Figure 5.1   The Mosaic browser

of these is the Frame tag (see Figure 5.2)—which happens to be supported by the newest versions of both Netscape's Navigator and Microsoft's Internet Explorer.

In order to keep up with these developments, the HTML standard has been extended. First with HTML 3.0, and most recently with HTML 3.2 (May 7, 1996), HTML is slowly absorbing those features contained within HTML+ that are considered universally useful. Probably most significant was the inclusion of tables with the latest versions of HTML. So it's important to the Webmaster to know which version of HTML a given browser supports.

These varying standards leave Webmasters who want to sit on the fence of this ongoing debate with a dilemma. Do I design cool-looking pages with the latest HTML+ gizmos that only some people can see? Or do I design less interesting HTML-compliant pages that everybody can see? Luckily the question isn't totally black and white. Often it is possible to design pages in a way that incorporates the new gizmos for Web hotshots, while producing an acceptable layout for strictly HTML-compliant browsers. The best way of achieving this is to have at least two different

BROWSERS

■ **Figure 5.2 Frames**

browsers available—one that can render the desired HTML+ tags and another that strictly adheres to HTML 3.2 to check for multiple compatibility. Making this easier, many of the compliant browsers are available for free, such as NCSA's Mosaic.

Images and Graphic File Formats

Certainly hyperlinking is a big step up from some of the earlier protocols like FTP and gophers, but the fact that multiple file formats are available is another important reason behind the Web's popularity. Web browsers, unlike a gopher client, can display files other than just ASCII text files. The most widespread among these are graphic files, incorporated within and around text to make for a better looking presentation of information.

Graphic files come in a large variety of formats, but only a few are standard for the Web. Some browsers can render more graphic file formats than others. The two most important and widely supported formats are GIF and JPEG files. Other formats, such as TIFFs, are supported by very few browsers and are not widely used on the Web. GIFs and JPEGs are the most important and each one has slight advantages over the other.

BROWSERS

GIF

GIF, or Graphics Interchange Format, is currently the most widely used graphic file format on the Web. The GIF format was created by Compuserve back in 1987. GIFs have their advantages and disadvantages. GIFs incorporate LZW (Lempel-Ziv & Welch) compression, leaving a file size up to five times smaller than the original picture file. This high compression is achieved in conjunction with a conversion of the picture file into 8 bits per pixel, or 256 colors.

This compression is obviously helpful for transmission across the Internet, but it also has a downside in the reduced image quality of GIFs. Luckily, this degradation of quality is relative. If an image is made available for others to download and high quality is a must, GIFs may not be the best option. However, if the image is merely going to be displayed on a Web page—like most graphic files on the Web—GIFs are a good solution.

Other formats also use compression techniques, so compression alone is not the sole reason behind the preference for GIFs. The big advantage of GIFs is their versatility. GIFs can obviously be used for basic picture files, but the latest version of the GIF format—GIF89a—has some nice additions packed in. First, GIFs work off something called *index color,* as opposed to RGB or CYMK. Since each color is indexed on a strict color table not affected by compression, color integrity is easily maintained. Why not make one of those colors—say the background—none, or transparent? This is exactly what the GIF89a format is capable of, allowing the display of an in-line picture without a border. Better yet, these transparent GIFs can appear to float above a background image.

Another interesting and useful feature of the GIF89a format is that these files can be layered with multiple pictures. That is, the same file can contain more than one image. Netscape has exploited this feature so that each image contained in the file is shown sequentially. The result is an easy way to create animation on a Web page without the need for scripts and CGI. These animated GIFs can also be formatted to play infinitely with a special Loop Animation Bloc embedded within the file—once the sequence plays all the way through, the loop bloc starts the process again. Most browsers support single-image GIF87a and will only recognize the transparency flag of GIF89a and nothing else. The main exception is Oracle's Power Browser which has followed suit by including support for animated GIFs. Many other browser developers are sure to follow in the near future.

JPEG

The second most popular graphic file format that is almost universally supported among Web browsers is the JPEG (Joint Photographic Experts Group) format, pronounced as "jay-peg." The level of compression

BROWSERS

possible with the JPEG format is unbeatable. Typically, JPEGs can achieve 10–20 to 1 compression without a visible loss of quality. If small defects are acceptable, 50 to 1 compression is possible. In fact, 100 to 1 is possible for very low quality displays, such as for previews. Obviously the JPEG format has many uses.

Like GIF files, there are different formats within the realm of JPEG. Increasingly popular among Web browsers is support for what are called *progressive JPEGs*. These progressive JPEG files contain the same information as a regular JPEG, the difference being the way that information is arranged. In the progressive format, the image is loaded by a supporting browser in layers, very much like interlaced GIF files. A rough image is loaded and in subsequent layers, the image slowly comes into focus and sharpness. This is different from the regular way, where the image is loaded from top to bottom, making it hard to tell how large the image is going to be until it is finished loading.

Listed below are two Web sites that can help you get what you need to create animated GIFs and progressive JPEGs. These sites provide documentation, how-to information, and lists of products you'll need to create your own files in these hot new image formats.

Animated GIFs

GIF Animation on the WWW

http://member.aol.com/royalef/
gifmake.htm

Progressive JPEG

The JPEG Playground

http://www.phlab.missouri.edu/
~c675830/jpeg_tests/testgrnd.htm

Browser Features

Aside from varying abilities to render many different document formats, some Web browsers have better navigating (or exploring) capabilities than others. There are many features that make surfing the Web easier and give the Web client more control.

An often overlooked capability is whether a browser works on line or offline. What was that, you ask? What's the point of viewing offline? Well, some browsers only work offline—not many, but they do exist. Certainly the other way around is also true—some only work on line. For those creating Web pages, having the capability for both is the best situation. It is often advantageous to create pages on a computer that is not a Web server. This may save you connection time costs. Naturally, you'll want to view your work before uploading it to a server. Most browsers come equipped with both online and offline viewing capabilities.

A feature that is essential to Webmasters is the capability of viewing the source file of any given Web page. That is, a browser ought to be able to provide the rendered page as well as the real HTML file with the raw scripting tags. There are myriad reasons for wanting to see the source file.

BROWSERS

Perhaps the document contains information you need desperately, but an HTML error—lack of an end table tag after a table full of vital information, for example—has scrambled the text. Probably the most common reason for using this feature is to find out how some new trick was achieved by peering behind the scenes. But no matter what the purpose, source file viewing is a very valuable feature. Most browsers have this capability, but it's also good to check and make sure.

Bookmark files are very convenient for anyone who's been on the Web more than a week. Even if you can start at the same place everytime, remembering your way through the maze of hyperlinks and waiting for each page to load to finally reach the spot you are looking for is no substitute for just typing the location in. However, URLs are long and easily forgotten, and even if remembered correctly, typing in URLs is not something anyone wants to do more than is absolutely necessary. The tried and true solution to this problem is to use *bookmark files*. These files are lists of your favorite and most often viewed sites—all equipped with hyperlinks for easy access.

Of course, almost all browsers currently available contain some sort of bookmark scheme. But some are better than others. How many Web pages can you store? Can you create multiple categories within your bookmarks? How easy is it to add and delete bookmarks from this file? These are some of the important questions to think about when looking at a new browser.

Related to bookmarks is a list of places that you have just visited—basically a viewing history for the current surfing session that allows you to jump back quickly to pages you've visited recently. This relieves you of the annoying task of pounding away at the back arrow that most browsers use to move back through previously viewed pages. Many browsers have a pop-down menu of some sort listing all the places you've been, either during that session or in recent sessions. This feature is very handy for speedy navigation.

More often than not, the back-arrow button is not the only button available. Browsers tend to have several command buttons, usually located at the top of the browser window in a toolbar. How the toolbar is designed and which commands it includes can be of great service. Usually things like Back and Forward are included universally. Other command buttons to look for include: Home Page, Source View, Stop Transmitting Data, Print Page, Refresh Page, Add Page to Bookmark File, Reload Images, and many others. If at all possible know which features you use most and find a browser that supports those commands from an easily accessible toolbar. Most browser's toolbars come equipped with a display of your current Web location, but not all. Needless to say, this is very useful information. Also useful is a toolbar that is configurable. Why let

BROWSERS

someone else pick and choose what features are easily accessible? The ability to create a custom toolbar is a very nice feature.

If you use a modem to connect to the Net, and perhaps even if you don't, it's very convenient to know how big a file is and how long it is taking to load. In your browser, look for some sort of information about loading pages. For example, Netscape Navigator displays a calculation of how many bytes are being loaded by a given Web page, an approximate transfer rate and an estimated time of load completion. This is can be very helpful. Nothing is more frustrating than waiting a long time for a Web page to load and having no idea when it might be finished. Should you go make some coffee or sit tight?

File size information is useful when performing another popular Web task: downloading directly from the Web through a browser. Most browsers will perform this task, but some are more upfront than others about the time that will be required. Often the file you're downloading is something large, like a shareware program. Some browsers will commit to the download, but neglect to inform the client how big the file is or how long it will take. As an example, try NCSA's Mosaic. All it displays is a processing icon—an hourglass or wristwatch depending on the system you use. Should you get a bite to eat, drive to the store, or take that much-needed week-long vacation while waiting for the download? A little information in this area can save a good amount of stress and frustration.

Last but certainly not least in the area of browser features is a memory cache. Again, most current browsers support some sort of caching system. Memory caching is very useful, especially if you have a few sites that are viewed with any regularity. A cache will store the Web page information on the computer where the browser is located. When the site is brought up again, a memory cache will retrieve the information from your computer instead of across the network, saving both the Web client and the Web server time and energy. When looking at new browsers, make sure that the memory cache size is adjustable. No one wants the browser's cache eating up all your hard-drive space. At the same time, it's nice to be able to expand it to fit your needs.

Plug-ins

The Internet is packed full of different platforms, formats, and file types. Even if a browser were to provide support for all known formats for all known data types, it still would often be outdated the day after its release. New and often better formats emerge all the time. To cope with this fast-paced reality, many browsers have the capacity to expand their list of supported formats with what are known as *plug-ins*. These plug-ins—often developed by third parties—can be integrated within browsers set up to

BROWSERS

handle them. Currently only a handful of browsers come ready-made with this capability.

Plug-ins can be very useful for those Web page developers that want something that deviates at all from the norm. Things like RealAudio files, Shockwave, and other plug-ins will be examined in another chapter, but suffice to say that plug-ins are very popular and the number of plug-in formats will only increase in the future. Table 5.1 describes some of the plug-ins popular today.

Helper Applications

In the same genre as plug-ins are *helper applications.* Helper applications differ from plug-ins in that they are stand-alone programs that deal with specific file formats not handled by the browser itself. Probably the most basic helper application is a text editor, often used to view HTML source files. Other uses of helper applications include processing sound files, video, unusual picture formats, compressed files and many other file types. The best browsers can identify the format of a given file, know which helper application is needed for the job, and execute that application. Other browsers without this capability leave more work for you to do. In this case, it is still possible to use the files, but all of the work must be performed manually, first downloading the file then opening it by hand. If you spend any time on the Web retrieving files, you'll come across some common ways of denoting a particular type or format of file.

The most common file name suffixes found throughout the Web are shown in Table 5.2. All of those listed can be all uppercase or all lowercase.

Web Security

Security on the Internet is a very hot topic, mainly because it is severely lacking. Information is very easily accessible on the Internet, and the Web

---

■ Table 5.1 List of Some Popular Plug-ins

Product	Description
ABC QuickSilver	Developed by Micrografx, QuickSilver allows users to interact with object graphics from within Web pages. Currently available for Windows 95 and Windows NT.
ISYS HindSite	Developed by ISYS/Odyssey, HindSite acts like the ultimate bookmark file, remembering every site you've ever visited. These sites are indexed and searchable. Currently available for Windows 95, Windows NT, and Windows 3.1.
PointCast Network	Developed by PointCast, this plug-in provides access to a free service that includes up-to-the-minute news, weather, sports, and other information. Currently available for Windows 95 and windows 3.1.
ToolVox	Developed by Voxware, ToolVox brings high-quality speech audio to Web pages. ToolVox provides 53 to 1 compression. Currently available for Windows 95, Windows 3.1, and Macintosh.

BROWSERS

■ Table 5.2   Decoding File Endings

Suffix	Description of Format
.gif	A GIF picture format. You'll need a program that can read GIF formats to view the picture. .jpeg, .tiff, and .pict are other (and different) picture formats. If you see these suffixes, then the file is a picture.
.gz	Known as the "gunzip" compression format—a variant of the PKZIP format for Unix systems. Try **gunzip** *filename.gz* to uncompress at a Unix prompt.
.hqx	A Macintosh format that needs BinHex for decoding.
.mpeg	This is a movie file; that is, it contains moving pictures and usually audio to boot. You'll need a MPEG viewer to watch the show.
.pgp	This is a text or binary file encrypted with PGP (Pretty Good Privacy). You'll have to use PGP and know the password to unencrypt it.
.ps	A PostScript document (in Adobe's page description language). You can print this file on any PostScript-capable printer.
.tar	Yet another Unix format, often used to place several related files or complete directory trees into one big file. Use the "tar" command to create and extract these types of files. Often, a "tarred" file will also be compressed with the .z/.gz method.
.txt	Basically, a text file. By itself, this means the file is a document, rather than a program. Sometimes seen as .doc.
.wav	This refers to an audio file. You'll need a program that can deal with audio files to listen to it.
.z	A file compressed by the Unix pack utility. Type **unpack** *filename.z* or **gunzip** *filename.z* to decompress it.
.zip	This suffix indicates the file has been compressed with a common MS-DOS compression program called PKZIP. Many Unix systems will let you decompress such files with a program called unzip.

is no exception. Since information on the Internet is often routed through many different computers before it reaches its destination, how can it remain secure as it passes through these untrusted intermediaries? For companies interested in using the Internet for business purposes, this is a very unpleasant and potentially dangerous situation.

It's no picnic for customers, either. How can a company expect potential customers to send their credit card numbers over a medium that is not secure from eavesdropping? Credit card information is just the tip of the iceberg: There are many types of transmissions across the Web that people need to keep private.

The first company to tackle this daunting task was Netscape Communications Corporation. The Netscape Navigator (see Figure 5.3) was the first browser to incorporate SSL, or Secure Sockets Layer. The SSL protocol was developed by Netscape, but is now licensed to many other Web browser companies. SSL works as a buffer layer between the application layer, such as the Web browser, and the network layer, or TCP/IP.

First, SSL uses a new URL access protocol method, https, instead of the standard http, to connect to HTTP servers. For those interested in ports, http uses port 80 and the new https uses port 443. SSL actually uses two protocols: the SSL Record Protocol and the SSL Handshake Protocol. The Handshake Protocol is used to authenticate the server and negotiate an encryption scheme. Once a secure channel of communication has been established, the Record Protocol is used to send the encrypted data. This scheme anticipates and undermines three different security problems: bogus servers, eavesdropping, and interference with data integrity.

BROWSERS

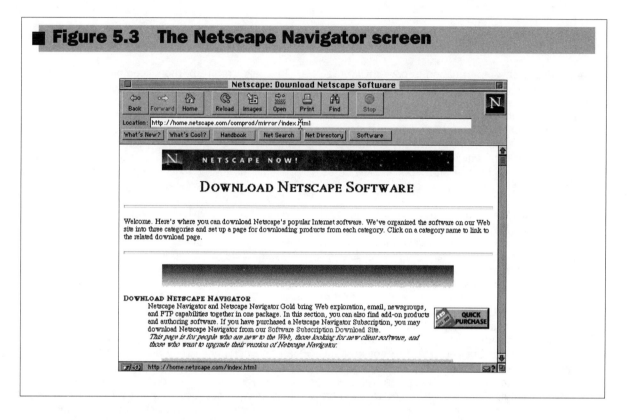

■ **Figure 5.3   The Netscape Navigator screen**

SSL is not the only secure channel for communication. Many browsers use another security measure known as the Secure Hyper Text Transfer Protocol, or S-HTTP for short. S-HTTP was developed by Enterprise Integration Technologies in cooperation with RSA Data Security. Like SSL, S-HTTP also supports end-to-end secure transactions by incorporating encryption schemes.

So how safe are these security measures? Both SSL and S-HTTP use public-key encryption developed by RSA Data Security. The largest and most secure algorithm allowed by U.S. law is a 128-bit key size domestically (any exportable version of software must be equipped with no larger than a 40-bit key). This sounds pretty technical, so what does it mean? A 40-bit key, on average, takes 64 MIPS-years to break. In other words, it takes a 64-MIPS computer a year of dedicated processor time to perform a brute-force crack of the key. A 128-bit key is not 3 times as secure, but rather 2 times more secure than the 40-bit key. That sounds good, but it is by no means totally secure. Teams of crackers have recently broken much larger keys. But it is certainly better than no security at all.

BROWSERS

■ Cryptography

An old adage says: Information is power. Cryptography is a way to harness this power by controlling access to information. The basic premise of encryption is to lock information under a shroud, revealing itself only to a select few. The way this is accomplished is by transforming the information into something completely indecipherable. The selected viewers are then given a special "key" that unlocks the encryption, exposing the once-hidden information.

This power is something that the U.S. government has been trying desperately to control. How can it allow groups of people to develop encryption schemes that no one can crack? A few years ago, the U.S. government proposed a plan to deal with encryption. This took the form of a computer chip, called the Clipper Chip. This chip, according to the proposal, would be installed in any machine that transmits information. The Clipper Chip is based on an algorithm—known as SkipJack—developed by the National Security Agency. The government argued that this solved the encryption problem. It would provide encryption for those that require it, and the government would hold a key to all information encrypted with the Clipper.

This met fierce opposition from a wide range of groups who asked some hard questions. First, why should the government allow itself to view any document it pleases? Secondly, the SkipJack algorithm is classified. How secure is it? No one knows. In the face of this opposition, the government has temporarily dropped its proposal.

To make matters more complicated, a man named Phil Zimmerman has entered the story. He is a civil libertarian who developed an encryption program called Pretty Good Privacy (PGP). The algorithm used in PGP is one of the most secure available today. Zimmerman created this program, uploaded it on the Internet, and made it freely available for anyone to use. This was the proverbial Pandora's box, serverely damaging the government's ability to control encryption.

This story is obviously long and complicated. Zimmerman was prosecuted by the U.S. government for making the PGP algorithm available because it is illegal to export encryption schemes of over 40 bits. The PGP algorithm uses a 1,024-bit key. Recently, the government dropped all charges against Zimmerman. Congress is still pursuing legislation to deal with this problem.

A large number of Internet-related companies, including Netscape, also oppose the government's ban on encryption. They argue that these restrictions hinder their ability to compete in worldwide markets. In fact, Netscape now develops two versions of every product to comply with the ban—one product for domestic markets and one for international markets. But the one developed for overseas is extremely weak, using only 40-bit encryption. These companies argue that a much higher level of encryption is necessary to ensure security for buyers of their products. Needless to say, the fight over encryption is far from over. ■

Scripting Languages

As has been stated before, HTML is a very static tagging language. For those that want more interactivity and control over the Web environment, HTML is a dead end. In the past, this led Web developers to use CGI scripts, but they can end up being a big burden on the server's processor. For these reasons, a growing number of browsers are supporting scripting languages that can be embedded within HTML. The browser then extracts the script and executes the code. Some of these languages now include JavaScript and Visual Basic. These scripting languages solve

BROWSERS

both problems, moving the execution of code from the server side to the client side.

Already the most widespread of these scripts is Netscape's JavaScript, which is often confused with Java. JavaScript syntax and built-in functions are modeled on Java, but that's where the relationship ends—JavaScript is entirely independent of Java. Java is a stand-alone language, whereas JavaScript is wholly dependent on Netscape's Navigator 2.01 and later versions for execution. Netscape licensed Java from Sun Microsystems as an extension language and developed LiveScript in-house as a scripting language. Combining the two, LiveScript was renamed JavaScript. This language provides a programmable API that allows cross-platform scripting of events, objects, and actions. Web masters can access events such as start-ups, exits, and client mouse clicks.

Not to be left out, Microsoft has also introduced its own scripting system. The Internet Explorer (see Figure 5.4) incorporates the Visual Basic Scripting Edition (VB Script) into its ActiveX Control system. VB Script is a subset of the Visual Basic language, very much like JavaScript is to Java. And like JavaScript, VB Script allows for more control over interactivity, such as forms, program linking, animation, and more. ActiveX acts as an interface between the browser and other supporting applications. As an example, ActiveX can open documents formatted for Excel, directly within the browser.

Of course, what discussion of Web languages would be complete without a mention of Java? While Java is all the rage, there are still only a handful of browsers that support Java applets. Java applets, unlike VB Script and JavaScript code, are not embedded within HTML documents. Unlike these scripting languages, Java pre-compiles its applets into byte-code prior to runtime. But like these others, Java requires a compliant browser to run the applets—they are not stand-alone applications. Sun and Netscape are currently working together so that the next release of JavaScript will be capable of interacting with Java applets, creating an even higher level of control over Web pages. This will allow, among other things, several applets on one page to pool information and manipulate objects such as forms within the page.

The first browser to support Java applets was Sun's HotJava. HotJava supported the then-released alpha version of Java. HotJava, so far, has not been updated to deal with beta versions or the new release of Java 1.0. This will likely change soon. Other browsers that now support Java applets include Netscape's Navigator 2.0, Microsoft's Internet Explorer 2.0, Spyglass Mosaic, Oracle's Power Browser, and IBM's WebExplorer (later versions of these products are also Java-enabled).

BROWSERS

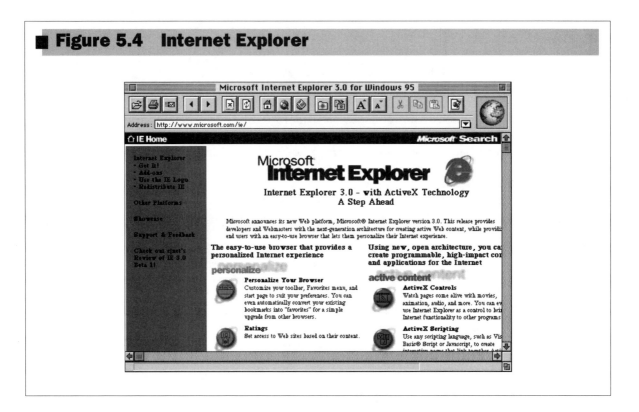

■ **Figure 5.4 Internet Explorer**

After reading the section above, it should be fairly obvious that scripting languages, while providing a very powerful tool, have a severe limitation. HTML was originally designed to be as universal as possible, usable by as many platforms and devices as possible. These scripting languages are inherently proprietary and so far, fairly exclusive. Currently, Java-Script will only work on a couple of browsers, such as the newest versions of Netscape Navigator and Microsoft Explorer. The same is true of the other scripting languages as well. This will likely change as other browsers enter the world of embedded scripts. If you need some more information on these scripting languages, try one of the sites below, all of which offer good documentation. This is an extremely short list considering the sheer volume of material available on line.

Netscape JavaScript documentation	http://www.netscape.com/comprod/products/ navigator/version_2.0/script/script_info/ index.html
JavaScript Index	http://www.c2.org/~andreww/javascript/

BROWSERS

Microsoft Visual Basic **Scripting Edition**	http://198.105.232.4/VBSCRIPT/
Sun Microsystem's **Java page**	http://java.sun.com/

Other Supported Protocols

Certainly the Web is not the only way to access the Internet. Many other protocols exist besides the Hypertext Transfer Protocol (HTTP). Many documents on the Internet that were established before the introduction of the Web are not in HTML form. To access these types of documents, browsers need to support either the FTP protocol, gopher, or both. Nearly every HTML browser available has this support.

Transferring and viewing documents is not the only thing people do on the Internet. In fact, most of the information that flows across the Internet is done through e-mail. Current projections forecast that Web traffic will outpace e-mail traffic in the not-so-distant future; still, e-mail will likely remain the cornerstone of Internet communication. So wouldn't it be nice if all Internet services were bundled into one application? Many browsers are attempting just this.

Access to e-mail is fast becoming a common feature among Web browsers. Just point and click your way through your e-mail inbox. Features to look for in e-mail–extended browsers are common e-mail standards, ease of setup, and good control over the presentation. Standards to look for include MIME format, POP3 and MAPI (For more on these standard formats and protocols, please refer to Chapter 7). Some browsers come packaged with little or no advice or support when it comes to setting up access to your e-mail account. This situation can easily become frustrating and a little help can go a long way. Good features that are always welcome include address books, signature files, and customizable configuration. Other protocols that more and more browsers are supporting include NNTP (newsgroups), Telnet, and IRC. Depending on personal interests, these features can be very convenient.

Platforms and Connections

As with any other application, Web browsers are coded for specific platforms. Microsoft's Internet Explorer ported for Macintosh will not run on Windows 95. Many of the most popular Web browsers are ported for many different platforms. The most popular platforms include the usual suspects: Windows 95, Windows NT, Windows 3.1, Macintosh PowerPC, Macintosh 68x, and various flavors of Unix. Keep in mind that not all browsers are written for all platforms.

The same holds true for types of connections to the Internet. Some browsers may only work on a LAN (local area network). Some may only

BROWSERS

work via serial connection. Having said this, nearly all browsers support the standard TCP/IP connection, including SLIP and PPP connections. Many surfers access the Web through modems. Not all modem connections support SLIP or PPP, limiting you to serial connection–based browsers, such as Lynx or SlipKnot.

Price

The cost of Web browsers is an obvious factor in deciding which one is best for the job. Luckily, the price of browsers is relatively small. A large number of browsers are available for free. Most of these are somewhat limited or scaled-down versions of commercial browsers that cost a modest sum. For those that are not free, the prices range from less than $10 up to almost $200—averaging around $80. Usually the more expensive browsers come with a variety of extra features outlined above, such as e-mail and newsgroup readers, HTML editors, and other built-in goodies.

The Best Browser

So which browser is best for you? This depends on two things: what do you have and what do you want? Your choice is limited by the type of platform and connection you have. What you want is only limited by how much you are willing to spend. For a listing of available browsers and supported features, please refer to Appendix E.

6 PLUG-INS

WEB BROWSER PLUG-INS are vastly expanding the ability of Web masters to support new and exciting forms of resources. Perhaps you are searching for multimedia and animation support. Are you looking for a way to display a document in a favorite format, say Excel? Or maybe you are looking for support of an unusual sound or graphic format. Plug-ins are an easy solution.

PLUG-INS

What Are Plug-ins Good For?

So what are plug-ins exactly? In brief, they are software packages that work in conjunction with Web browsers, allowing Web clients to render and display formats not included in the regular line-up of features of the browser. As an example, take Netscape's browser. It supports a number of good and useful graphic file formats, like GIFs and JPEGs. But what if you want to display a TIFF image? Since Netscape's browsers currently do not support TIFF files, plug-ins make a handy solution to the problem. Plug-ins, as the name implies, are dependent collections of software that add functionality to the browser, such as providing the necessary support to display TIFF images. They are said to be "dependent" because plug-ins can't operate as stand-alone programs like helper applications can. Instead they depend on the browser to function, in much the same way as your stereo depends on being plugged into a wall socket in order to play music.

Netscape's Navigator 2.0 was the first browser to implement this new plug-in technology, but many others are now following suit. The reason for this is simple: Plug-ins provide an easy solution to a complex problem. The number of plug-ins has exploded recently, topping 100. This number will only increase as more and more browsers move to support plug-ins.

Plug-ins are what many refer to as *second-wave* Web technology. The first wave is obviously HTML. In the days before plug-ins, any file format not supported by browsers had to be handed off to a helper application. The file was displayed, not as a component of the Web page, but rather rendered in a window separate from the originating page. Plug-ins, however, allow for unusual file formats to actually be embedded within the Web page. No separate windows are needed. This gives the Web master much more control over layout and design.

All of this begs the question: What about Sun Microsystems' Java? Aren't some of the solutions that plug-ins deliver also promised by Java? The short and easy answer is yes. The full answer is a bit more complicated. Plug-ins are carving out territory that many thought Java would dominate. The important difference is on emphasis and focus. Plug-ins are developed for those who author Web content; they are tools for display. Java, on the other hand, focuses on the computer programmer. In other words, if your intent is just to display something like animation, plug-ins are the easiest solution. But if the problem is programming related, plug-ins offer little and Java is called for.

Usual Unusual File Formats

Of the file formats not normally supported by Web browsers, some are more likely to be rendered with plug-ins than others. For the sake of simplicity, these plug-in–supported file formats can be placed into six basic categories: graphics, multimedia and animation, sound, three-dimensional

PLUG-INS

imaging, document support, and the grab-bag category of productivity. Perhaps other categories will emerge in the future, but for now these are the common areas that plug-ins support.

Graphics

Following close behind GIFs and JPEGs in graphic format popularity are TIFF (Tagged Image File Format) files, although TIFFs have some severe limitations. They can't store vector graphics or text annotation, nor are they easily streamable like JPEGs. On the other hand, there are many good things built into TIFFs. TIFFs were originally designed by developers of printers, scanners, and monitors as a raster data interchange. They tend to contain more information, such as colorimetry calibration and gamut tables, than many other graphic formats. Basically TIFFs tend to be better, yet bigger graphic files.

The standard for graphics file formats tend to support raster files, like GIFs, JPEGs, and TIFFs. Raster files, also refered to as bitmapped files, contain data described as pixels. But this isn't the only choice: Corel's CMX format uses a vector format instead. Vector files contain graphic information described as mathematical equations. Computer Graphics Metafiles (CGM) also deviate from the norm, providing encoding that is oriented towards stroke-drawn graphics, such as polylines, markers, and filled polygons. Infinet's Lightning Strike has developed a new type of compression for graphics. While most graphic file formats use a ccompression technique—such as the Discrete Cosine Transformation (DCT)—that is based on the Fourier analysis method, Lightning Strike uses a new approach which adapts a wavelet method. The differences between these methods are obviously technical, but suffice it to say that each one has its advantages. Infinet claims that their scheme produces better looking images because the wavelet method more closely resembles the human visual system. Of course "better" is most often subjective.

For the chemical engineer (or masochist), there are a wide variety of file formats for displaying chemical structures within Web pages. Some of these formats include the Brookhaven Protein Databank (PDB), MDL Molfile (MDL), IEMBL Nucleotide Format (EMBL), Rasmol Script File (SPT), Chemical Structure Markup Language File (CSML), MDL Transportable Graphics File (TGF), and many others for your viewing pleasure. Other technical formats include DWG and DXF (Drawing eXchange Format) which are used to display a representation of AutoCAD files.

PLUG-INS

Multimedia and Animation

Multimedia and animation files are becoming more and more numerous on the Web. Higher average connection speeds, better software development, and the simple fact that these files make the Web come alive, are all important reasons why these file formats are becoming increasingly popular. A couple of the most common of these types of files include ASAP Word Power and QuickTime files. ASAP WordPower is a product developed by Software Publishing Corp. and is designed to display and print reports and presentations rich in graphics and sound. ASAP WebShow is the plug-in used to display these WordPower documents via Web browsers. These files are identified with the .asp extension. QuickTime is a type of multimedia architecture developed by Apple. It is used to store, edit, and play synchronized graphics, sound, video, text, and music. QuickTime is not limited to Macintosh, but will also run on Windows and other platforms. Figure 6.1 below shows QuickTime's home page, but fails to capture the excitement of the moving pictures you'll find at their site.

Arguably the most popular animation and video file format is MPEG. MPEG is an acronym for *Moving Pictures Experts Group*. MPEGs have

■ Figure 6.1   QuickTime's home page

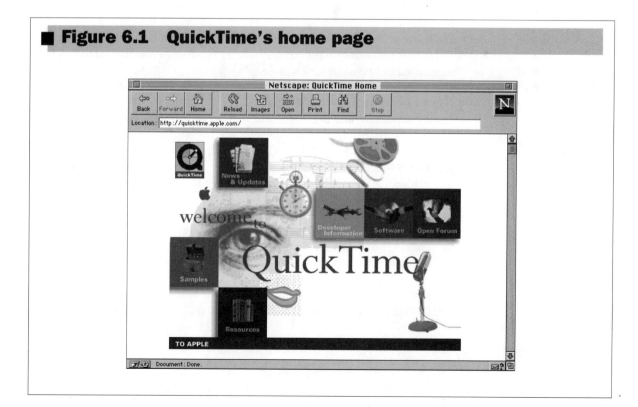

PLUG-INS

little to do with JPEGs despite the similarity in names. One is for animation and video, the other for still graphic images. MPEGs are a very popular choice because, like JPEGs, they offer very good compression ratios. The compression technique is a little complicated, but the basic idea involves predicting motion from frame to frame. The average ratio is about 26 to 1 without much visible loss in image quality. Obviously, this is extremely useful video format.

Sound

Established in 1983 by the International MIDI Association (IMA), the Musical Instrument Digital Interface (MIDI) is a sound format supported by a wide number of plug-ins. WAV sound files (.wav) are more widely available than MIDI files and are supported by many browsers, but MIDIs have a definite quality advantage. Basically, MIDI is an interface between many different devices, like keyboards and guitars, providing a common way to communicate. Unlike WAV files, MIDI files actually have different signals and codes, or channels, for different instruments; WAV files just throw everything together. MIDIs sequence these channels, and the result is music. While MIDI files can be converted to WAV files, the reverse is not true for obvious reasons—the MIDI files contain much more data. Sound for sound, MIDI files tend to be larger in bandwidth but are much more versatile than WAV files. One example of a MIDI plug-in is MIDPLUG, shown in Figure 6.2. If you put your ear *real* close to the page, you might even hear something!

Three-Dimensional Imaging

The most popular and prevalent three-dimensional imaging format is the Virtual Reality Modeling Language (VRML)—pronounced as an acronym or sometimes as "vermel." The extension for VRML files is .wrl. The goal of VRML is to develop an infrastructure for a multiuser space for virtual worlds. Check out Silicon Graphics's pioneering plug-in at their home page shown in Figure 6.3.

The basic components of three-dimensional graphics include geometry, transformation, attributes, shading. The geometry is the most basic component, providing an X, Y, and Z coordinate system. This static base is given life with transformation—the ability to scale, rotate, and translate objects in relation to each other. To lend a realistic look to the scene, attributes provide information on how light should be reflected off or transmitted through each object. The final component, shading, controls how

PLUG-INS

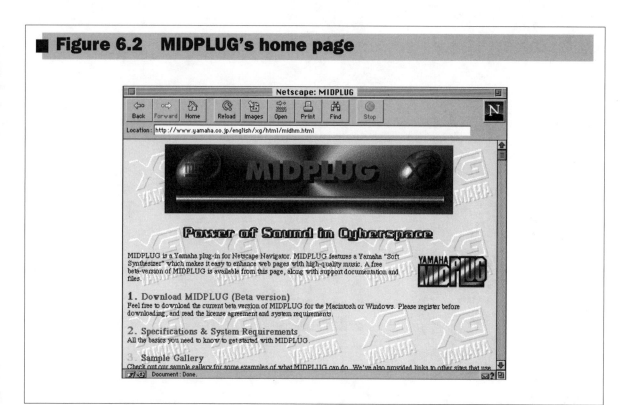

■ Figure 6.2   MIDPLUG's home page

objects are colored, including textures and surfaces. Listed below are some URLs that provide specific information about VRML.

VRML Frequently Asked Questions	http://vag.vrml.org/VRML_FAQ.html
VRML 1.0 Specs	http://vag.vrml.org/vrml10c.html
VRML 2.0 Specs	http://vag.vrml.org/vrml20info.html
Authoring tools	http://www.sdsc.edu/SDSC/Partners/vrml/repos_software.html
Survey of 3D-Rendering Engines	http://www.cs.tu-berlin.de/%7Eki/engines.html
WWW Test Page	http://www-dssed.llnl.gov/documents/WWW test.html

PLUG-INS

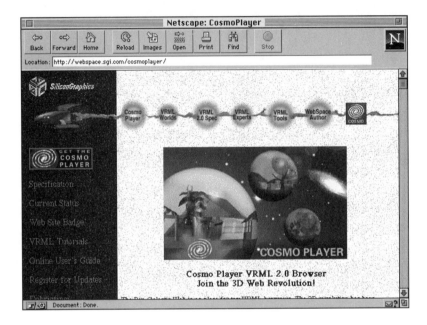

Figure 6.3 The VRML plug-in Cosmo Player's home page

Productivity and Document Support

Aside from actual file format support, some plug-ins work as utilities, offering better productivity. In other words, they simplify work in some way. This type of plug-in comes in a variety of shapes and sizes, offering remote control of another PC via the wWeb, e-mail spell checkers, and displaying time zones around the world.

If you like to do research, ISYS/Odessey's ISYS Hindsite is a great utility. It acts as a giant Web elephant, remembering, indexing, and saving all the content of every URL visited within a configurable time frame. Another useful plug-in utility is Pointcast's Pointcast Network, which delivers personalized news, stock quotes, weather, and other information directly to your browser. No need to visit multiple sites searching through piles of archives, and the service is free.

Another service performed by plug-ins is document support. Some plug-ins can display documents created in Excel and Microsoft Word 6.0 and 7.0. Arguably the most popular document on the Web is the Portable Document Format (PDF). Developed by Adobe, PDF is a system of adding hypertext features to PostScript files. Adobe's PDF plug-in is called

PLUG-INS

Acrobat. PDF is used on sites run by such agencies as *The New York Times, The Los Angeles Times,* and *PC Week.* It is necessary to use Acrobat to view many documents available on these pages; an example is shown below in Figure 6.4.

Plug-in Developers and Where to Find Them

Hunting for plug-ins can be quite a chore. This is especially true now that there are so many companies developing so many different plug-ins. For a list of some of the many companies currently developing plug-ins for Web browsers, including their Web address, see the charts in Appendix F. For now, nearly all plug-ins only support the latest versions of Netscape. A growing number of these companies are now branching out, producing plug-ins for more than just Netscape browsers.

If you can't find something suitable in the appendix, there are other places to look for browser plug-ins. A good place to start is Netscape's plug-in page, shown below in Figure 6.5, (http://home.netscape.com/comprod/products/navigator/version_2.0/plugins/). It contains a growing

■ **Figure 6.4 A page from the magazine *Acropolis* viewed with Acrobat**

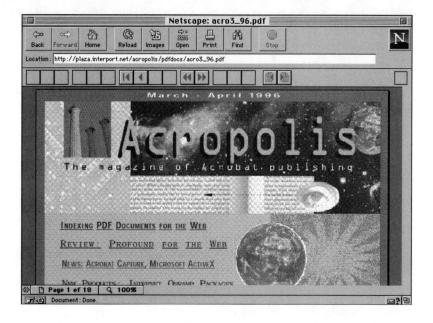

PLUG-INS

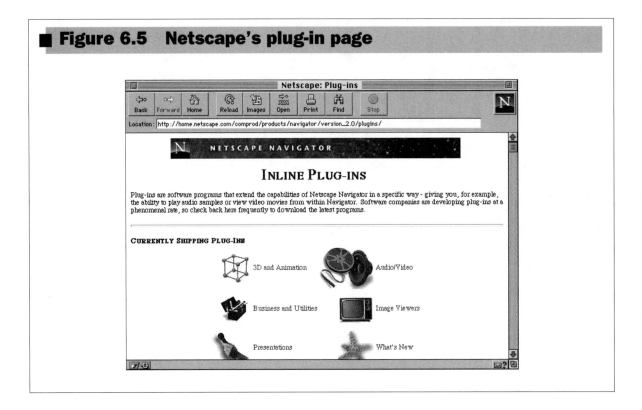

■ Figure 6.5   Netscape's plug-in page

list of plug-ins, categorized by function, that are supported by Netscape browsers. Another starting point is BrowserWatch's Plug-in Plaza (http://browserwatch.iworld.com/plug-in.html). This site provides a great reference tool for people interested in currently available plug-ins and those that are still in development.

Building Your Own Plug-in

There are obviously a large number of developers creating plug-ins for many varieties of file formats and platforms. But what about a favorite format that is not yet supported by current plug-ins? Should weary Webmasters throw up their arms and be overcome with a sense of futility and cyber-angst? Despair is not needed, thanks in part to folks at Netscape who pioneered support for browser plug-ins. Netscape has been kind enough to provide the necessary tools for writing your own plug-ins for whatever format is desired.

PLUG-INS

The Essentials

There are four essential components for creating and installing plug-ins from scratch. First and foremost is a copy of a plug-in compatible browser. In the following examples, this will be assumed to be Netscape Navigator. Second, is Netscape's Software Development Kit (SDK), which is available as freeware at http://home.netscape.com/comprod/ development_partners/plugin_api/index.html. The SDK contains an overview of plug-ins, including design and architecture; a step-by-step tutorial on making a plug-in, including all necessary information; a description of the Application Programming Interface (API); and an explanation of known problems. Third, a C++ compiler is required. For the following examples, this will mean Microsoft's Visual C++ 2.1 compiler. Last and certainly not least, is a minimum working knowledge of C++ and interfacing with the desired file format type.

In other words, the plan is to use these tools to talk to each other. Ultimately, the browser ought to be able to communicate with and understand the target file type. To get from here to there, C++ will assist with the communication, providing all the necessary coding to make it happen. This code will also eventually become the main component of the plug-in. The final step is getting the C++ code to communicate with and understand the browser, that is, a newer version of a Netscape browser. This is where the SDK comes into the scene. This isn't exactly everything, but is an overview of the basic procedure. Other necessities will be discussed a little later on.

Where to Start

Unfortunately, each browser is platform-dependent. For the following examples, it will also be assumed that the platform is Windows. The first thing to do is to create all the necessary directories for all the files that will be needed. Create a directory for the plug-in project—for example, "myplugin." Uncompress and place the Windows Sample Source Code into this directory. Two subdirectories within myplugin, AVI and shell, are automatically created. The shell directory contains the basic files used to create a new plug-in. The AVI directory contains example files for creating an AVI movie plug-in. Next create another subdirectory within myplugin for working on a specific plug-in. As an example, call it plugin1. Copy over all files and directories from the shell directory and place them within the newly created working directory, plugin1. This is also where the plug-in code will reside once it's written. Make sure that your Netscape directory also contains a plug-ins directory. This should have been automatically created, but if it hasn't, do that now.

PLUG-INS

Configuring Files and MIME Types

Once the correct directory structure is achieved, the next step is to properly configure certain files that the necessary components will use. Using the Visual C++ compiler, open the existing makefile in your working directory. There are actually two makefiles (.RC2), one for 16-bit applications (NPDLL16.RC2) and one for 32-bit applications (NPDLL32.RC2). It is very important to edit the proper resource file for the given platform environment. After the proper resource file is determined, go into the appropriate one and change the MIME type and the file extension values. The resource file should look something like this:

```
VALUE "MIMEType",      "application/x-myplugin\0"
    VALUE "FileExtents",    "xxx\0"
    VALUE "FileOpenName",    "My First Plug-in (*.xxx)\0"
    If there are more than one MIME types included, a vertical bar can be used
to separate multiple types. For example:
    VALUE "MIMEType",      "application/x-myplugin | app2/x-plug2\0"
    VALUE "FileExtents",    "xxx | yyy\0"
VALUE "FileOpenName",    "My First Plug-in (*.xxx) | SecPlug (*yyy)\0"
```

This of course begs the question, what if I want to create a new MIME type? In other words, what if no proper file extension exists for the proposed format? In this case, there are a couple things that are worth doing. First and foremost is registering the new extension with the Internet Assigned Numbers Authority (IANA). There is a mailing list devoted to this subject, accessible at ietf-types@cs.utk.edu. Also see the Network Working Group memo on Media Type Registration Procedure available at http://home.netscape.com/assist/helper_apps/rfc3.html. If you are using a new file format extension, you'll also have to let your browser know about it.

A Walk through the Plug-in Park

For a plug-in to be of any assistance to the browser, the unusual file format must exist and the browser must be able to reference the given file. So the first thing to do is to create an HTML file to make this reference. The example will be plugin-test.html. Inside this HTML, place the following tag:

```
<EMBED SRC = "test-file.xxx" WIDTH = 300 HEIGHT = 300>
```

To invoke and display any plug-in, the EMBED tag must be included. The EMBED tag is very much like the IMG tag. Like the IMG tag, the EMBED tag includes attributes that name specific characteristics of the resource file. Unlike the IMG tag, some of these attributes require definition. As in the example above, width and height attributes need to be defined—in this case, 300 pixels wide and 300 pixels tall. For a detailed description of the EMBED tag, see Table 6.1.

These are merely the standard EMBED parameters. Many plug-ins can deal with their own predetermined parameters. For example, many

PLUG-INS

■ Table 6.1   The Embed Tag

Syntax	Attributes	Description
<EMBED SRC WIDTH HEIGHT PALETTE>	SRC="name of data file"	This specifies the referenced data file or object. Often, this attribute includes file location information such as a URL. This attribute is required.
	WIDTH="value"	This specifies the width of the area that the file or object will be drawn in. This is required.
	HEIGHT="value"	This specifies the height of the area that the file or object will be drawn in. This is required.
	PALETTE="background or foreground"	This attribute defines whether the file or object will be rendered as a background or foreground palette. This attribute is usually used when more than one plug-in file exists on a page. The default value for this attribute, if none is given, is "background." Therefore, this tag is not necessarily required.

plug-ins use a parameter supported by Netscape called PLUGINSPAGE. This value will contain the URL for the location of the embedded plug-in. If the Web client does not have the necessary plug-in, PLUGINSPAGE goes into action. The client is given a warning about the problem and is given the choice of visiting that URL. The PLUGINSPAGE is more universal than most other parameters. Many plug-ins support unique parameters and the corresponding values that may be necessary to properly display the plug-in supported files.

This is only one of the three ways that a plug-in assisted file can be displayed. With the EMBED tag, the file or object is embedded within an HTML document. Again in this case, the file or object behaves very much as if it were a GIF or JPEG referenced with the IMG tag. The other two options are full-page and hidden display. A full-page display might be a viewer that can operate outside of HTML documents. A good example is Abode's Acrobat viewer. For this display, the viewer will take over the entire browser window in order to properly represent the data object. The last option is currently not implemented—a hidden plug-in. In this case, a sound file, for example, will run in the background. Since most plug-in objects are included within HTML, our example will stick to the embedded option.

Returning to the plugin-test.html example, attempting to load this document will return an error called "Illegal Operation performed." Why? There are a number of things missing, the first of which is the referenced data object. In the example, this is test-file.xxx. Creating this file, then, is the next step. This assumes that .*xxx* is the chosen extension of the new MIME type, and *test-file* is the name given to the example that will be used. After this file is created and accessible to the browser, loading it again will still not complete the task, although something has changed: Now instead of an error, the broken resource icon is displayed.

PLUG-INS

The next step is to let the browser know about the new extension—extension.xxx. So far, the browser has no idea what .xxx means. In Netscape, it is fairly easy to tell the browser what a new extension means. Under the Options menu, choose General Preferences. Within this section is another option called Helpers. Within Helpers is a button for Create New Types. This where Netscape finds out about new file extensions. Type in the following:

```
Mime Type:     "mime-type name"
```

In the edit box called File Extensions, type in the new extension. In this case, type **.xxx**. Now although the browser can identify and recognize the new file format and its corresponding extension, it is still incapable of dealing with or understanding the new format. Now is the time for the C++ code to help out.

What is needed now is a Dynamic Link Library (DLL) file. This is a file that the browser will load (or plug in) to understand and display the new data format. This is the guts of the plug-in, giving the browser all the information it needs to support the new format. Once this file is created, navigating back into the File Extensions section of Netscape is necessary so that the browser will know what to do with the new file format when it comes across that extension.

Creating a DLL file

Open the npshell.cpp file. This compilable shell file provides the structure for creating a new plug-in. Working within npshell.cpp, all that is needed is to fill in the necessary code for basic plug-in functionality. In other words, the npshell.cpp provides a basic skeleton to work from. This is where Visual C++ comes into the picture and the real work begins: coding the plug-in. In the npshell.cpp, write the code for the functions needed to properly deal with the new file format. Looking at the npshell.ccp file in the AVI directory might be a helpful example as to how to create a plug-in.

Netscape provides a plug-in authoring guide for developers that is very helpful for the novice. Included in this support are class libraries provided by Netscape, which can save you a good amount of work. This guide is available online at http://home.netscape.com/eng/mozilla/2.0/handbook/plugins/toc.html. The list of methods in the library is accessible via the standard C++ syntax:

```
#include <npapi.h>
```

PLUG-INS

These methods include functions originating on the plug-in side as well as on Netscape's side. A list of these methods follows.

Plug-in Methods	Netscape Methods
NPP_Destroy()	NPN_DestroyStream()
NPP_DestroyStream()	NPN_GetURL()
NPP_HandleEvent()	NPN_MemAlloc()
NPP_Initialize()	NPN_MemFlush()
NPP_New()	NPN_MemFree()
NPP_NewStream()	NPN_NewStream()
NPP_Print()	NPN_PostURL()
NPP_SetWindow()	NPN_RequestRead()
NPP_Shutdown()	NPN_Status()
NPP_StreamAsFile()	NPN_UserAgent()
NPP_Write()	NPN_Version()
NPP_WriteReady()	NPN_Write()

When the code is finished, save the npshell.cpp file. Now, build the project with the compiler. This will create the DLL file. Copy the DLL into the plug-ins directory, which ought to exist at the same location as the Netscape program (netscape.exe). You must restart Netscape for the new plug-in to be loaded. All plug-ins that reside within the plug-ins directory at the time of execution will be loaded. It's a good idea to check and make sure that this actually occurred. To do this, choose the Help menu from the Netscape browser, then choose About Plug-ins. This ought to produce a list of all known MIME types and corresponding plug-ins. With that, load the plugin-test.html document. The new plug-in is now finished.

7

E-MAIL APPLICATIONS

WHAT WOULD THE INTERNET BE without e-mail? Not much. Electronic mail is the most basic and prevalent means of communication available on the Internet. The many uses of e-mail are readily apparent to anyone who spends any time at all on the Internet.

E-MAIL APPLICATIONS

E-mail is a fairly broad category. The most basic definition is electronic mail, but this comes in a variety of forms, of which the most widely used is *Internet mail*. Internet mail is unique in that it must conform to Internet standards, because it will likely travel across many machines, running many different platforms. Another type of e-mail travels within the confines of proprietary online services. Examples of this type include America Online, CompuServe, and Prodigy mail functions for sending messages to other members of the online service. For this kind of e-mail that is merely traveling within the realm of an online service, the services often have their own systems of exchange. The last type of e-mail travels through local area networks (LANs). Very similar to online service mail, LAN-based e-mail can have limited outside accessibility. This allows these systems to run protocols that are useful to their specific needs but which are not necessarily universal.

This chapter will focus on Internet mail and the applications used to send and receive this type of mail. Internet mail operates by using certain protocols, some of which are more widely used than others. There are many different types of e-mail applications, known technically as *Mail User Agents* (MUAs). In terms of protocol support, connections, and features, some MUAs are better than others.

E-mail Standards: SMTP

So how does e-mail work? The most widely used e-mail protocol—though there are others—is the Simple Mail Transfer Protocol (SMTP). Basically, the SMTP process starts with a MUA request: "This message needs to be sent there." The mail server—known technically as the SMTP-sender—receives this request and then establishes a two-way communication channel to a SMTP-receiver.

This receiver can be either the ending destination or an intermediary mail server. A variety of commands are sent to the SMTP-receiver, such as MAIL and RCPT commands. If you are at all interested in more of these commands, refer to Table 7.1 below. While other commands are available, this table details the minimum commands required of an SMTP-server.

If the SMTP-receiver finds these commands acceptable, it returns an OK message to the sender. The mail data is then transmitted and the message is sent on its way. This may occur a number of times before the mail actually reaches its destination, traveling from host to host in between.

Perhaps this is a bit on the technical side, but knowing what is under the hood is helpful in determining which e-mail application you need. All e-mail is not created equal; different e-mail applications support different e-mail protocols. Knowing what protocols are available and which ones are accessible on your system are important factors in choosing an e-mail application right for you.

E-MAIL APPLICATIONS

■ Table 7.1   Minimum SMTP-Server Commands

Command	Description
HELO	This field should contain the host name of the sender-SMTP, and is used to identify the sender-SMTP to the receiver-SMTP.
MAIL	This is the initial command for starting a communications channel between two SMTP servers. Often, this command will also contain the sender's e-mail address.
RCPT	This field contains the identity of the recipient(s) of the mail data. This takes the form of an e-mail address.
DATA	This is the field for the mail data—the actual message—to be sent. This data must conform to ASCII character codes.
RSET	This is a command for aborting the current mail transaction.
NOOP	This is a command for checking the SMTP connection. It does not affect any mail, but instead requires the receiver-SMTP to send back an OK reply.
QUIT	This command requests that the receiver-SMTP return an OK reply and then close the communication channel.

X.400 versus SMTP

For those who design these e-mail protocols, a running debate emerged some time ago about which protocol was better: X.400 or SMTP. Some e-mail applications use one and not the other. Although each has its advantages and disadvantages, SMTP is by far the most widely used and accepted protocol for sending and receiving e-mail.

While the name may sound like a new household cleaner, X.400 is actually a rival protocol to SMTP, created by the International Telecommunications Union (ITU), an agency of the United Nations, and the International Standards Organization (ISO). SMTP, on the other hand, was given birth by the Internet Engineering Task Force (IETF). The key difference between the ITU/ISO and the IETF is the fact that ITU/ISO standards cost money because they are copyrighted. The IETF is a volunteer organization which upholds the opposite philosophy: All their standards are (and must remain) freely available over the Internet.

Aside from this political difference, X.400 and SMTP are designed differently. SMTP is limited to information tramsmission based on the American Standard Code for Information Interchange (ASCII) character set. This means that e-mail is limited to text-only transmissions. Certainly many servers today allow the transmission of other file types (such as binary files). This is not a result of an improving SMTP, but rather is the product of other systems at work, such as MIME (MIME is explained later in this chapter). X.400 does not have this restriction as it is a binary format. Consequently, X.400 makes it much easier to send binary files—like images—without encoding them.

X.400 has other advantages over SMTP. When a message is sent with SMTP, the SMTP-sender passes the responsibility for getting the message

E-MAIL APPLICATIONS

to its destination on to the next server in line. There is no mechanism for the final receiving host to notify the original sender that the message was received. X.400 does not have this limitation and supports delivery notification. This is very much like America Online's return receipt system. SMTP is much more limited in this area. If a message is rejected or returned without delivery for some reason, the SMTP-sender will be notified. But often account names are left in the system even after the account is no longer in use, and in such cases the server will accept the mail even though there is no true recipient for it. If this happens, SMTP has no system to notify the sender that the message was lost in a cyber black hole.

For high bandwidth servers, SMTP is also limited by the fact that its mail queue is a first-come-first-served system. However, if it takes the server a substantial amount of time to process messages due to large volume, it is nice to be able to assign priorities to messages so that important ones reach their destinations quickly while less important ones are handled at a more leisurely pace. X.400, unlike SMTP, has such a system of priority markers. The X.400 system has three levels of priority to allow messages deemed important to receive service before others listed as less important.

In the area of security, X.400 and SMTP have differing approaches. SMTP is very much a basic protocol. It does what it's supposed to do: get mail from here to there and not much else. If SMTP users are interested in closing the security hole, SMTP offers nothing. SMTP must be layered with something else, in a fashion very similar to dealing with binary file transmissions. The issue of security has become very important recently, and there has been an explosion of new security applications. Many schemes can be used in conjuntion with SMTP. X.400, on the other hand, has an actual framework for security. It supports a security label to specify which scheme is used. Although there isn't a single security standard uniformly used, some sort of security scheme is inherent in the X.400 system, and the security labels notify the receiving-server as to which scheme should be applied.

SMTP Extensions

It may seem surprising that SMTP is more popular than X.400—considering the many advantages of X.400—but sometimes something simple is better. TCP/IP is a great example. It doesn't really do anything exciting—that's the beauty of it—but it provides a good, albeit simple working system that is the foundation for the Web protocol (HTTP) built on top of it. This is very similar to how e-mail has evolved with SMTP. Other systems are layered on top of it, making it better and more effective.

E-MAIL APPLICATIONS

One of the problems with SMTP is that it requires mail users to have direct contact with the mail server. But what if you want to view your mail from a remote location? Perhaps you want to view mail from your home computer or at a computer that is not directly connected to the main network at work? SMTP does not directly support remote mailbox access. As a result, other protocols have been added to change this situation.

POP   The first of these new protocols is known as POP, or Post Office Protocol. POP is the oldest addition to SMTP and is probably the best known. POP supports offline mail processing. Offline means that mail is delivered to an SMTP-server, and the user of a remote computer can periodically connect to the main server and download all the mail in the queue to the remote machine.

There are three version of POP: POP, POP2, and POP3. POP3 is the newest and most widely used of the three. It supports extensions not included in the earlier versions, such as Xtnd and Xmit. These extensions allow POP3 to actually send mail, bypassing SMTP altogether. The advantages of POP over other protocols are that it is simple and easy to impliment, and it is widely supported in a large number of mail clients. Z-Mail is one example of a MUA that supports POP. See Figure 7.1 for Z-Mail's graphical user interface.

IMAP   The Internet Message Access Protocol (IMAP) is another support mechanism for remote mailbox access. Like POP, IMAP can also support offline processing. IMAP goes a step farther, supporting online operations as well. Online remote access refers to a system where mail is delivered to a remote system—just like the offline system—but the operation is more interactive. The key difference is that the messages from the main server are not copied, sent, and deleted all at once. Instead, messages can be moved around at the whims of the mail user as if the user had local access.

Like POP, there are different varieties of IMAP: IMAP2, IMAP3, and IMAP4. IMAP3 is practically unheard of and is rarely seen. IMAP2 is probably the most prevalent of the three, and IMAP4 is the newest addtion to the family. IMAP4 extends the protocol by helping the server recognize MIME messages. The advantages of IMAP are that it provides management of multiple mailboxes, better control over message storage, and support for communcations other than e-mail, such as Usenet News.

Other Protocols   Three other protocols worth mentioning are the Distributed Mail System Protocol (DMSP), the Interactive Mail Support Protocol (IMSP), and the Messaging Application Programming Interface (MAPI). IMSP is actually just an extension to IMAP. It can complement

E-MAIL APPLICATIONS

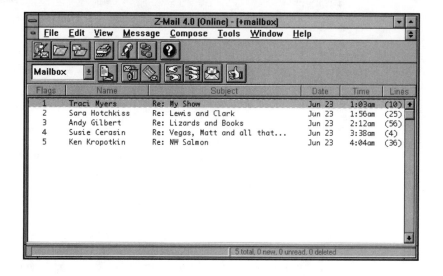

■ **Figure 7.1 Seen here, Z-mail is one of many e-mail applications supporting POP.**

IMAP by providing e-mail services not currently supported by IMAP alone. DMSP is limited in use to a single application, PCMAIL. DMSP supports a "disconnected" remote access system based on the idea that mail users use multiple stations. These stations—usually desktop computers—are given what is essentially a directory of messages. When a user connects to the server from one of these stations, the directory is filled with the corresponding messages. MAPI is a protocol for the Windows world. Many applications ported to the Windows platform will support MAPI.

What about Those Strange File Formats?

As mentioned above, SMTP is limited to the 128 characters in the ASCII set. What do you do about binary files, such as pictures and sounds? Sending these types of files with SMTP would cause it to choke and wouldn't give pretty results at the other end, either. To rectify this situation, there is something called the Multipurpose Internet Mail Extension (MIME). Its basic function is to provide a means for interchanging data that is

E-MAIL APPLICATIONS

encoded in languages with different character sets (like binary and ASCII). MIME can usually handle the following types of files:

- Non-ASCII character sets (such as ISO and/or Unicode)

- Images

- Sounds

- tar files

- PostScript files

- Encapsulated messages

- Enriched text

Instead of just plain text files, MIME allows users to create e-mail with audio, images, and other non-text content. Better yet, these files can work across many different platforms. There are other products that support non-text content, but MIME was the first to support platforms nearly universally.

Unfortunately, MIME support is a very broad label. Some e-mail applications offer more MIME support than others. In other words, to be MIME-compliant means that, at a minimum, the e-mail agent is able to identify non-text content and ensure that the user is not exposed to the raw data. Usually these applications merely capture the unsupported data and attach this information as separate files. Some MIME-supporting MUAs use MIME fully, actually identifying the content type and displaying that content instead of hiding it. The level of MIME support totally depends on the mail agent you're using.

Help is available for testing mail agents. The E-mail MIME Test Form is accessible at http://www.dsed.llnl.gov/documents/tests/e-mail/e-mailform.html. This form provides a variety of tests to see how good your MIME reader really is. WAV sound files, GIFs, MPEGs, QuickTime files—all these are waiting to see how confused your mail agent can get. With the click of a button, this Web page will automatically e-mail the desired formats to the destination of your mail program.

File Encoders

What if you need to send a binary file or some other non-ASCII-based file to a destination without MIME support? Perhaps you don't even know if MIME support exists at the other end? Instead of sending such a file hoping it makes its way there intact, it's time to think about the old phrase, When in Rome…. In the case of e-mail, it's an ASCII world, so doing it in ASCII is the most secure way to deal with the situation. There are a couple of ways to solve this binary/ASCII dilemma.

E-MAIL APPLICATIONS

The first tried and true method is to use UUencoding. UUencoding stands for Unix-to-Unix encoding. While this encoding scheme was born in Unix, it is now available on most popular platforms such as Windows, DOS, and Macintosh. UUencoding is a way of encrypting binary data into ASCII's character limitations. In this way, binary files can be hidden within ASCII, sent through e-mail, and reassembled (UUdecoded) into binary at the other end. UUencoded files will usually use .uue or .uu as the file suffix to identify its encoding.

Another method, called Binhexing, is usually associated with Macintosh. Binhex was developed by Yves Lempereur back in 1985. Binhexed files use the .hqx extension. Macintosh files often have both a data fork and a resource fork; additional information is also stored in the Desktop database. However, many other encoding schemes do not support multiple forks and will corrupt the file. For this reason Binhex is often used in conjunction with Macintosh file transferring. But Binhex is not limited to Macintosh and can be used on a variety of platforms.

E-mail Applications

Now that you've meandered your way through the wild frontier of e-mail protocols and extensions, it's time to move out from under the hood and get behind the wheel of e-mail applications. From the bare-bones to the gold-plated and gizmo-infested, these applications come in a variety of shapes and sizes.

The Basics

There is obviously a minimum number of features that any e-mail application worth its salt will support. Probably the most basic e-mail application is the MAIL program developed for and available on most Unix systems. This program does nothing more than the basics: sending and receiving e-mail. To compose mail, the From and To fields must be hand-typed. A text editor is basically nonexistent, and each line needs a carriage return. You may despise the old and cryptic Unix editors like VI, but even they look good compared to this system. What was that command for sending the message, you ask? Better get a manual—this program is not menu-driven in the least. It's free and it works, but that's about all you can say for it.

Usual Features

The next generation of mail applications brought in some very helpful features. Pine and Elm are the best examples of this style of e-mail agent (see Figure 7.2). Once you get used to them, there is no way you'll go back to MAIL! For starters, something as simple as a word wrapper can be a godsend. Have you ever gotten caught up writing a flame and forgotten to hit the return key before the line begins to melt into the edge of the screen? An automatic word wrapper makes writing messages a good deal easier.

E-MAIL APPLICATIONS

■ **Figure 7.2   Pine is a standard fixture on most Unix platforms. It's a simple, no-nonsense e-mail application.**

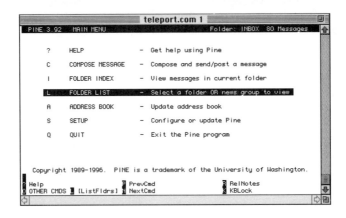

Now that composing is easier, why not make reading e-mail easier? Instead of just displaying a long list (assuming you get a reasonable amount of mail) of e-mail messages, how about a method for sorting the messages in the inbox so that they are easier to access? This is exactly what many e-mail applications now support. They will usually sort messages by subject, data, senders, and perhaps other categories.

If you have spent any time at all working with e-mail, you probably have saved messages. If you subscribe to listservers for example, saving subscription information is very important. When a message enters your inbox that is worth keeping, a scheme for managing these saved files is a good feature. Many e-mail applications support some sort of folder management for storing messages based on personally chosen categories.

For just about everyone, typing in e-mail addresses is a tiresome chore fraught with frustration for the fumble-fingered. It is especially tirseome when you have to type in the same long address several times a day. To solve this problem, many e-mail applications provide an address book. This takes the form of a file containing addresses and corresponding names of people that are frequent recipients of your electronic compositions. Instead of typing in the entire address, these address books usually let you choose from a directory or merely type in a predetermined nickname—the application then fills in the complete address.

E-mail is a fairly homogenous medium. From, To, Date, and a message—that's about the size of it. Or is it? Many applications support some

E-MAIL APPLICATIONS

sort of customization settings for e-mail messages. This might include support for custom headers—instead of just the basics, why not add your own personalized headers? At the other end of your e-mail messages, you can add a *signature file,* currently all the rage with e-mail cognoscenti. Many e-mail applications will automatically append such a signature message at the tail of your messages, though if you've ever seen a signature more than a page long, you might begin wishing for a world without signature files.

The final usual feature is very useful: file attachment support. If you want to send anything more than your short rantings via e-mail, file attachment is a must. Perhaps you're interested in sending your thesis to a friend. Instead of retyping 100 pages or cutting-and-pasting your way through the dilemma, you can just attach the file containing your thesis and the problem is solved. If you made it through the section above on MIME, then you know that it is not quite this simple. While attachments can open a whole new can of worms, they are more often than not a lifesaver.

Customizing Your E-mail Environment

If you're happy with the features mentioned above and would be scared by anything more complicated, then programs like Pine and Elm for Unix are probably for you. They are basic, simple, and reliable. Best of all, they are most always freeware. If you are not yet satisfied, there are plenty of other gizmos available.

The first big step up from menu-driven applications is a nice graphic interface. For those that are partial to the world of Windows and icon-driven events, Pine and Elm probably look like relics from the Stone Age. Do not despair, help is available. Many applications support toolbars for common commands and pull-down menus for most everything else. If that's *still* not fancy enough, a select few mailers even offer customized toolbars. A good example of this style of e-mail agent is Eudora. (See Figure 7.3.)

Although pointing out spelling errors in e-mail messages is considered bad netiquette, reading messages full of unintelligible and random letter associations is no picnic. To alleviate this situation, some e-mail applications are nice enough to include a built-in spell checker. This feature is extremely useful to just about everyone. Of course, like most extremely useful things, this feature comes at a premium and usually costs something more than nothing. Other useful features include importing files, return receipts, printer support, and searching capabilities.

So you say you are still not impressed? Looking for that free set of Ginsu knives as a bonus? A handful of e-mail applications have pulled out all the stops and included so many interesting features that it verges on overkill. First off is a feature providing multiple windows for viewing mail. Most people, it seems, can only read one message at a time. But for those

E-MAIL APPLICATIONS

■ Figure 7.3   Eudora is arguably the most prevalent e-mail application for personal computers. Eudora Lite (shown here) is a limited version of Eudora Pro.

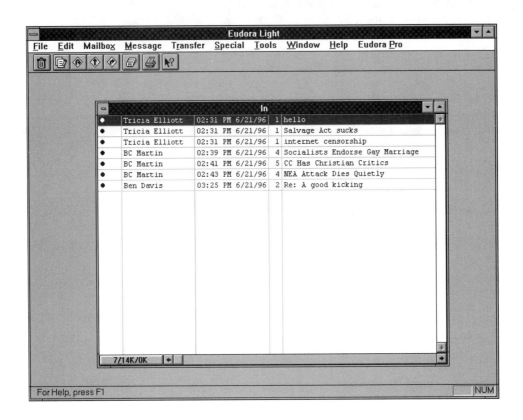

who are always doing six things at once, multiple windows are available. For people who can't click on icons, some applications offer drag-and-drop execution. For those who live for frills rather than thrills, there are even e-mail applications that will talk to you. Yes, audio is now an option.

The All-in-one Applications

More and more Internet software comapnies are developing applications that perform a wide variety of functions. For these applications, the slogan (as seen on Saturday Night Live) is "It's a dessert topping and a floor wax!" Many of the most popular Web browsers support more protocols

E-MAIL APPLICATIONS

than just HTTP. Often these meta-applications support HTTP, NNTP, FTP, gopher, Telnet, and a variety of e-mail protocols. This can be very helpful to people that like to keep a variety of functions operating at once, without the need for two, three, or four different programs.

Hardware and Platform Limitations

Already mentioned was the different ways for e-mail applications to inter-act with mail servers: on line, off line and disconnected. Depending on constraints imposed by the system at hand, there is also the question of how this interaction is established. The two main methods of connection are serial and TCP/IP (along with SLIP and PPP). Often the method of connection is an imposition of circumstance, rather than an actual choice. So it's important to choose an application able to operate in your environment. Many e-mail applications are ported to many of the popular platforms, but others are limited to a small number of systems, perhaps even just one. Obviously your chosen platform will limit your choices of e-mail applications.

Price

In keeping with the dominant Internet culture where most necessary com-ponents for commnication are free, a large selection of e-mail applications are available as freeware. Even a number of commercially developed soft-ware packages are given away freely. The rest are made available mostly as shareware. Very few e-mail programs require payment without a free test-drive offer. Obviously those programs that deviate from the norm, offering frills, gizmos, and support for unusual or propietary protocols are most often the ones that cost real dollars.

Which Mail User Agent Is for You?

Picking an e-mail application is very much limited by your environment. What platform do you have? What type of mail server do you connect to? Last but not least, what type of connection links your computer to the server (or perhaps these computers are actually one and the same). If you are limited to a basic university shell account with a serial connection, the choice is extremely limited. Running a computer from home via a SLIP/PPP connection greatly improves the selection. Whatever your situa-tion, you should be able to find a number of e-mail application options in the comparison charts in Appendix G that would be right for you.

8

GRAPHICS SOFTWARE

GRAPHIC IMAGES ARE AN INTEGRAL PART of the Web and help distinguish it from many of the other Internet protocols. Pictures, icons, and logos all add a bit of artistry to what was once a text-dominated medium. Now, Web pages come alive with style, flair, and creativity.

To create these masterpieces of design, the Web artist requires the proper tools. Brushes, canvas, and paint are substituted with electron guns, monitors, and keyboards. The smell of turpentine is replaced by the sound of a whirling hard drive. Standing at the center of it all, providing the interface between cyber-artist and hardware, is the graphics application. This component is the key to producing visually pleasing Web material.

GRAPHICS SOFTWARE

The Basic Graphics Application

Graphics applications come in a variety of shapes and sizes and generally perform one of three primary tasks: graphics conversion, viewing, or creation. Conversion applications are primarily concerned with turning one file format into another. Perhaps you have scanned in a photograph using scanning software that only allows you to save the file as a TIFF. Instead of requiring visitors to your Web page to use a plug-in to deal with the TIFF image, you can convert the TIFF into a more widely supported format, such as a GIF.

The second major type of graphics application functions as a graphics viewer. Your scanned image may exist as a file, but that doesn't mean you can see what it looks like. A graphics viewer will turn the file data into a graphic image that is displayed on a monitor. Usually such programs come with added goodies such as magnification and cropping tools.

Finally, some graphics applications provide the actual means to create your own graphics. Using one of these programs, you can manipulate scanned images just about any way you want. You can also fill the beckoning blank screen with logos, icons, or your own doodling. The best of these graphics powerhouses provide tools for area selection, blending, filling, painting, drawing, burning and dodging, and contrast and brightness manipulation.

The separation between these three categories of software is not too sharp, however. Programs in the third category usually support viewing and conversion as well, and so-called viewing programs usually also provide conversion features. In other words, there are some very basic features that nearly all graphics applications support.

File Conversion

File conversion is the most necessary feature of any graphics application. There are a large number of formats available, just about one for every letter of the alphabet: BMP, CGM, CLP, CVG, DCX, DL, DIB, FIF, FITS, FLI/FLC, GIF, GRP, HP-GL/2, ICO, IFF, JPEG/JFIF, MacPaint, MSP, MSX, PAC, PBM, PCD, PCX, PIC, PIC-Atari, PIC-Lotus, PICS, PICT, PM, PNG, QDV, RAS, RIFF, RLE, SCX, SGI, SHP, SOFTIMAGE, SPU, SUN, TGA, TIFF, TINY, VFF, WMF, WPG, XBM, XWD, 8BIM, 8BPS, and others. Out of this mighty list, four are most commonly supported by graphics applications: GIF, JPEG, TIFF, and EPS (Encapsulated Post Script).

Graphics programs were largely developed for things other than the Web. In other words, these applications were designed to produce good output from a printer but not necessarily to produce good images on a monitor. Because of this emphasis, graphics software tends to prefer the TIFF and EPS file formats supported by most printers rather than the GIF and JPEG formats common on the Web.

GRAPHICS SOFTWARE

■ Carberry Conversion Machine

Have a file format that you want to convert but no conversion software? The Carberry Conversion Machine may be just the thing for you—it converts file formats right over the Web. All you need is a URL for the file. Once you let the Conversion Machine know where your Web-accessible file resides, it will do the rest.

Presently, the Conversion Machine is relatively limited in the number of formats it can import and export. It can import CGM, HPGL, DXF, GIF, and JPEG files. It can only export from the above list into CGM, GIF, and JPEG files. If this machine sounds useful to you, check out Carberry's page at http://www.ct.ebt.com/ convmach.html. ■

It makes little sense to create a masterpiece for your Web page using a program that only gives you the option of saving it into an unusable file format. The GIF and JPEG formats have important subcategories. The GIF89a format is capable of displaying an inline picture without a border, making it appear to float above a background image. This type of GIF also supports layering of multiple images. Exploiting this feature properly yields a basic form of animation—each image contained in the file is shown sequentially. A progressive JPEG file arranges the image data in a different order from a regular JPEG. The progressive format allows a slow-loading application—such as a Web browser—to load the image in layers. This is very much like interlaced GIF files. A rough image is loaded and in subsequent layers the image slowly becomes sharper.

Much of the scanning software available will place the scanned data into a TIFF format and little else, whereas desktop publishing software packages tend to only offer EPS output. An EPS file is not a graphic file at all—it is really just command tags for printer output. Obviously, EPS files are great if a printer is the target, but for the Webmaster this isn't the case. A good file converter that can deal with at least the four of the formats listed above is an absolute necessity.

Graphics Creation

There are two basic ways to create graphic images. The first is to scan in images. Scanned images are usually cleaned up in some fashion, cropped, and exported into a usable format. The other way is to start from scratch using different graphics tools to create entirely new images and icons. Of course, these techniques can be, and often are, used in conjunction with one another.

GRAPHICS SOFTWARE

Scanned Images

A scanned image starts out as hard-copy—that is, the original image exists on some sort of paper medium as a photograph, a newspaper clipping, a hand-drawing, or something along those lines. The image is placed on or in a scanner and the information from the hard-copy is transformed into computer data. That's not the end of the story, though. Scanned images often need cleaning up to remove rough edges, fix discontinuities in lines, and erase marks caused by dirt on the scanner or original image. Fortunately, there is plenty of software available to help you manipulate the scanned data to get the desired result. You also need software to convert the scan into an acceptable format, such as a GIF or JPEG. See Figure 8.1 for an example of an image as a raw scan and after clean up.

■ **Figure 8.1   (A) The raw scan; (B) The same image after being cleaned up.**

A
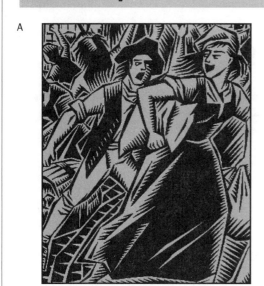

B

Formatting Features   Arguably the most important feature for this type of work is a way to vary the brightness and contrast of an image. A scanner is very similar to a photocopier. Anyone who has photocopied an image knows that, as in any conversion process, quality suffers. To minimize this problem, you can adjust the brightness and contrast. See Figure

GRAPHICS SOFTWARE

8.2 below for an example of a typical brightness/contrast controller. This is very much like the brightness and contrast controls found on many photocopiers. The key difference is that photocopiers require such information before the image is processed; with software, the brightness and contrast can be manipulated over and over after scanning until the desired result is achieved.

■ Figure 8.2   A typical brightness and contrast controller

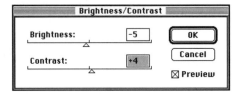

Some graphics software offers control over color tint, similar to the tint control on a television. Obviously this is reserved for color scans. Often manipulating color tint can bring dead-looking images to life. This control can also aid in the image quality, helping to provide better definition.

Perhaps you have a black-and-white image to which you wish to add color, or perhaps the opposite is true. This is where a feature to change between grayscale and a variety of color settings is beneficial. Grayscale refers to images, commonly referred to as black and white, whose pixels are either black, white, or various shades of gray. Color images vary in the number of total colors they can display; possibilities include 2 colors (1 bit), 4 colors (2 bit), 16 colors (4 bit), 256 colors (8 bit), 32,768 colors (16 bit), and millions of colors (32 bit).

Inversion is a feature that allows the artist to flip the data of an image—usually a black-and-white or grayscale image. Inverting such an image will produce an image similar to a photographic negative.

Similar to inverting is mirroring and rotation. Mirroring manipulates the image data to produce a mirror image of the graphic. Usually you can specify a vertical mirror or a horizontal mirror operation. Rotating an image is fairly straight-forward. Of the applications that support rotation, some are limited to fixed degrees of rotation, such as 90, 180, and 270 degrees. Others offer any amount of rotation, perhaps even providing a manual rotation device where the user can watch the image as it spins around. See Figures 8.3, 8.4, and 8.5 for examples of inversion, mirroring, and rotation.

GRAPHICS SOFTWARE

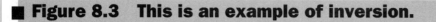
Figure 8.3   This is an example of inversion.

Formatting an image is not confined to its basic appearance. Among the supported features, control over file size is absolutely necessary. The file size is related to both the image size and the resolution, which is measured in dots per inch (DPI). The image size is represented with basic units of measurements, such as inches or pixels. Control of DPI levels and image size is paramount to control over the byte-size of an image file.

Basic Tools   Tools for specific manipulations to graphic images are usually found on a toolbar in the graphics application. These tools tend to offer more micro-focused features than the overall formatting features discussed above. In other words, the toolbar provides capabilities that affect a specified region of an image rather than the overall look of the image as a whole.

Most common of the tools is the crop. Since it is difficult to accurately define the exact borders of an image you want scanned from within the scanner's preview, you usually scan in an area slightly larger than the image you really want. You then use a cropping tool to remove this "border" and pare the scan down to the image you wanted. See Figure 8.6 for an example of cropping.

GRAPHICS SOFTWARE

6Ring6.gif (1:1)

169K

Drawing tools allow you to actually add material to the image. They usually include at the very least an eraser, a pencil tool, and basic shape tools. The eraser is self-explanatory: It erases parts of an image. A pencil tool allows the artist to draw lines as you would using a pencil on paper. The better graphics applications will include multiple pencil tools of different sizes. Finally, any basic graphics program ought to support a few predefined shape design tools, typically including tools for drawing circles and squares.

Finally, any decent graphics application should include an eyedropper. This is a treasured tool among computer-aided graphic artists and is used to select a color by clicking on any pixel in the image. This allows the artist to fill in pixels to smooth out edges without the guesswork that is required when matching colors by sight.

Advanced Manipulation Tools

There are entire books that explore the features of some of the best known graphics applications like Abode's Photoshop and Macromedia's FreeHand. Suffice it to say that this section will only cover those tools that are fairly common to the advanced programs—pointing out behavior most helpful for Web developers.

GRAPHICS SOFTWARE

■ **Figure 8.5   Here's a graphic that's been mirrored then rotated.**

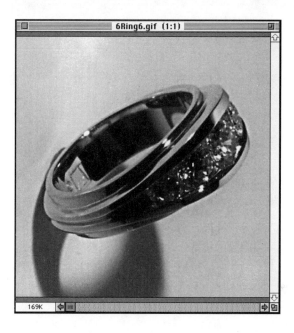

Included in the features described below are tools found only in programs like Adobe's Illustrator and FreeHand. These graphic applications were not written for the express purpose of Web graphics, but are rather tools for professional graphic artists. Because of this, they usually offer little support for common Web formats like GIF and JPEG. For example, FreeHand supports EPS and TIFF. If you want to place a FreeHand image on the Web, there are two solutions available: a plug-in or a conversion program. Shockwave is a plug-in for Netscape that will display images created in FreeHand. If you are not interested in forcing your Web viewers to download extra software, you'll have to acquire another program to convert the TIFF output from FreeHand into a GIF or JPEG. Having said this, the new Illustrator 6.0 does support JPEG, saving you the extra conversion.

Selection Tools
Selection tools are those that allow you to select a very defined area for manipulating. For example, let's say you want to change the brightness

GRAPHICS SOFTWARE

■ **Figure 8.6   Cut your way out of irregular shaped borders with the cropper.**

and contrast of a small region of an image. You have to select that region first. Some selection tools are better than others. Most applications will support a very basic selection tool that allows for a click-and-draggable box or oval area. This has a very limit application. You can't select an irregularly shaped area, like part of a person's body, for example.

Tools to remedy the situation are the Lasso and Wand. The Lasso feature, which is fairly common, allows you to hand-draw the selected area. In this way, your selection options are much greater than when using a simple rectangular or circular area. The most powerful selection tool is the Wand tool, such as found in Adobe's Photoshop. This tool will select areas based on contrasting colors and shades. This tool is far less common than the other types of selection tools, but very helpful. It allows you to grab entire areas along their border for moving and manipulating, as shown in see Figure 8.7.

GRAPHICS SOFTWARE

■ Web Image Tips

There are some basic rules to follow when creating and formatting images for display on the Web. Already alluded to is the fact that the Web is a much different medium than other standard output devices like a printer and requires a different approach. In this section we will discuss things you can do to make your Web images more enjoyable for viewers.

Formatting for Monitors

Printed images, whether output to paper or film, require fairly high resolution images since "photographic quality" is often a goal. This is not the case when dealing with images on the Web because such images are meant only to be displayed on monitors, not to be printed. The resolution capabilities of a monitor are far more limited than printers: A typical printer has a minimum resolution of 300 DPI, but a monitor has a maximum resolution of only 72 DPI. Many printers go way beyond 300 DPI resolution, with resolution as high as 4800 DPI, but anything over 72 DPI is just wasted information for images targeted for the Web.

For example, let's take an indexed-color image that is 5 inches by 5 inches. A typical magazine resolution is 1200 DPI. At that resolution, the file is a whopping 34.3MB. With a 28,800-kbps modem, that would take nearly three and a half hours to download! Even at 300 DPI, the image is still overwhelming at 2.15MB. Take it all the way down to 72 DPI and the file size shrinks to 127K. This is much more acceptable. This is especially true when taking compression into account. For example, that same 127K image shrinks further into 28K when compressed into a GIF format. The file could be even smaller with a strong JPEG compression.

So which file format is better? It really depends on a number of things, including the content of the image. Sometimes GIFs are better, sometimes JPEGs are better. Typically, Web surfers will have a 256-color monitor, and it's safe to say that GIFs usually appear crisper in this setting. With higher resolution monitors this is not always the case because a JPEG typically contains more image information than a GIF. The best advice is to set your monitor to 256 colors and test images in both formats to see which one looks better. For more information on GIFs and JPEGs and how to manipulate file size, see the Bandwidth Conservation Society page at http://www.infohiway.com/.

A Better Appearance

72 DPI is certainly not the best resolution, but there are ways around this limitation. The best technique is *anti-aliasing*, which allows low-resolution images to appear much more clear and less blocky. See Figure 8.8 for examples of this method in action.

In the illustration above the words *Anti* and *Alias* are both 36 point type and the magnification is 4 to 1. This allows you to see how this technique works. The regular type ("Alias") is made up of very rough edges and looks very blocky. The other word (Anti") has a fuzzy-looking edge instead. When the magnification is normal, this will make the image appear to be smoother. Some argue that this technique allows 72 DPI images to appear as good as 1200 DPI. This might be a bit of exagerration, but it's true that anti-aliasing does make for better appearing graphics.

Of course there is a serious drawback to anti-aliasing—anti-aliased graphics are not usually compatible with a transparent GIF. The problem stems from the fuzzy edge, which inherits qualities from the background it is created on. In this case, the fuzzy edge is made up of gray (black and white) pixels. If the image text was blue on a yellow background, the anti-aliasing would be green. Therefore it takes some tricky moves to produce good-looking anti-aliased images that are also transparent. Just keep in mind the target environment. Also important to understand is the fact that anti-aliasing works on sharp edges, like text. It may not be of use for many other situations. ■

GRAPHICS SOFTWARE

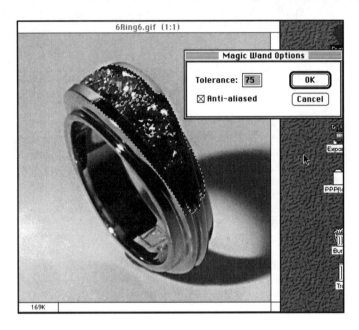

■ **Figure 8.7 The Wand tool works like magic, grabbing color and tint-specific areas without much effort.**

Painting

Painting tools are those that allow you to draw shapes onto the canvas area of an image. The most basic of these have been discussed, such as pencil and brush tools. Many applications support better control over these tools, offering control over the size of the brush, for example. Other tools include the ability to render shapes, such as lines, circles, and boxes. Finally, the Paint bucket is a common feature that will fill a selected area with a predetermined color. An airbrush tool, such as the one found in Photoshop, creates an effect similar to that created by a real airbrush— a fuzzy rather than a solid stroke of color. Usually such a tool can be modified to control the size of the spray and the rate of the virtual-paint. This control allows for the introduction of transparent (non-opaque) layers of color to images.

Manipulation

So far, the features we have discussed have been the most basic tools. By themselves these tools are not very useful unless you like stick figures. To move a step further you need tools for manipulating areas of images.

GRAPHICS SOFTWARE

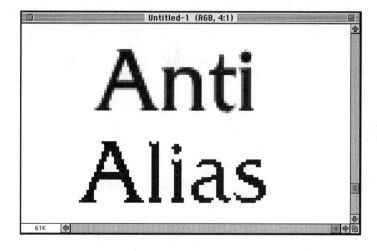

■ **Figure 8.8   Anti-Aliasing can improve your text graphics dramatically.**

These include the smudge, sponge, and burn and dodge tools. The smudge tool often appears on the toolbar as a finger icon. This tool works very much like a finger on chalk. The sponge tool works, not surprisingly, like a sponge. It allows you to control color saturation in a selected area by mopping up excess color. The burn and dodge tool allows for darkening and lightening of selected areas.

For the more adventurous graphic-masters there are rubber stamp and gradient tools. These also manipulate areas, but with more deliberate effects. The rubber stamp picks up images like Silly Putty does on comic strips. It can paint one selected area onto another. See Figure 8.9 for an example. The very useful gradient tool acts as a type of blending tool. Multiple colors can be preselected and filled in an area as a blend.

Output Control

Contrast and brightness controls give only very limited control over the image tones and tints. Other features to look for are control over output levels, curves, hue, and saturation. Levels and curves allow for very complex command of the image tones and channels. With these features, you can make the blackest black more gray without affecting any other area or color of the image. Hue and saturation controls allow control over which colors will appear and how bright they are.

GRAPHICS SOFTWARE

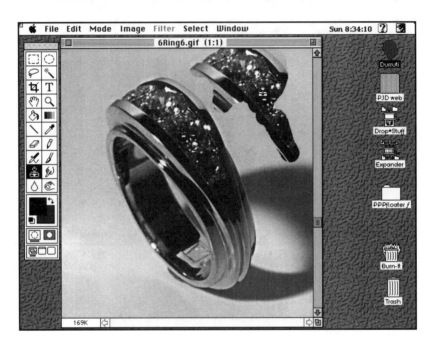

■ **Figure 8.9   The rubber stamp tool is an example of more advanced graphic software capabilities.**

Distortion Effects

Distortion effects are helpful features that manipulate portions of images, creating distorted representations of the original area. Areas can be stretched and scaled in many different ways. Some applications support more distortion features than others.

The most useful distortion tools for Webmasters are those that are used in conjunction with text. Stretching and scaling are just the tip of the iceberg. Serious graphics software, such as FreeHand and Illustrator, can give complete control over text positioning. These types of programs allow you to create paths of any shape to which the target text will conform. This provides unlimited possibilities. See Figure 8.10 for an example of such a distorted image.

GRAPHICS SOFTWARE

■ **Figure 8.10 Some graphic software allows you to work with text as objects; a good example is FreeHand.**

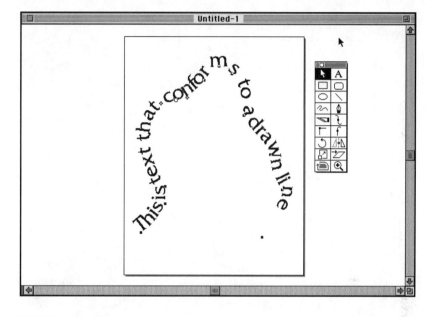

Filters

Filters are a broad category of features that do unusual and unique manipulations to images or portions of images. Fully describing all available filters would take up an entire chapter of its own. Some filters offer different techniques for sharpening images. Others support different varieties of blurring. There are also a wide variety of distortion and stylist filters. See Figures 8.11 and 8.12 for examples of Photoshop's Polar Coordinates and Wind filters. The Polar Coordinate filter takes the x and y coordinates and imposes the data on a polar coordinate system. The results are interesting. The other figure is an example of the Wind filter. This filter creates the simulation of wind and offers custom options for wind strength and direction.

Plug-ins

Like Web browsers, some graphics applications offer plug-in capabilities. This allows a graphics program to support features that are not written into its original lineup of tools. Netscape is to Web browser plug-ins as Photoshop is to graphics plug-ins—this is the pioneering application.

GRAPHICS SOFTWARE

■ **Figure 8.11   Frog in a blender anyone? This is what the ring looks like through a Polar Coordinate filter.**

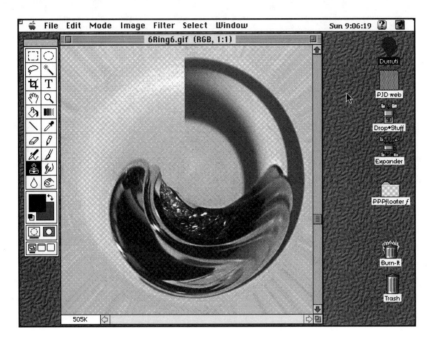

Other programs now support plug-ins, but nearly all are developed with Photoshop in mind.

Plug-ins tend to lend support in two main areas, the first being file formats. Photoshop does not have built-in support for transparent GIFs or progressive JPEGs, but this can be remedied with plug-ins. The other major area where plug-ins are used is in new filters. The most popular of these filters were developed by a third party and are known as Kai's Power Tools. They provide an impressive list of new stylistic and distortive filters for creating amazing images. There are 18 categories of filters in this package, and each category often has multiple types. An example of these filters is one for creating 3-D textures.

GRAPHICS SOFTWARE

■ **Figure 8.12   Here's what your wedding ring might look like in a tornado.**

Extra Features

If that's still not enough gizmos for you, some applications offer other tidbits that can make life easier for the overworked Webmaster. Some programs combine many tasks into one application, some support sound and video. This is very helpful for multimedia developers. Other programs offer a slideshow effect, so that you can see all images in a selected directory. This is helpful if you are not sure which of several images to use. Also useful in this regard are programs that create catalogs of thumbnails of your images. This makes for easy selection when there are quite a number of them.

Many of the superpowered and high-priced graphics programs neglect a screen capturing feature. For those Web designers that want to offer any sort of computer tutorial on line, this is a severe disadvantage. If you are using a Macintosh, a screen capture feature is built into the system software (Command-Shift-3). For PC and Unix users there are multiple options. For a comparison chart of these and other types of graphics applications, see Appendix H.

GRAPHICS SOFTWARE

Price

Unlike some of the other software categories, graphics applications have a very skewed price range. Some are available as freeware; others are as much as $1,000 or more. The key to not overspending is to decide what the purpose of the program is. Many of the higher priced applications are developed for professional graphics artists—not Web page designers. These types of software usually have more gizmos than a Webmaster will likely ever use. On the other hand, many of the freeware and shareware programs give significantly less control over images. Once you work out the amount of image control your Web site will demand, you should be able to find something that's right for you in terms of both price and features.

9 WHAT IS A WEB SERVER?

A *WEB SERVER* is simply the server that handles requests from Web browsers on the World Wide Web. The World Wide Web is divided into *clients*, also known as Web browsers, who request files, and *servers* which deliver the requested files. The client and server communicate using the Hypertext Transfer Protocol (HTTP). An HTTP connection is initiated by a Web browser requesting a document from a Web server. When the Web server receives this request, it usually responds by returning the requested document to the Web browser. Of course a simple document request like

WHAT IS A WEB SERVER?

this is the easiest type of transaction the Web server deals with—Web servers must also be equipped to handle more complicated tasks such as responding to invalid requests, executing CGI scripts, and logging requests. Many Web servers are also able to handle image maps, secure transactions, and multiple domain names.

If you want to run a Web site from your own computer, you will have to install and configure a Web server on your machine. In the early days of the Web, there were not many Web servers to choose from. Now, however, the amount of Web server software is abundant, making the choice somewhat more difficult. With the vast number of Web servers available, you have many options to find the right server for your needs.

What to Look for in a Web Server

A few years ago, your choice of a Web server was limited to a few possibilities. With so many Web servers currently available, the decision can be quite daunting. Even though this gives you many options, you may have trouble deciding which Web server to use. The best way to determine the right Web server for you is to think about your Web site and what features you want to have. For example, do you want to include image maps on your site? How about online financial transactions, such as the purchases or sales? Or perhaps you will be running a Web hosting service, in which case you would want to have the ability for one Web server to handle requests addressed to multiple domain names.

Once you have compiled the list of functions that you want for your Web site, the choice of Web server becomes easier. Many of the desired functions in your list will necessitate certain features in your Web server. For example, if you will be having image maps on your Web pages, you may want a Web server that has built-in image map support. For processing of online purchasing, you would want a Web server that has some support for secure transactions. And as for serving multiple domain names, you would clearly need a Web server that offers this as a feature. You should be able to take most of your functions list and translate it into a features list of what to look for in a Web server.

Below, several of the most popular Web server features are discussed. As you look over these features, think about which ones you need to provide the desired functionality for your Web site. After reading through them, you should be able to narrow down your choices for a Web server by looking for one that has all the features you have selected.

The Web Server's Platform

The best way to begin narrowing your choices is to see what platform the Web server runs on. It does little good to find a great Web server that provides every feature you need, but does not run on the machine you have.

WHAT IS A WEB SERVER?

By making the Web server's platform your first priority in making your decision, you can quickly eliminate many servers from your list.

If you have not already purchased a server machine, you will want to evaluate the hardware first before making a decision about the software. In the early days of the Web, almost all Web servers were available for Unix machines only— running your Web site from a Windows NT machine was simply not an option. Today, with the abundance of Web servers for all platforms, you do not need to compromise your hardware choice in order to get the Web server features you desire. Virtually all Web server features are available for all the major hardware platforms.

Hosting of Multiple IP Addresses

Web site hosting is a business that developed from the practice of the early Internet Service Providers leasing out space on their Web servers. At that time, the Web servers were only equipped to handle a single IP address. For leased space, providers would set up a subdirectory in the document root for that user's Web pages. If customers wanted to use their own domain name, they had to lease a dedicated Web server just for themselves, at a much greater cost than leasing space on a shared server.

Now, however, many Web servers provide the ability to handle requests from multiple IP addresses and domain names. This provides the ability to set up multiple Web sites on the same server machine using the same Web server software, but having different IP addresses and domain names.

This feature would be most important to you if you plan on hosting other people's Web sites. By using a Web server with this feature, you can keep your hardware and software costs low and still provide your customers with the ability to have their own domain names for their Web sites. You might also be interested in this feature if you need to have multiple Web sites yourself.

One important consideration though, is the amount of traffic for your Web server. Even if your Web server can host multiple domains and IP addresses, you may not want to use this feature. If your sites, or the sites you are hosting, generate a lot of traffic, then it would be better to run the sites off separate machines or Web servers to reduce the amount of work a single Web server has to do, thereby making your sites faster for your users.

Logging of Requests

Web server logs can be a useful source of information about your Web site and the documents that are requested from it. All Web servers offer some form of request logging, usually in the CERN and NCSA *common log format*. While this format has been the standard for Web servers, many of the newer servers offer more flexibility in logging.

WHAT IS A WEB SERVER?

One feature that some Web servers offer is the ability to customize the information that is entered in the log for a normal request. Normally, the Web server logs requests in the common log format. This format contains basic information such as the domain name or IP address of the remote client, the date and time of the request, the object requested, the status returned by the Web server, and the number of bytes sent to the remote client. However, this is only part of the information the Web server receives with a request from a Web browser. The Web servers that offer this customization allow you to choose from all available data what information will be placed in the log file for each request, letting you track the information that is most important to you.

Two of the most popular fields to log (which are not usually logged in the common log format) are the *referrer* and the *browser.* The referrer is the URL of the last page the user had loaded into the Web browser. By logging referrers, you can keep track of links to pages within your Web site. The browser field is the name of the Web browser being used to make the request. Most browsers broadcast a unique name that can be entered into the log file. For example, the Netscape browser refers to itself as Mozilla. Since not all browsers support the same features, you can use this information to determine what features you want on your Web site. For example, it would not make sense to incorporate Java applets in your Web site if the majority of the Web browsers being used on your site do not have support for Java.

Another logging feature that some Web servers offer is the ability to generate multiple log files. This is convenient if you want to be more organized with the information that is logged and is especially important if you will be running multiple Web sites from the same server. You could separate the requests by the IP address or domain name that was receiving the request and keep the log files separate.

A few Web servers even enable you to track individual users as they move through your Web site. In normal log entries, you can only guess and extrapolate which pages were viewed by a single user and in which order. Some Web servers have a built-in function to do this tracking of users automatically, generally through the use of *persistent cookies.* A *cookie* is a persistent object for storing *state information* on the client side. State information is just information from previous requests that under normal circumstances is lost. For example, if you wanted to track a user's requests through your Web site, your Web server could assign a username to the user. This username would be the state information stored by the Web browser, usually in a file. When the Web browser requests another document from your Web site, it will send that username as part of the normal HTTP request header. The use of such a username will thus allow your Web server to track the user's requests.

WHAT IS A WEB SERVER?

When choosing your Web server, take a close look at what logging features it has. Most will offer the ability to log in the common log format. However, not all can capture such useful information as the referrer and browser data. You will also want to choose one that is quite flexible, allowing you to capture the information you need in the form that best suits your needs.

A Built-In Scripting Language

Almost all Web servers have support for the Common Gateway Interface. This interface allows you to write programs that can be called from your Web pages to perform certain tasks, such as sending you the contents of a feedback form or generating an access counter for display on your Web pages. CGI gives you a way, albeit not necessarily the most efficient one, to extend the functionality of your Web site. Since CGI scripts operate as a separate process and require a separate environment to function, they aren't always the most elegant solution to a problem. Also, CGI scripts do not give you unlimited ability to customize the functionality of your Web server. For those reasons, many Web servers now offer a built-in scripting language which enables you to add functionality at a much lower level than a CGI script.

Native Image Map Handling

In recent months, a new form of image map has arisen called *client-side image maps*. These image maps are handled on the client or browser side instead of by the Web server. Even with these types of image maps, your Web server will still service many requests for server-side image maps, since not all Web browsers support client-side image maps at this time. Therefore, choosing a Web server with built in image map handling will greatly improve the overall performance of your Web server, since a CGI script will not have to be called every time a server-side image map is used.

Browser Uploading of Files

A new feature which is gaining popularity is the ability to upload files from the Web browser to the Web server. This enables you or the users of your Web site to add pages to your Web site. Without this feature, it is not possible to upload documents to a Web site.

This feature is implemented using the PUT method in HTTP 1.1. Although this method was defined in the earlier versions of HTTP, it was poorly defined and essentially unimplemented. Now, Web servers which support HTTP 1.1 can accommodate the PUT method, thereby enabling users to add material to a Web site through their browsers.

WHAT IS A WEB SERVER?

There are many benefits for having a Web server with this feature. First, it allows an easy way for your Webmaster to add or replace files on your Web site. Also, if you are hosting other people's Web sites, it provides you with an easy way to allow your customers to make changes to their sites. Finally, it provides an avenue for your users to send you files, either for use on your Web site or simply as a way to get information to you. For example, if your Web site provides technical support for software products, you could enable your users to upload error logs from your products to your Web site and at the same time leave a message for the technical support staff.

Support for the Windows CGI Interface

If you will be running your Web server on a Windows machine, you may want to choose a Web server that has support for the Windows CGI Interface. The Windows CGI Interface is an extended CGI which enables you to take advantage of the features and software of the Windows environment. The normal Common Gateway Interface was developed and optimized for the UNIX environment; the Windows CGI extends the normal CGI to integrate better with commonly used Windows application development tools, such as Visual Basic and Delphi. Since these tools are already widely used to develop front ends for various business applications, the Windows CGI provides an easier way to integrate these business applications into your Web site through the development tools. For more information about the Windows CGI, see the Windows CGI protocol definition at http://www.city.net/win-httpd/httpddoc/wincgi.htm.

Native DBMS Support

Like native image map handling, native database management software (DBMS) support can greatly improve your Web server's performance if you will be interfacing it with a database. Normally, to interface with a database, you must use a Common Gateway Interface script between your Web server and the database. This adds the additional overhead of running another program and having an extra step in getting data back and forth between the Web server and the database. Also, writing the CGI script to do the interfacing can be quite complicated and time-consuming.

Because of the many advantages you gain by having Web servers and databases work together, many Web servers are now including native DBMS support. The DBMS is a program that manages the database, controlling input to and output from the database. Native support in the Web server removes the need for a CGI script to interface with the DBMS. Typically, Web servers that have this feature will open a link to the database upon startup and maintain the connection as long as the server is running. By keeping this connection up and running, database queries are

WHAT IS A WEB SERVER?

much faster than through a CGI script. If you need to have a lot of interaction between a database and your Web site, you should look for a Web server that has native DBMS support for your database.

Source Code Access

Many of the free Web servers and a few of the commercial ones provide source code for the server software. The advantage of having the source code is that you can make changes directly to the server software. Typically, to extend the features of your Web server, you must write either a CGI script, or a native scripting language extension to the server. However, some changes may be easier, more efficient, and faster to accomplish by simply making some changes to the source code. Having the source code also provides you with greater flexibility in customizing changes since you have complete control over the resulting software.

Being able to obtain the source code for the Web server is not something everyone will need. Also, changing the source code for the Web server opens up the possibility for introducing bugs into the software. Perhaps the most important reason for wanting the source code is to have the ability to compile it yourself. This would be more important to Unix users than users of the other platforms. Since there are so many versions of Unix, it is possible that you are running a version that does not provide you with many options for a Web server. By having access to the source code, you can make any changes necessary for your specific system. However, doing so will require a great deal of programming expertise.

Ability to Act as a Proxy Server

Since the Internet brings with it the possibilities of computer hacking and the compromising of networks, many companies and individuals choose to place their local networks behind a *firewall* before connecting to the Internet. A firewall is usually a single computer which is running specialized software to refuse all requests coming in from the outside network. In this way, the local network behind the firewall is protected from unauthorized access. However, this also restricts the availability to the Internet of any information from behind the firewall because all incoming requests are blocked.

When a Web server is set up by a company or individual that has a firewall, the Web server is either placed on the outside of the firewall, or a *proxy server* is used. A proxy server is just like a regular Web server, except that it resides on the outside of a firewall and does not handle requests directly. Instead, the proxy server receives a request and passes it on to the real Web server behind the firewall. This is done so that data can be safely stored behind the firewall. Once the real Web server finishes

WHAT IS A WEB SERVER?

processing the request, the results are sent back through the proxy to the Web browser which sent the request.

If you will be running your Web server from behind a firewall, you will need to run a proxy server on your firewall machine. Thus, you need to find a Web server which can run as a proxy server as well as a regular Web server.

Setup and Configuration

When the Web first came into being, setting up and configuring a Web server involved editing a few configuration files. Now, most Web servers allow configuration from a graphical user interface, making it much easier to get your Web site up and running as soon as possible. However, after the Web server is up and running, you may need to make changes to the configuration from time to time. To make this easier, many Web servers also provide remote maintenance of the Web server. This allows you to log in remotely and make changes to the system. However, not all Web servers allow remote maintenance. If you will need to make changes to your Web server's configuration from machines other than the Web server machine, then you should make this feature a top criterion in your selection.

Security

As you probably know, most information passed over the Internet is not secure. This means that anyone with enough programming expertise can potentially gain access to your information. Although this is not as easy as you may have been led to believe, it can happen.

In order to prevent this from happening with information being passed in HTTP communications, both the Web server and Web browser must use some manner of protocol that protects the information being passed between them. Since security concerns are seen as the major barrier to online commerce, many companies have dedicated a lot of resources to developing these secure protocols. So far, there are three main protocols currently in use: SSL, S-HTTP, and PCT. Each of these protocols is briefly described in the following sections.

If you will be needing a Web server with a secure protocol, the best choice is the one that is supported by the most browsers. Although each protocol provides the necessary layer of security to ensure secure transactions, recall that in order for HTTP communications to be secure, both the Web server and the Web browser must be using the same protocol. Therefore, it is in your best interest to choose a Web server which uses the protocol that the majority of Web browsers support. At this time, the majority of Web traffic is with browsers that support the SSL protocol.

WHAT IS A WEB SERVER?

Secure Sockets Layer (SSL)   The *Secure Sockets Layer* protocol allows Web servers and browsers to communicate without the possibilities of unauthorized viewing, listening, manipulation, or message forgery. With the SSL protocol, you are ensured that the connection is private. As soon as communication is established between a Web browser and the Web server, a secret key is defined. From that point on, all data is encrypted based on that secret key. By using this key, the identity of the remote client can be authenticated. Also, the communication will always be reliable because of built-in integrity checks of the data being sent.

Secure HTTP (S-HTTP)   Like SSL, *Secure HTTP* provides secure communications for Web servers and browsers. S-HTTP provides security mechanisms to ensure communications confidentiality, reliability of the data being sent, and authentication of the user sending the data. The S-HTTP protocol has a strong emphasis on flexibility when it comes to the Web browser and Web server choosing a method of key management, security policies, and cryptographic algorithms. In other words, the protocol is flexible in allowing you to specify what degree of security you want in the Web server, which will in turn specify degree of security to the Web browsers.

Private Communication Technology (PCT)   The *Private Communication Technology* is very similar to SSL and provides private communications between Web servers and Web browsers. Every PCT protocol connection begins with a handshake phase. It is during this phase that a session key is assigned for the connection and authentications are being performed. All transmissions after the handshake phase are encrypted using encryption keys which are derived from a single master key that was exchanged during some point in the handshake phase. The PCT protocol also verifies the integrity of all data transmitted between the Web browser and Web server.

User Authentication

Authenticating users is the process of identifying users and authorizing their access to the Web pages on your Web site. Many Web servers provide ways to restrict access to Web documents to authorized users. The most common methods of doing this are user name and password authentication and IP address or domain name restriction.

User Name and Password Authentication   You may find it necessary to place documents on your Web site that you only want certain people to have access to. You could simply place such a document somewhere within the document root of the Web site, without linking to it in any of your

WHAT IS A WEB SERVER?

other Web pages, and then tell only certain people about it. However, this will not ensure that only those individuals will be able to access it.

A better way to restrict access to such documents is by assigning a user name and password that must be entered to gain access to the documents. Web servers that have this feature will require a valid user name and password every time a restricted document is requested by an unauthenticated Web browser. An unauthenticated Web browser is a browser which has not yet sent the valid user name and password during the current session. For example, when a Web browser first requests a restricted document, the Web server will prompt the user for the user name and password. When these are correctly entered, the browser is authenticated, and the Web server will not require the user name and password for that restricted area or document to be entered again from that browser during that session. However, once the Web browser is shut down—the program is exited—the Web browser will no longer be authenticated. Authentication only lasts during the Web browser's current session.

IP Address and Domain Name Authentication   Access to Web documents can also be restricted by IP address or domain name. Web servers with these features will only handle requests (or deny requests) from specified IP addresses or domain names. Since specifying a single IP address is not highly efficient, wildcards can be used to specify a range of valid (or invalid) IP addresses. For example, if access to a directory called Webclass was given the restriction of 199.104.43.*, then every request coming from a machine with an IP address beginning with 199.104.43 will be handled by the Web server. The same restrictions can also be placed on domain names.

Price of Software

Many of the Web servers that are available are distributed for free. Although there is no cost for the software, the products are not by any means inferior to their commercial counterparts. Just because a Web server costs thousands of dollars does not mean that it is a better product than one that is being given away.

Often the differences in cost will be reflected in the types and number of features the Web server offers. Features such as the ability for secure sessions, built-in DBMS support, and the existence of a scripting language are usually reserved for the more expensive commercial servers. However, this is not always the case. Even some commercial Web servers are given away, with the only charge being for support.

10 WEB MANAGEMENT TOOLS

SINCE MOST WEB SITES undergo constant changes, there is a lot of management that must be done. Even a simple change, such as deleting a file from the Web site, can often impact several other documents. The entire concept of the Web is based on interconnectivity of documents, and simply removing the document will not necessarily remove all references to that document. As your Web site evolves, your Web pages can quickly become outdated, containing invalid links and old information.

WEB MANAGEMENT TOOLS

THERE ARE SEVERAL WEB management tools that offer features to simplify managing your Web site. These tools provide useful features such as graphical and hierarchical views of your Web site and management of all your hyperlinks. Some even have built-in authoring tools that can help you in the construction and maintenance of your Web pages.

Most Web management tools are separate software packages that run independently from your Web server. However, several Web server manufacturers are beginning to incorporate Web management tools in the Web server software. Providing tools for administering and managing the Web site is a natural extension of the Web server and is a key selling point for these Web servers.

Web management tools typically do not have to be run on the same machine that is running your Web server software. This provides you with maximum flexibility in choosing a Web management package, since you are not limited to the platform your Web server is running on.

What to Look for in Web Management Tools

There are several Web management tools currently on the market, with more becoming available all the time. However, not all tools offer the same features. As for Web server software, you should evaluate what you need to accomplish and then choose the tool which has features appropriate to your objective.

Most Web management tools offer the same basic features—ones that are fundamental in maintaining a Web site. For example, all Web management tools offer some method of verifying and updating hyperlinks in your Web pages, because maintaining valid hyperlinks can be one of the most time-consuming jobs for a large, dynamic Web site. However, even though all Web management tools have this capacity, they do not all manage links in the same way. The most basic tools may simply check all the hyperlinks on your Web pages and display a list of any that are invalid. The more sophisticated Web management tools will maintain the hyperlinks within your Web site for you by changing the links whenever you rename or move a Web page.

The following sections present some of the features you'll find in Web management tools. Since not all Web sites are the same, many of the features described will be unnecessary for your Web site. If you already have a running Web site, keep track of the maintenance tasks you already perform and look for a Web management tool that can help you with those tasks. If you have not already set up your site, think about how large a site you plan to have and how often you will be making changes to it. Then, look for features that will help you make those changes. Refer to the comparison chart in Appendix J to find a tool suited to your needs.

WEB MANAGEMENT TOOLS

List of All Files on Your Site

Since your Web site is composed of files, often of many different types and stored in several different places, a very basic function of most Web management tools is maintaining a listing of all the files making up your Web site. In order to effectively manage your Web site, the Web management tool must know what files make up the Web site. Typically, all your files for your Web site will reside under the document root. The document root of a Web site is the highest-level directory for the documents on your Web site, which will not necessarily be the highest-level directory on your Web server machine. However, users accessing your Web site with a Web browser will not be able to request any documents that reside above the document root directory.

Within the document root, there can be as many subdirectories as you wish to create. Of course, if you were to place all your files in the document root directory, you would not have any trouble keeping track of all your files for your Web site. However, unless your Web site is rather small (fewer than about twenty Web pages), it is usually a better idea to organize the files into subdirectories.

Any script files you have for your Web site will usually be stored outside of the document root, most commonly in a cgi-bin directory somewhere on your Web server machine. If you lease shared space on a Web server that is running other people's Web sites as well, very often your CGI scripts will be placed in the same directory as these other people's CGI scripts.

As you can see, it is very easy to have a Web site with files spread out in several subdirectories, and not all within the document root. Rather then keeping track of the names and locations of all your Web page files yourself, it is much easier to assign that task to your Web management tool. Then you can display all the files that compose your Web site in a highly organized, accurate manner. There will be no chance of overlooking a section of your Web site when you need to make changes.

Graphical and Hierarchical Representations of Your Site

Although your Web site is composed of individual files, it is the interconnections between these files that are the most important aspect of your Web pages. Unfortunately, these links are also the part of your site that is most likely to become outdated quickly. Since all the files on a Web site are interconnected with hyperlinks, changes to one page will often affect many other pages. For example, if you delete one page, you must also remember to delete links to that page remaining in your other pages. Deleting a page may also cause you to lose links to other documents that were only connected to your Web site through the document you deleted. With even a medium-sized Web site, it can be difficult to keep track of how the documents are interconnected.

WEB MANAGEMENT TOOLS

Many Web management tools provide very useful graphical and hierarchical views of the Web pages on your Web site to help you keep track of how your Web pages are interconnected. A hierarchical view of your Web site will show you the names of your Web pages organized in an outline view. For example, the home page of your Web site would be at the top level of the hierarchical view. Indented underneath the home page would be the names of all the Web pages your home page links to. Then, indented underneath each of these second-level pages would be the names of the Web pages linked to the second-level pages. This structure continues until all the Web pages have been represented.

A graphical view of the Web site is similar to a hierarchical view, except that it represents your site as a flow chart rather than an outline. For example, the home page would be represented by an icon. Then, usually to the right or beneath the icon representing the home page would be icons representing other Web pages. Links among the pages are represented with lines so you can easily see how your Web pages are interconnected.

Real-Time Monitoring

Real-time monitoring of traffic and users on your Web site enables you to see what is happening at any given moment on your Web site. For example, you can have access to the number of files sent, the IP addresses or domain names of the users requesting the files, the most recent files sent from your Web server, the most frequently requested files from your Web site, and a list of URLs from which users are accessing your Web site, commonly known as *referrals*. Traditionally, this type of information about requests sent to your Web server was written to a text file access log, which you could view at a later time to gather information about your Web site. In order to gain specific information, such as the most frequently requested files, from these log files, you had to run a log analyzer program on the log file which would generate these types of statistics. Every time you wanted to update the information from a log file, you had to rerun the analyzer to create a new report. With real-time monitoring, you have this information available to you immediately within the Web management tool, without having to generate static reports from your log files. Of course, to view this real-time information, you will need to be connected in some way to the machine running your Web server. This could be just an open HTTP communications channel, or it could mean running the Web management tool on the same machine as the Web server.

WEB MANAGEMENT TOOLS

Creation and Management of Hyperlinks

Hyperlinking is the connection of documents on your Web site with HTML links. These hyperlinks enable users browsing your site to move among your Web pages and other Web pages on the Internet. This ability to interlink your documents is fundamental for a Web site.

When you first put up your Web site, you will need to create hyperlinks between your documents and other Web pages. These other Web pages can be on your own Web site or on someone else's. Some Web management tools provide autolinking capabilities that can greatly reduce the effort required to construct your Web site. Autolinking is the automatic creation of the hyperlinks. To autolink your Web pages, the software will actually read in the content of Web pages, index the content by keywords, and then generate suggestions for possible hyperlinks based on the indexing.

After your Web site is running, your hyperlinks will need to be managed to ensure none of them are invalid. An invalid link is one that connects to a document that does not exist. This can happen for several reasons. One possibility is that the document has been moved or renamed. Perhaps you deleted a document that contained information you no longer wanted on your Web site, but you neglected to remove all references to that document as well. Somewhere, in one or possibly many of your other documents, there may be hyperlinks to this deleted file. To prevent invalid links, you need to edit all the other files that contain such hyperlinks and delete them. As you can imagine, it is easy to overlook a few hyperlinks in large Web sites. Your Web management software can aid you with this task by verifying all the hyperlinks on your site and notifying you of any invalid hyperlinks. Some management tools can even automatically update hyperlinks when you move or rename a file on your Web site.

Features for Multiple Web Authors

Large Web sites often require the work of more than one individual to keep Web pages up-to-date. Also, companies with a large amount of legacy data that they want placed on their Web site will need multiple developers to convert the information and place it in Web pages. Some Web management tools accommodate this need for multiple developers by including features which enable multiple users to work together efficiently on the same Web site.

One such feature offered by a few Web management tools is a facility for a to-do list. This enables the group leader to plan out the tasks needing to be accomplished and assign them to various Web developers. The developers can then check the list and work on their projects. When they are finished, they can update the to-do list to reflect the completed status.

WEB MANAGEMENT TOOLS

This greatly facilitates the management of a Web site by providing a tool for effectively distributing and managing the workload. Some Web management tools even provide wizard features which will generate tasks for the to-do list automatically.

Database Integration Management

As Web technology progresses, more and more people are choosing to interface their Web sites with a new or existing database. For example, if you have an existing database full of information about your company that is updated frequently, it makes better sense to generate your Web pages dynamically from this database each time they are accessed rather than create static versions that would have to be updated by hand whenever a change is made in the database. Another advantage of connecting your Web site to a database is that you can add to your database information supplied by users browsing your Web site.

In the early days of the World Wide Web, it was relatively difficult to make this connection between a Web server and a database. Typically, it involved creating a CGI script that would take information and requests from the Web server, translate them into commands the database could understand, and then return any results from the database in HTML or text format to be displayed in the user's Web browser. With the many different databases in use, these scripts had to be highly specific to integrate directly with a specific database, and the amount of scripting could be relatively high.

Now, Web servers and database software have progressed to make this interaction easier. Many database software manufacturers have created existing gateways which link their databases to the Web servers without needing custom scripting. However, setting up the interaction between the Web server and database software can still be relatively complex.

Naturally, many Web management tools are building in features to manage this interaction. Since not all Web servers have native support for a database, the level of control your Web management tool has will depend on your choice of Web server and database software. Some Web management tools provide methods for developing complete interaction with the database within the Web environment by automatically generating Structured Query Language (SQL) statements and providing wizards and templates to easily set up dynamic Web documents with data being supplied from the database. If serving information directly from your database is of great importance to you, take your existing database into consideration when shopping for your Web server and Web management tool so that a seamless integration can be obtained.

WEB MANAGEMENT TOOLS

Firewall Support

Firewall support can be a very important feature for your Web management tool if you operate from behind a firewall and your Web server runs on the other side of the firewall. Many companies that have internal networks choose to create a firewall between their network and the Internet before connecting the entire local network to the Internet. The firewall provides protection for the local area network from unauthorized access. A firewall is usually a computer that connects the local area network to the Internet and runs special software that refuses attempts for connections which come from outside the firewall, across the Internet. However, documents and requests can be sent out from the local area network through the firewall to the Internet.

Often when a company running a firewall wants to set up a Web server, it does so by placing the Web server machine on the outside of the firewall. This way, the Web server can easily handle requests from the Internet. However, this can make it difficult to access the machine from behind the firewall.

Typically, when communication needs to be established between computers on opposite sides of a firewall, say while communicating with your Web server through a Web management tool, a channel has to be opened up in the firewall to allow the information to flow through. By opening a channel in your firewall, though, you are compromising some of the security provided by the firewall. This is addressed by a few Web management tools that provide support for firewalls within the tools themselves, thereby enabling you to manage your Web site without compromising security. Most Web management tools do not yet provide any kind of firewall support, and those that do are usually limited to a single firewall software package.

Integrated Authoring Tools

The line between managing a Web site and placing new information on that Web site is somewhat blurry and is becoming more so as most of the Web management tools now have integrated authoring tools that help you create and add to your Web site. There are many authoring tools available for creating content for your Web site. In fact, it is getting easier to create a site without knowing anything about coding HTML. However, these basic authoring tools lack the Web site management features that can keep your Web pages from having invalid or out-of-date information. By having authoring tools incorporated into your Web management tool, you can rely on a single package to do all of your content creation and site management.

WEB MANAGEMENT TOOLS

HTML Editing   Hypertext Markup Language, or HTML, forms the basis for all information that is placed on the Web. HTML is a subset of the Standard Generalized Markup Language (SGML), which is a language that specifies document types and how to display the various types. HTML consists of various tags that describe to the Web browser how to display the information contained within the document. Every hypertext document on the World Wide Web is published in either HTML or SGML.

Although HTML coding is not difficult, it can be time-consuming, especially if you are trying to convert a large amount of existing data into HTML format. There are several HTML editors which make the task of creating HTML files much easier (see Chapter 15 and Appendix O for more information on HTML editors). Many of these require no knowledge of HTML whatsoever. Since many HTML editors are available for purchase separately, it is not imperative that your Web management tool have one built in. However, if you want a management tool that does have HTML editing capabilities built in, there are a few features you should look for.

First, you want to make sure the HTML editor is current with the latest standards. This is vital if you do not know HTML at all and want the editor to do all the work for you. If the editor does not have the latest tags, you will have to learn the HTML codes for them yourself and insert them manually, if you want to use them. You may want to specifically look for an integrated HTML editor which supports the latest Internet Explorer or Netscape Navigator advanced tags, since these tags tend to be highly useful and provide you with many more capabilities in HTML page layout and design.

Also, many HTML editors being incorporated into Web management tools have a feature known as WYSIWYG, which stands for "what you see is what you get." You are probably already familiar with this type of editing, since it is the way most common word processors operate. When you tell the editor to display text in bold italics, you will see it that way in the editor, and the HTML file will be displayed that way within a Web browser. This is the most intuitive way to create HTML pages, and if you are familiar with word processing programs, it will be the most comfortable way. Typically, with WYSIWYG HTML editors, you will not see the HTML tags unless you specifically request to display them.

Finally, when looking for a Web management tool with a built-in HTML editor, you may want one that offers direct editing of the HTML documents. To do direct editing, you will need to know HTML tags and how to insert them. While this may sound more difficult, it is often the best way to do some final tweaking to your Web pages—even the best HTML editors fall short when trying to obtain a very specific layout for your Web pages. Also, since new tags are constantly becoming available,

WEB MANAGEMENT TOOLS

your HTML editor will not support all possible tags. The only way you can make use of the very latest tags is to insert them manually in your HTML document. Of course, to do so, all you really need is a simple text editor program such as Notepad for Windows, Simpletext for the Macintosh, or vi for Unix. However, you may want to do your direct editing all within the environment provided by your Web management tool. If this is the case, then you will definitely want direct editing capabilities.

Image Conversion   As with HTML editors, image conversion is not a task that is restricted to Web management tools. Chances are that you already have a graphics software package that will save images in several different formats. If you don't have one, obtaining one is as easy as downloading a shareware program from your nearest shareware archive. However, you may want the added convenience of image conversion and management within your Web management package. If so, you will need a Web management tool that provides these capabilities.

On the simplest level, a Web management tool may just provide simple image conversion capabilities. The tool may read in several different graphics file formats and convert the existing format into either GIF or JPEG format, which are two graphics file formats supported by most browsers for in-line images. If you have a lot of files to convert, this conversion feature can be very useful.

On a more advanced level, some Web management tools provide complete image manipulation, from image creation to saving the file as either a GIF or JPEG file. Since image editing is not the primary focus of a Web management tool, these editors typically will not have many of the advanced features found in stand-alone graphics software packages like Adobe Photoshop and are best suited to making only simple changes.

Image Map Creation   One of the most practical uses of graphics on a Web site is in *image maps*. An image map is a normal graphic that also contains multiple hyperlinks. Various sections of the graphic can be designated as links to other documents and other locations within the same and other documents. The portion of the graphic that represents a link is designated by coordinates, which are usually stored in a *map file*.

To create a map file, you typically use a software tool that does most of the work for you. These tools will allow you to select a region of the image and specify the location of the document you want it to link to. As with all the authoring tools, if your Web management tool does not include an image map component, you can easily download a shareware one from the Internet. However, if your Web management tool does contain an image map creation tool, then you can use it to create image maps for your Web site.

WEB MANAGEMENT TOOLS

Automated Wizards and Standard Templates Even with HTML authoring tools, it can still be very time consuming to create Web pages for anything larger than a very small Web site. Templates and automated wizards can help you through the process. Standard templates supply a basic design for a Web page to which you can add your own information, eliminating the need for you to create the entire page design yourself. Like a WYSIWYG HTML editor, you will usually not need to know any HTML to use a template—you simply provide your specific information where needed. For example, many Web sites have a feedback form which enables users of the Web site to send questions and comments to the owner of the Web site. Since this is a common feature, and most feedback forms look more or less the same, a standard template of a feedback form can be used. Then, to customize your feedback form, you simply enter your or your company's name and information into the form template instead of having to create the entire form yourself.

Often automated wizards are used in conjunction with standard templates to automate the process of inserting your specific information into the template. An automated wizard is an interface, usually done with dialog boxes, which prompts you for information to be entered. The information you enter in the dialog boxes is then entered into the template automatically for you. You do not need to directly edit the template unless you want to do something more than the automated wizard will allow. For example, with the aforementioned feedback form, you would be prompted for your or your company's name in a dialog box. Once you entered that information into the dialog box, the wizard would insert the information into your feedback form HTML file.

Automated wizards and standard templates can be a very quick and easy way to create pages for your Web site. However, due to somewhat limited ability in generating truly unique-looking customized work, you may wish to either design your Web pages without them, or have a Web designer create your Web site for you. If you are planning on designing a Web site with a truly unique look and feel, these features should not be an influencing factor in choosing your Web management tool.

11 E-MAIL SERVERS

ELECTRONIC MAIL, more commonly known as e-mail, is usually made up of textual messages that are sent across computer networks from one e-mail address to another. E-mail has been around for several decades and currently accounts for the majority of bandwidth traffic on the Internet. E-mail operates in a similar manner to other Internet software, in that there are both e-mail clients and e-mail servers. The *e-mail client* is the software utilized by the e-mail users to read and compose messages (see Chapter 7 for more information on e-mail clients). The *e-mail server* is the software that is responsible for sending, receiving, and storing e-mail messages until they are received and deleted by the e-mail user.

E-MAIL SERVERS

TO SET UP YOUR OWN E-MAIL SERVICES, you will need to install and configure an e-mail server for your domain. Your e-mail server will receive incoming messages addressed to users within your domain and route outgoing messages from users within your domain. Unlike e-mail clients, your e-mail server needs to reside on a host machine that maintains a constant connection to the Internet. Otherwise, incoming e-mail will get returned to the sender because your e-mail server was not available.

What to Look for in an E-mail Server

E-mail server software can vary widely from manufacturer to manufacturer. As with all the server software you will be using, your first concern is finding an e-mail server that runs on the server machine and operating system you have. After narrowing down your choices by hardware platform, you will want to look at several other features. For a chart comparing the features of several e-mail servers, see Appendix K.

The first feature you will want in an e-mail server is ease of configuration and maintenance. Even if you are not a novice computer user, you can save a lot of time and frustration if the software is easy to configure. Many of the early e-mail servers were configured through text-based configuration files. Now, with many of the e-mail servers operating from a GUI environment, the configuration is much easier. Also, the ease of maintaining the e-mail server once it is operating is important. Under most circumstances, you will need to make frequent changes to the e-mail servers configuration, such as adding or deleting users. In the "Easy Configuration and Management" section below, the most common easy ways to configure and maintain your e-mail server are discussed. As you read through the section, take note of the various ways of working with your e-mail server and look for an e-mail server which offers the methods you prefer.

Many e-mail servers offer automated response options. These can be very useful and time-saving features for both individual users as well as your organization as a whole. If you plan on supporting your company's products or services via e-mail, or if you will be servicing many users with e-mail accounts, you may want to consider using an e-mail server which offers automated responses. In the "Auto Reply Capabilities" section below, the most common automatic response options are discussed. Take note of which ones would work well in your organization and look for an e-mail server that offers them.

There are several other features of e-mail servers that may be useful to you, depending on your needs. For example, if you already have a medium to large size e-mail system on a local area network, you may want to look for an Internet e-mail server that has built-in compatibility with your legacy e-mail system. You may also want an e-mail server that was engineered modularly, to allow easier upgrades and add-ons. Other basic features that most e-mail servers offer, and that most of your users

E-MAIL SERVERS

will find useful, are support for nicknames, mailing lists, and the forwarding of e-mail messages. You may also need your e-mail server to be able to handle multiple domains. Each of these features are discussed in the sections below.

As with all Internet servers, your e-mail server's security is of major importance. You will need to protect both the privacy of your user's messages as well as prevent unauthorized access to both your e-mail server and your host computer. Since e-mail security issues are not new, you have many options for security. Even if you will be running a small server with only a few users, it is still important to utilize as much security as you can. The "Security" section discusses the main security features most e-mail servers offer. Your best option is to choose an e-mail server that offers the most security possibilities.

Finally, you will also want to look for an e-mail server that supports most of the standard protocols used with e-mail. In order for communication to take place on any network, the software must be running the correct protocols. Every e-mail server on the Internet must use the Simple Mail Transfer Protocol (SMTP). However, many e-mail servers are also integrating several other protocols which enable many other features for your e-mail system. In the "Support for Standard Protocols" section, the various protocols are discussed. This section should give you an idea of the advantages you gain by having support for the different protocols, which should enable you to choose the ones you want your e-mail server to support.

Easy Configuration and Management

The last thing you want in an e-mail server is something that is difficult to configure and maintain. To make configuration and maintenance easier, many e-mail servers now allow configuration and management to be done through HTML forms or e-mail messages.

Some e-mail servers have built-in HTTP support that enables them to interface with HTML forms. This is done specifically so that forms can be created which will guide you through the configuration of your e-mail server. Many e-mail servers also have the capability to receive configuration settings from within an e-mail message. With these types of servers, making changes to your server is as easy as sending an e-mail to your e-mail server. All you need to know are the appropriate commands and parameters to send and the password which authorizes you to make those changes. Typically, the available commands can be obtained directly from the e-mail server by sending a help command within an e-mail message. The e-mail server will send back a message containing the usage for all the commands that are available.

E-MAIL SERVERS

User-Managed Accounts   One feature that many newer e-mail servers are offering is the ability for users to manage some aspects of their account. This takes some of the load off the system administrator and lets the e-mail user make certain changes when appropriate and necessary. For example, if an e-mail user is going on vacation and wants to have his account automatically reply to all messages that he is on vacation, he would be able to make these changes himself, usually by either sending a configuration e-mail message to the e-mail server or by using an HTML form. Either way, this eliminates the need for the system administrator to become involved.

Having the ability to let your e-mail users manage their own accounts is a valuable resource. You will save your system administrator a lot of extra work, as well as enabling your e-mail users to feel in charge of their account. They will also appreciate the freedom of being able to make changes whenever they want, without having to bother someone else to do it for them.

Auto Reply Capabilities

Most e-mail servers now have built-in automatic reply capabilities that allow you to set up an automatic reply to incoming messages. An automatic reply is a message that gets sent by the e-mail server whenever it receives any message for an e-mail account which has the automatic reply feature enabled. For example, many companies that receive a lot of e-mail messages every day have an automatic reply feature which will send a preset reply to all messages that are received. This preset reply is usually just a note letting the sender know that the message was received and to expect a reply within a few days.

Many e-mail servers offer various automatic reply options, such as Vacation, Reply, and Echo. The Vacation automatic reply is for use by e-mail users who are going to be on vacation and not checking their e-mail. When an e-mail account is placed on Vacation automatic reply, the server will automatically reply to every message it receives for that account with a message stating that the e-mail user is on vacation. This stock reply can usually be customized by the user to provide specific information about how long the user will be gone, or an alternate person to contact. A nice feature some e-mail servers offer with the Vacation automatic reply is the ability to send only one message in reply to an e-mail address, no matter how many messages are sent from that address.

When an e-mail server's automatic reply function is set to Reply, it will usually just send a preset message to every e-mail it receives. This can be a very useful feature, especially for companies that provide additional information about services or products via e-mail. With this feature, you can set up an e-mail address where customers can send queries for additional information. This e-mail address could then simply respond

E-MAIL SERVERS

automatically by sending out the preset additional information to every e-mail address it hears from. At the same time, you can accumulate e-mail addresses of individuals who are interested enough in your company's products or services to send for additional information. Typically, if you are using this approach, no person is actually reading the messages that are being sent, a fact you might want to mention in the preset message you send back to the user. However, you can also set up the system so that someone does receive and review all the messages after the e-mail server has already sent the initial, automatic response.

Another feature that many e-mail servers' automatic responders have is an Echo setting. This setting will simply return all messages that it receives with a preset message attached. This is different than the Reply setting, which will not typically return the contents of the sender's original message. The Echo setting is most useful for notifying senders that their message was *not* received for some reason. For example, when an e-mail account is removed from your system, you can set up the server to have an Echo reply notify everyone who sends a message to that e-mail address that the account has been deleted. You could even place a forwarding e-mail address in the preset message to let the sender know the new e-mail address for the individual.

Modular Design

With the fast pace of Internet server software development, you may want to consider an e-mail server that is engineered for easy upgrading when a future version offering new features becomes available. As with all software, e-mail servers are constantly changing over the years. When you choose to upgrade your existing software, it is simplest to just install the upgrade over your existing version, saving your current configuration. Many e-mail server software manufacturers are planning for these upgrades by creating modular software which can be easily upgraded without compromising the existing installation.

Compatibility with Legacy E-mail Systems

If you already have an existing e-mail system running on a LAN or WAN, you will probably want your new Internet e-mail server to be compatible with your legacy e-mail system. Such compatibility will enable your users to send Internet e-mail using the same e-mail client program they have always used, and they will be able to receive Internet e-mail into their existing legacy e-mail account. For this situation, your Internet e-mail server would be acting more as an Internet mail gateway than an actual Internet e-mail server. Thus, if you already have an e-mail system, you should evaluate whether you really need an Internet e-mail server or whether you just need an Internet mail gateway for your legacy e-mail system.

E-MAIL SERVERS

Ability to Handle Multiple Domains

If you currently service multiple domains, or if you plan to do so in the future, you will probably want an e-mail server that can handle the multiple domains. Just as with Web servers, it is much simpler to have a singe e-mail server handle all the e-mail services for all the domains you serve. This is especially useful if you are planning on leasing space on your server machines to other people or organizations, each with their own domain. You would be able to have a single e-mail server handle all the e-mail services for everyone who is leasing server space from you.

Support for Nicknames

A *nickname,* also commonly known as an *alias,* is an alternate name that can be used for addressing e-mail messages and is a feature provided by most e-mail servers. For example, most Web sites use the alias "Webmaster" as one of their e-mail addresses. Typically, there is not really an e-mail account with the address Webmaster. Rather, Webmaster is a nickname for the e-mail account of someone on the system who is in charge of the Web site—instead of having users send mail to JohnDoe@wacky-web.xyz.com, they can simply address mail to Webmaster@wacky-web.xyz.com, and it will be routed to John Doe's account. This is really convenient if John Doe happens to leave the company. If so, then you can change the Webmaster@wackyweb.xyz.com to route to Jane Doe's e-mail account, for example. Your customers will never have to use a different e-mail address or even be aware of the staff change.

Another nice part about nicknames is that they allow your users to select multiple e-mail addresses for themselves without requiring you to set up e-mail accounts for all the names. For example, suppose John Doe has an e-mail account JohnDoe@wackyweb.xyz.com. Now, people who know that John Doe works for wackyweb.xyz.com, but who don't have his e-mail address may try to send him e-mail at addresses like jdoe@wacky-web.xyz.com, johnd@wackyweb.xyz.com, or John_Doe@wacky-web.xyz.com. All of these are possiblities based on conventions typically used with e-mail addresses. By setting up all these other possibilities as aliases that route to JohnDoe@wackyweb.xyz.com, most e-mail addresses the customer tries will get to John Doe's e-mail account.

Support for Mailing Lists

A mailing list is sort of an automatic mass mailer that enables one e-mail message to be sent to many people by addressing the message to the name of the mailing list. The distribution list for the mailing list is a list of e-mail addresses of users who have subscribed to the mailing list. For example, if you had a mailing list called email-users and your domain was mail.com, then you would send a message to the list by addressing an e-mail message to email-users@mail.com.

E-MAIL SERVERS

Typically, users can add and remove themselves from the mailing list by sending e-mail messages to the mailing list software with commands in the body of the e-mail message. This enables the users to maintain their own status without bothering the system administrator who is maintaining the e-mail server.

Mailing lists are an easy way to establish a sort of community based on a common interest in a subject. Mailing list software can be purchased separately, but if you have plans to provide a mailing list, you could look for an e-mail server that provides this functionality built in.

Easy Forwarding of Messages

From time to time, users on your e-mail system may need to forward messages to another e-mail account. In the early days of the Internet, when most e-mail systems were on Unix systems, users could easily forward their e-mail messages to any e-mail address by placing that address in a .forward file in their home directory. Now, with many options for the hardware platform on which to run your e-mail server, users may not have a home directory or even a login account, for that matter. However, it is best to leave the responsibility for forwarding messages in the hands of the individual users, rather than assigning this task to the often overloaded system administrator. When choosing your e-mail server, check to see how forwarding of e-mail messages is set up, and try to choose a server that enables users to assign forwarding addresses themselves.

Security

As with all Internet services, you must take security into consideration when choosing your e-mail server. A poorly secured e-mail server can provide an avenue for an unauthorized user to gain access to your e-mail server machine. This unauthorized user could acquire passwords and e-mail messages from users on your system and could even install a program to send the intruder copies of all messages sent out from your system. This could compromise sensitive information contained in e-mail messages, or at the very least, destroy the confidence of your users in the security of your system.

There are many ways e-mail servers can provide security for both the e-mail server machine and the messages stored on or sent through it. On the most basic level, all e-mail servers provide some password protections, for both configuration and management and for users to obtain their waiting e-mail messages. Also important is how the e-mail server software is run on the host computer. These security issues are discussed in the next sections, along with some enhanced security features such as limiting access to the e-mail server and the encryption of e-mail messages.

E-MAIL SERVERS

Password Protections   At the most basic level of security is password protection. All e-mail servers require a valid password for all users when they retrieve their e-mail messages. This provides security for the messages themselves, ensuring that the intended recipient (or someone given the password by the intended recipient) will be the only person retrieving the e-mail messages.

Most e-mail servers also require some kind of password to configure and make changes to the e-mail server. Often this can simply be a valid system account with high enough access privileges to make changes to the e-mail server. However, for those e-mail servers which provide HTML forms or e-mail message–based configuration and management, this means a password that must be included in either the HTML form or in the body of the e-mail message. Also, for those e-mail servers that provide user management of the user's e-mail account, the e-mail server requires a password for verification. This will usually be the same password that the user provides when retrieving e-mail messages.

Any system that relies on passwords for security also needs some mechanism for monitoring possible instances of account tampering. Passwords can be intercepted or even guessed, thereby granting unauthorized users access to the e-mail server. Most e-mail servers provide features to monitor the e-mail server for suspected tampering. For example, if a user repeatedly tries to make changes to the e-mail server's configuration by submitting an HTML form with an invalid password, then the e-mail server can automatically send a message notifying the system administrator of the invalid attempts to change the configuration. This way the system administrator is made aware that someone is trying to tamper with the e-mail server and can take necessary steps to ensure the unauthorized user does not gain access.

Host Computer Security and Software Privileges   The way in which the software runs on the host computer can be just as important, if not more important, than layers of password protection for protecting your system. Since the e-mail server is a piece of software running on the host system, unauthorized access into the e-mail server could mean unauthorized access into the host system as well.

The most important security feature for an e-mail server is the ability to run as a non-privileged user. Under most circumstances, programs that are run on a host computer run with the same privileges as the user who starts the program. If the system administrator is the user starting the software program, as would be the case with an e-mail server, then the software would be running with the same privileges as the system administrator. However, if an unauthorized user were to gain access to the host system through some security flaw in the e-mail server, then that user would have the same privileges as the e-mail server, which would be the same as

E-MAIL SERVERS

the system administrator. With those privileges, the unauthorized user would be able to access and make changes to any part of the system within the system administrator's purview, which is usually the entire system.

Because of the security risk, system administrators specify what user privileges a software program will run under. That way the software will not necessarily have the same privileges the system administrator has. Although some e-mail programs require high-level system privileges in order to run at all, this is not the case with all e-mail servers. Thus, you should look for an e-mail server that does not need to run as a privileged user.

Some e-mail servers also have the ability to run independently of the host computer. By doing so, any unauthorized access through the e-mail server will not expose the host computer system. Although this is a nice feature if you can find an e-mail server that offers it, it is not as critical as making sure the e-mail server does not need to run as a privileged user.

Limiting Access   One effective method of security is limiting access to your e-mail server by accepting requests only from machines in certain domains. For example, if your domain at work is company.com and you limit access to your e-mail server to the company.com domain, then no one, whether they have correct passwords or not, will be able to access the e-mail server from a machine outside of the company.com domain. In most instances, this means you cannot access the e-mail server from any machine not at the office. While this method of security is highly effective, it can be inconvenient for individuals and employees who need or want access to their e-mail at any time from any machine. If this is the case with your users, you will not want to enable this feature on your e-mail server.

Access can be further limited in systems with user-maintained accounts by limiting the HTML forms or e-mail commands available to each user. For e-mail servers that have HTML form–based configuration and maintenance, there is always the risk of passwords being discovered and users tampering with the e-mail server. If the HTML forms available to each user provide only the set of functionalities that should be available for that user's privilege level, you have less risk of the user performing actions which he or she is not authorized to do.

By far one of the best ways to limit access for security purposes is to not allow e-mail account users to have login privileges to your server machine. Most early e-mail servers required a valid account on the server machine in order to have a valid e-mail account for a user. In these cases, the login password would be the same as the e-mail message retrieval password. Although steps can be taken to keep these users from being able to log in, this creates more work for the system administrator. Several of the newer e-mail servers are removing the requirement of having a login account in order to have an e-mail account. These servers maintain a separate database of user names for e-mail accounts only. This prevents the

E-MAIL SERVERS

users from having any access to the server machine itself and minimizes the amount of work the system administrator must perform. Since the average e-mail user for both personal and business accounts does not need login access to the server machine, this is one of the best solutions to maintaining tight security for both your e-mail server and your host machine.

Encryption   Most of the previously discussed security measures are designed to protect the system and the e-mail server from unauthorized access and tampering. All are concerned with the security on the host machine. However, once an e-mail message is sent by one of your users, it 16leaves your host machine and travels across several other machines en route to its final destination. There is always the possibility that somewhere along this path the contents of the e-mail message will be read by an unauthorized individual. For most messages, this represents an annoying loss of privacy but is not a matter of great concern. However, in cases where sensitive or confidential information is being sent, such snooping can be a major problem.

The most logical way to protect the privacy of an e-mail message sent across the Internet is to use some method of encryption on the contents of the message. Many e-mail servers are beginning to utilize encryption methods to encode the data while in transit. For encryption to work, though, both the e-mail server and the e-mail client must support the same types of encryption, and the e-mail client must be able to authenticate itself to the message for it to be decoded. Since most e-mail clients do not yet support encryption standards, the use of encryption on e-mail messages cannot be widely used at this time.

Support for Standard Protocols

As with all software on the Internet, e-mail servers must support certain protocols to properly function. On the most basic level, all e-mail servers must have support for the Simple Mail Transfer Protocol, or SMTP. However, there are a few other standard protocols that many e-mail servers are beginning to support and which will provide those e-mail servers with additional features you may find useful.

HTTP   The Hypertext Transfer Protocol (HTTP) is the protocol used on the World Wide Web. Some e-mail servers have begun to support HTTP to provide support for configuration and management by HTML forms. As mentioned above, many e-mail servers provide HTML forms that can be filled out within a Web browser which, when submitted, will make changes to the configuration of the e-mail server. Such servers use the HTTP protocol to receive the data from the HTML forms and make the appropriate changes to the server's configuration. If you will be choosing

E-MAIL SERVERS

an e-mail server that offers HTML form–based maintenance and configuration, it will have support for HTTP.

SMTP   SMTP (Simple Mail Transfer Protocol) is the standard protocol for transferring all e-mail messages across the Internet. It is the communications protocol used by e-mail servers to send and receive messages from other e-mail servers. It does not handle e-mail message exchange between the e-mail server and an e-mail client, however. This is handled by the POP3 (Post Office Protocol Version 3) protocol, which is discussed below. In order for an e-mail server to function on the Internet, it must support SMTP. Since there are some e-mail servers designed solely for use on LANs and WANs where SMTP is *not* required, you must make sure your choice of e-mail server supports SMTP or it will not function with Internet e-mail.

MIME   MIME stands for Multipurpose Internet Mail Extensions; it provides a mechanism for varying media types to be sent via an Internet e-mail message. Typically, e-mail messages contain simple text and are easily handled by both e-mail servers and e-mail clients. E-mail messages can also have *attachments,* which could be files of many other types, such as graphic image files or executable programs. Since e-mail messages are text messages by default, the e-mail server needs to know the document type of attachments in order to handle the file correctly. Otherwise, the e-mail server will treat the attachment as text, which usually results in the text version of the file being appended to your e-mail message. MIME types enable the e-mail server to correctly handle the attachments by identifying to the e-mail server what type of document is attached. E-mail servers with MIME support know how to handle the files defined by the MIME types.

MIME is also being used now to allow richer content types within e-mail messages. Rather than sending an image as an attachment, many e-mail clients are now including support for displaying rich media types within the body of the message. As with attachments, however, your e-mail server will still need to be able to handle the MIME types to correctly transfer the included media objects.

IMAP4   Internet Mail Access Protocol Version 4 (IMAP4) is a protocol to provide remote connectivity features for e-mail clients. It must be supported on both the e-mail client side as well as the e-mail server. Some of the features IMAP4 provides are the partial downloading of e-mail messages, mailbox synchronization, and off-line usage. When your users are connecting over a slow modem connection to check their e-mail messages, it is sometimes convenient for them to download parts of messages to see if they need to read the whole e-mail message. *Mailbox*

E-MAIL SERVERS

synchronization and *off-line usage* are actually closely related. Off-line usage refers to the ability to download the messages from the e-mail server to the e-mail client, deleting the messages from the e-mail server. Mailbox synchronization provides for what is known as *disconnected usage.* With disconnected usage, the user downloads a copy of the e-mail messages from the e-mail server, leaving a copy on the server. The user will then disconnect from the server to read and delete some or all of the messages from within the e-mail client. The mailbox synchronization occurs the next time the user connects to the e-mail server. At that time, the messages stored in the mailbox on the e-mail server are synchronized with the user's mailbox in the e-mail client—any messages that were deleted in the e-mail client while the user was disconnected are also deleted in the e-mail server.

POP3   POP3 or Post Office Protocol Version 3, is a protocol used for transferring e-mail messages between an e-mail server and an e-mail client. It is similar to but not as robust as IMAP4. The POP3 protocol does not provide all the remote connectivity features that IMAP4 does. Instead it allows for the retrieval of messages, with either deletion or saving of the messages on the e-mail server. POP3 is actually considered a subset of IMAP4. However, many more e-mail client programs support the POP3 protocol than the IMAP4 protocol. To plan for the future, choose an e-mail server that has support for both POP3 and IMAP4.

12 FTP SERVERS

FTP, OR FILE TRANSFER PROTOCOL, is the standard means of transferring files over the Internet. FTP has been around for nearly the entire lifetime of the Internet itself, and is very efficient in terms of bandwidth for doing file trans-fers. As with the other major Internet services, FTP is divided into both client and server programs. The *FTP client* software is the program used by FTP users to send and receive files from any FTP server on the Internet. The *FTP server* is the software that manages a FTP site. An FTP site is the location where files are stored for downloading by an FTP client. FTP sites are also capable of accepting file uploads.

FTP SERVERS

AN FTP SESSION IS INITIATED when an FTP client sends a connection message to an FTP server. If required, the FTP client will be prompted for a username and password to log in to the FTP server. Once the FTP connection is established between the FTP client and the FTP server, the client sends requests for files on the server. When a file is requested, the FTP server sends it to the client as long as the client has the correct permissions set to request the file. If the FTP server allows file uploads, the client can also send files to the server to be added to the server's file system.

To use FTP, you will need an FTP client and a connection to the Internet. This will allow you to send and receive files from FTP servers already up on the Internet. If you want to set up your own FTP site for users to send and receive files, you will need to install and configure an FTP server. The type of FTP server you get as well as the way you configure it is dependent on the type of FTP site you wish to set up. You might want an FTP site for just you and your coworkers at your company, not for all the users on the Internet. Or you may be interested in setting up an FTP site with files accessible to the entire Internet. This chapter focuses on the various features of FTP servers to help you select the features you need in order to achieve your FTP site goals.

What to Look for in an FTP Server

The purpose of your FTP site will largely determine the features you need in your FTP server. If you will be running a private site just for the employees of your company, the anonymous login features described below will probably not be that essential. However, you will still need high security to restrict people from outside your company from accessing the files on your FTP site. The following sections present descriptions of the most common FTP server features that will allow you to determine how the feature will benefit the FTP site you are planning.

Configurable Logging

Most FTP servers provide some way of logging sessions. This could be as simple as keeping a log of which users logged in at what times. Some FTP servers also can log all the commands issued by every user. Probably the most important logging feature you should look for when shopping for your FTP server is the ability to configure the logging that you want performed. Although logging every command issued will probably gather the data you are interested in viewing, it may also gather more data than you need or want—placing undue strain on your FTP server and wasting disk space for the log files. Also, you or your log analysis program will have to wade through lines of information that is of no interest to you. Look for an FTP server that not only has the ability to log the information you want to track, but also lets you choose what information is written to the log file.

FTP SERVERS

Security

Security should always be a concern, no matter what type of Internet service you will be providing with your FTP server. In general, FTP servers do not provide many means by which unauthorized people can access the host computer. However, there are still several security risks involved with running an FTP server. For example, perhaps you want to provide files and information to employees in your company via an FTP server. Naturally, you would not want sensitive data to be downloaded by unauthorized individuals. Typically, this would be handled by simply using password protections to prevent unauthorized access to your files. However, if you want to run an anonymous FTP site and make files available to everyone on the Internet, you need to take precautions to ensure that important system files are not accessible to anonymous FTP users. Access to these files could result in allowing unauthorized users to gain access to your FTP server machine through direct logins. The following sections cover basic security features that should be requirements for your FTP server software.

Passwords   Usernames and passwords are the most common means of providing basic security. Naturally, if the username and password are discovered, an unauthorized user can gain access to the system, but generally password protection offers a good level of security for the system.

Typically for an FTP server, each user will have his or her own username and password. However, you may need to set up a group account where all the users in the group share the same username and password. To allow the entire Internet community access to the files on your FTP server, you would set up an *anonymous account*. Anonymous FTP accounts allow any user to log in to the FTP server and download files that are in the FTP file system. This process is called *anonymous FTP* because the username supplied is "anonymous." With anonymous FTP, users do not have to enter a specific password. In some cases, no password is required at all. The standard is to request the user's e-mail address as the password. Some FTP servers have the ability to do some rudimentary checking on the validity of the e-mail address. This checking just verifies that what the user has entered conforms to the specifications for a valid e-mail address. If not, the FTP server will deny access to the user until a password is entered that does conform to the valid e-mail specifications.

This added security of requiring a valid e-mail address for anonymous users can be very useful, especially if you are logging all the commands and transactions performed by every user, because it gives you the ability to track which files are being accessed by whom. Also, if you have an area of your anonymous FTP server that allows file uploads, it allows you to know who loaded which files onto your system.

FTP SERVERS

IP Address and Domain Name Restrictions   IP address and domain name restrictions are an effective method of preventing access by unwanted users. To place one of these types of restrictions on your FTP server, you would specify a range of IP addresses or domain names that you either do or do not want to have access to the files on your FTP server. Typically, you specify a range that *will* have access to the server, thus denying access to all other users on the Internet. However, the ability to specify a range of IP addresses or domain names that you do *not* want to have access to your server can be very useful if you need to ban certain users from your site. This would be the case if you encountered abuse of your FTP site by particular users, who either uploaded dangerous or frivolous files, or made repeated attempts to breach security.

This type of restriction is much more secure than a username and password scheme, since it is very difficult to fake an IP address. Also, unauthorized users will not usually know the correct IP address range in order to gain access to the FTP server files. The major drawback to this method is that it is extremely limiting. Even authorized users will not be able to gain access to the FTP server if they are using a machine that is outside the acceptable range, such as in the case of using a computer at a friend's house. However, it is better to have FTP server software that gives you the option of placing these types of restrictions, especially if you are planning on serving sensitive or confidential material from your FTP server.

Individually Configured Read/Write/Modify Privileges   If you will be running an FTP site that will be providing many different services for different levels of users, you will want the flexibility of being able to assign read, write, and modify privileges for each individual user, group of users, and class of users. *User groups* and *classes* are described later in this chapter in the section "Groups and Classes of Users."

The read privilege allows a user to see what files are in each directory. In some directories, such as an inbox where users place files for you only and not for access by any other users of your site, you will want to remove read privileges so users cannot see the files in the directory. However, you may want to have areas for workgroups in which files can be placed and retrieved by any member of that group. If your FTP server has the capability for flexible configuration of privileges, you can give that workgroup read access to the files in the directory but leave all other users without read access. You can also have different *index files* for the different groups and classes. Such index files describe which files are available for the user when he or she logs in; users will only see the index file for which they have read privileges.

Write privileges allow users and groups and classes of users to upload files into a directory. Even if you will be allowing uploads to your FTP file system, you do not want users to be able to place the files anywhere in the

FTP SERVERS

directory structure. Instead, you will want a specific directory where users can upload files. You can also create different directories for uploads from the different groups and classes, to further organize your system. With the flexibility to assign different write privileges to different users, you could even distribute the administration of the FTP site by having various users manage the available files.

Modify privileges are distinct from the simple read and write privileges. Modify privileges let users delete and overwrite existing files on the FTP server. Typically, if you have an inbox or another area where any user can place files, you will want to remove any modify privileges for general users. This ensures that files will not be accidentally overwritten just because they have the same name. Also, as with the write privileges, you can assign different users to have modify rights to various directories and place them in charge of managing the files in those directories.

Directory Mapping and Virtual Path Names   Directory mapping and the use of virtual path names are important features for an FTP server that will be serving information to the entire Internet. Directory mapping makes the root directory of the FTP file system appear as the top level directory for the entire system. This is an important security feature. When the root directory gets mapped to the top of the FTP file system, the FTP server does not know of the existence of any directories above that top. This ensures that users are not able to use the special directories like .. to change to a directory that is above the top of the FTP file system. Such protection is important because if unauthorized users gain access to files outside or above your FTP file system, they may be able to access system files that could let them obtain even greater access to your server machine and the files that reside on it.

Virtual path names are another feature that provide some of the same security that directory mapping provides. A virtual path name means that the path specified to a file is relative from some other point in the directory structure. By using virtual path names, you can keep the actual directory structure of your system hidden. This adds one more layer of security by denying potential intruders information they could use to gain unauthorized system access.

Ability to Disable Account in Response to Bad Passwords   As mentioned in the section "Passwords," usernames and passwords can only provide security if the correct password is not known. Often, individuals will try to gain unauthorized access by guessing passwords. Given enough time and opportunities, most passwords can be stumbled upon simply by trying combinations of valid characters. A simple program could be constructed to repeatedly try possibilities until the password is discovered. Since the process is automated with a computer program, the detection can be very fast.

FTP SERVERS

Many services which provide username- and password-level security have some built-in mechanism for disabling the account if incorrect passwords have been entered a certain number of times, typically three times. By disabling the account, even if the correct password is eventually tried, access will not be provided. In fact, a disabled account would not even let the user trying to login know that the password is valid.

This feature is extremely valuable to deter discovery of passwords by trial and error. Some FTP servers let you choose the number of times an invalid password can be entered before the account is disabled. It is not a good idea to set this number too low, since it is relatively easy to mistype a password a few times in a row. The standard of three times provides users with the flexibility of a few errors and still guards the account against continued attempts. Also, as mentioned earlier, three times is the usual amount of invalid attempts allowed by most services. By sticking with the standard, most of your users will already be familiar with how many erroneous attempts they can make. That way, if they have already entered it incorrectly twice, they can sever the connection and try again rather than risk a third error and have the account disabled.

Multiple Simultaneous Users and Transfers

Unless you are planning on running a small FTP service to only a few users, you will need an FTP server that supports simultaneous users and transfers. Most FTP servers can handle many simultaneous FTP users. There are a few that charge on a per user capacity basis, though. If you will be choosing one of these servers, you should have a good idea of how many connections you will want to start with. As the popularity of your FTP site grows, you can purchase additional licenses to accommodate more simultaneous users.

Allowing your users to do multiple simultaneous file transfers is another feature you should consider. This ability lets your users do several downloads, uploads, or a combination of downloads and uploads, at the same time. Typically, users connecting to your FTP site via a slow connection, like a 28.8-kbps modem, would not want to do too many simultaneous transfers because of their limited amount of available bandwidth. However, it is better to give users the option of doing so rather than forcing them to perform only one transfer at a time.

Groups and Classes of Users

To set up a secure FTP site with minimal security risks, you must assign specific access privileges to all your users who will be accessing the site. Rather than having an account set up for every possible user, most FTP servers have the capability to create groups and classes of users. A group consists of several users whom you want to have the same access privileges. For example, if a group of people at your company are working

FTP SERVERS

together and you want to set up a directory for their use on your FTP server, you can create a group with the correct privileges for that directory and assign all the users in that workgroup to the group. By using groups, you can minimize your time spent configuring accounts by setting privileges for a few groups rather than for many individual users. Also, if you ever need to change the permissions for a group of users, you will save time by only having to change the settings once for the whole group.

Classes are categories that describe the level of the user and the access privileges assigned. Classes are similar to groups in that you can assign privileges for the entire class rather than each individual user. The most common classes of users are *real users* and *anonymous users*. A real user is a user who has an FTP account on the FTP server with a username and password. When logging in to the FTP server, a real user will have access to the majority of the machine, depending on his or her account privileges. Typically, a real user is someone you work with, although this does not have to be the case.

Anonymous users are users who do not have a username and password for the FTP server. Instead, these users use "anonymous" as their username and their e-mail address as their password. Since anonymous users can be anyone who has network access to your FTP server, users in this class should be severely restricted to a certain part of the file system.

When setting up groups and classes, most FTP servers let you specify options about the various groups and classes that can help to configure their access privileges. For example, when setting up a group of users, you could specify a domain range for valid users in that group. That way, any user logging in from that domain range would be automatically assigned the privileges of the group, without you having to explicitly place that user's username into the group. Also, particular attention should be paid to limiting the number of simultaneous connections from any single group or class of users, especially if you are running an anonymous FTP server. Since anyone on the Internet can log in to an anonymous FTP server, you can quickly stress both your server machine and available bandwidth by having too many simultaneous connections. Allowing too many simultaneous anonymous connections can also block real users from gaining access to the machine to do maintenance or work.

Most FTP servers allow you to set a maximum number of simultaneous connections for any single group or class of users, so you could set a maximum of 200 simultaneous connections for anonymous FTP users to ensure that not too many users connect at the same time. Since separate restrictions can be placed for each group or class, connections by users in other groups and classes will only count toward the limits in those other groups and classes.

FTP SERVERS

Resume Option Capabilities

The FTP specification includes a feature called the resume option. Resume allows users to continue an aborted file transfer from the point at which it was halted. This keeps the users from having to start the download all over again. It will also help to save your bandwidth since you will not have to resend bytes that the user has already received. Although resume is part of the FTP specification, not all FTP servers implement it. This feature may be especially important to you if you will be offering large files for downloading from your FTP site. Since most users will typically be accessing your site over a modem connection, the transfer for a large file can be quite lengthy, and if the transfer gets temporarily aborted, it is convenient for the user to have the option of continuing it rather than starting over.

Configurable Messages

When signing on to an FTP server, the available files and directories are displayed to the user. Typically, an index file is included in the root directory to inform the user of the files that are available on the FTP server. However, the user has to download and read the file to find out what it contains. A much better way to keep users logging in to your FTP server informed is to have the FTP client software display information for them immediately, without need for the user to select, download, and open a file. The FTP specification allows for such messages to be included for various events, such as logging in, logging off, and changing directories.

When users log in to your FTP server, you should provide them with some information about the server, such as your name or your company's name, the files that are available on the server, and any other important information about finding files. This is also a good place to include announcements about upcoming server changes or planned outages. This information will automatically get sent to users every time they log in to your server and is usually displayed in a separate window of the FTP client software.

Although not as important as a login message, many FTP servers allow a short message to be sent to the user upon the user's request to log off. Like the login message, these messages can also contain announcements to remind the user of planned outages or major changes that will be affecting the service.

A change directory message is another useful message to send to the user. This message can inform the user of the files that are available in the new directory and what subdirectories to go to for other files.

FTP SERVERS

Timeout Feature

Most FTP servers have a feature which will time out a connection if it remains idle for a specified amount of time. This is an essential feature if you will be assigning maximum numbers of simultaneous connections. If your FTP server does not clear idle and hung processes, they contribute to the total number of active connections, thereby decreasing the number of actual transactions being performed. FTP sessions can become idle or hung for a number of reasons. If the FTP client does not properly close the connection when shutting down, or if the computer running the FTP client crashes, the FTP server may not close the connection. This idle or hung process lingers as an active process even though it is not performing any actions. If the FTP server does not clear these processes itself, the system administrator will need to check for these idle connections on a regular basis, manually killing the processes. For a busy FTP site, this can mean several minutes of administration a day just in killing idle processes.

Multihoming

Multihoming is the ability for a single FTP server to handle requests for multiple IP addresses and domain names. It is similar to the multihoming of several World Wide Web sites on the same Web server. When a user logs in to an IP address that is served by your FTP server, he or she will be given access to a specific file system that you set up. Typically, this file system will be different than the file system for the other FTP sites that are served by your FTP server. For the user, it will be entirely transparent that more than one FTP file system exists on that FTP server. For example, suppose you want to set up an anonymous FTP site that handles both Windows and Macintosh software with the domain names of ftp.windows.com for the Windows software site and ftp.macintosh.com for the Macintosh software site. The same FTP server can handle both of these sites and have different directory contents depending on which domain name the user specifies. If a user logs in to ftp.windows.com, he or she would see three subdirectories: win31, win95, and winNT. A user logging in to ftp.macintosh.com, however, would see the subdirectories sys7 and sys75. The directories for both the Windows site and the Macintosh site would exist somewhere within the file system defined for the FTP server.

Although multihoming is a great feature if you will be running more than one FTP site, you should consider whether the one FTP server can handle the load of all the FTP sites you will be running. Initially, you may not have a lot of traffic to your site. However, as it grows, your FTP server may be overstressed depending on the number of simultaneous transfers it has to process.

FTP SERVERS

File Checks and Restrictions for Uploads

One of the major reasons for having an FTP site is to allow users to up-load files to your system. This can be a convenient way to get necessary files from clients and coworkers who are not in the same office. Also, if you will be hosting an anonymous FTP site, uploads allow users to place files on your FTP site so they are available to everyone else with access to your site. Naturally, allowing files to be stored on your FTP site can generate some legal concerns, such as copyright violations for pirated software. Whether or not the operator of an FTP site is responsible for the content made available from the site is a matter that has not been totally resolved in the legal system yet, and may not be for some years.

Normally, most FTP servers do not offer any features to fine-tune restrictions on file uploads—the only restriction these servers offer is an across-the-board ban on file uploads. However, some FTP servers are now incorporating some features with increased flexibility in deciding what files get uploaded. These features are commonly referred to as a *duplicate checker* and a *not-wanted list*.

A duplicate checker in an FTP server will refuse to accept any file with a file name that already exists somewhere in the FTP file system. This is extremely useful for keeping duplicate files from being placed on the FTP server, which is a waste of disk space. This feature automates the administrative task of purging any duplicate files.

Not-wanted lists are lists of file names that your FTP server will not accept for uploading. If you know of some common files that you do not want added to your system, you can just add the names of the files to the not-wanted list and not have to worry about searching manually for them. This is especially useful if you will be supporting anonymous uploading of files and wish to put some general restrictions on what files get uploaded. Of course, the person uploading the file can always change the name and try again, but this offers a basic level of deterrence.

13 NEWS SERVERS

TO UNDERSTAND NEWS SERVERS, you must first understand what news is. On the Internet, *news* is a generic term that refers to Usenet News. Usenet News consists of news articles that are made available for reading by anyone with access to the Usenet News server. Usenet News is not news as you may be used to, such as what is provided on the news programs on your television. Instead, Usenet News is more like a bulletin board, where messages can be posted, read, and replied to.

NEWS SERVERS

USENET HAS BEEN AROUND for a long time. It was first created in 1979 through the work of graduate students at both Duke University and the University of North Carolina. This early version of Usenet was written in Unix shell scripts and utilized the UUCP (Unix to Unix Copy Protocol). Soon after its initial release, the software was rewritten in C and began to propagate to other universities.

As more and more universities began running Usenet News, the volume of news traffic began to increase dramatically. To accommodate the increased news traffic, the Usenet software was constantly updated and enhanced. New features like the moderation of groups were added to help prevent unnecessary news messages from bogging down the already overloaded news servers.

In 1986, a new Usenet News software package was introduced that made use of the Network News Transfer Protocol (NNTP). NNTP enables news hosts to pass news articles using TCP/IP connections rather than the UUCP connections required previously. It also enables the news software to be divided into clients and servers, thereby enabling clients to read and post news articles from machines that are not running the entire Usenet News software package. The news clients can send and receive messages from a news server that is running the Usenet software. Naturally, by removing the requirement that all news articles be stored on a local machine, and by enabling non-Unix systems to read and post news articles, the NNTP version of the program dramatically increased Usenet News traffic.

News servers are software packages that include the Usenet News system. The entire Usenet News system operates in a distributed way. New news articles get posted to a single news server, which then propagates that article to other news servers, which in turn propagate to more news servers. This continues until the message has reached all the news servers that carry that *newsgroup*. A newsgroup is a discussion group focused on a single topic. The news articles are categorized into these discussion groups to make it easier for users to read only the messages they are interested in. Not all newsgroups are carried by all news servers.

For users to read news articles, they must run a news client program, also known as a *news reader,* on their local machine and connect to a news server. Only articles in the discussion groups carried by the news server are available. When a user enters a discussion group, the news reader displays summaries of all the articles in that group. When the user wants to read one of the news articles, the news reader requests it from the news server and displays it.

NEWS SERVERS

What to Look for in a News Server

News servers are distributed, but for the most part they all handle the same basic information. Thus, the first thing you need to decide is whether you need your own news server. If you just want to set up your own newsgroups that will be distributed across the Internet, you do not have to set up your own news server—you can simply establish the newsgroups on your Internet service provider's news server and have them propagated. If, however, you will be acting as an Internet service provider, then you will probably want to set up your own news server. You may also want to set one up if you work for a large organization that wants to access newsgroups more quickly than is possible through your connection to your Internet service provider's news server, which can often be very busy. Finally, you will want to set up your own news server if you are planning on running private newsgroups which will not be propagated to other news servers across the Internet.

Once you have decided what type (public or private) of newsgroups you need to offer, you need to find a news server that can accommodate your needs. A private newsgroup is one that you do not want to be accessible to everyone on the Internet. A public newsgroup, on the other hand, is distributed to all other news servers that carry it and will be accessible to anyone who wants to read it. If you want to set up a news server that carries only public newgroups, any news servers will provide this basic functionality. If you are looking to establish some private newsgroups, you will want to consider the various features that are available to ensure that your private newsgroups are not subject to unauthorized access. These features are discussed in the section "Private and Public Newsgroup Settings" below.

Security might also be an issue for you, depending on how you will be operating your news server. Many of the latest news servers offer the ability to configure the server remotely through a Web browser and HTML forms. Without proper security precautions, your configuration information, including user names and passwords, could be intercepted. Also, if you have plans to run private newsgroups that will contain sensitive information, you should look for a news server that provides some sort of encryption when passing news articles between the news server and clients. Security issues are discussed in more detail in the "Security" section of this chapter.

On a very basic level, you will want your news server to be able to both accept and send newsfeeds. Since this is really the foundation of the Usenet News system, all news servers should offer this feature. However, some of the newer news servers also include many options on how these newsfeeds operate. These options are described in the section "Features for Incoming and Outgoing Newsfeeds" below.

NEWS SERVERS

Most news articles contain only a text message with text-based header information. There has been a growing trend, though, to allow more data types to be included in news postings. Being able to accommodate such data types could be very important to the clients for whom you will be providing news access. The "Rich Content Postings" section details what additional data types are being enabled by some news servers.

Thousands of news articles are posted to Usenet newsgroups every day. Clearly, these messages cannot remain posted indefinitely. It would be a tedious chore to remove messages manually, due to the sheer number of messages that are posted each day. Rather than leaving this job to the system administrator, the ability to expunge old articles has been built into the Usenet system. In addition, as with the accepting and sending of newsfeeds, several of the newer servers are exploring new and more efficient methods for getting rid of expired articles. These methods are discussed in the section "Expiration and Deletion of News Articles" later in this chapter.

As with other Internet servers, all news servers will require periodic administration. However, the methods used to accomplish this administration differ from news server to news server. The "News Server Administration" section below discusses some of the growing trends that make administration easier.

In the early days of Usenet, news servers were only for Unix machines. Today, with the growth of Windows NT as a server platform, many developers are making versions of their news servers for both platforms. Some of these servers also will work seamlessly together no matter which platform the server software is running on, allowing you to distribute the news server load among several machines. This gives you the most flexibility in deciding which machines you will use for serving news. The section "Transparent Multiplatform Support" describes this kind of server in more detail.

As mentioned above, news servers see a lot of news article traffic every day. In fact, for most news servers, the amount of disk space required to store all of the unexpired news messages numbers in the hundreds of megabytes. Many of the news server manufacturers are working on methods to help reduce the amount of required storage space and to make better use of storage techniques to optimize server performance. These methods are discussed in the "News Item Storage" section later in this chapter.

Private and Public Newsgroup Settings

In general, there are two main types of newsgroups: private and public. Typically, a private newsgroup is a discussion group set up on a server that is not propagated to other news servers. This would be the case when

NEWS SERVERS

an organization sets up its own news server to run newsgroups for use solely by members of the organization. A public newsgroup is usually a newsgroup that is distributed across the Internet and can easily be read by anyone with access to a news server that carries that newsgroup.

However, setting up a news server with private newsgroups will not ensure that news articles posted to the group are inaccessible to unauthorized individuals. Unless you place restrictions on who can access the news server, anyone with Internet access to the news server machine will be able to retrieve the newsgroups and news articles from that news server. Of course, this can always be averted by placing the news server behind a firewall. However, this then restricts access to only users behind the firewall. In some cases, you may have authorized individuals who are outside the firewall but still need access to the news server.

Most news servers already provide a mechanism for setting up individual newsgroups to either propagate or not to propagate to other news servers. This individual configuration of newsgroups allows both public and private newsgroups to coexist on the same news server. Many news servers are also incorporating features that enable the server operators to establish access control for individual discussion groups, to ensure that unauthorized individuals are not able to access the private newsgroups. Some of the methods that are being used for access control are the assignment of a user name and password for a newsgroup and restricting access to the newsgroup to only certain IP addresses or domain names. This allows the server operator to dictate which outsiders will have access to the newsgroups rather than eliminating outside access altogether.

Security

Security is not a crucial concern with a news server unless you will be administering it remotely or will be using private newsgroups containing confidential material. In both of these cases, information will be passed across the network to your news server, and it is important for the data to be secure while in transit. As with other Internet servers, the primary method of securing data in transit between two Internet locations is through encryption.

Encryption   Encryption is an effective deterrent to random and casual eavesdropping on data that is sent across the Internet. Depending on the encryption method used, it can even block calculated attacks by someone specifically targeting that data. However, in order for encryption to work, both the clients and the server must be able to use the same encryption methods, and must know the key to encrypt/decrypt the message. Otherwise, the data will not be decoded on the receiving end. This necessitates the use of standard encryption methods for both clients and server.

NEWS SERVERS

One encryption method, Secure Sockets Layer, has begun to see widespread acceptance on the Internet, especially on the World Wide Web. With some news servers, SSL is supported to facilitate secure communications for both restricted newsgroups and for administering the news server from across the network. As mentioned above, though, an SSL-compliant client software program must be used when communicating with an SSL news server.

Features for Incoming and Outgoing Newsfeeds

The propagation of messages over the Usenet system results from *newsfeeds*. A newsfeed is the news server from which your news server accepts its news articles. To run a Usenet news server with some or all of the popular newsgroups, you will need to have at least one newsfeed. Your news server may also act as a newsfeed for someone else's news server.

Naturally, when choosing your news server software, the ability to both accept and send newsfeeds is crucial. Even if you will be running only private newsgroups for your own organization, news article traffic can grow rather quickly. As your organization grows, you may find it necessary to run multiple news servers to handle all the news traffic generated. In this case, your news servers will need to be able to handle newsfeeds to keep the news servers synchronized.

Some news servers are enhancing their newsfeed capabilities to allow *smart feeding* of news articles. Traditionally, when a newsfeed is set up, all the news articles from the newsfeed server are sent to the receiving news server. With all the newsgroups available, and all the traffic on these newsgroups, this can amount to a huge amount of information being sent between the two servers. This can greatly degrade the performance of your news server during the newsfeed process because of the extra work being done by the news server and the extra bandwidth that is consumed by the newsfeed.

Smart newsfeeds help to alleviate this large burden on the news server by selectively sending and requesting news articles, rather than sending all the news articles available. News servers with smart newsfeed ability let you specify the newsgroups from which to accept news articles. A few news servers even have the ability to automatically request only news articles from newsgroups that are actually read from your news server. One company that distributes a news server with this capability estimates that this reduces the amount of network bandwidth used to 10 percent of the previous amount and reduces the disk space used on the news server machine to between 5 and 10 percent of the previous amount used. Reducing the number of unread articles stored on your news server will also speed up the expunging routines that are automatically run by your news server.

NEWS SERVERS

Rich Content Postings

Most news articles contain simple text messages from the person who posted the message. However, some news servers allow various MIME types to be used in posted articles. For example, news servers that support MIME types can receive articles that are written in HTML or contain GIF or JPEG images. The addition of these media types to news articles greatly enriches the content of the messages and makes Usenet News a much better medium for communicating.

Expiration and Deletion of News Articles

With over 10,000 Usenet newsgroups currently available, you can probably imagine the extremely large number of news articles that are posted each day. Since these articles are all stored on the hard drive of the machine running the news server, adequate disk space can be a great concern. Typically, newsgroups have criteria set by the news server administrator for when articles will expire. This way, the news server software can automatically delete articles when they meet the expiration criteria, making the administration of the news server much easier.

A few news servers have a feature referred to as *smart expiration* that makes the expiration and deletion of articles more intelligent. Rather than just having a number of days to keep all articles, these news servers can adjust the expiration criteria depending on several key factors. For example, when available disk space on the news server machine becomes low, smart expiration would change the criteria so that news articles expire sooner. Another feature offered by smart expiration is the ability to set expiration criteria based on the number of news articles that are in the newsgroup. Typically, you want to reduce the time for an article to expire in a newsgroup that contains a lot of news articles.

News Server Administration

Like all Internet servers, news servers require administration, both when they are initially set up and on an ongoing basis. A growing trend among Internet servers that is also being seen with news servers is the ability to administer the server through HTML forms. This allows you to have a highly graphical interface with all the administration parameters clearly presented to you, rather than the older methods which required you to make changes in a text-based configuration file. Web-based administration also lets you administer the news server from anywhere across the Internet, provided you have set the proper permissions for the domains that can administer the news server.

Another key feature that some news servers are incorporating is the ability to recover the news system from a remote system after the news system has crashed. This enables you to bring up the news server from

NEWS SERVERS

any machine even after a crash. If you will be running a news server that must be available every hour of every day with no interruptions, this is definitely a feature you will want to have.

Most early Usenet News servers only provided administration for the news server as a whole. Many modern news servers are placing more control into the administrator's hands by enabling the administrator to not only configure the whole news server, but also to set configurations for individual users, groups of users, and newsgroups.

Transparent Multiplatform Support

After you set up your news server, you may soon realize that a single news server isn't enough for your needs. Whether running private newsgroups solely for your organization or a public news server for several thousand users, the news traffic can quickly tax a single news server to the point that connections get refused or are extremely slow. As you go to set up another news server, you may decide that you want to run the new news server on a different platform of server machine than you used previously. Although you can easily set up your news servers on different platform server machines and establish a newsfeed between them for synchronization, using a server program that provides different versions based on a common architecture for your various platforms can achieve better integration between your servers.

Many software vendors who distribute news server software have different versions for most of the commonly used platforms—primarily Unix and Windows NT. Some of these versions provide a common architecture for both the platforms. This allows the news articles from any of the carried newsgroups to be easily moved from one news server machine to the other, providing the system administrator maximum flexibility in deciding which newsgroups will be served from which news server. Also, with this type of configuration, the system administrator is able to manage both news servers from a single administrative console on either machine, rather than having to administer both news servers independently.

If you are planning on only running a single news server that will handle all traffic, or if your organization runs on a homogeneous platform, this feature will not be a major concern for you. However, if you already have multiple platforms for your server machines and you want to maximize your options on which machines you use as news servers, you may want to consider a news server that is available for the platforms of machines you have and that can work seamlessly with another version of the same news server running on a different platform.

NEWS SERVERS

News Item Storage

How a news server stores news articles is an important feature of your news server. While many newsgroups do not experience many postings, there are just as many that see hundreds of messages a day. Every news server carrying a newsgroup must store all the unexpired articles for that newsgroup. This can amount to hundreds of thousands of news articles being stored on your news server machine. Conservatively, this could amount to 200 to 400MB of disk space being used just for news articles. Since this is a major concern for news server operators, some news server software vendors are coming up with more efficient news article storage mechanisms.

Traditionally, news servers store all news articles as individual files on the news server system. Each newsgroup has its own directory within which all its news articles are stored as files. For relatively small newsgroups, this is adequate. For example, if you will be running private newsgroups with few postings for your organization, this method of storage should be adequate for your needs. However, if you will be receiving newsfeeds for most of the available newsgroups, this kind of storage can greatly limit your system's performance. Whenever a file is written to or read from your news server machine, the news server software has to open and close that file. When there are hundreds of thousands of files, this can cause a noticeable strain on the news server. Additionally, systems are limited in the number of files that can be written to the hard drive. Even if there is still disk space available, if the maximum number of files has been reached, no more files can be created until some of the existing files are deleted. Since news articles are usually relatively small files, you can easily reach the maximum number of files before reaching your disk's full capacity.

An alternative to storing news articles as individual files is to store the news articles in database blocks, with a single block containing several news articles. The news server handles the administration of the database and writes new articles into the same block in the database until the block is full. It creates new database blocks as needed. By storing the news articles in this way, the amount of opens and closes for system files is greatly reduced, with the reduction being proportional to the number of news articles that are stored in a single block. For example, if a block can store 100 news articles, then the number of file opens and closes required under the database block system will be $\frac{1}{100}$ that of the individual file system. Additionally, the system will be less likely to reach the maximum number of files before reaching its full disk capacity. Continuing the example of storing 100 news articles per database block, the number of files stored would also be 1/100 that of the number of files with a news server that stores articles as individual files, making better use of the available disk space.

14 WEB ADMINISTRATION TOOLS

IN THE EARLY DAYS of networked Unix computers, Unix system administrators were called *superusers*. There was no such thing as a Web server, only Unix computers and system administrators given the superuser privilege for all operating system commands. Unix system administrators were responsible for adding users, managing privileges, implementing security, checking distributed computers to make sure they were running, and performing all tasks involved in keeping an operating system and applications functioning smoothly. Today, with the advent of the World Wide Web, Webmasters have taken on many new system administration roles, and the

WEB ADMINISTRATION TOOLS

tools for performing basic system administration have gotten much more advanced and efficient. This chapter will help you decide what kinds of Web administration tools you would find useful and will offer tips on the best ways for you to use those tools. Once you know what you're looking for, the comparison chart in Appendix N will help you find appropriate tools.

Before the development of Web servers, administration tools were provided within operating systems such as BSDI, IRIX, or Solaris. In 1993, Mosaic Communications Corporation created a graphical interface to the World Wide Web which required the superuser to act as the administrator of the Unix operating system and to provide a second layer of administration through the use of newly developed *Web server* software. Early on in the growth of the Web, the three popular Web server software programs were CERN, LINUX, and Netscape's Communication Server. These early Web server programs provided administration tools for managing domains; establishing HTTP protocols; and creating FTP, news, e-mail, proxy, and Telnet servers.

Because of the explosive growth of the Web, Web server administration has had to become truly distributed across a variety of individual programs performing each of the tasks listed above; the term "Web server software" now refers to the collective group of programs that allow you to connect your Web server to the worldwide network of Web servers.

What Are Web Server Administration Tools?

Web server administration tools can be described as the toolkit of programs and/or commands necessary to administer, update, secure, and monitor the performance of a running Web server. Web server administration can be performed by one person or a team of people responsible for administering a Web site. A Web site for the purposes of this chapter can be described as a computer or collection of computers containing some or all of the following components: Web server software, database engines, electronic commerce software, legacy interface applications, and proxy or firewall servers. All of these components function as a cohesive unit to serve the information needs of users distributed over a network.

To graphically depict what Webmasters may be asked to administer, Figure 14.1 illustrates the components of your Web site that may possibly require Web administration.

While the model depicts operating systems as separate from Web server software, some operating systems, such as IBM's S/390, offer Web server software as part of the operating system. In this chapter, we will explore only those administration tools that are separate from Web server programs.

WEB ADMINISTRATION TOOLS

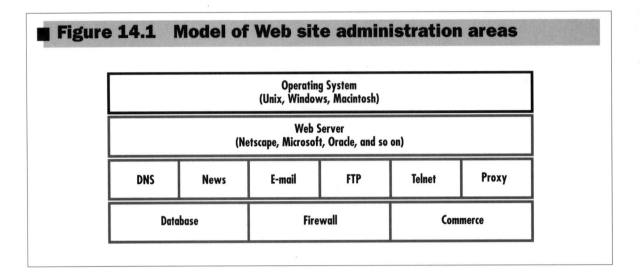

■ Figure 14.1   Model of Web site administration areas

Operating System (Unix, Windows, Macintosh)					
Web Server (Netscape, Microsoft, Oracle, and so on)					
DNS	News	E-mail	FTP	Telnet	Proxy
Database		Firewall		Commerce	

The Benefits of Administration Tools

As the number of intranet applications expands, so will the tasks falling under the Webmaster's purview. With ever increasing demands, the most successful Webmasters will find tools to make their jobs easier and more efficient. Administration tools can accomplish that end by

- Saving time

- Forcing consistency

- Establishing a minimum level of security

- Reporting performance and site visit summaries

- Implementing fault tolerance

- Providing backup

- Offering user management

- Saving money by working within existing corporate legacy environments

- Reporting load balancing to plan future capacity

- Organizing HTML file structure

- Offering distributed and remote server monitoring

WEB ADMINISTRATION TOOLS

The very best place to search for Web administration tools is the Web itself. Search engines like Yahoo and Altavista can yield many URLs for administration tools and products. To preview a list of all the available search engines, go to http://home.netscape.com/home/internet-search.html.

Types of Administration Tools

Administrative tools cover a wide range of categories. Tools on the market fall into categories such as the following:

- User management tools

- Security tools

- Remote resource management tools

- Collaboration tools

- Programming tools

- Database tools

- Content tools

- Client software

- Web server software

- Hardware tools

- Routers and connection monitoring tools

However, since other chapters of this book discuss several of these categories of tools, in this chapter we will only investigate the administration tools not packaged with Web server programs. These include third-party and vendor add-on products not included in the Web server bundle. These administration tools are described in Table 14.1 below.

Choosing Administration Tools

Your choice of administration tools is limited first of all by the operating system running on your Web server. The more flexible tools are operating system–independent (that is, they work seamlessly across Unix, Windows, and legacy platforms). The platform containing the richest selection of admin tools is Unix because Unix was the platform for which early Web server software was developed. The late entry of Microsoft into the Internet software development game means there are fewer tools available for DOS or Windows platforms. Industry experts predict that Unix will remain the platform of choice for sites with the largest hit volumes because DOS-based operating systems are not robust enough to handle

WEB ADMINISTRATION TOOLS

large volume transactions. Mainframe operating systems offer the weakest selection of administration tools because they are not open architectures, do not follow native Unix standards, nor have many third-party developers been willing to develop specifically for such closed platforms.

Other factors determining your choice of administration tools involve the kind of Web site you are supporting. Web sites fall into one of three functional categories depending on size and function of the Web site. These categories are described in Table 14.2.

Depending on the size and function of the Web site, administration tool choices will be swayed by the Webmaster's mission in serving either external customers, internal corporate customers, upper management, or development and Webmaster staffs reporting to an administrative manager. Clearly the need for administration tools increases as the complexity of the Web site grows. Web sites of the third type (those with multiple administrators and multiple domains) absolutely depend on quality administrative tools for effective administration.

■ Table 14.1   Web Administration Tools

Category of Tool	Purpose of Tool	Description
Basic Tools	User management HTTPD DNS (Domain Name Server) Activity log Multiple domain management Site tracking Performance monitoring HTML file system management System shutdown/restart	Basic tasks involve managing user accounts, domain names, performance reporting, site tracking, and server monitoring and shutdown. The best tools minimize the use of hand-performed operating system commands and automate entire series of operating system–level functions.
Remote Resource Management	Network computer status Network printer status Printer queue editing Distributed file system support Partitioning of workloads across servers Shared resource management Load balancing	In multiserver Web site environments, it becomes crucial to be able to monitor, update, reboot, load balance, and configure remote resources in a distributed network. These tools give one-screen access to multiple resources on an administrator's distributed network.
Commerce	SET (Secure Electronic Transfers) standard SSL (Secure Sockets Layer) compliance Auto credit card swipes	These tools allow for sending secure credit card information from the Web server to credit card clearinghouses. Tools that conform to the industrywide SET standard and SSL (Secure Sockets Layer) protocols are the most useful.
IP Address Management	Elimination of one-to-one IP mapping Multiple-domain IP addressing	These tools allow you to manage IP address allocation and multiple connects through a single modem.
Web Site Mapping	Graphical display of all Web page hierarchies Repair of broken links Interface to content corrections	These tools let the Webmaster see a graphical description of all the Web pages in the site. They allow for consistency management of page layout and give the Webmaster a high-level view of the hierarchy of all the pages associated with a Web site.
Access Restriction	Limitation of access to particular users Exclusion of particular potential users Limitation of resources available to users	These tools define boundaries for Web site use, allowing limitation of access by time of day, IP address, domain name, application, e-mail address, or use of a filter. Such restrictions allow management to focus employee use of the Internet.

WEB ADMINISTRATION TOOLS

Many companies dictate the operating system platform to which Webmasters must conform. But in other cases, the Webmaster is given the freedom to choose the platform and tools he or she prefers. In either case, whether setting up a new Web site or expanding the functions of an existing site or group of sites, administration tools greatly improve the efficiency of Web site management. Below is a discussion of tool types describing what to look for in a tool and what services the tool offers beyond those provided in Web server programs. For a more complete comparison of individual products' features, see the chart in Appendix N.

Basic Tools

Basic tools involve user and group management as well as domain configuration management. For Internet service providers who are selling domain name management as a service, these tools become critical to monitoring size limitations per user. They also help Webmasters proactively manage the smooth operation of these domains. While many Web server products offer basic tools, some tasks have been ignored by these packages. Tasks covered by these basic tools include easy drag-and-drop management of user and group hierarchy, status reporting, user disk-space usage, maintenance of an audit trail, security threat detection, importing/exporting passwords and user IDs, and domain quota and license management.

The Webmaster who can quickly perform the most basic of administrator functions can devote time and resources to the more difficult problems of Web site management. Webmasters' demands for basic function management are growing and their time is becoming increasingly valuable as they become more crucial to companies' information infrastructure. The most notable benefits of using these basic tools are that Webmasters can delegate responsibility for these basic tasks to less educated staff members who can use these simple tools effectively without going through a lengthy learning curve.

■ Table 14.2   Web Site Types

Web Site Type	Example
Single administrator	Small to medium-sized business with a single domain Web site
Multiple administrators for single domain	Fortune 500 or large corporate Web site
Multiple administrators for multiple domains	Internet service providers (ISPs) Telecommunication firms offering Internet services

WEB ADMINISTRATION TOOLS

Remote Management

The type of remote management tools you need depends on the kind of Web site you are managing. For large sites, look for remote management tools that poll running servers and give detailed status descriptions about the server and any resources connected to it such as printers and network resources. For small Web shops, remote management tools help the Webmaster treat all the Web servers in a single network as a unit and give a graphical overview of all those machines. Most remote management tools support activity logs, but the more sophisticated tools will filter the reports for exceptions and alert the Webmaster when a particular server fails or goes awry. The remote management tools currently available are minimal compared to what Webmasters need; the tools should really creep into the lower levels of hardware monitoring such as ISDN and T1 line monitoring. For Webmasters who work for an Internet service provider, tools that monitor functioning of dial-up modems would be an amazing resource.

Commerce Tools

In many companies there is a strong initiative to incorporate electronic commerce into the basic functioning of the Web site. *Commerce tools* are used on such sites to sell products directly to the customer and process financial transactions efficiently. Before the Web era, our society functioned on a basis of mass production and mass delivery. However, since the incorporation of commerce tools into Web sites, the system has significantly changed. Now our society can function according to the principle of custom production for mass delivery.

Because commerce tools and intranet infrastructures allow for seamless information sharing between corporate divisions, manufacturing departments, and customers, the customer is now able to request a custom product built to the customer's specification and have it delivered much more quickly. This is reshaping how we think about customer service and gives customers more direct access to internal information systems. This demands a greater attention to security, a focus on speed of delivery, and an eye for maintenance of the product's quality.

For many companies the promise of Internet profits lies in using the Web to process financial transactions. For the first few years of Web growth, there were no standards for commercial transactions. However, since the introduction of the SET (Secure Electronic Transfer) standard, commerce software and vendor support of commerce add-ons to Web server programs have flourished. Especially for Internet service providers, support for electronic commerce is crucial to their future. ISPs may charge per-transaction fees for processing financial transactions through their gateways. This creates a "service bureau" approach to commerce

WEB ADMINISTRATION TOOLS

and releases individual companies from relying on in-house electronic data processing or on providers using the older Electronic Data Interchange (EDI) technology.

For companies wanting more control over their commercial transactions, several EDI vendors are adding Internet-based value-added products that will allow the consumer to maintain their own commerce software tools running on their own servers. As the Internet grows in complexity, many have predicted that electronic commerce and the need for security surrounding the passage of financial data over the Internet will become the greatest challenge to the success and growth of the Web as a backbone for high-speed financial transactions. Because large banks can afford to set up virtual private networks (VPNs) and use an intranet approach to passing commerce data over their own network, the threats of sending data over the larger Internet are lessened. By the year 2000, companies unable to absorb Internet-based commerce technologies into their own information infrastructure will experience serious competitive disadvantages versus those companies embracing such commerce tools.

Administrators should look for commerce tools that perform securely and conform to the SET standard. Tools that connect to back-end financial clearinghouses are also useful because they eliminate the need for a manual credit card swipe by performing that swipe electronically. For sites advanced enough to present users with a form screen for credit card purchases, these commerce tools can automatically verify the credit of the cardholder and move on to real-time processing of the order.

IP Address Tools

Due to InterNIC rationing of IP subnets and addresses, Webmasters are often in a crunch for available IP addresses. Tools that manage IP address allocation and actually eliminate the need for one-to-one mapping of users to IP addresses are very useful to administrators. For Web sites with a single ISDN router and dedicated or dial-up access, a tool that allows multiple workstations to connect through a single IP port is useful. In Appendix N, the reader will find two useful tools specifically focused on IP addressing and managing those tasks.

Access Restriction

With the recent passage of the Communications Decency Act, Web site administrators suddenly became responsible for ensuring that content considered indecent was not distributed to minors. Rather than use this act as a way for government to become a regulatory agency over Internet content, Web protesters have lobbied heavily to approach the problem of pornographic or indecent content through administrative tools that provide access restriction. Especially for Web sites focused on educational purposes, the use of access restriction tools very nicely circumvents the

WEB ADMINISTRATION TOOLS

problem of users accidentally happening upon sites with lewd material. There is another use for access restriction tools: For corporations wishing to grant employees Web access but to limit access to business uses, these tools can effectively filter out game or extracurricular Web sites. Access restriction is approached in one of two basic ways:

- Permit sites approved and restrict all others.

- Restrict sites unapproved and allow all others.

One of the limitations of these tools is that they may accidentally restrict a broader range of sites than the user desires. Because the tools work simply by word detection rather than by trying to understand the context of the word, relevant sites may unfortunately be ignored. For these tools to advance, they will have to delve into the realm of natural language processing and gain some "understanding" of a Web site's content rather than merely perform restriction based on the presence of a particular word on the site. See Appendix N for tools that perform access restriction.

Mapping Tools

A Web site's HTML pages can grow into many thousands of individual files and folders and become too unwieldy for content creators to manage. Web site mapping tools allow graphical viewing from a high level of the site's file structure and allow moving and deleting files that are no longer needed by the site. Advanced tools make the interface easy enough that nonprogrammer content creators such as graphic artists or department managers can manage their own portion of the Web site hierarchy and reduce the burden on the administrator.

The most advanced tools for Web site mapping work on an open systems architecture methodology, seamlessly meshing with both Web server and Web browser programs. Programs that find broken links and perform some level of compiling, testing, and repairing of Web sites are especially productive and eliminate the tedium of scanning HTML commands for errors. Mapping tools provide these capabilities and are often not found in traditional web content creation tools.

Wish List for Administration Tools

In writing this chapter, it became clear that vendors haven't quite understood the market demand for administration tools separate from the Web server and uniquely stand-alone. While much press and attention goes to the server software suites, little attention is paid to the gaps in those products and the functions that Webmasters are forced to handle either by hand or not at all. The reason administration tools must remain stand-alone products is that they will soon need to perform across multiplatform Web server environments. Although administration tools, like all

WEB ADMINISTRATION TOOLS

other Web products, are advancing, there are still a few things on Webmasters' wish lists. The top three seem to be the following:

1. Development of secure cross-platform standards for the way Web administration is handled in a corporate setting.

2. Administration tools that are accessible to or operable by anybody within a company, not just Webmasters or people with a technical background.

3. Tools that work seamlessly across Web server platforms and within multiserver environments

Vendors could benefit from walking in the shoes of Webmasters of large enterprises. Web server vendors rushing to get new software to market might achieve greater success by simply polling corporate Webmasters for their true feelings on tools still required to manage large-scale Web development shops. As intranets continue to become the information system architecture of choice, vendors may find that Web administration tools or the lack thereof are the determining factors for why Webmasters choose a particular company's product suite. Hats off to Webmasters everywhere who perform miraculously despite the buggy Internet software products available on the market today, and may more complete admin tools arrive soon to aid the burden of Web site management!

3

PROGRAMMING TOOLS

HTML Editors

Authoring Tools

Java Authoring Tools

CGI Tools

VRML Tools

15 HTML EDITORS

WRITING HTML DOCUMENTS and creating Web pages is a funny business—you basically want your HTML coding efforts to go unnoticed. The best pages combine skilled designs and well-oiled mechanics in such a way that the user hardly realizes the complexity of the HTML code, unless it is to appreciate, or appropriate, it. A Webmaster needs to be an insatiable tinkerer, someone who likes to make things happen for their own sake. However, even dedicated tinkerers are likely to find tedious long hours of poring over nearly identical documents in pursuit of a great new HTML trick, so a tool that minimizes the typing required in HTML coding

HTML EDITORS

and frees you to concentrate on creating functional design is a godsend. A real boon would be a tool that looks and feels like a graphic design application but allows access to the HTML document for fine-tuning. Happily, these tools exist. Of course, they come in a variety of degrees of functionality and can never, despite their claims, do away with the need to know HTML.

In this chapter we will define HTML, look at where you can find the latest innovations, and examine and compare HTML editors for Macs and PCs. We will discuss some sources on the Internet where shareware and freeware editing tools can be acquired and cover the basic features of the most popular and commonly used commercial editors on the market.

Hypertext and HTML: A Few Necessary Definitions

Having assembled all of the necessary design and delivery tools, you must now set to the task of assembling your page layout. This is where the HTML editor comes into the play. But before you start editing, you need to know what HTML is.

- *Hypertext* is the dynamic relationship between a group of documents (text, images, sounds, video clips, and animations) that can often be accessed in a non-linear fashion.

- *Hypertext Markup Language* is the set of instructions that tells the client browser which files to download and where to place them within the viewing window. With HTML you will create links to other documents on your server and the entire Internet. Skillful use of the language can create works of art that possess a visual beauty as well as an intuitive means of accessing content. Your job as Webmaster is to directly compose these links and describe the page's composition. For this reason we recommend that you take the time to learn the basics of HTML. While you may not necessarily need to know the proper tags for embedding a video clip, when a link leads to a 404 (file not found) error, you will need to be able to find and fix the problem. There are many books that can teach you the basics of HTML; one excellent design-oriented book is *Designing Killer Web Sites* from Hayden Books.

- *HTTP,* Hyper Text Transfer Protocol or Hyper Text Teleprocessing Protocol, is the system for managing communications between servers and clients. It is a method for addressing another machine in much the same way as when you dial a telephone number to reach a friend.

- *HTTPD* stands for HTTP daemon, which is the software set that runs at all times on the server and responds to all inquiries from client machines. To take the telephone analogy one step further, the daemon is what checks to see if the number is a right or wrong number. HTTPD comes in two flavors: CERN and NCSA.

HTML EDITORS

Keeping Ahead of the Pack

HTML has been around for the last five years, but its development has been greatly accelerated over the last year or so by Netscape's creation of their own *extensions.* Extensions to HTML are tags that are generally created to be recognized only by a particular browser; however, if the tags are successful and widely used, they often become integrated into other browsers and recognized by the Internet Engineering Task Force and HTML Editorial Review Board of the W3 Consortium. (The W3 Consortium is a group of companies in the industry that have gotten together in order to create and promote standards for HTML-based products.)

HTML is now in its third revision, what is known as HTML 3.0. As with any language or software program, "revisionitis" takes over—we are currently up to HTML 3.2. Netscape's Navigator 2.0+ and 3.0.1 and Microsoft's Internet Explorer 3.0 are the two primary browsers you will be designing for.

For the latest in HTML extensions check out Netscape's Web site which offers all of their latest additions, as well as working examples with the source code explained. You should also keep your eye on the MicrosoftNetwork, Microsoft's online service and Web site, as they too are releasing extensions and beta versions of their software quite frequently now.

Microsoft Internet Explorer 3.0 is the first browser that supports most HTML 3.2 standards, while at the same introducing some of its own like cascading style sheets, CSS, and ActiveX. ActiveX is an enabling technology with a set of controls or protocols for integrating everything from multimedia to database administration. ActiveX as a meta-architcture has yet to be rounded out, but you should familiarize yourself with it now.

Something for Everyone

HTML editors come in three basic flavors: text-based, draw-based, and WYSIWYG. Within each of these categories, editors vary in terms of the features they offer and their ease of use. Of the editors tested for this book, high performers were the text-based BBEdit 4.0.1 editor, and the now-in-beta Adobe PageMill 2.0 and Microsoft FrontPage 1.1, both of which are very powerful programs that may appeal to users who prefer a WYSIWYG environment. As is the case for most software these days, when upgrades to the editing programs become available, they are generally placed on the company's Web site for download. In this chapter, we'll discuss the features of six popular HTML editors: Adobe PageMill 2.0, CorelWEB.DESIGNER, HoTMetaL PRO (shareware edition), BBEdit 4.0.1, Navigator Gold 3.0, and FrontPage 1.1. Keep in mind, though, that some of the authoring tools that will be discussed in Chapter 16 can also be used as HTML editors.

HTML EDITORS

Text-Based Editors

Text-based editors can be any word processing program that allows documents to be saved as ASCII files. Before HTML editors, production was done with Notepad and SimpleText programs, which have no built-in support for HTML. These simple text editors require you to have a complete understanding of HTML, and you'll probably want to keep reference materials handy for the less commonly used intricacies.

Today the most powerful text-based editor is BBEdit, by Bare Bones Software. Versions 3.5.2 and 4.0.1 of BBEdit offer a drag-and-drop HTML extension toolbar and sophisticated *GREP* (global/regular expression/print) and find/replace functions which are found more commonly on Unix and LINUX machines. The only drawback to this great editor is that you need some in-depth HTML knowledge.

Draw-Based Editors

Draw-based editors are a new thing to the Web world. Up until recently all options for Web page creation programs have been text-based and WYSIWYG, but this was primarily due to the lack of very fine control in HTML interpretation. Though it has always been possible to tweak things to near perfection, doing so has almost always called on code dragged out of obscurity.

Currently the only draw-based editor is provided by NetObjects in their Fusion Site Publisher which will be covered in the next chapter, "Authoring Tools."

WYSIWYG

WYSIWYG (what you see is what you get) is a form of editing whereby you insert your text and images at their desired positions on the page and assign them functions, letting the editing program fill in the HTML for you. Most WYSIWYG programs integrate graphics editing and file format conversion capabilities to do away with the hassle of switching between different programs. Unfortunately, WYSIWYG editors are often not up to date with current HTML extensions.

Features to Look for in an HTML Editor

Your choice of editor will be determined in part by the environment you feel comfortable working in (text-based or WYSIWYG), in part by the operating system you will be using, and in part by the features you demand in your editor. Users who are less comfortable in HTML will probably want a toolbar for inserting HTML code while competent HTML programmers will perhaps be more interested in advanced find and replace features or support for HTML 3.2 standards. Once you've determined the features you're looking for, use the comparison chart in Appendix O to find editors that fit your bill.

HTML EDITORS

Operating System

HTML editors are available for Windows, Macintosh, or Unix systems. Some editors have different versions for the different platforms, but some of the best, such as BBEdit, only support one platform (Macintosh, in the case of BBEdit). Thus your choice of editor will be somewhat restricted by the operating system of the computer you plan to use for your page creation. Netscape Navigator Gold 3.0 and SoftQuad HoTMetaL Pro are available for Macs and PCs and Adobe and Microsoft have plans to follow suit shortly.

Drag-and-Drop Editing

Most editors can accept elements which have been highlighted and dragged over the construction window from within a document or from outside. You will find this very useful when converting existing documents into HTML. Some larger software manufacturers also provide an expanded capability for integrating their own products.

One of the best implementations of drag-and-drop editing, one which goes beyond the norm, is found in PageMill 2.0 which features the *pasteboard.* By selecting an area in the browser window and dragging the selection to the pasteboard window, you can drag and drop elements that are repeated in your Web site's design. When stored in the pasteboard, linked elements will retain their links no matter how many times they are used. One limitation is that there are only five pages on the pasteboard, though the window can be resized and more than one element can be stored on a page. It can speed up the process of applying navigation bars and links, copyright notices, and recurring imagery throughout your site.

Toolbars

Toolbars provide instant access to all major page and site creation tools. The editors vary in the complexity and usefulness of their toolbars from Navigator's surprisingly sparse and very ordinary one to HoTMetaL PRO's three floating toolbars which can be turned off to provide more room for the page on screen. BBEdit also provides an extensive floating palette of HTML tools, shown in Figure 15.1.

If you plan to work within a WYSIWYG environment, you can count on using the standard toolbar setup which allows you to assign multiple attributes to a given highlighted element with great ease. If you tend toward a programming interface you will appreciate the expanded capabilities of BBEdit's HTML Tools Palette as a time saving device.

User Interface

Although a great user interface doesn't always signify a great editor, if you hate an editor's interface, you will probably find the program difficult and unpleasant to work with, no matter how complete its set of features is.

HTML EDITORS

■ **Figure 15.1   The BBEdit extension toolbar can be positioned anywhere on the desktop. Clicking on buttons with ridges, holding down the mouse button, and dragging enables you to place elements anywhere you choose.**

A great example of a well-designed user interface is PageMill 2.0 with its standard word processor–based toolbars working in conjunction with the Attributes Inspector and pasteboard floating palettes. The availability of these tools at all times combined with the ability to keep many pages open will be of benefit to those working on large sites.

At the other end of the spectrum is the standard Windows interface. The CorelWEB.DESIGNER user interface is similar to most Windows-based word processors and is structured like all common Web browsers. If you are comfortable in any WYSIWYG word processor, you'll feel right at home in CorelWEB.DESIGNER.

Other editors like HoTMetaL PRO and BBEdit are less user-friendly in their interfaces. Having very little in the way of user interface, while not necessarily a bad thing, makes HoTMetaL PRO more difficult to use than most of the other editors tested. This is due in part to the graphical representation of HTML tags. Furthermore, the Preferences settings, which in most other programs allow you to control certain aspects of the

HTML EDITORS

interface, provide no real control over anything important. What control is offered is very minimal at best.

The BBEdit 4.0.1 interface is not very inviting, and there is no subsequent layout tagging provided. Such conventions are unnecessary for programmers and generally hinder document proofing and troubleshooting. However, you can customize your work environment through the Preferences window. By assigning text colors to general HTML, anchors, images, and comments, it's easy to find the precise point in the document that needs adjustment. Other customizable settings include window layout, built-in mail and FTP functions, and a disk browser similar to a Web browser that allows you to enter or select any document, including PICTs, from your local or network hard drive and view its contents before opening it.

Multilevel Find and Replace Functions

Find and replace capabilities are provided by nearly every HTML editor. PageMill and FrontPage offer the most effective of the standard find and replace functions and allow for path name and file name replacement with automatic link updating.

With advanced multilevel find and replace functions, you can search multiple documents and directories for similar elements and perform global changes. BBEdit offers the most complete find and replace functionality of any editor available today. BBEdit's ability to search by file group is a function you would need a Unix terminal to emulate. The power of BBEdit's find and replace function makes it an excellent site management tool, enabling the Webmaster to make subtle changes to any document on the server.

For searching within documents and groups, BBEdit offers several options, as shown in Figure 15.2. You can search for specific words and/or characters with or without case sensitivity, search using variable strings, search by file type including text, PICTs, letters, and project files, and find and compare differences that are then displayed side by side or as predefined in the Preferences area. You also have a wide variety of search options such as GREP, Start at Top, Wrap Around, Backwards, Selection Only, Entire Word, Case Sensitive, Multi-File Search, and Batch Find, which can be used to search within documents and throughout entire sites, including CGIs and logs.

GREP stands for *global/regular expression/print*. What a GREP search does is conduct a global search through a file for a prespecified *regular expression* that is then displayed. A regular expression is a string consisting of two elements: ordinary characters and special operators. Ordinary characters are all lower- and uppercase letters, numbers, and other characters such as ~ ' ! @ # - : ; = , and /. Special operators include \ . * $ [and]. By combining ordinary characters and special operators into strings and then combining strings, you can search for almost anything with the push of a button.

HTML EDITORS

Figure 15.2   The unbeatable BBEdit Find and Replace dialog box

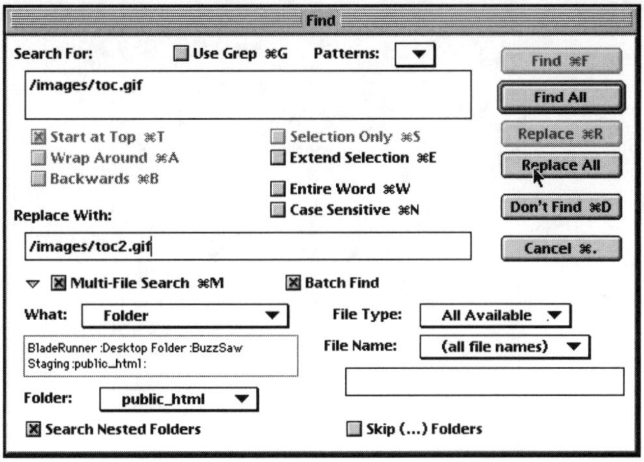

```
┌─────────────────────────── Find ───────────────────────────┐
│                                                             │
│  Search For:      ☐ Use Grep  ⌘G   Patterns:  [ ▼ ]   ( Find  ⌘F )  │
│  ┌───────────────────────────────────────────┐             │
│  │ /images/toc.gif                            │  ( Find All )       │
│  └───────────────────────────────────────────┘             │
│                                                  ( Replace ⌘R )     │
│  ☒ Start at Top  ⌘T      ☐ Selection Only  ⌘S                │
│  ☐ Wrap Around  ⌘A       ☒ Extend Selection  ⌘E  ( Replace All )    │
│  ☐ Backwards  ⌘B                                             │
│                          ☐ Entire Word  ⌘W      ( Don't Find ⌘D )   │
│  Replace With:           ☐ Case Sensitive  ⌘N                │
│  ┌───────────────────────────────────────────┐  ( Cancel  ⌘. )    │
│  │ /images/toc2.gif                           │             │
│  └───────────────────────────────────────────┘             │
│                                                             │
│  ▽ ☒ Multi-File Search  ⌘M      ☒ Batch Find                 │
│  What:  [ Folder          ▼ ]   File Type:  [ All Available ▼ ] │
│  ┌───────────────────────────────┐                          │
│  │ BladeRunner :Desktop Folder :BuzzSaw │ File Name: [ (all file names) ▼ ] │
│  │ Staging :public_html:         │                          │
│  └───────────────────────────────┘  ┌──────────────────┐    │
│  Folder:  [ public_html  ▼ ]         │                  │    │
│  ☒ Search Nested Folders         ☐ Skip (...) Folders       │
└─────────────────────────────────────────────────────────────┘
```

Used in conjunction with another BBEdit feature, Internet Config, BBEdit's search capabilities make it possible to edit and update CGIs and JavaScript and modify Web pages remotely from within the same work environment. The online documentation offers easy to understand information on writing search strings; you might also want to pick up a good Unix book (just for reference, of course).

Integrated Graphics Tools

Some editors include tools for editing graphics and performing graphics format conversions. PageMill 2.0 supports animated GIFs, and most programs provide image-mapping and hotspot tools. If no graphics tools are provided, an editor may integrate an outside graphics tool as in the case of Navigator Gold 3.0. The Image View window shown in Figure 15.3. gives you an idea of some of the graphics tools available in PageMill 2.0.

The most typical image tools can be found in FrontPage 1.1. After an image has been placed in the page it can be highlighted to activate its options. Selecting a circle, square, or polygon will determine the type of hotspot to be created.

Browser Preview

This feature allows you to use outside browsers to preview your page and test for cross-browser compatibility. With most HTML editors, when it is time to preview your work in progress you are limited to either the

HTML EDITORS

Figure 15.3 PageMill's multifunctional Image View window provides tools for everything from hotspot creation through setting the color bit rate to accepting and saving files as GIFs and JPEGs.

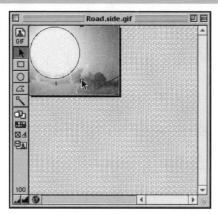

built-in browser or a default. However, some editors allow the use of more than one browser for preview purposes.

Depending on your editor, such a feature may or may not be necessary. For instance, CorelWEB.DESIGNER does not offer an outside browser preview, instead relying on the WYSIWYG editing environment to provide an adequate representation of what the document will look like when loaded. When tested, CorelWEB.DESIGNER performed well and accurately previewed the page layout as seen by major browsers. Navigator Gold 3.0 offers a browser preview function, the benefit of which is obvious—as Netscape is the most widely used browser, basically you get a great browser integrated with text and graphics editing capabilities.

With BBEdit when you select the Preview button on the floating palette you are presented with a list of all the browsers in your system from which you must select the default browser. If you press the Preview button and get a system sound, you need to define the default by simply selecting a browser from the pull-down list to the right of the Preview button. This makes multiple browser testing a button click away.

HTML 3.0+ and Netscape Extensions

Given the speed with which everything related to the Internet moves, you want to make sure that your editor is as current as possible. You should be able to insert a <SCRIPT> tag in the header and control body

HTML EDITORS

attributes such as layout, <BLOCKQUOTE>, <FORM> <H1-6>, <P>, <LI>, <TABLE>, <BR>, and embedded objects such as <IMG>, <EM-BED>, and <APPLET>. Of course you will also want full font control.

As described above, Netscape was the first browser development company to go out on a limb and develop extensions to HTML. Extensions they introduced are <BASEFONT>, <BR>, <CENTER>, <FONT>, <HR>, <IMG>, <UL>, <LI>, <GIF89>, <TABLE>, and <FRAME>. Microsoft Internet Explorer 3.0 offers full support for these and more.

FrontPage blows away the competition in the integration of the latest HTML extensions. Although FrontPage caters to the Microsoft-related extensions and the Internet Explorer 3.0 browser, it also covers most of those introduced by Netscape. HoTMetaL PRO provides free updates to the latest extensions at the SoftQuad Web site. However, it is a WYSI-WYG editor and the WYSIWYG editors are usually not the best choices for users who demand support for the very latest HTML extensions.

Netscape Navigator is an Open Architecture application, meaning that it allows for the expansion of its own capabilities through the use of plug-ins. With Navigator 3.0 it is possible to integrate almost any third-party technology, such as Shockwave, QuickTime, PDF, AVI movies, Real-Audio, and others. PageMill 2.0 supports direct use of some Netscape plug-ins (most of the same ones used by Navigator 3.0), including Shockwave, QuickTime, PDF formats, and sound files such as AIFF, WAV, SND, and AU.

Support for Tables and Frames

Support for tables and frames ranges from PageMill's completely WYSI-WYG, drag-and-drop functions, including support for nested tables, HTML 3.0 table tags, and template-based frame creation, to Corel-WEB.DESIGNER's lack of any native table or frame function. However, CorelWEB.DESIGNER and some other programs do allow you to import and format tables and frames created in word processing or spread-sheet applications. An example of this would be a spreadsheet from Excel that can be opened within CorelWEB.DESIGNER and retain its layout information. Microsoft distributes the Internet Assistants (see Chapter 16) which do the same thing for free for their Office suite.

Java Applets and ActiveX

Today's Web sites are becoming virtual computers made up of non-platform specific executable applications and a browser plug-in architecture. PERL script and Sun's Java programming language are the driving force behind this development, but other programming languages are also used. If you plan to include many programs on your Web site, you'll need good support for a variety of programming languages. In this area, BBEdit is far and away the best choice. Originally designed for software programmers,

HTML EDITORS

BBEdit has an amazing set of libraries that work with C, C++, Pascal, FORTRAN, PERL, Java, and recently, HTML. The high-powered nature of BBEdit can be daunting at first, but after using 4.0.1 for a time you will be able to fly through the creation of entire Web sites.

Microsoft's Internet Explorer uses ActiveX as the framework for supporting third-party technologies such as Java and PERL. Many editors allow you to import and place applets and ActiveX controls without ever having to touch the code or write the parameter settings. Be sure to look for packages that offer library integration if you are going to be designing on an expanded network.

Font Control

Editors with font control let you control the size and attributes of text appearance. In most editors, you can change the text font size and color of individual characters, rather than only whole paragraphs or pages. Also commonly provided is a means for changing the base font. The minimum level of control you should look for is the <FONT> tag with its attributes SIZE, COLOR, <B>, <I>, <STRIKE>, <SUB>, and <SUP>.

Recently, with the release of Internet Explorer 3.0 and its browser-specific technology, cascading style sheets, true font control became possible over the Internet. A style sheet works by acting as a set of instructions to the browser that direct it to search the client's system font directory for preferred fonts. The viewable text is then displayed according to specifications in the style sheet. This gives the designer a higher degree of control over the style of the document than ever before. Microsoft even provides fonts which have been optimized for the screen, not paper.

The comparable Netscape tag is <FONT FACE> which can be set to your first, second, and third choice of font. When you design pages that take advantage of system fonts remember that most people won't have the exotic fonts you might have as a designer. Good use of existing system fonts will look far nicer than the standard browser fare.

The Programs

Each of the six editors covered in this chapter has its pluses and minuses, but all offer support for the more common HTML 3.0 features. Most are similarly priced, ranging from free to $150 for the cheapest version of FrontPage.

CorelWEB.DESIGNER's inclusion of HTML 3.0 tags, easy switching between preview and HTML documents, client-side and server-side image mapping, and the ability to seamlessly convert word processing layout are the base level of functionality you should consider. Corel-WEB.DESIGNER also provides easier access to HTML documents for text editing. These are all handy tools but some of the more advanced capabilities of the competition leave it lacking in comparison.

HTML EDITORS

Now available for both PC and Macintosh, Netscape Navigator Gold 3.0 serves as the central tool in your Web-building toolbox. Although Navigator Gold 3.0 is primarily a browser, it provides a WYSIWYG editing environment and boasts an in-line JavaScript editor for the creation of custom cross-platform applications, a starter Web site where you can learn by example, and prefabricated page templates. Navigator Gold 3.0 is available as a stand-alone editor/browser or as a component of the larger site authoring suite from Netscape: LiveWire and LiveWirePro, both discussed in Chapter 16.

Working within the Navigator browser, you select Editor Preferences in the Options menu and proceed to create your work environment by setting your preferences for General, Appearance, and Publishing controls. In the General preferences area, you set the text and graphics editing applications in much the same way you do when selecting helper applications and plug-ins within Netscape. As shown in Figure 15.4, I set the preferences to open BBEdit and Photoshop and can now access these tools through Netscape directly.

Navigator Gold also offers a Publish preferences area that gives you some control over path names and the saving of remote documents. The choices offered are to maintain links and to keep images with the docu-

Figure 15.4   General preferences settings in Navigator Gold 3.0 designate path names to other programs, allowing you use Navigator as the central tool in your Web construction tool set.

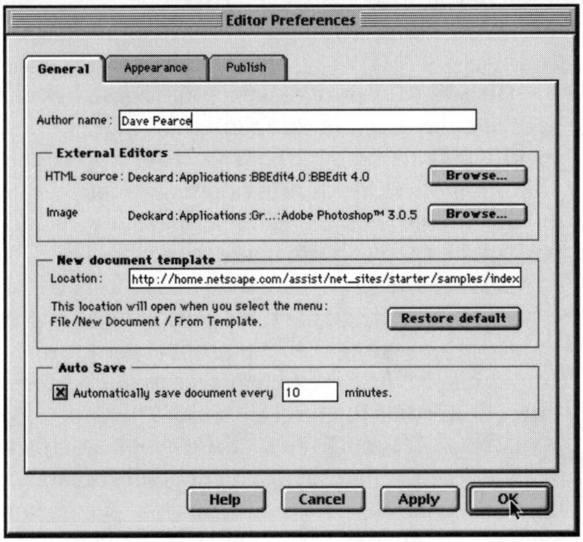

HTML EDITORS

ment. Maintaining the proper path name in your Web site is important, but there are some differences between the way Unix and the Macintosh OS read characters. Commonly used Unix syntax such as periods (.) and slashes (/) are not recognized by the Mac when they precede a string. Therefore, if you are writing your Web site on a Macintosh you will need be aware of these differences. Though Navigator Gold 3.0 is free to the public, for full technical help from Netscape you must purchase a subscription generally priced around $100.

SoftQuad's HoTMetalPRO series has been around for a few years now and has made a point of offering the standard set of features including automatic word processor conversion, word processing tools, multiple browser previews, and the latest extensions to HTML, but to take advantage of the full range of capabilities you need to register your freeware or buy the latest version. The freeware version was used for the test and unfortunately it offers little support for current HTML standards. For the fully enhanced version, go to http://www.softquad.com and expect to pay $159.

For serious programmers with a Mac, you can't beat BBEdit. It's a general purpose programming tool that can be used for high-octane development at a very reasonable price of $110. Although the program assumes the author is a code mechanic, it does provide a plethora of built-in tools for aiding the troubleshooting process, as well as an extension that allows you to correct mistakes made by PageMill 1.0.

However, BBEdit itself is *not* a WYSIWYG editor! All you see while you work is a text document. It also provides nothing in the way of image processing other than HTML coding. Conversion to GIF or JPEG, creation of transparencies, and image mapping all must be done in an outside application. If you plan to use a lot of image maps you might consider a WYSIWYG editor like PageMill.

BBEdit 4.0.1 provides awesome control over most current HTML 3.0 tags, and the drag-and-drop interface makes it a very worthwhile investment if you are doing serious Web development. Furthermore, its ability to work in most major programming languages including Java is a bonus. If you do your Web design on a Mac but with another program, BBEdit can still be used as a site maintenance tool.

As far as WYSIWYG Web page editors go, Microsoft FrontPage 1.1 is one of the best available tools. Part of what makes it so good is its accuracy in representing the final product while you are constructing the page. In this respect FrontPage manages to out perform PageMill, though the latter does come in at a close second.

Microsoft FrontPage 1.1 offers you a complete set of easy to use editing tools within one environment. Unfortunately, figuring out how to use those tools can be a little difficult since the documentation is just a brief pamphlet that familiarizes you with the various viewers and editors. To make up for that lack, there are online tutorials at MicrosoftNetwork

HTML EDITORS

(http://www.msn.com) and quite an extensive built-in help function that has hypertext to related issues. As with CorelWEB.DESIGNER and Adobe PageMill 2.0, FrontPage 1.1 does a great job of incorporating pre-formatted text from word processors such as Microsoft Word 7 or Word Perfect. FrontPage will also import and convert Rich Text Format (RTF) documents to HTML, as well as automatically convert images to GIFs.

FrontPage 1.1 is toolbar– and push-button–driven, with most of its options being, at this time, standard across applications. You have push-button control over links, tables, font attributes, alignment, lists, tabs, and form creation. FrontPage also includes hotspot editing in the toolbar, allowing you to create image maps in the primary editor window.

For those who wish to avoid as much HTML as possible the greatest advantage to FrontPage is that it ships with a healthy selection of wizards and templates to meet a variety of needs. There is a Frames wizard, shown in Figure 15.5, and a Form Page wizard that works in conjunction with the Save Results Bot (discussed in Chapter 16) to automate the gathering of information on your site. Wizards and templates are provided for Employee Directories, Feedback Forms, Press Releases, Searches, Surveys, User Registration, and more.

If you think FrontPage is what you are looking for, call Microsoft sales and get a price quote for the package. At the time of writing, FrontPage 1.1 could be purchased for $159, but there was mention of the price increasing to as much as $650.

Choosing an Editor

If you are like most people, you will prefer to work within an integrated environment that lets you have quick access to the tools you will be using most. These will most likely be a text editor, graphics editor, image-mapping tool, and preview browsers. We have looked at six of the most commonly available freeware and commercial HTML editors, several of which possess the four tools within one program, and Netscape Navigator Gold 3.0 which combines its WYSIWYG editor with individual settings for external editors.

Regardless of the HTML editor you choose to use most for your Web page production, you need to learn HTML because eventually you will need to diagnose or fix a problem, such as an omitted closing quote in an <A HREF="*"></A> tag, that your HTML editor has missed. The basics can be learned in a day by spending time on line with tutorials provided by Netscape (the URLs of a few of the best resources for Web-related information and products are included in the sidebar below) and by viewing the source files of the pages you like. And, above all, you need to keep up with the development of the language and implement changes as they happen.

HTML EDITORS

Figure 15.5   The FrontPage Frames Wizard selects from a range of preset FRAMESETs or allows customization of the layout by dragging the bars within the page frame.

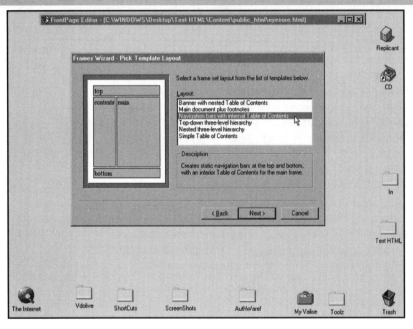

HTML EDITORS

■ Online Resources

Netscape's Web site (http://home.netscape.com) gives you access to many online HTML resources. Under the Assistance header, select the Creating Sites link by clicking on it with the pointer. There you will find information divided into the categories Authoring Documents, Adding Functionality, and Developer Tools. In Developer Tools you will find links to most of the tools needed to maintain your Web site. Examples of extensions and aesthetically pleasing layout are available for close examination.

Mentioned earlier, the Microsoft's Web site offers online HTML tutorials (http://www.microsoft.com/workshop/) that cover ActiveX and style sheets; the site also has online documentation for Microsoft FrontPage 1.1. As with Netscape's site, Microsoft provides many browser-centric tips for getting the most out of Internet Explorer, now at version 3.0. More important tools can be found at http://www.windows95.com where there is a wide collection of 32-bit freeware and shareware including Eudora Light, WS_FTP95, Graphic Construction Kit, WinZIP and more Internet-specific goodies as well as cool toys for modifying your desktop and system.

Useful URLs include the following:
http://www.w3.org
(W3 Consortium, Latest developments in HTML)
http://www.yahoo.com/
Computers_and_Internet/
http://www.yahoo.com/
Computers_and_Internet/Software/
http://www.yahoo.com/
Computers_and_Internet/Internet/
World_Wide_Web/HTML_Editors/
http://www.yahoo.com/
Computers_and_Internet/Internet/
World_Wide_Web/Authoring/
http://www.webmonkey.com
(tips and tricks for cutting-edge Web techniques)
http://www.cnet.com/howto/
(very useful information on current Web techniques)
http://www.microsoft.com/msoffice/
frontpage/productinfo/brochure/front2.htm
http://www.msn.com
http://www.adobe.com/
http://www.barebones.com/bbedit.html   ■

16 AUTHORING TOOLS

SO, YOU'VE MADE IT THIS FAR and still want to get involved in Web site production, but the mass of information you need to master is daunting. Servers, modems, T1, T3, ISDN, video, audio, DNS, FTP, plug-ins, and firewalls—how are you ever going to track and edit your site on a global level, and keep all the pieces organized? One answer is site authoring and publishing programs.

AUTHORING TOOLS

SITE AUTHORING AND PUBLISHING PROGRAMS come in a variety of levels of usefulness and sophistication offering more toolset combinations to choose from. When considering these packages, which claim to incorporate most of the tools you will need to maintain a site, remember that no authoring program is going to help you write HTML pages using tags it doesn't know. In other words, look for the authoring tool that provides the best support for current HTML standards (HTML 3.0 or higher) or plan on manually tagging the bulk of your documents.

That said, we can move on to examining a few of the commercially available site authoring applications. In Chapter 15 we examined and compared the features of the most popular and commonly used commercial or shareware HTML editing tools. We defined a handful of key features required for Web page production, features which are equally relevant to our discussion in this chapter, since most of the applications we will look at here include built-in HTML editors.

Site Authoring Considerations

Having covered your HTML editing requirement what do you look for next in a site authoring program? Tools for creating an information hierarchy? Managing a wide sprawling site? Integrating multimedia and databases? Support for third-party technologies? Embedding a movie or a Shockwave file is one thing, setting the parameters to a Java applet is another. You might be surprised to know that some site authoring packages can do all of the above. To find out more about these kinds of programs and the features they include, read on. To help find a tool that fits your needs, see the comparison chart of authoring products in Appendix P.

Flowcharting

The first thing you want to look for is a good flowchart program. A flowchart diagrams the structure of your site in such a way that it is easy to understand the relationship of the individual elements to the whole site. A typical example resembles a plant root system with multiple paths branching out from the central point of the trunk or home page. A high powered flowcharting tool will be one of your most valuable tools for designing the flow of information on your site and how the user will access it.

Look for a program that supports drag-and-drop for easy experimentation with flow. A site authoring program that has this capability built in is a plus, but if you need to find one outside, some are better than others. For the Macintosh, Inspiration 4.1 is great. For Windows, Flow Charting PDQ, Flow Charting 4, Org Plus, and Visio 4.0 will all do the job. Of the built-in tools, NetObjects's Fusion SiteArchitect Editor lets you easily create the flow of the data you wish to provide, as well as communicate that structure to others. The SiteArchitect Editor is drag-and-drop and visually restructures itself with each change you make. The saved structure is

AUTHORING TOOLS

then used as the skeleton for the elements/assets created in the Page-Draw Editor and SiteStyles Manager and it can be restructured anytime. This environment offers the choice of a structural or an outline view, and provides a specialized properties palette, though many of its functions can be performed within the window.

A slightly less user-friendly interface is Microsoft's FrontPage Explorer. FrontPage Explorer allows the Web designer to view and structure their Web site in an Outline or Link view. The two views are very useful when used in conjunction with one another. When a document is selected in the Outline view, the Link View shows you links to that page as well as the links from that page. In the Outline view window, World Wide Web links are denoted by a globe icon with the full URL listed.

Link Management

The task of link management needs to be approached in a couple of ways. First, there is the testing of the site that must be done before going live. For this you will need to be able to view the entire site's links and their status. Some of the applications we will look at offer what they claim to be trustworthy link managers. While this may be true, the only way to know for sure is to let yourself and your associates hammer away at your site for a day or two before going live.

Another consideration when dealing with link management is the amount of day-to-day upkeep your site will require. Are you going to be searching your site for specific links that need to be updated? If so, you will want to consider options that provide strong find and replace tools. None of the site authoring tools are as powerful in this area as BBEdit 4.0.1, which was covered in the last chapter.

The two programs offering the best control in link management are Fusion and FrontPage, although they do so in very different ways. With Fusion the elements or *assets* are either files, links, or data objects. By simply highlighting a particular asset you can make global changes to your site from within the Properties palette. FrontPage allows you to classify and view site links along three lines: links to images, repeated links, and links inside a page.

As with NetObjects Fusion, when in Adobe SiteMill you can rearrange and rename files, sort them by name, and modify the date, all without losing any links. This comes in handy as your site matures in structure and content. As you edit links between your pages and develop the global graphic iconography of your site, you can ensure correspondence between elements from page to page.

AUTHORING TOOLS

Interactivity and Multimedia

Adding dynamic content to sites today is almost an imperative. Whether it is something as simple as an e-mail address or an interactive Java applet, interactive sites offers more than static, one-way sites. There are many online resources for CGI scripts, JavaScripts, and applets offered for public use, as well as tutorials on writing your own. While found and "borrowed" scripts are convenient, they tend to reappear on many sites. Some of the authoring packages come with compilers or with automated functions that can be used throughout the sites you build. If your Web site is on an ISP's server, call their Webmaster to find out if there is support for CGI scripts and if so, which ones and whether or not they are CERN or NCSA.

Fusion provides the easiest insertion of multimedia elements and ships with a few of its own. Prefab Java applets are provided in the Plugins directory of the Parts folder. Those that are there to use are very basic: an LED clock, a counter, and a tickertape applet. If used conservatively, these common applets can be tasteful additions to your site. To insert an applet within the page you simply click on a button and draw a box where you want it placed.

Those who have gone to the trouble to download huge video files of their favorite bands will most likely prefer to stream and view the clip within their browser window. But many people will want to go beyond mere moving pictures to be able to create an interactive environment— an environment that, through a combination of sounds, images, and scripted functions such as forms or JavaScript enhancements, provides different ways to access information for those who will come to their site. Movie and sound files are pretty easy to work with, but choosing the best way to serve one or both in a form that will be most widely received requires knowing a little about the different technologies.

The new Shockwave with Streaming Audio plug-in delivers fairly high-fidelity sound with controls that you design and script in Director. RealAudio controls the streaming audio market and supports *multicasting,* or the serving of multiple streams simultaneously. Whereas with RealAudio products, server software is required, with Shockwave none is necessary, making it more convenient to serve. Both require a third-party plug-in or application for playback, although Navigator 3.0.1 streams various audio formats automatically with its LiveAudio architecture.

Third Parties: Macromedia Shockwave

One year ago the hot topic was Netscape's integration of Java applets and Shockwave within the Navigator 2.0 environment. The announcement from Netscape virtually rocketed the Internet frenzy into, well, cyberspace. Shockwave is part compression scheme, part MIME type that uses

AUTHORING TOOLS

a plug-in to take advantage of Netscape Navigator's open architecture. Macromedia provides the Shockwave Afterburner application which highly compresses files for maximized Web download. These files then open and perform a wide range of scripted functions within the browser page, even interacting with the server in some cases. Afterburner is available free at Macromedia's Web site. A MIME extension allows a document to retain its original media type when communicated over the Internet via HTTP. Different MIME types are denoted by different extensions to the file name, such as .gif and .jpg for image files; .aiff, .au, and .ra for audio files; and .mov, .qt, and .mpg for video files.

Originally Shockwave was only available for Director 4.0, but now you can use it with three of Macromedia's bestselling applications: Director 4.0+/ 5.0, Freehand 5.5 and Authorware 3.5. Though the applications themselves are expensive, they are quality tools that can be used for many purposes.

Configuring Your Server   To support the new Shockwave MIME type, you will need to tell your server how to recognize it. This is what is known as configuring your server. To configure your server to support a Shockwave MIME type you first need to determine the platform (NCSA, Netscape, Apache) and then update the relevant files. The correct way to configure an NCSA server is to open the srm.conf file and add:

```
AddType application/x-director dir
AddType application/x-director dcr
AddType application/x-director dxr
AddType image/x-freehand fh4
AddType image/x-freehand fh5
AddType image/x-freehand fhc
AddType image/x-freehand fh

AddType application/x-authorware-map aam
AddType application/x-authorware-seg aas
AddType application/x-authorware-bin aab
```

Different brands of servers will need to be updated with variations on this format (for more information, go to http://www.macromedia.com/support/technotes/shockwave/servermain.html).

Shockwave for Authorware and Database Support   Authorware 3.5 is an interactive multimedia application that is used for many different projects and is now Shockwave-compatible. Authorware 3.0 comes with ODBC drivers for Windows that allow you to connect to most major databases from the Authorware applet. Unfortunately, at this time Authorware is only Shockwave-compatible for intranets.

AUTHORING TOOLS

The Low Cost Animation Solution—GIF89a

If you are looking for an inexpensive solution to Web animation that also respects the limits of your bandwidth, you need to look into GIF animations accomplished through the use of the GIF89a graphic format. Any series of images can be converted to a scripted GIF animation that can retain attributes such as delay settings on individual frames, transparency, and loop. To save the bandwidth that would be consumed by a Shockwave or QuickTime or AVI movie, convert them into numbered PICT files which in turn can be saved as GIFs. GIF89a files are stored in the browser's cache and and do not require external plug-ins or appllictions to play. Both the Microsoft and Netscape browsers support the GIF89a file format. Try to find an animated image on the Web, save it to your hard drive, and open it to learn about different settings.

For this kind of animation, GIFBuilder 0.4+ for the Macintosh and GIF Construction Set and Autodesk Animator for Windows are useful products. Reports have it that Netscape will offer support for audio-enhanced GIF animations somewhere down the road.

The Programs

The four site authoring programs covered here all offer the basics for HTML editing, but vary in the quality and number of other authoring capabilities they provide. All are WYSIWYG, but only NetObjects Fusion is drawtool-based. LiveWire, with its healthy supply of development tools, will appeal to those who like to tweak code by hand while Adobe SiteMill will force you to do all your tweaking with no tools. For the quick and dirty corporate site, Microsoft FrontPage does the job. NetObjects Fusion will also work, and if you are part of a team that includes engineers and designers, Fusion's Assets Manager and DataObjects and SmartObjects Libraries will make site design less tedious.

Most Netscape extensions are supported by all the programs, except that SiteMill lags behind its HTML editor sibling, PageMill 2.0. JavaScript, Shockwave, and ActiveX integration can be had in various combinations though the most useful one to have is JavaScript support. Tools for handling the other two can easily be added manually.

The pricing of the products ranges from $100 for the LiveWire packages to $650 for NetObjects Fusion. SiteMill retails for $299 and FrontPage comes in around $150, but only the latter supports HTML 3.0 and 3.2 standards.

Netscape LiveWire 1.0 and LiveWire Pro

Netscape's LiveWire and LiveWire Pro are Web site authoring and management tool suites based around Netscape Navigator Gold 3.0 (which was covered in detail in Chapter 15). LiveWire is available for Windows 95, Windows NT, and Unix and offers connection to all the most commonly used databases from Illustra, Informix, Oracle, and

AUTHORING TOOLS

Sybase. The heavy-duty version, LiveWire Pro, is only available for Windows NT and Unix and comes with a developer version of the OnLine-Workgroup high-performance SQL database from Informix.

Though this is a powerful set of tools, it is not for those afraid of programming, not to mention that the LiveWire Pro package occupies *85MB* of disk space on an NT machine and 50MB on a Unix machine! With either of the LiveWire packages, you get tools for site and link management, and for connecting your site to a database, and a JavaScript compiler. The LiveWire Site Manager, like NetObjects Fusion, uses drag-and-drop technology for restructuring the flow of information on your site. Link maintenance is covered by an external link checker and a global link updater. As with the other available applications, you can import your existing Web site for editing in LiveWire and then publish the updates to your site with the push of a button. You can also compile JavaScript applications to run on Netscape's FastTrack 2.0 and Enterprise 2.0 Web servers.

Microsoft FrontPage 1.1

Chapter 15's discussion of Microsoft FrontPage concentrated mainly on the text-based FrontPage Editor and the built-in Web creation tools. In this chapter we will discuss FrontPage's site management capabilities along with some of its expanded page and site construction functions such as *bots* and wizards. Bots are scripted functions that work with pre-fabricated PERL scripts and search engines provided by Microsoft. As always, Microsoft benefits from selling the operating system and from being a primary software provider for said OS. FrontPage integrates easily into Windows 95 and takes advantage of pre-existing packages such as Microsoft Office to provide convenient importing of Word documents and to work automatically with Excel databases.

Internet Assistants

Not long ago database interaction on the Web was primarily one way: Information was submitted by the browser and sent to a database by the CGI script where more likely than not, some poor intern was responsible for cleaning the "dirty data." With Microsoft's Internet Assistants, allowing Web browsers to access information stored on server-side databases is as simple as using any of Microsoft's Wizards. Microsoft Internet Assistants are a set of extensions to FrontPage that allow you to create inline access to Excel databases, PowerPoint presentations, and Word documents. The Internet Assistants are easy to use, template-based integration tools that minimize the need for scripting and Java. They are also available for Microsoft Word on both Windows and Macintosh platforms and Schedule+ for Windows only. Unfortunately the standard versions for Word only output as HTML 2.0, but for Internet Explorer 3.0 users there is a version that supports HTML 3.0.

AUTHORING TOOLS

NetObjects Fusion 1.0

NetObjects has predicated the construction of Fusion around what they see as a four-step site building process: creation of structure and navigation, creation of pages, application of style, and the publishing of the site. Most of the tools required for accomplishing all these tasks are incorporated in the Fusion package. When performing the layout of your site, the page is divided into three parts: the header, the body, and the footer. The designs you create in these three sections of the page, which are physically separated by maneuverable bars, are interpreted as HTML and then assembled when you post or preview. This is extremely convenient when producing a site with standardized headers and footers such as navigation bars and ad banners.

There is an elegance to the ease of use of the draw-based interface that can't be matched. You can drag text blocks, images, and media files anywhere on the page and adjust their size using the control handles on the window. Fusion handles importing all the most popular commercially available word processor formats, maintaining layout and font properties seamlessly. The insertion of the most common forms of Web-based multimedia such as sound, movie, JavaScripts and applets, ActiveX, and Macromedia Shockwave files are just a click of a button away. Correct tagging for linking to and embedding these files is provided with parameter controls accessed in the Properties palette.

Site publishing within Fusion is unbelievably simple. Having defined the site structure, created sectional templates, imported RTF documents from various word processing applications, incorporated multimedia files, and applied global styles to your site, you are ready to test your site. Through the Properties palette you are able to publish full and text-only versions of your site to a local or remote server. You are given the option of only staging changed assets for site maintenance. As Fusion manages and tracks all links and relationships between elements throughout the creation process it automatically knows which elements to update when necessary. The final word on NetObjects Fusion is that with a street price of approximately $650, it's a little steep but definitely comes chock full of power.

Adobe SiteMill 1.0

When evaluated for its site management abilities, SiteMill falls short of the mark established by Microsoft FrontPage and NetObjects Fusion, which both offer a multitude of administrative tools, as well as direct publishing of the site to the server. Instead, SiteMill functions more as a site design and construction environment and even there it suffers from lack of a true design or flowcharting tool. However, the SiteMill window is an improvement over the FrontPage Explorer window, leaving behind the clumsy flowchart structure for a stripped-down view that is easier to manage. SiteMill establishes a set of icons to communicate the condition of

AUTHORING TOOLS

global and local links centered around the Incoming/Outgoing Links buttons. You should probably wait until the next version is released, because it will incorporate more up-to-date HTML and should be available for Windows systems.

The Final Word

Site authoring entails a multitude of responsibilities that are best divided between a few individuals rather than left to one person or any single application. The programs discussed are enticing in the tools they offer, but for the most part they are still only page design programs, regardless of how they assemble the final product. And with this in mind, take the time to learn HTML. Any potential Webmaster who is looking for a way to avoid learning HTML will be hard pressed to keep up with the latest developments of the language, let alone deal with the inevitable problems that arise in staging and testing a site. If you are or plan to be a freelance Webmaster/designer you will need to create customized environments with scripted functions that require more than these applications offer, though Fusion and FrontPage make it easy to integrate your own customized style libraries. If you have those skills covered, then both of these programs can offer a lot to make your job run much smoother. The Internet Assistants that integrate with the Microsoft Office and FrontPage packages can speed the process of creating sites for corporatations, many of which already use the Office products. Both FrontPage and Fusion offer the ability to automate the inclusion of headers and footers and to integrate with all major databases. Finally, both come stocked with a healthy supply of templates.

If total integration is what you are looking for, you might want to give LiveWire 1.0 Pro a spin. It integrates with its own server software package and offers many of the same tools as NetObjects Fusion 1.0 and Microsoft FrontPage 1.1. Full database support and the built-in JavaScript compiler makes it a handy development environment. Microsoft also sells server software to complete the entire package.

Where true authoring comes in is in the creation of the flow of information on your site and built-in methods for accessing that information. Don't feel that you need to create a fancy site with all sorts of bells and whistles just to keep up with technological innovations. The best service you can do yourself and users of sites you create is to create a functional, intuitive method of navigation and an engaging mode for delivering content. Fortunately (and unfortunately, in some cases), there are no tried and true standards to fall back on. Every situation presents you with a different set of variables ranging from aesthetic choices to bandwidth considerations. Hopefully, you have the right tools for the job.

17 JAVA AUTHORING TOOLS

IF YOU'VE EVEN THOUGHT about building Web pages, chances are good that you've heard of Java. It is also likely that what you've heard has described Java as a supernatural gift from God—able to leap tall virtual buildings in a single bound. Unfortunately, the hype is so thick that the truth about Java is often hidden from view.

JAVA AUTHORING TOOLS

THIS HYPE HAS LED SOME to think of Java as a solution to all kinds of problems; sometimes there are easier solutions than Java, such as browser plug-ins and pre-existing CGI programs. It really depends on the situation at hand. If your problem involves rendering an unusual format—such as a TIFF file—developing a plug-in might make more sense. If you want to allow users of your pages to see how many times your pages have been accessed, a Perl script might be an easier solution than a Java applet. Java is extremely versatile, so if another solution is elusive, Java is likely the right choice.

Crazy Little Thing Called Java

So what is Java? No, it has nothing to do with coffee or an island in Polynesia. Here's a simple definition: It's a general purpose, object-oriented programming language. Obviously Java has much more going for it than just being a new language; it's only one among many. The nifty thing about Java is that its design makes it ideal for programming applications on the Internet and the Web.

Java was developed by a team at Sun Microsystems. They were interested in creating software applications for small, portable, and distributed electronic devices. Sun first attempted to use C++ to create these applications, but abandoned this approach because programs written in C++ have to be recompiled for each chip native to each particular electronic device: In other words, C++ programs have "closed" architecture. Programs in compiled languages like C are transformed into *bytecode;* the file holding this bytecode information is then executeable. On the other hand, programs written in interpreted languages like Perl remain in the language form until they are needed; at that time, the interpreter is called to perform the transformation.

By 1992, Sun decided that a new language was needed, and Java was born. Java was designed to solve the main disadvantage to compiling: Programs written in Java do not need to be recompiled by different chips—the language has "open" architecture.

An interesting aspect of Java's popularity is that there is nothing really new in Java. Java, in fact, is very similar in syntax to C and C++, and Java is not even the only architecture-neutral language. Not wanting to reinvent the wheel, Java's developers incorporated the best features from many of these older languages.

The Buzz About Java

"Architecture-neutral" is just one of many buzzwords that appears in Sun Microsystems's white paper on Java. Java is described as a "simple, object-oriented, distributed, interpreted, robust, secure, architecture-neutral, portable, high-performance, multithreaded, and dynamic language."

JAVA AUTHORING TOOLS

That's quite a mouthful! But what does it really mean? For the programming-lingo impaired, please refer to the handy Java-jargon-to-English dictionary, Table 17.1.

The relationship between Java and the Web is symbiotic, each helping to build and support the other. Java and the Web emerged at about the same time, and the popularity of the Web led the development team at Sun to see great potential in Java for the Internet: The Internet, and the Web in particular, is a distributed system lurking within myriad platforms. Since Java coding supports both multiple platforms and distributed systems, it is a logical choice for applications in this environment.

Today, Java is everywhere. Many of the most popular Web browsers support Java (see Chapter 5). Books abound on the subject of Java programming. Java is worming itself into all kinds of areas of the Internet, from business applications to VRML. For example, Java is being used by businesses to respond to customer orders right over the Web. Java can be

▪ Table 17.1   Java-Jargon-to-English Dictionary

Buzzword	English Equivalent
Simple	Java is relatively easy to learn because the number of language constructs has been kept to a minimum. Also, they are largely modeled after those of C and C++.
Object-oriented	Refers to a language that is built around objects. Instead of focusing on procedures, in the object-oriented paradigm the code-writing focuses on the data and methods to manipulate that data.
Distributed	Designed to support applications on networks. The Java.net package allows applications to access foreign files as easily as local files.
Interpreted	Java is actually both compiled and interpreted. You must compile Java source code, which creates Java bytecode. This bytecode soup then must be interpreted to execute.
Robust	Means that the language is highly reliable and that problems in the code are often caught at compiling time. Another programming buzzword for this is "strongly typed."
Secure	Takes security seriously. Java places a number of restrictions on memory allocation and bytecode verification in order to ensure that distributed code is not tampered with. It's worth pointing out that no language is entirely secure.
Architecture-neutral	The compiled bytecode produced by the Java compiler is not dependent on architecture. In other words, this bytecode can be interpreted on any number of machines: PCs, Macs, Unix machines and others.
Portable	Related to architecture neutrality. Java has no implementation-dependent aspects and has its own graphical user interface (GUI) structure, so you don't have to rely on the architecture of a particular machine, like the Macintosh, for example. The windows and boxes will work on any machine that can compile and run Java; you don't have to mutate your widgets for each platform your program is ported to.
High Performance	This refers to the language's relative speed of execution. Actually Java is nearly 20 times as slow as C! This is because Java is an interpreted language—compiled languages tend to be much faster than interpreted languages. But as mentioned above, Java is both. If speed is imperative, Java just-in-time compilers can be used to increase its speed to rival strictly compiled languages like C.
Multithreaded	Can work on more than one task at once. Most people take for granted the fact that their computer can run more than one application at a time—this ability is a result of multithreading.
Dynamic	This means that Java is adaptive. Classes can be loaded as needed, even across networks. Many key components are not bound until runtime: New objects can be dealt with even during runtime. In other words, not everthing in Java code needs to be set in stone before you run the program; Java can adapt to varying situations.

JAVA AUTHORING TOOLS

used to ask customers what they are looking for and then generate Web pages based on their answers. If customers like what they see, they can place an order right then and there.

Java's Cousin: JavaScript

There is some confusion about the difference between Java and JavaScript. They are very similar, but not synonymous. JavaScript was developed by Netscape (see Figure 17.1), who licensed Java technology from Sun. JavaScript, as the name implies, is a scripting language. Unlike Java, it is strictly interpreted (that is, interpreted without first having to be compiled).

■ **Figure 17.1 JavaScript was created by Netscape and Sun Microsystems. Netscape provides the best documentation for JavaScript.**

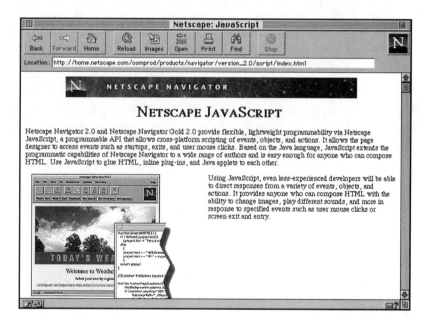

Both Java and JavaScript can be executed from within a Web browser—JavaScript is strictly interpreted from source code, while Java must exist in its bytecode form for a browser to deal with it. Both languages use similar code syntax and types. If you learn one, it is easy to learn the other.

Unlike Java, JavaScript programs live within HTML documents. Java programs can be called from HTML files—like CGI (Common Gateway

JAVA AUTHORING TOOLS

Interface) programs—but Java code does not inhabit these text files. Java-Script resembles a scaled-down, limited version of Java in basic syntax and types. It doesn't include Java's static typing and strong type-checking. Java-Script is said to be object-based, as opposed to being object-oriented—it uses built-in objects without classes or inheritance. For a list of Java-Script information resources on the Net, see Table 17.2.

Applets and Oranges

Java code can be used in two forms: applications and applets. A Java application is Java code that is independently executable. A Java applet, on the other hand, is dependent on a Web browser to run. The two forms use the same language, but are structurally different. Applets are usually—though not always—simpler in design. Applets exploit Java's inherent client/server advantage to its fullest: Programs can be loaded and run right over a network.

Applets are extended from the applet class package function that is built in to the Java language. Applets have more security restrictions than applications do. This is a result of the fact that applets are inherently distributed. Basically, Sun designed Java so that untrusted code can be run in a trusted environment. Applets exist at one location and can be called, loaded, and run at another location. This type of environment is very insecure—normally you would not want to download random programs that can run on your machine. That could be disastrous. To limit this danger, applets are severely limited in areas of potential security risk. If you are interested in applet security, take a look at Sun's Applet Security FAQ (http://java.sun.com/sfaq/index.html).

Applets are by far the most widely used form of Java on the Web today. Applets tend to be easier to write than stand-alone applications, which are used for Web development, but are most often limited to a CGI environment. Using stand-alone applications in conjunction with CGI can defeat many of the advantages of Java—other languages, like C++ and Perl, are usually better suited for CGI programming. C++ tends to

■ Table 17.2 JavaScript Resources

Site	Address
Netscape's JavaScript Documentation	http://home.netscape.com/eng/mozilla/3.0/handbook/javascript/index.html
JavaScript Index	http://www.c2.org/~andreww/javascript/
JavaScript Resource Center	http://jrc.livesoftware.com/
Gamelan's JavaScript Archive	http://www.gamelan.com/pages/Gamelan.javascript.html

JAVA AUTHORING TOOLS

execute faster than Java and Perl tends to be easier to learn. Also, both have larger libraries of preexisting programs available for use (see Chapter 18). Applets, like browser plug-ins, have the advantage of passing program execution from the server to the client. This can vastly ease processor strain inherent in CGI by distributing the work load onto many computers, instead of just one server.

Applets versus Plug-ins Applets also have a definite advantage over browser plug-ins (see Chapter 6). Plug-ins are a good solution for problems that involve file format compatibility because you can easily write and distribute plug-ins for formats that you intend to support on your Web site. But plug-ins are very limited in functionality and versatility because they have to be converted and developed for each platform they will run on. Applets, however, can be written once and ported to any machine with a Java-enabled browser.

You can write plug-ins to read in and display database documents created in applications like FileMaker Pro. Applets, however, allow for even greater possibilities. For example, with applets you can create your own unique database program configured any way you prefer.

The most significant advantage plug-ins have over applets is that plug-ins only need to be downloaded once, whereas applets are downloaded each time they execute. Downloading an application and data is obviously slower than downloading data alone. On the other hand, while many of the installers for plug-ins are very large—Adobe's Acrobat is nearly 5MB—applets tend to be significantly smaller, making for relatively fast load times. If you find Java applets irresistible and want to know more about Java, refer to the Java Resources listed in Table 17.3 below.

■ Table 17.3   Java Resources

Site	Description	Address
JavaSoft	Here's where it all began. The current version of the JDK (Java Development Kit) lives here.	http://java.sun.com/
Digital Espresso	All the news that's fit to print about Java. This is the place to follow news, trivia, and opinions about Java.	http://www.io.org/~mentor/jnIndex.html
Gamelan	The biggest archive of Java applets around.	http://www.gamelan.com/
Sun's Online Java Tutorial	Want to find Java documentation? This is the place to start.	http://java.sun.com/tutorial/index.html
Presenting Java Online Bibliography	This is a growing list of the books available on Java.	http://www.december.com/java/bib.html
Elliotte's Java FAQ	If you have questions, this document has answers.	http://sunsite.unc.edu/javafaq/javafaq.html
Java Resource List	One of the best resource lists available	http://www.rssi.com/info/java-info.html

JAVA AUTHORING TOOLS

Attack of the Killer Applets

If you find yourself trembling with fear at the thought of doing your own programming, there is an alternative. Namely, have someone else do it for you. There are a wide variety of Java applet resources available to save you the trouble of developing and implementing your own programs. There are large collections of code already written and freely available for you to download and reuse.

Much of this is available as source code, which you can modify to suit your needs without having much programming experience. In the same vein, there is a good amount of prepackaged software for sale. Packages of popular applets are bundled and sold by a variety of companies. Some of these packages offer customized or easily modified applets.

Applets for Many Purposes

There are now a growing number of applets available for use in Web pages—most of which are free. They include thousands of useful, if not extravagant, programs that add functionality to your pages. These freely available applets perform amazing tasks, limited only by your imagination and programming skill.

CGI Replacement Applets can deal with most of the problems CGI was designed to handle; for example, applets can create dynamic Web pages that generate information based on user input. Say you want to provide a search engine for your Web pages. An applet can prompt the Web user for the keyword and search through all the files you program it to search. You can also use this power to respond to user input and generate Web pages on the fly; with the click of a button, as another example, an article can be displayed in a different font size, background color, or font.

Graphical Interfaces Exploiting Java's graphical user interface, many applets use Java's built-in Advance Windows Toolkit (AWT) to create attractive graphical interfaces. Such interfaces are easy to build because Java provides packages for common interface components, such as buttons, frames, panels, and windows, with most of the programming work already done for you—although you can easily customize any component for your specific purpose. If you find a custom applet interface that you like, chances are good that the source code is available to examine. This can make development of your own gizmo much easier than you imagined.

Animation Java's popularity and fame is tied to Java applets' ability to load and render multimedia information on Web pages. While the GIF89a format has spread like wildfire through the virtual depths of the Web, Java applets have a distinct advantage when it comes to rendering full multimedia since. GIF89a is limited in animation capabilities, and is

JAVA AUTHORING TOOLS

clueless when it comes to synchronizing sound. Applets can clear this hurdle with elegant ease.

Games and Puzzles   A lot of the Java applets you'll come across are games or puzzles. If you want to attract the masses to your pages, why not include the proper virtual opiates? Today there are hundreds of options, from the very simple to fast-paced arcade-style games. The simple early puzzles like the one shown in Figure 17.2 have had to take a back seat to the new games now emerging that are comparable to regular arcade games. Icebox is one of the latter (see Figure 17.3).

Figure 17.2   This Rolling Cubes puzzle is a sure crowd-pleaser. Just click your way into gaming bliss.

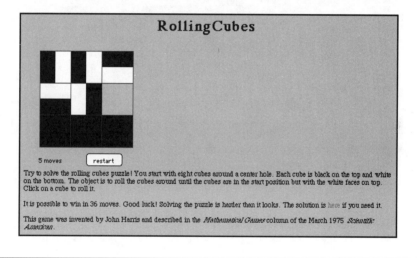

Dynamic Data Management   The real power of Java is its ability to handle dynamic data management. Games, puzzles, and multimedia are exciting, but Java is more than a cyber-circus clown. It is a powerful language capable of handling complex business applications. A great example of Java at work is the Automated Travel Agent (see Figure 17.4). This applet prompts the user for desired airline travel specifications (departing location, destination, date, and time), then searches databases for availability and price information, which it returns to the Web client. This is just one example of how Java can solve complex problems.

JAVA AUTHORING TOOLS

■ **Figure 17.3 Grumble no more, video heads: Applet arcade action has arrived to waste away your days on the Internet.**

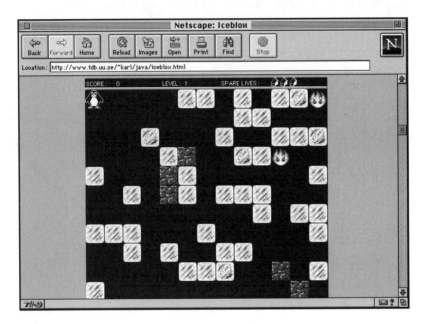

Finding Applets

Adding Java applets to your Web pages is a very simple task, but first you must get your hands on them. You can build them yourself, which we will cover in the next section, "Java Development Tools," or you can buy them in commercially-bundled packages. The easiest way to get them, however, is to download them from Java resource sites on the Internet. Arguably the biggest and best selection of applets is available at the Gamelan site (see Figure 17.5). This site houses thousands of applets—approximately 3,000 at the time of writing—broadly categorized by subject. Perhaps half of these applets also provide source code.

Java Development Tools

If you're a trailblazer on the cyber-frontier, you may be itching to build your own applets, but you'll need a few things to get started. Obviously the first thing you need is a working knowledge of the Java language. Refer back to Table 17.2 for a list of some popular online Java resources.

JAVA AUTHORING TOOLS

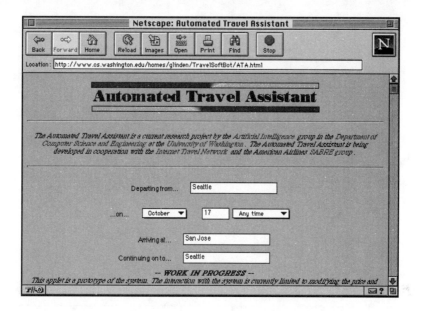

■ **Figure 17.4   The Automated Travel Agent is just one example of Java's power at work on the Web.**

These sites can help you in areas in which your programming skills are lacking. Online tutorials and FAQs are the best places to start, but there are also nice bibliographies available for those who want to curl up with a Java book.

The second thing you'll need is a Java-enabled browser or some other way to view applets. There are now a number of browsers that can load and run applets, including Netscape Navigator, Microsoft Internet Explorer, and Oracle's PowerBrowser. Another option is the applet viewer that comes with Sun's Java Development Kit (JDK). Another Sun browser, HotJava, is not a great choice because although it was the first browser to handle Java applets, it was designed to understand the alpha-release of Java and has not been updated to the current release of Java. Unfortunately, applets created with the current version of Java (1.0+) are not compatible with the alpha-version and vice versa. If you are having problems viewing an applet using HotJava, check the version to verify compatibility.

The third thing you'll need is a set of Java development tools. These consist of a variety of required or recommended tools, such as text editors, compilers, debuggers, GUI tools, and just-in-time (JIT) compilers. A

JAVA AUTHORING TOOLS

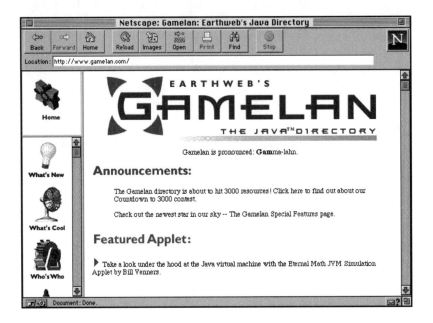

■ **Figure 17.5   Gamelan is the premier Java applet center. It provides information on more applets than any other site.**

text editor and a compiler are absolutely essential for creating and developing your own applets. The other tools are not required products, but can be extremely useful.

The Bare Necessities

A text editor is used to write Java source files. Just about any type of text editor will do. The only thing to keep in mind is that word processing programs like Microsoft Word and WordPerfect that add formatting must have a feature for saving the file without any program-specific tags. For example, Microsoft Word can be used if you save the file as "text-only;" if you save the file as "normal" it will not be usable by a Java compiler. If you are using a word processing program, you should use text files to code your Java source file.

The second necessity for writing Java applications is a Java compiler. There are now a large number of compilers available. The most basic is Sun's Java Compiler—now in version 1.0.2—which is included in Sun's JDK. This is a no-nonsense and barebones compiler that gets the job

JAVA AUTHORING TOOLS

done without the frills. The compiler is used to generate bytecode file that is readable and executable by applet viewers and Web browsers. These bytecode files have the .class extension, meaning that if you take a Java source code file called calculator.java and feed it to the Java compiler, the compiler will spit out "calculator.class".

Programming Profligacy: Java Junk Food

There are an increasing number of products available to ease your work and add to your programming power. There are a plethora of products to help you write better code, ease the creation of application components, and link your programs to other systems like databases and file servers. These gizmos are usually known as IDE (Integrated Development Environment) tools.

Better Compilers and Debuggers In the calculator example above, a successful compile was assumed. If you've spent any time at all programming, you'll know that this success never comes easy—even when working with relatively simple problems. You have to fight your way to coding nirvana and a good debugger is a great help in this struggle. When your car won't start, you turn to a mechanic to find out what's wrong; likewise, when your compiler chokes on your code, without any explanation, you look to your debugger for help. A debugger's job is to identify where the code took a wrong turn. The more information a debugger offers, the better it is.

Sun's Java Compiler comes equipped with a limited debugger. If a problem is found by the compiler, it will let you know which statement is the culprit and on which line it lives. Commercially available debuggers will do much more. Many will analyze your code, looking for both compiling errors and possible runtime errors. Many are also capable of offering optimization advice so that your code can achieve better memory utilization, speed, and efficiency. Going a step further, the better debuggers have visual tools, allowing you to find those errors more easily and wield more power in fixing them.

Compilers are not all created equal—some are better and faster than others. Commercial Java compilers tend to operate at much faster speeds than Sun's JDK. The compilers that stand alone are the just-in-time (JIT) Java compilers. A JIT compiler allows programmers to develop high-performance applications that need to be fast—faster than an interpreter will allow. A Java JIT compiler increases the speed of execution by a factor of 10, closing the speed gap between Java and C++. JIT compilers, unlike standard compilers, transform source code directly into native code—skipping the intermediate bytecode state.

JAVA AUTHORING TOOLS

Visual Tools   A source code editor is usually just a text editor with features especially designed for programmers. Some provide auto-indenting; indenting in a programming language is very different than indenting for text, and having this done automatically is a nice touch. These editors tend to support color-coded text in order to distinguish functions or classes from each other. Full-function source code editors also offer split-screen editing of multiple parts of a file at once. This is a nice feature for tracking down mismatched types and other elusive bugs.

A graphic class browser creates a graphical representation of the class hierarchies of your Java programs. This is a great tool for developers of larger applications and applets, since keeping track of a large number of subclasses and superclasses can become daunting. With a class browser, you can easily keep track of a variety of components—files, classes, data, functions, and source code.

So you want to build a nice GUI for your program, but you're getting frustrated because you can't seem to get it to look exactly they way you want. Since you have to keep compiling the file, over and over, to see the changes you are making, you're wasting a lot of time. You can save time by using a WYSIWYG (what you see is what you get) GUI tool. This sort of tool allows you to add text fields, buttons, panels, check boxes, and the like with the click of an icon. It's like using PageMaker to design your applets!

A project manager allows you to make better use of your time by organizating and automating frequently used tasks. Symantec Cafe's Project Manager (SPM) is a good example of this useful feature. It allows Java developers to drag and drop files between projects and supports multiple projects at once. It also keeps track of all your files in nested directories and remembers which files were used recently for easy access.

Extras   Still looking for more goodies to make programming Java easier? Some programs provide a built-in Java tutorial. So if you are rusty in a certain area, you can learn it as you're coding. For serious developers, many commercially available products include support for native functions for a variety of platforms. Many products also include easy methods for integrating functions written in your favorite language, like C++ or AppleScript, into your Java code. Finally, for high-end Java applications, there are products like BulletProof's JAGG to support ODBC (Open Database Connectivity) data integration, and the JDBC (Java Database Connection) Advanced Programming Interface developed by Sun.

JAVA AUTHORING TOOLS

Things to Look For

There are all kinds of features available in Java development tools. The trick is to isolate the ones you'll really need from the fad gadgets. If you're just interested in developing relatively simple applets for Web pages, then some of the features listed above are probably overkill for your purposes. Obviously those needing special features should know what they are looking for. It's safe to say that if a product is advertising an acronym you've never heard of, you probably won't ever use it.

Just as for any other kind of software, your chosen platform will limit the choice of products available to you. Up until recently, almost all Java development tools were written for either Windows 95 or Unix. This has now changed dramatically. Java is now ported to many other platforms, including Macintosh and Windows 3.2. Commercial developers of Java tools have followed suit and are now providing products for the major platforms.

The really useful products will provide speed, efficiency, and simplicity. Speed is very important: Who wants to sit around waiting for code to compile when you could be doing other things? Speedy compilers make your life much easier. The speed of just-in-time compilers is really only necessary for those who plan on using Java for real- life applications. They have little use for Web-related projects. Efficient graphics tools for controlling your development environment are a useful feature. They can help you find conflicts before they happen, and may help you out of problems when they do happen. And why write all your code by hand when you can click a button? Simplicity is at the heart of the programmer's credo: "Keep it simple, stupid." Development tools ought to follow the same rule. They should be organized around a logical design for easy, intuitive interaction.

Before jumping on the Java bandwagon, you ought to decide whether or not Java is useful for your needs. There are now many different possible solutions to typical computing and networking problems. Plug-ins, GIF89a, and freeware CGI programs all are possible shortcuts that avoid diving into Java. If your problems are such that Java is the only (or best) solution, the next step is to look into pre-written Java applets instead of reinventing the wheel. These programs are easy to use, but are often limited in their application to simple and popular computing tasks. If you are building a programming solution to a fairly unique problem, then the Java IDE's (Integrated Development Environment) are something to look into; the tools offered in it can make programming in Java much easier. To help decide what tools are right for you, see the comparison chart in Appendix Q of useful Java products.

18 CGI TOOLS

IF YOU'VE SPENT ANY TIME at all on the Web, you've probably visited one of the popular search engines like Alta Vista, Yahoo, or Inktomi. These sites provide an incredible volume of information, and would be extremely cumbersome if the information was limited to the static world of HTML. It would take literally hundreds of thousands of Web pages to catalog all the references they maintain.

CGI TOOLS

You are person number

0 1 2 3 8 1

who has tripped this counter since August, 1995

OF COURSE THIS IS NOT the way search engines operate. They use
something called CGI—Common Gateway Interface. *Gateways* are programs designed to handle requests for information from Web servers.
These programs then return the appropriate information to the requesting client. CGI is not a program, but rather a specification for how gateway programs should operate. In other words, it provides a common
language that allows Web clients, servers, and programs to communicate
with one another.

The ability to link HTML documents to executable programs creates
limitless possibilities. When a Web daemon retrieves an HTML document, the document is inherently static and does not change. On the
other hand, when a Web daemon accesses a CGI program, it can retrieve
dynamic documents which can do just about anything. For example, it is
nearly impossible to display the current time and date on a Web page
using HTML alone—you would need an army of people churning out
pages for every minute of the day. With CGI, however, all you have to do
is write a program that calculates the time and date when requested, orga-
nizes the information into a displayable form, and sends the information
back to the browser. This is the power of dynamic documents.

Popular Applications of CGI Programs

The clock example above is just the tip of the CGI iceberg. There are
many different ways to use this tool to create information for Web clients.
In fact, there are many ways to display a clock. The information can be
sent in the form of text. Even better, images can be created to represent
the digits 0 through 9. These images can then be used to create graphic
clocks that load onto Web pages. Taking this a step further is the ever-pop-
ular page counter. The number images can be used in conjunction with a
counting program to display the number of times a particular Web page
has been accessed. See the illustration below for an example.

Forms are arguably the most common application of CGI. They allow
Web clients to enter information that is processed in some fashion by a

CGI TOOLS

CGI program. Typically, this information might be the client's name and address. This information is passed to a program that catalogs the information for use by the owner of the Web page. Forms are also used to create a variety of documents that are e-mailed to a chosen destination by a CGI program. For an example of a form, see Figure 18.1.

■ **Figure 18.1 A form for making travel reservations**

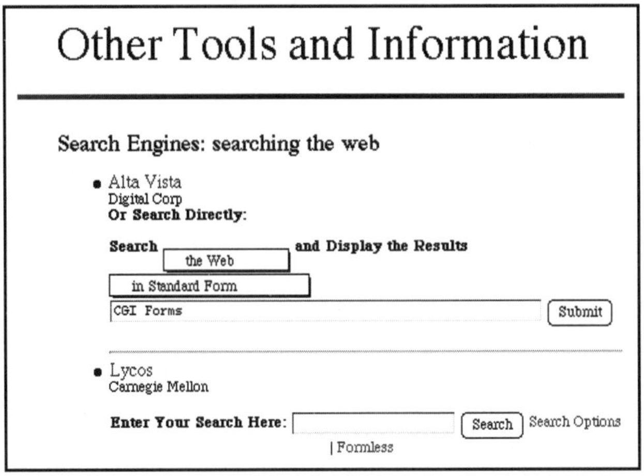

Forms are constructed within HTML using the <FORM> tag. Within the <FORM> tag are variables which include a METHOD and an ACTION. The *method* determines how the information is transmitted to the CGI program and the *action* determines which CGI program will receive that information. Here's an example of an HTML form line:

<FORM METHOD=POST ACTION="/cgi-bin/mailmerge.pl">

In this example, POST is the method used; another likely candidate is the GET method. The action is a reference to a program; in this case, it's mailmerge.pl. The ".pl" extension means that the file contains Perl code. This reference also contains a path to the program, which is in the cgi-bin directory. In other words, this command line passes information from the user through the POST method to the mailmerge program.

CGI programs can also be used to interface with non-HTML documents, such as databases. Suppose you use FileMaker Pro to maintain

CGI TOOLS

lists of people, products, or other information. You also want to make this information available to viewers of your Web page. A CGI program can solve your problem easily. All you have to do is write a program that reads in information from the FileMaker Pro document, turns the information into an HTML document, and sends the finished product to the browser. No need to produce tons of pages, no need to update the information daily—the program does it all for you.

As mentioned, search engines are very popular. If you maintain pages with large amounts of information, you might want to allow clients to search for information by subject. A CGI program can be made to search all the relevant documents by subject and return a list of possibilities to the browser.

These are just a few common examples of uses for CGI programs. There are many more, such as image maps, URL redirection, on-the-fly document creation, and animation. CGI is really limitless—if you can program it, CGI can deal with it. See Table 18. 1 for a list of sites that provide hosting information on CGI programming.

Under the Hood of CGI

So how does CGI work? CGI is a communication link between various components: the browser, the server, and the program. Since the program can be accessed at any time by many different browsers, most of the information destined for the program is contained within CGI environment variables. See Table 18. 2 for a list of common variables. The CGI program

---

■ Table 18.1   Sites Providing Further Information on CGI Programming

Site	Location
Web Developer's Virtual Library: CGI	http://www.stars.com/Vlib/Providers/CGI.html
NCSA's CGI Specifications	http://hoohoo.ncsa.uiuc.edu/cgi/overview.html
A CGI Programmer's Reference	http://www.best.com/~hedlund/cgi-faq/
The CGI Frequently Asked Questions	http://www.best.com/~hedlund/cgi-faq/faq.html
Learn to Write CGI Forms	http://www.catt.ncsu.edu/users/bex/www/tutor/index.html
CGI Environment Variables	http://hoohoo.ncsa.uiuc.edu/cgi/env.html
CGI.pm—A Perl5 CGI Library	http://www-genome.wi.mit.edu/ftp/pub/software/WWW/cgi_docs.html
CGI Debugging Tips	http://www.btg.com/scat/cgidebug.html
The CGI Programmer's Reference Library	http://www.eff.org/~erict/Scripts/reference_library.html
The Common Gateway Interface	http://www.stars.com/Seminars/CGI/
Server Side Includes	http://www.webcom.com/~webcom/help/inc/include.shtml

CGI TOOLS

can also access any HTTP request headers received by the Web server from the browser. Finally, the program can receive information via standard input through the POST form method, mentioned earlier.

All information sent by the browser is URL encoded, just as data input into HTML forms is.

This encoding entails turning spaces into + marks, special characters like the tilde (~) into their hexadecimal equivalents, and separating name/value pairs with an equal (=) sign. Such pairs are then separated from one another with an ampersand (&). The CGI program must then extract the information it needs from this digital soup. See Figure 18.2 below for an example of how Alta Vista sends information to the search engine through URL encoding.

■ **Figure 18.2   A simple query in URL encoding**

Location: `http://altavista.digital.com/cgi-bin/query?pg=q&what=web&fmt=&q=CGI+Forms`

After the CGI program receives and processes the information, it returns information to the server. It does this with parsed headers. Any information in these headers not specific to the server is then passed on to the browser. Most servers allow CGI programs to bypass the server, returning information directly to the browser. If this mode is used, then

■ **Table 18.2   CGI Environment Variables**

Environment Variables	Description
AUTH_TYPE	Authentication of web browser
CONTENT_LENGTH	Length of string representing user input
CONTENT_TYPE	Type of data accompanying the CGI request
PATH_INFO	Additional path information for the CGI script
QUERY_STRING	User data when the request method is GET
REMOTE_ADDR	IP address of the requesting Web browser's host
REMOTE_HOST	Requesting Web browser's host
REQUEST_METHOD	HTTP request method
SCRIPT_NAME	Virtual path and name of the CGI script
SERVER_NAME	Domain name or IP address of the Web server's host

CGI TOOLS

the program must supply a nonparsed header. This header is made up of HTTP response headers that the browser can understand. See Table 18.3 for a list of some of these headers.

Alternatives to CGI

CGI is only one way to create dynamic documents for Web browsers—there are other alternatives. Other server-side systems for calling programs are Server Side Includes (SSI) and Application Programming Interface (API). Each has its advantages and disadvantages. These systems can often be used in conjunction with one another.

SSI works by way of server command lines included within a HTML document. When the Web server finds such a command tag, it inserts the dynamic data into the HTML document as it is transmitted to the browser. SSI has an advantage in that its command lines are extremely easy to change if necessary, and are therefore very adaptable. This ease of use and adaptability is the trade-off for their inherent lack of power.

API is a system where code is loaded directly into the Web server. The code used to generate dynamic documents does not exist as a separate entity. Instead, the code exists as part of the Web server's code, effectively extending its capabilities. Because of this, API can do things that CGI can't. The main advantage of API is that it tends to need less processor overhead than CGI and SSI. API applications are actually loaded at server start-up time and run alongside the server. This advantage is also API's drawback: As part of the server system, a bug in the API can affect the server itself. Thus, there's a great deal more work involved in setting up and maintaining API extensions than in some other methods of creating dynamic documents.

Other alternatives to CGI programming include moving the processing of dynamic documents from the server to the client. This topic is discussed in the Chapters 5 and 6. Whenever possible, moving processing to

■ Table 18.3   HTTP Response Headers

Header	Description
CONTENT-ENCODING	Identifies type of encoding used
CONTENT-LENGTH	Byte length of the returning document
CONTENT-TYPE	Type of returning data, such as text/html
DATE	Creation date of the requested object
LAST-MODIFIED	Date of the last modification of the requested object
TITLE	Document title

CGI TOOLS

the client is a big advantage, resulting in less strain on the server side. But CGI is much more flexible and can handle many problems that have no solution on the client side.

CGI and Security

CGI can do what it does precisely because you are allowing others to run programs on your system. This is not the safest situation. All CGI programs need your utmost attention when it comes to the issue of security. Otherwise, your system could become a playground for cyber-intruders.

The first step in securing your CGI environment should be to create a special directory for all CGI programs. This is usually called the cgi-bin directory. This directory can be configured so that you—and no one else—can create new programs in this area. In fact, many system administrators do not allow users any access to this directory, thereby preventing potentially disastrous mistakes.

SSI command line tags, if available, should be disabled from program directories. Having SSI available in conjunction with CGI programs that collect input from users can be dangerous because instead of inputting the information your CGI program requests, such as a name or mailing address, someone could input an SSI command. For example, the following line of SSI code could retrieve the password files from your system if entered as input in a CGI program:

```
<!--#exec cmd="cat /etc/passwd" -->
```

To protect against security breaches, the safest method is to write security into your program code. For instance, you can easily write a routine that checks all user input for SSI statements like the one above, rejecting them if found.

This is one of the advantages of client-side scripts—the Webmaster has fewer worries about security when programs are executed on another machine. In that situation the security issue is passed to the Web client, who now must take appropriate steps to secure his or her system.

CGI for the Non-programmer

CGI can still be useful even if you have little or no experience with programming. A large amount of software is already written and readily available—much of it for free. Obviously, such programs are rather generic and perform only basic tasks. Anything unique or customized for a particular purpose requires some individual programming input.

Freely available CGI scripts support many popular tasks, including counters, clocks, shopping carts, search engines, and URL redirection. There are many other CGI scripts available as well. They are usually

CGI TOOLS

packaged and compressed into tar, gunzip, or PKzip documents. All you usually have to do to use them is download the files, uncompress them, place them in proper directories, configure a file or two if necessary, and include a call to the program within your HTML files. Everything else ought to have been done for you.

This assumes that your system is set up to deal with CGI and whatever script the program is written in. If you are unsure about whether or not CGI is supported on your system, ask your system administrator. Your system administrator should also be able to tell you how to configure your CGI scripts so that they are executable. This entails letting your system know that the script files are programs and telling the system how to execute them. If the script is written in Perl, for example, the system needs to know that and also to know where the Perl interpreter is located.

If you are interested in browsing CGI software libraries, see Table 18.4 below, which lists some archives of popular CGI programs. Figure 18.3 shows the CGI Collection page where you can find many freeware or shareware CGI products.

In addition to free CGI software, there are also commercially available products. Typically these products are better supported, more customizable, and perform more tasks. For a comparison chart of available freeware, shareware, and commercial CGI programs, see Appendix S.

CGI for the Programmer

To build your own CGI programs, the first requirement is that you have to know how to program in at least one language. The more you know, the better, but one is the minimum. You'll have to understand CGI environment variables so that you can get your Web components to speak the same language. You'll have to know how to code headers for output so

■ Table 18.4   CGI Software Archives

Name	Location
Chris Stephens's CGI archive	http://128.172.69.106:8080/cgi-bin/cgis.html
CGI Scripts at NCSA	ftp://ftp.ncsa.uiuc.edu/Web/httpd/Unix/ncsa_httpd/cgi
Perl Modules List	http://perl.com/perl/info/cool_modules.html
Matt's Perl Script Archive	http://worldwidemart.com/scripts/
Otis's Perl Scripts	http://www.middlebury.edu/~otisg/Scripts/index.shtml
Selena Sol's Public Domain CGI Scripts	http://www.eff.org/~erict/Scripts/scripts.html
The CGI Collection	http://www.selah.net/cgi.html
The IntrAnet Resource Site's CGI Script Pages	http://www.frontiertech.com/swebres/VB.HTM

CGI TOOLS

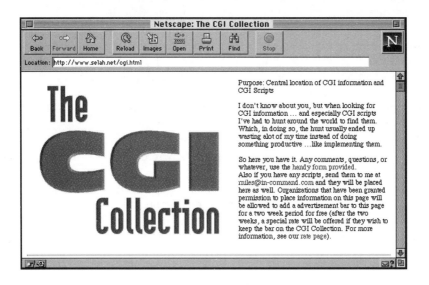

■ **Figure 18.3   The CGI Collection is a great archive of freeware and shareware programs that you can use with your Web pages.**

that communication between server and browser can occur. It's also a good idea to be familiar with <FORM> tags.

The second requirement is the necessary software. Aside from the programs you will write, you'll need additional software to deal with your code. Namely, you'll need either a compiler for compiled languages like C and C++, or an interpreter for a language like Perl. You'll also need an HTTP server that is compatible with CGI.

The first real programming step is deciding what task you want accomplished. Perhaps you want to develop a customized form that receives input from users and e-mails the results back to you. Check around to find out if such a program already exists. Why reinvent the wheel? If it does and it's free, then you may not want to write a new program yourself. Even if the program is not perfectly suited to your requirements, it may be similar enough so that you can modify the code instead of starting from scratch.

Once the task is identified and you know that there are no similar programs already available, then it's time to think about writing one yourself. The next decision is which language to use—unless you only know one! It is worth pointing out that some languages are better suited for certain tasks than others. The most popular languages used for CGI programs include

CGI TOOLS

Perl, TCL, Visual Basic, C, and C++. Two others worth mentioning are AppleScript and Unix Shell script—both are popular but platform-specific.

While popular languages like C and Perl are not platform-specific, it is important to pick a language that is readily usable on your platform of choice. For example, if you program on Windows, yet don't feel like paying for a fancy compiler, you may not want to choose C.

The next thing to address when choosing a language is which one is best suited for the task at hand? Simple tasks can be accomplished with less complex languages like Perl, while a language like C++ is better suited for extremely complex tasks. Of course these decisions are subjective: What do you know, what do you have, what are you willing to learn, and what are you willing to spend? If you're still not sure, take a look at Table 18.5 for the addresses of information archives on some popular CGI languages.

Perl

Perl is an acronym for Practical Extraction and Report Language—though some claim it stands for Pathologically Eclectic Rubbish Litter. It was created and developed by Larry Wall as a language for processing text. Since then Perl has evolved into something much bigger. It is now a full-blown programming tool, borrowing some of its structures and syntax from C.

Perl is by far the most popular language for CGI. In fact, CGI programs are often referred to as CGI *scripts*. This is a result both of Perl's popularity and the fact that it is an interpreted language. Perl code is written and placed into text files, known as scripts. These scripts are read into an interpreter at runtime, as opposed to languages like C that are compiled before runtime into executable byte-code.

The fact that Perl is interpreted means that, task for task, it is slower than compiled languages. This also means that if you have a Web server

■ Table 18.5   Sites with Information on Popular CGI Programming Languages

Name	Location
Perl Resources on the Net	http://infoweb.magi/com/~steve/perl.html
TCL FAQ	http://www.sco.com/Technology/tcl/tclFAQ/ part1/faq.html
The C Programmer's Pages	http://pitel_lnx.ibk.fnt.hvu.nl/~rbergen/cmain.html
VB FAQ	http://www.smartpages.com/faqs/visual-basic-faq/ general-info/faq.html

CGI TOOLS

that is overburdened with heavy traffic, Perl may make matters worse because it requires extra processor resources to interpret for every execution. But Perl's disadvantages are often overshadowed by its positives. Perl has strong string matching which makes it ideal for CGI tasks. Perl also makes it extremely easy to develop software quickly (as opposed to a language like C), making it a likely choice for basic CGI applications.

TCL

TCL stands for Tool Command Language. It was created and developed by John Ousterhout at the University of California at Berkeley in 1988. TCL, often pronounced "tickle," is a useful language because of its portability. In other words, it can be run on many different types of platforms, like Unix and Macintosh.

TCL in many ways resembles Perl. It is interpreted and has strong string manipulation capabilities just like Perl. Like Perl, TCL is freely available for anyone to use. The key difference is that TCL has better support for a graphical user interface. TCL is often available as TCL/TK, where TCL is the basic programming language and TK refers to the Tool-Kit of widgets. Widgets are graphical objects, like other components of a GUI. TCL has an advantage over other languages that use graphical objects because it doesn't require C or C++ to manipulate the widgets.

However, most CGI scripts do not have a need for graphical interfaces—HTML takes care of that. So TCL is not often touted as the best tool for CGI. The real advantage of TCL is that it can talk to many other languages. If you have libraries written in another language, TCL can readily use that code. Packages now exist so that TCL can interface with C, C++, Unix Shell scripts, Modula-3, Prolog, and Perl.

C/C++

The C language was developed by Dennis Ritchie in 1978 for the original Unix platform. C derives its name from its predecessor, language B of Bell Laboratories. When it was created, C differed from its counterparts in that it was not machine- or platform-specific. It could be used on a variety of systems. Today, C is just one of many platform-independent languages.

C++ is based on C, and as its name hints, it has some pluses. C++ was originally called "C with classes" and was developed by Bjarne Stroustrup. It is a fully object-oriented language, meaning that programs are structured on objects or representations of data. C++ implements all the buzzwords of the object-oriented programming paradigm: encapsulation, inheritance, dynamic binding, and polymorphism. The differences between the two languages are large enough to make the transition from C to C++ a challenge for programmers.

CGI TOOLS

C and C++ are not for the programming novice. They are both complex and powerful languages whose advantage is speed: Both are compiled programs. This is a real plus for CGI programmers. Many CGI applications can cause a strain on processor resources. C's speed can lessen the burden, calling on the processor for much shorter periods of time. Typically, a compiled language like C is ten times as fast as an interpreted language.

Visual Basic

Visual Basic, or VB, is a programming language developed by Microsoft. VB was created with the intent of providing a language for quick and easy development of applications for Windows. Visual Basic accomplishes this objective by providing a graphic, drag-and-drop programming environment. This environment allows you to construct a user interface that is easily constructed and code is then used to bond the elements together.

VB, like C and C++, is a compiled language. It is therefore faster executing than Perl or TCL. Visual Basic has an advantage over C and C++ in that it is easier to learn—programming novices will become productive much faster with VB. Unfortunately, this ease also means that VB is not as powerful as C and C++—more complex programming tasks will usually require C or C++.

Compilers and Utilities

When looking for a compiler for your favorite language, there are some key differences to be aware of. Some compilers are strictly bare-bones— they compile (if you are lucky) and that's it. Others come equipped with a variety of utilities to make the programmer's life much easier.

A debugging tool is a programmer's godsend. If you've ever tried to compile programs without one, you'll know why this is so important. When your program doesn't compile, you're left to guess what the problem is unless you have a debugger. A good debugger will assist you through the code, pointing out problems as they arise. The best debuggers will analyze your code, finding ways to improve it, and saving memory by making your code faster and more concise.

A graphical programming interface is also a nice touch. Drag-and-drop features are very helpful. A toolkit makes programming GUIs from scratch much more enjoyable. GUIs are usually not necessary for CGI programs, but when they are a GUI utility is helpful.

CGI TOOLS

Summary

It should be apparent that building CGI programs from scratch isn't so much about purchasing products as it is gathering a knowledge base. The only product really necessary is a compiler or interpreter. The rest springs from your knowledge and creativity.

Certainly the price of a product will be a major influence. But more than in the other categories in this book, choosing a compiler or an interpreter really is rooted more in what you know (and can use) than the bottom line. For example, a Perl interpreter available for free is of little use to you if you know nothing about programming in Perl. For a comparison chart of many popular compilers and interpreters, see Appendix R.

19 VRML TOOLS

SINCE THE WEB'S FULL COLOR DEBUT in 1994, the Internet community has been chanting the mantra "Cyberspace is upon us." *Cyberspace* is the term coined by William Gibson to represent a networked computer space where people will someday communicate and interact. The Web facilitated such a network of human to human communication via computer networks, and people often refer to sites as being "here" or "there," someplace to visit or return to, like a real place. We have "home" pages and "work" sites—the spatial metaphor is ubiquitous.

VRML TOOLS

BUT THERE IS NO REAL "SPACE" in a two-dimensional hypertext creation, since there can't be space without a third axis, usually called the *z axis,* to provide three-dimensionality. *VRML,* or *Virtual Reality Modeling Language,* is the standard tool for putting the *space* in cyberspace and bringing three dimensions to the Web in what is commonly known as *virtual reality* or *VR.* VRML is a text-based file format that specifies how to make shapes (objects) and position these objects within 3-D networked *worlds* and *rooms.* It also specifies how to add sound, video, animation, lighting, camera angles, and more. The latest version of the specification, VRML 2.0, is thick with VRML possibilities. As a leading-edge Web designer, it's imperative that you know what VRML is and how to navigate it, but more importantly, how to build with it.

This chapter is all about VRML. It covers everything from what VRML is, how to use it, and the tools to create it, to the browsers available to see it. Keep in mind that VRML is a young industry and the tools are mostly just entering the prototype stage (with a few exceptions). This chapter was written using information from pre-releases, projected features specifications, prototypes and white papers. The material covered is most likely to change to some degree. However, the identity of most of the major-player companies, most of which are discussed here, is not likely to change. The best way to get updated information about these companies' products and new developments is to regularly check their corporate Web sites—all the URLs are included in the VRML tools comparison chart found in Appendix S.

How It Began

Knowing a bit of VRML's history, what the original vision of its developers was, and how it has evolved, will give you a broader understanding of VRML's functions and why it's such a revolutionary and valuable technology. I firmly believe that VRML is, as Tony Parisi, co-creator of VRML has often said, "as important as the invention of the wheel."

Of course people have been dreaming about 3-D networked worlds for some time, but VRML, as it is known today, began in late winter 1993 with a living room conversation between graphical interface expert Tony Parisi and networks superhero Mark Pesce. Both had a vision of 3-D networked environments that would improve data visualization, but more importantly would build community and improve human to human communication. Encouraged by prospects for the future success of the World Wide Web, Parisi and Pesce immediately set out to build a browser to view 3-D over the Internet and a few months later had a working copy of Labyrinth, the first VRML browser, viewing a 3-D banana. The browser and their idea for a 3-D Internet standard based on their work was presented to the First WWW Consortium in Geneva, Switzerland, and

VRML TOOLS

quickly gained the support of Tim Berners Lee (founder of the Web) and the Internet community.

Brian Behlendorf of *Wired* started a VRML mailing list to solicit ideas for a 3-D Web standard, and from there the official standard was born. With the input of a few dozen hypergeeks and the critically important Open Inventor 3-D file format from SGI (made public through the efforts of Gavin Bell and Rikk Carey), the VRML 1.0 specification became a reality in May, 1995.

The second version of the specification, VRML 2.0, was finalized at SIGGRAPH 1996, in New Orleans (SIGGRAPH is the oldest, and most widely respected computer graphics conference). It is this version, 2.0, that has sealed VRML as the official 3-D standard for the Web. Both Netscape and Microsoft have acknowledged it as such, along with hundreds of other Internet and 3-D hardware- and software-related companies.

Perhaps the most beautiful component of VRML is the original vision of community that inspired Parisi, Pesce, and VRML's early adopters. It's been noted that no other Internet standard or technology has evolved as quickly or as fluidly as VRML, which is probably due, at least in part, to the fact that this vision was maintained, even at some dark political hours. The camaraderie of the VRML community encouraged companies like Microsoft, which has traditionally relied on closed systems architectures (proprietary solutions) to gain power, to contribute its ideas and technology research to the collective standards setting process. Literally, the VRML Architecture Group (VAG) and the VRML mailing list made a mockery of those companies unwilling to share and participate, and for the sake of saving face more than a few businesses did in fact change their attitude. Silicon Graphics, for example, earned itself a bit of a reputation for trying to dominate the standard, and its heavy-handed efforts were quickly squelched, again by the VAG and the VRML mailing list. Because VRML also had the solid support of Netscape, a company also built on the idea of open standards and community-based technologies, the Internet business community had little choice but to support VRML and its non-traditional methods of development—Everyone who was anyone needed to be close to Netscape and follow its lead.

This idea of a real community in a virtual world is important to developing your own patch of cyberspace. Creating virtual worlds is significantly more complex than just plugging in objects and pretty backgrounds. You'll need to think as much about social engineering, psychology, and community as about nuts-and-bolts programming, and worlds built with this in mind will be dramatically more successful than worlds slapped together simply for the sake of building worlds. Just as cottage industries have arisen to celebrate the worst of the Web—those static home pages with pet pictures and CD collection listings—worlds built without human

VRML TOOLS

factors deliberately added into the equation will most likely fail. Use VRML tools in conjunction with a solid development plan and a strong awareness of social space to help create an amazing cyberspace.

What Are You Going to Build?

It's a common misconception that VRML, as with many new technologies, offers strictly entertainment-based possibilities. This is because the entertainment industry is traditionally the first business class to reach out to emerging technologies. Several gaming companies, including Sega, Sony, 3D0, Electronic Arts, and more, are planning either to build VRML worlds or participate in other corporate worlds, to provide 3-D, interactive, multiuser gaming. Additionally, Hollywood staples like Warner Brothers, Fox, and Paramount will most likely provide movie theaters, 3-D sitcoms, and entertainment spaces very soon. Sony has already launched a multiuser Cable Guy VRML site. It's easy to imagine rock concerts, cartoons, and live chats with movie star avatars (an *avatar* is a three-dimensional representation of a person).

VRML will also be used for education, both in the traditional schooling sense (community outreach, long distance education, and seminars) and in technical training areas as well—Gateway 2000 has been using VR for years to teach its technicians how to remove and install memory chips, video cards, and other products. VRML provides an excellent forum for educating those living in long-term medical facilities and those who cannot leave their homes due to physical limitations, aging, or illness. Imagine visiting a VRML site sponsored by Toyota that teaches you how to change your oil. Maybe you want to visit a museum and see all sides and angles of its latest sculpture exhibit. Or perhaps you might like to browse through a local library and meet with your kids in the story reading room, from work!

And let's not forget the business applications. Advertising is hot for VRML. Corporate branding on the Internet will take a whole new turn as companies pop 3-D Coke cans into nightclubs, or create Zima bottles that follow you home. *Data visualization,* a hip buzzword as of late, is another business application that would visually reorganize traditionally flat concepts like files, database fields, and catalogs. Maybe you'll soon browse a 3-D J. Crew database catalog, only instead of just seeing those snappy new khakis on your screen, you'll have a custom avatar, built to your size, that can try the pants on. Speaking of J. Crew, it's not a wild speculation that virtual malls are just around the corner, with virtual salespeople, virtual cars to test drive, and yes, virtual ATM machines. VRML is loaded with application possibilities.

VRML TOOLS

Today's VRML

It would be nice if browsing VRML was as easy as browsing the Web. Someday it will be as simple, but you're going to have to sit tight for a few more months. Be prepared for system crashes and memory-hogging behemoth browsers to cause a few headaches, not to mention the fact that not all worlds work with all browsers, despite the push for industry standards.

VRML, like HTML, now has proprietary extensions in addition to the set of commands included in the VRML 2.0 standard. Browsers that support the VRML 2.0 standard do not all support the proprietary extensions, and browsers that do support VRML extensions do not all support the same ones. This means that a world built and optimized for SGI's browser, Cosmo Player, might not look so good when viewed in Netscape's Live 3D browser. And while you might be able to view streaming video with streaming audio in the OZ Virtual browser, the same world might crash with another browser.

Navigation is also a challenge for VRML, mostly because the technology is so new, and so few people are familiar with navigating three-dimensional spaces. While it seems simple to veteran game players—push your mouse forward to go forward—you might be surprised at how many people pick up the mouse and wave it in the air, expecting to move. Also, while it is a standard feature on most Windows 95 VRML browsers to right-click and get a menu with walk, run, fly, and spin options, how many people really knows what those options mean? Running in most browsers is not all that much faster than walking, flying usually leaves users lost several "miles" from the original world, and spinning will most likely just cause nausea, at least until you've done it for a while.

Another navigation headache comes from clunky motion due to poor rendering speeds. Although it may seem optimal to maximize your browser window, making full use of that 17-inch monitor on your workstation, beware. Larger browser windows equal slower processing time because you have that many more pixels to re-render every time you move your mouse. Remember, VRML is not a static image of a 3-D space, it *is* a 3-D space that needs to change its perspective as you change yours. Unfortunately, the best way to view VRML, if you don't have a 200MHz machine with at least 80MB of RAM, is with a teeny tiny window, which of course squeezes much of the life out of those beautiful graphics that some poor artist spent weeks or months rendering.

Choosing a Browser

Never mind how difficult it can be to traverse VRML-land, it's equally challenging to pick the right type of browser for your needs. Browsers come in two main flavors, stand-alone and plug-in (meaning it "plugs in" to an existing Web browser), each with its own set of advantages.

VRML TOOLS

The plug-in variety seems to be the best option for many at-home VRML users because it's usually smaller in hard-disk space and memory requirements and lives inside your existing Web browser. This is beneficial because it facilitates easy linkage between VRML worlds and Web sites, making a near seamless transition between all the two-dimensional hypertext and three-dimensional VRML functions. There are many plug-ins for both Netscape and Internet Explorer. Additionally, both Netscape and Internet Explorer have VRML solutions now built directly into the browser, making a separate browser plug-in seemingly not necessary. But remember that different browsers support different functionalities. So even though Netscape and Internet Explorer support VRML, other plug-ins might better suit your browsing needs. For example, the spin function in Netscape's solution doesn't always work that well, and Internet Explorer's solution is often slow. Also, some people won't like the Netscape or Internet Explorer VRML interface, either because of aesthetics or placement of navigational tools.

Choosing a browser is like choosing a car: Some people like molded corners, some people like flashy colors, some people like cars that talk, while others rely heavily on a built-in digital compass. And while all cars share some standard features—steering wheel, four wheels, a carburetor—they also have all sorts of extra gizmos that are unique to the model of car and only relevant to personal preference. As far as browsers go, use the comparison chart in Appendix S to find browsers that supply the functionalities you desire, then test-run the browsers (they're all free anyway) to see which ones have the most pleasing design and most intuitive navigation for you.

For the best match of functionality and feel, some people may opt for a browser that doesn't function as a plug-in or sit inside an established Web browser. While these stand-alone browsers may be more taxing on your system resources, demanding more memory and more hard-disk space, they may support features you like or need for specific projects. Usually these browsers have faster rendering speeds and support both VRML and proprietary technologies. This is especially important to people who were working in the VR community pre-VRML and who have 3-D Web sites already up and running using a non-standards-based technology. Using a specific company's browser will enable you to not only browse that company's non-VRML 3-D worlds, but may also let you view VRML worlds. Many stand-alone browsers support hypertext functionality as well, enabling users to view both Web sites and VRML worlds from within the VRML browser. Unfortunately, most of these hybrid browsers aren't as up to date as Netscape or Internet Explorer in HTML support. If you're using a stand-alone browser, you'll probably have to open up a second browser at one point or another to maximize your Web experience.

VRML TOOLS

Features to Look for in a VRML Browser

Most VRML browsers support what's called *points of entry* or *viewpoints*. Points of entry can be preprogrammed positions within a VRML world (set at the time of the world creation) that lead users from view to view, or custom locations that you set yourself. The preprogrammed points of entry are helpful when visiting a site for the first time. Instead of wandering about on your own, you can select the next viewpoint or go back to the previous viewpoint to get a quick tour of the offerings. This, of course, is based on the assumption that the world's creators programmed in these viewpoints. Some browsers also let you add in viewpoints to create custom hot lists of areas within the world that you want to revisit in the future. Additionally, most browsers have a special option called Entry Point that will take you back to the first position in the world from wherever you are.

The walk, run, fly, and spin options (available in a menu that pops up by right-clicking in Windows 95, or by holding down the mouse button on a Mac) are self-explanatory, though different browsers handle these functions with different levels of competency. It's usually best, especially when first visiting a world, to select the walk option and use the arrow keys (as opposed to the mouse). While it's a little slow at first, walking will help you gain your bearings.

Lighting controls are also handled slightly differently by the various browsers. While most browsers offer the option to add or subtract all of the lighting in a world or just highlight specific areas, some perform these functions better than others. Additionally, when building a world, some browsers are generally lighter or darker, and it may be necessary to test several before finding the perfect one for you.

The wire frame feature is a nice option for people who want to zip through VRML worlds without bandwidth-hogging textures. The wire frame option removes the textures and replaces the geometry with wire frame images (a cube would look like it's shaped with wires instead of solid material) which dramatically increases rendering speeds due to the smaller file sizes of wire frames.

Some browsers have maps in the browser interface, others have extra window frames for chat, multimedia presentations, bookmark files, and additional options. And now there are even a few browsers that come with browser, avatar, and real-time world editing features built in. This furnishes more advanced users and developers with the opportunity for customization based on specific project needs. For example, if you were a developer and wanted to add an extension to the VRML standard, but didn't want to take the time to build your own browser to accommodate this feature, you could use such features. There are a few browsers that ship with a toolkit that includes browser pieces that can be added to or

VRML TOOLS

assembled in a variety of ways (assuming you know Java or C++). Eventually these toolkits will be simple enough for easy consumer customization as well. Likewise, custom avatar builders will be an important feature in browsers of the future; some browsers already support this feature. When you enter a world and choose an avatar, you may not like the hair color, or body shape, or maybe even the species. If your browser (and server) supports avatar customization, you can easily change such physical characteristics. Additionally, some of the avatar editors also let users, quite gracefully, add in simple behaviors like body motion and facial expressions (controllable from the keyboard).

System requirements are similar among all the VRML browsers: Most require a 32-bit PC running Windows 95. At the minimum, that PC had better have 12MB of RAM and 5 to 7MB of hard-disk space available. These are low estimates. It's common to use as much as 20MB of RAM to keep your browser from crashing, especially if you want to move smoothly through the space or support any type of animation, sound, or video. There are a handful of browsers for the Unix platform, and a precious few for the Mac. Additionally, SVGA monitors and graphics accelerator cards are highly recommended. Most browser companies are making claims that they will be fully cross-platform by 1997, so Mac and Unix users will just have to cross their fingers and hope the manufacturers make good on those claims.

Tools for Building VRML Worlds

Tools, tools, and still more tools. If you thought picking a browser was a difficult decision, try picking a VRML creation tool. It's been an industry-wide fact that it's almost impossible to create compelling VRML worlds (at this stage of the game) with a single tool. While there are a few simple authoring tools that output VRML 1.0 and 2.0 respectively, all you will get with simple products are simple worlds. That's not to say those worlds won't be beautiful, but textures and images will be significantly enhanced if you have the budget to support a few different types of tools.

Basic Editing Tools

There are several basic VRML editing packages, some with more features than others. An editing package will, at the most basic level, allow you to create shapes, position those shapes in a three-dimensional perspective, and move them around. Of the more advanced editors, some have libraries of JPEGs that can be cleverly substituted as textures (to keep file sizes low and image quality high), while others have libraries of existing rooms that are easy to rearrange, reconstruct, or redecorate with different colors and image choices. Still other editors have libraries of objects such as furniture, cars, clothing, avatars, and pets. A few editors have all of these

VRML TOOLS

features. Very few consumer-grade editing packages support actual rendering. The price of a solid editor without advanced rendering capabilities starts at $50, but if you add in modeling capabilities (the ability to create advanced shapes and textures), advanced behaviors, and intelligent agent properties (*intelligent agents* are objects that actually learn behaviors), you could easily spend several thousand dollars, never mind the cost of the hardware to support such gizmos. Some other basic editing features common to many software tools include a variety of camera angles to give the designer any desired perspective, drag-and-drop libraries, and familiar icons for cutting and pasting, relocating objects, and assigning URLs to objects in the space.

Almost all existing editors can export basic geometry using functionalities defined in the VRML 1.0 specification. Some have partial 2.0 functionality, which might include the ability to create animation and incorporate multimedia; a select few have full 2.0 functionality. Expect most editors to fully support VRML 2.0 by spring 1997. Most editors can also import a variety of 3-D file formats, so if you are lucky enough to have a rendering package you can create 3-D models, import them into your editor to add VRML functionality, and then export complete VRML files.

Rendering Programs   Some rendering packages themselves can export VRML files, denoted with the .wrl file extension label. While some rendering packages output VRML 2.0 files, most are designed to output VRML 1.0 files—which means geometry and textures only. In most cases, output to VRML 1.0 is acceptable since 2.0 functionality has more to do with multimedia and behaviors than geometry and textures. There are a number of converters (the most popular is available free from SGI's Web site at http://vrml.sgi.com) that convert 1.0 files to 2.0 files, if this is something you need. But again, most of the differences between VRML 1.0 and 2.0 are irrelevant to the modeling and rendering process. As long as your package exports VRML 1.0 files, you can add in the behaviors and animation either by hand or with a 2.0 conversion package like Cosmo WORLDS from SGI. The best rendering and modeling products to output VRML are 3D Studio Max from Autodesk, Extreme 3D from Macromedia, Lightwave, Power Animator 7.5 from Alias Wavefront (which is great for animations), Strata for the Mac, Pioneer, True Space, Fountain from Caligari, and Soft Image. A company from Iceland, OZ, has also made freely available a utility called Soft2Vrml which translates models and spaces from the Soft Image 3-D rendering package to VRML. You can get this small and easy to use utility at the OZ Web site (http://www.oz-inc.com). To use it, all you need to do is start the program and open the Soft Image file, and it will spit out VRML. The SGI converters for translating VRML 1.0 to 2.0 work the same way. It doesn't get much simpler than that!

VRML TOOLS

Customizable Editors   A few of the advanced editors for worlds, behaviors, and avatars are built in Java or C++ and are fully customizable with editor toolkits. This is handy for developers who know what extra functionality they want in an editing package: By putting together combinations of features, they can eliminate what they don't want, or add in extra goodies. For example, if you design a world for a record company that focuses on sound, you might want to add an "import digital music" feature to your editor to make it easier to add in these files than it would be to add them one by one by hand. Finding an editor that ships with, or is built as a toolkit would be of extreme benefit to you. Of course, these editing toolkits require that you, or someone on your team, know Java or C++.

System Requirements   Like the browser market, most editors are currently available for a Windows 95 PC. Editors take up about as much space and memory as browsers, so be wary of the specification label that says you only need 8MB of RAM to run the program. Sure, you might be able to get by with 8MB, but prepare yourself for ultra-slow rendering and processing speeds. Only a select few function reasonably well with 8MB. Unix and Mac editors are hard to come by, but they do exist, and somewhat surprisingly have a wide range of features, including full export to the 2.0 specification. SVGA monitors are nearly a must, as are graphic accelerator cards, and in some cases video cards.

Serving the World: VRML Servers

Now that we can see and build VRML, it's important to know how to serve it. VRML 1.0 is servable from almost any Web server, but networked VRML 2.0, which is essential for multiuser, shared-environment virtual reality, is a different story. While there are several proprietary solutions for world servers, only a few are heading down the open standards path. In most cases, server solutions need to be customized for specific world needs, and the only way to determine which server is right for you is to talk to the companies directly with a list of your basic technical needs.

Most multiuser servers will offer features to track usage statistics, enabling you to track the most popular areas of your VRML world. Some servers have been built to accommodate a database of user profiles too, and these servers will export the usage statistics directly to your database. Support for *shared states* is another important feature of a VRML server. Shared state means that when there are multiple people in a VRML world, if one person in the world turns on the light or moves a chair, everyone in the room will see the effect. Some more advanced servers allow window views into other worlds that are running the same server program. This means that if my server in Kansas from company X has a link to someone else's server in San Francisco, also built by company X, I will be able to see activity through a doorway or window into that other

VRML TOOLS

world. This is a critical feature in establishing life-like 3-D simulations. Looking through a doorway into a no man's land of blackness or endless blue horizon does little to enhance 3-D perspectives.

Servers are expensive and most companies are charging by server capacity rates—a server that will accommodate 50 simultaneous users in a world will be much less expensive than a server that can support 1,200 simultaneous users. To date, the simultaneous user maximum is in the range of 1,200 to 1,500 users and can cost anywhere from $40,000 to $100,000. Bear in mind, though, that most of these numbers are only estimates. The VRML server market has just begun, and no one is quite certain yet how much traffic they will be able handle or what the prices should be.

The servers available today run mostly on Windows NT or Unix, though servers for Pentium Pro–based Windows 95 machines and Macintoshes are on the drawing board. Memory requirements will depend on the capacity of your server, but to serve a 1,200-user world, expect requirements of a 200 MHz processor and at least 100MB of RAM.

Your VRML Team

Building a VRML world in most cases takes a team. And this team should be carefully formulated based on your expectations for the world. Obviously a small world that consists of a house and some furniture could be created by a single developer. But worlds with complex programming features and social functions will need many more people. Many people have compared creating VRML worlds to creating films: You'll need a director, a producer, a tech whiz (or two or three), artists, musicians, and people with skills in architecture (set design), urban planning (world concepts), and sociology will also help. If you can afford it, don't skimp in these areas. The people that build the first round of cyberspace are responsible for setting precedents for those who will follow. If you aren't going to do it right, better not do it at all.

VRML Information Resources

While VRML is an overused buzzword in the technical community, remember that less than 10 percent of the world is currently surfing the Web, which means even fewer people are ready for a 3-D cyberspace. Products and support are also limited. There are a few good Web sites that will keep you up to date on the happenings of VRML, in addition to the company Web sites listed in Appendix S. VRMLSite Zine is sponsored by Superscape and was founded by Aereal CEO Adrian Scott. VRMLSite lists new products, industry gossip, and news. Check it out at http://www.vrmlsite.com. Another great resource is ZD3D at http://www.zd3d.com. ZD3D has regular columns by Mark Pesce, Tony Parisi,

VRML TOOLS

and Genevieve Martineau, as well as new product information and demonstrations. And the ever expanding Yahoo site at http://www.yahoo.com/ has a tremendous VRML section with listings of virtual worlds, places to get help, and networking opportunities. Sign up for the VRML mailing list by sending a message to majordomo@wired.com with "subscribe" in the subject line and "subscribe <your e-mail address> VRML" in the body. There is also a help file for the mailing list at http://vrml.wired.com/listfaq.html. The mailing list delivers an insane amount of mail (40 to 70 messages a day), many with highly technical content. If you don't want to sift through an abundance of rants about nodes, textures, Java, and camera angles, don't join.

Being on the technological leading edge, for all the bugs and uncertainties, can be a rewarding and frequently enlightening experience, and these days VRML is about as advanced as the Web can be. VRML isn't just the next-generation application for cyberspace, it's the birth of a new concept. Learn now while the amount of information is still manageable.

PART

4

SERVICES

Internet Service Providers

Internet Presence Providers

Web Designers

Web Consultants

ISDN Services

20 INTERNET SERVICE PROVIDERS

INTERNET SERVICE PROVIDERS (ISPs) are still a fairly new business and their services are evolving every day. The technology you use to connect to these providers is also constantly changing. (For a review of these access technologies, please see Chapter 2). Since the services provided by ISPs are changing so rapidly there are as yet no standards of quality or cost that are universally accepted, so you must evaluate your needs before choosing a service provider. In such a changing market, judgment and comparison can be difficult. Our goal in this chapter is to familiarize you with the service provider concepts and services you must understand to be successful in your quest for a good ISP.

INTERNET SERVICE PROVIDERS

INTERNET SERVICE PROVIDERS didn't just spring up overnight, but since 1994 the number of businesses selling connectivity to the Web has mushroomed. There are currently at least 1,600 Internet access providers battling for both consumer and corporate cash. While the most significant growth has occurred within the last 18 months, there is a huge amount of commercial traffic now, and every telecom vendor is developing an Internet strategy.

Flavors of ISPs run the gamut. At the top of the food chain are the long-distance companies—MCI, AT&T, and Sprint—which each own their own high-speed lines and equipment. At the next level are nationwide access vendors such as BBN Communications, Netcom On-Line Communications Services, Performance Systems International, and Uunet Technologies. These companies lease raw lines from the phone companies, manage their own points-of-presence, and offer 56-kilobit T1 and T3 lines to end users and to other ISPs for resale.

Regional phone companies and computer companies are now undergoing an ISP metamorphosis. Last May, Pacific Bell and their merger partner, SBC Communications, spun off Pacific Bell Internet Services—a wholly-owned subsidiary that sells dedicated Internet access to large companies. This allows the company to print Internet charges on the monthly phone bill. Further down the chain are regional ISPs, which lease a limited number of trunks to parcel access to individuals and businesses. Start-up ISPs such as MindSpring in Atlanta sell dial-up links to local buyers.

Although the Internet is thriving, experts are saying that the window of opportunity for ISP entrepreneurs is narrowing as the local market becomes saturated, and few companies have enough capital to become national backbone providers. Nevertheless, there are still plenty of entrepreneurs intent on proving the experts wrong. With an ISP lurking around every corner, buyers don't have to venture far. Many users, however, find themselves unprepared to choose among them.

When choosing an Internet service provider, you might consider buying the most expensive solution, following the theory that you get what you pay for. In reality, once you have studied the question, the right choice might well turn out to be a much cheaper solution.

Choosing the right ISP requires that you first determine your needs and your budget. Then you must ask intelligent questions of prospective service providers about the quality of their service. Rarely will you be able to get answers to all your questions, but many can be answered just by reading brochures, calling the service provider, or viewing a demonstration. You also may want to go ahead and sign up with a service to check out firsthand what they provide. A few providers offer free trial periods, allowing you to take a look around before becoming a paying member. Keep in mind the majority of these online trials only provide a minimal period of free time (approximately ten hours), after which you will be billed for service at the going rate.

INTERNET SERVICE PROVIDERS

The perfect service provider probably does not exist. But with a little digging, you should be able to find a provider that meets your needs without breaking the bank. To help you clarify what your needs are, listed below are some features and services you will probably want to know about before deciding on a service provider.

System Security

Probably the single most important aspect to consider when choosing a provider is the security of their systems. The FBI estimates that each year as much as $5 billion is lost to computer crime. That's just the tip of the iceberg. Weaknesses in information systems can also be exploited to gain the upper hand in negotiations and to ruin reputations. Businesses both small and large should work with their provider to understand what kind of preventive measures are appropriate against security threats. If security is a serious concern of yours, present the providers with a site security plan and ask about preventive measures for ensuring against unwanted intrusions.

Check whether the computer systems of your service provider have a US National Computer Security Center "Orange Book" rating. If so, verify the level of their rating. Nearly all service providers meet security level C1 as defined in the Orange Book; if security is your prime concern, you should look for a service provider that can offer you security at a higher level such as C2.

Modem Speeds

The type of error correction and data compression you use can affect the performance of any communications protocol. Each of these factors affects file transfer operations and interactive sessions differently. Some features can increase throughput, which is desirable for transfers, while others provide faster response, which is desirable for interactive sessions. Fortunately, a modem pool can be optimized for either file transfers or interactive sessions.

Error correction and data compression should be used for large file transfers. With error correction, the modem stores data until the receiving modem acknowledges receiving it without error. When data compression is enabled, the modem monitors the data being transferred and compresses it whenever the resulting compressed data is smaller than the original data. Overall throughput is increased because the modem automatically corrects for line errors and reduces the amount of data being transferred.

Error correction and data compression are also advantageous for interactive terminal sessions. The error correction between modems eliminates the "garbage" characters associated with noisy telephone connections. Data compression increases the amount of information that can be quickly displayed, which is useful for rapid screen updates when editing.

INTERNET SERVICE PROVIDERS

However, when a network protocol such as Internet Protocol (IP) is used over a modem connection, having the shortest possible delay is typically more important than having a totally error-free link. Network protocols correct for errors and tend to rely on quickly receiving data acknowledgments. If the network link is used primarily for interactive terminal traffic, the additional delay introduced by error correction and data compression becomes significant, overriding the benefits.

Typically, providers oversell their connections, meaning they sell so many connections that they end up with information bottlenecks. The result is poor performance when downloading files, working in Unix, or reading mail and news. To avoid this frustration, do your homework up front and ask the service provider and existing users about the availability of connections during peak usage times. Also make sure the ISP can provide PPP and SLIP modem connectivity. PPP and SLIP are two protocols that allow you to attach to your service provider and work as if you were directly connected to the Internet (see Chapter 2, "Access Technologies," for more details).

PPP versus Slip

Point to Point Protocol, or PPP, software allows a Macintosh or PC to act as an Internet node. You can use Mac or PC applications to read news, send/receive mail, transfer files, and so on. The only hardware requirements are a modem and telephone line. Most providers today use PPP instead of SLIP because it is a newer, more robust protocol. If you are using a provider who recommends SLIP, save yourself the headaches and switch to PPP. PPP offers these advantages over SLIP:

- Built-in dynamic IP addressing, without the hassle of using the bootp protocol

- Larger packet sizes for higher throughput

- Easier authentication support

- Real error detection and correction

- Much easier to configure for both the ISP and you

- Runs over ISDN

- Runs on Macintosh, Windows 3.1, Windows 95, Windows NT, OS/2, Unix, and other platforms

If you are looking for a more effective way to communicate with the Internet, you should look for a provider that gives you separate modem pools for PPP and Unix shell account dial-up access. Nearly all Internet service providers today support modem speeds of 14.4 kbps, and many

INTERNET SERVICE PROVIDERS

are starting to support modem speeds as high as 28.8 kbps for part of their connections. Try to select a provider who supports modem speeds of 28.8 kbps on all lines.

Network Link Speeds

Some real strides toward better Internet capacity are being made. In March of this year, MCI began upgrading its portion of the Internet's backbone from a 45-Mbps T3 line to a 155-Mbps OC-3 asynchronous transfer mode (ATM) connection. MCI says that's still not enough—without question, they will wind up at OC-12 (622-Mbps ATM) by the end of this year or early next year.

While the upgrade will be sure to please MCI customers, there is concern that other service providers, large and small, won't soon follow suit. Indeed, the economics of bandwidth dictate that the private-sector stakeholders in the Internet will be slow to upgrade their piece of the data architecture beyond the relatively pedestrian 1.55-Mbps speed of a T1 line. For the corporate side, there is a big price discontinuity between a T1 line and the next thing up, which is a T3 line. If a T1 isn't enough for your needs, then you will have to shell out a large sum of money to get to the next level, and a lot of service providers cannot afford to do that. Members of the Internet Society agree that the estimated 35,000 Internet service providers will not put more bandwidth up out of their own goodwill, but eventually user demand may drive ISPs to do so.

To put Internet growth into perspective, compare MCI's separate data and voice networks. Their optical fibers for carrying telephone calls run at 3.7 Gbps and are being upgraded to 10 Gbps per fiber. That may sound like a lot of bandwidth, but consider the hundreds of thousands of gigabits per second of data on the voice network: There are 600 million termini on the voice system generating millions of calls. In contrast, there are only 10 million termini on the Internet. So you can see that the Internet has a long, long way to go before it becomes as demanding of bandwidth as the voice system is.

As you shop for an ISP, you need to keep in mind that network link speed is what's between you and your destination. The first thing to understand is that your network connection can only be as fast as the slowest link in the path. Therefore, investigate what your potential provider has in the way of bandwidth. Reputable national and regional providers will usually publish their connection speeds to larger connectivity providers such as Northwest Net or Sprint Link. In order for you to experience reasonable throughput you should look for a service provider that can offer T1 or T3 access to the Internet. If a service provider only offers 64K, 128K, or fractional T1 access to the Internet, be wary: Remember, two 28.8-kbps modems operating at full potential will flood a 64K line. In this case, if more than two people are using the service at full potential

INTERNET SERVICE PROVIDERS

at the same time, your Internet connections will be frustratingly slow and inadequate.

Virtually every reputable Internet service provider enables you to connect at 28.8 kbps, the minimum speed recommended for Internet travel. With prices for 28.8-kbps modems heading down toward the $100 mark and fast ISDN connections still somewhat pricey and hard to obtain, it's a 28.8-kbps world—service providers who only offer a limited number of 28.8-kbs modems and a handful of slower modems should be avoided.

Just because an ISP has 28.8-kbps modem connections doesn't mean you get equal performance from all services—traffic makes the difference. The Big Four service providers (America Online, CompuServe, Microsoft Network, and Prodigy) have millions of subscribers who suck up bandwidth as they view fancy graphics and access services. Many users report that during peak periods they are able to get only a slow connection, if they can connect at all. On the other hand, small providers with few subscribers may have traffic problems if they lack sufficient hardware to handle the peak volume of calls.

ISDN is the next step up in terms of speed—at up to 128 kbps, it offers the fastest practical connection for home users. But getting it to function requires a pricey terminal adapter, complicated installation, and a special phone line that only phone companies in urban areas will install. Of the Big Four online services, only Microsoft Network and CompuServe support ISDN—not even AT&T will have ISDN up and running until the end of the year. Also remember that service providers charge more for ISDN than for ordinary modem connections—typically twice as much.

Whether or not you have a fast connection, you could still face the mother of all slowdowns from time to time—a busy signal. How often you get one depends on an ISP's customer-to-modem ratio, which should be between 8 to 1 and 12 to 1. Because service providers tend to fudge their numbers when it comes to frequency of busy signals, for a more realistic answer you should ask some current users on the provider's network how often they have had trouble connecting with the service. While this type of query will not give you an actual customer-to-modem ratio, it will give you a feel for connectivity demand.

You will also want to ask whether the network you are evaluating is currently up and running. Some providers may show links that are not operational as part of their backbone capacity. Do not assume that just because there is a press release or marketing materials about a new high-speed network link that that link is actually operational.

INTERNET SERVICE PROVIDERS

Software Concerns

You need software for each of the four most popular Internet activities: exchanging e-mail, browsing the Web, downloading files, and reading Usenet newsgroups. With the Big Four online services, you get applications for all these activities under one slick interface. Other national ISPs generally offer separate, licensed versions of brand-name Web browsers, newsgroup readers, and other software. Local providers often supply you with shareware or simply recommend applications for you to buy.

Most experienced Net surfers value the ability to use any Internet application they like. No matter where you get it, you'll need a suite of software that includes the following:

- **Web browser.** The two best browsers are Netscape Navigator and Internet Explorer. In the past, the Big Four online services restricted you to whatever Web browser they supplied, but these days America Online, CompuServe, and Microsoft Network let you install any browser you choose.

- **E-mail software.** The Big Four have proprietary e-mail systems that let you send messages across the Internet. With other providers you can use the e-mail program built into your browser, but you'll generally get more and better features with a separate e-mail program. Programs such as Eudora and Pegasus are shareware mail readers which offer nice powerful interfaces for your mail retrieval.

- **FTP, Archie, Gopher, and WAIS software.** File transfer protocol (FTP) enables you to download files from remote computers—provided you know the address of the site where the file is located. Archie lets you search the Internet for specific files to download, then sends back a list of site addresses. Gopher goes further by allowing you to browse menus of available files, then download them. Wide area information servers (WAIS) are similar to Gopher, but use indexes to perform more intelligent searches. Either Gopher or WAIS combined with FTP are must-haves.

- **Newsgroup reader.** A newsgroup reader enables you to participate in Usenet newsgroups, which are bulletin-board-like discussions on every imaginable topic. You can follow *threads* (messages and their replies), automatically download new messages, stitch together multipart file attachments, and more. Most Web browsers have built-in newsgroup readers, but they can't match the capability of such excellent stand-alone readers as Forté's Free Agent.

- **Other software.** Other desirable applications include online chat programs, which enable you to exchange messages with other people in real time, and Telnet, which lets you access Unix-based text at universities and other institutions through terminal emulation. ISPs generally maintain download libraries that offer a host of other goodies, such as graphics viewers, video players, file converters, file compression utilities, and more.

INTERNET SERVICE PROVIDERS

Hardware Concerns

Look out for service providers who are looking for quick cash and quick returns. Sometimes their innovative cost-cutting measures result in questionable quality of services. There are many Internet service providers running their services from a no-frills homemade PC, usually a 486 or 586. While such Intel platforms are not necessarily underpowered, they do tend to have bottleneck problems when trying to service many demanding users. To make matters even worse, some of those homemade PCs run under public domain operating systems, which usually means unreliable or questionable system performance. While public domain operating systems such as LINUX and BSD/386 are good for learning the ins and outs of Unix, you should not bet on them for serious business. It is always to your advantage to query a service provider on the equipment and operating systems they use.

Most national service providers use Unix as their operating system platform. Since Unix was the original Internet operating system, it has the most support in terms of time-tested, native programs. Popular operating systems such as Windows NT and Novell are now entering the Web service market. Smaller ISPs usually migrate to these operating systems because they are a little less intimidating to administer and set up. These operating systems are very reliable and are growing in worldwide acceptance; if your service provider is using one, you should be fine.

Using top quality equipment is important, but so is protecting it. Check that the provider's front-line equipment is protected with uninterruptible power supplies and locked and secured computer rooms. Also ask your provider what their backup plans are. If you receive an answer like, "We don't have a backup plan because we are never down," be cautious—there is nothing more frustrating than not having access to your data. Most larger service providers have redundant systems that take over once a problem in the main system is detected. You will also find that larger service providers have documented disaster recovery plans. If up time is important to you (and it should be), then ask for verification of these plans.

Technical Staff

One aspect you should be sure to consider when choosing an Internet provider is the quality of its technical staff. These are the people who will get your connection going in the beginning, then keep it and the network running in the future. Typical questions you should ask of a provider are:

- Technical support hours

- Backgrounds of technical staff

- Escalation procedure and means of establishing priority of requests for tech support

INTERNET SERVICE PROVIDERS

- Cost for higher-level support contracts

- Cost for on-site support

- Number of full-time and part-time technical support people available

- The type of support available during off-hours (when normal technical support is not available)

Larger service providers generally take the long view and consider good technical support good business. You may find that smaller providers, however, cannot answer all of the above questions to your satisfaction.

Since few people have the luxury to roam the Internet during working hours, be sure that an ISP's telephone support will be available when you're most likely to need it—ideally, 24 hours a day, 7 days a week. And, of course, you'll want your phone tech support to be toll free. Quick customer callback and e-mail support may also be acceptable if your question isn't pressing. If your problem isn't preventing you from logging on, the most expedient solution might be the service provider's online reference, which typically includes Web pages of indexed advice with links to other resources. If the reference is intelligently designed, you may find your answer right away. Some ISPs also let you chat live on line with a technician; you can type messages back and forth until the problem is solved or repairs are ordered.

If you want to set up your own Web page, you'll find that most Internet service providers will give you the server space to do so, but only some provide training—an area where, thanks to proximity and fewer customers, local providers have an obvious edge. ISPs offer from 1MB to an unlimited amount of space for personal Web pages, and prices vary widely, so shop carefully if having your own Web page is a priority.

In the game of ongoing support, it generally costs four times as much to attract a new client as it does to keep an existing client. With this in mind, providers who value their relationship with the client will offer ready access to their technical support. They will also ensure that their technical support people are trained and efficient at helping the end user. Since the service provider market is growing by leaps and bounds on a daily basis, you will find that many of these technical services are highlighted as enticements to potential clients.

In order for the security technology or any other protection technology to be effective, it has to be properly managed. It must be operated by skilled professionals. Changes to the system have to be properly controlled, and the system must be physically protected. It must be tested, and auditing must be done on a regular basis.

The provider should have adequate staffing to cover the usual scenarios. Does it seem like the staff is large enough that there will always be

INTERNET SERVICE PROVIDERS

enough skilled people back at the office to handle things even if some of the staff go away for a convention? Or does it sound like tech support duty will devolve onto the shoulders of the receptionist if the tech guy gets a cold? Be suspicious when an ISP says their technical staff can handle questions even when out of the office by calling back in.

Find out what their technical staff turnover is. If people are leaving, find out why, and who is left to keep your connection operational. Many suppliers of service have problems keeping highly skilled support staff because their skills are so marketable; such turnovers can lead to unreliable or discontinuous support for you and can represent a weak area in your connectivity plan.

Value-added services are important to many users and help them make effective use of their Internet connection. Some access providers have a user services staff that provides documentation and instruction on how to use the Internet, as well as general help. If a network has staff dedicated to user services, you are more likely to get the latest information about developments on the Internet. Ask your provider what kinds of specific documentation, instructions, or other help is offered. Some typical functions of a user services group are:

- Outreach, including newsletters, reports, bulletin boards, and announcements

- Training in technical matters and how to use the Internet through user groups, manuals, or books

- Help in the form of answers to questions about things to do or how to do them, helpful hints on how to simplify work, and advice on finding new resources

- Maintenance of online archives of software, manuals, outreach information, and network statistics

Very few network providers have set up online help systems to answer common user questions and serve generally as information resources for their clients. Check to see if the provider has one and what kind of information is available on it.

Network Troubleshooting

Even the best networks fail occasionally, and all providers will have outages. The critical factor is the speed with which providers recognize and fix the problems. There are many network tools available to assist providers in monitoring their network and recognizing problems.

At a minimum, the provider should have some kind of Simple Network Management Protocol-based (SNMP) monitoring system. SNMP collects performance statistics on various computers throughout

INTERNET SERVICE PROVIDERS

the network, allowing providers to recognize problems within minutes of occurrence. This means that problems get fixed more quickly, perhaps even before you notice them. Most of the larger ISPs base their value-added sales pitch on their network performance monitoring. Companies like U.S. West guarantee network performance by having 7-day-a-week, 24-hour monitoring of their network. These larger service providers also offer redundancy with their circuits, which allows them to quickly switch to other network paths in times of high bandwidth utilization and circuit errors. While local service providers cannot guarantee these same network performance packages, they are most likely using larger service providers who will provide this higher-level monitoring.

While system maintenance is important to keep the system up-to-date and in top performance, it should be done with the concerns of the customers in mind as well. Some providers perform system maintenance during regular office hours for their own convenience, but if you have a choice, you should look for one that carries out their maintenance at users' convenience—that is, very early in the morning, during holidays, and at other non-peak times.

System backup should be done every night, and copies of the backup should be kept both on site and off site to minimize failure. Service is everything in the information business. If system maintenance and upgrades mean service interruption, the provider should notify its customers well in advance and schedule the changes on a regular basis so there are no surprises.

Costs

When shopping for an Internet service provider, first make sure that you won't have to pay long-distance fees while you're connected. If a prospective provider doesn't offer a toll-free or local access number in your area, look elsewhere: Long-distance charges will quickly eat whatever savings you may get from signing up with a low-priced provider in another area code. Those who frequently travel with a laptop should opt for a national provider with lots of local access numbers—one in every likely destination, if possible. In this area, the Big Four online services (America Online, CompuServe, Microsoft Network, and Prodigy) and AT&T have an edge because they have the most local access numbers.

Next, figure out how much time you spend on line and compare charges based on that. Do you seldom spend more than five hours wired per month? If you're an AT&T long-distance customer, you can't do much better than AT&T's offer: five free hours per month for your first year of access. If you're connected less frequently and you like the style and content of an online service, $9.95 buys you five hours of access per month on either America Online or Prodigy. But beware: They both charge $2.95 for each additional hour. Even AT&T charges $2.50 per hour when you exceed five hours per month.

INTERNET SERVICE PROVIDERS

If you spend more than eight hours per month on the Net, you should start sifting through the mountain of payment plans available. The simplest are the unlimited access plans. For example, AT&T charges its long-distance customers a flat rate of $19.95 for as much time as you care to spend on line per month—an offer that several other national providers match, including EarthLink, PSINet Pipeline USA, and SpryNet. (Wow from CompuServe actually beats AT&T's rate, as do many local providers.) Or you can opt for a plan with a high hourly limit per month, which can work out to as little as pennies or as much as a few bucks per hour, depending on which ISP's plan you choose, how much time you actually spend on line, and whether you go over the limit and start racking up surcharges.

Some ISPs, particularly local providers, also charge an initiation fee, but you often get low rates in exchange. Illuminati Online (a provider in Austin, Texas), for example, hits you with a $25 startup fee, but charges a mere $15 per month for 30 hours of access.

All fees should be clear to users. Options and service packages should be put together in the simplest form and not to confuse the users. Watch out for providers who give you a low startup or monthly fee, but actually set a limit to your storage. They charge you a phenomenal rate when you exceed the limit.

If you use the system often, a program that charges high minimum usage fees and offsets these with low hourly connect charges may save you money. However, if you do not use the system often enough to justify the high monthly charge, you might be better off paying a higher hourly rate and a low usage fee with some other service providers.

Comparison Shopping

Price is important when choosing an Internet service provider, but it should not keep you from looking at other conditions. Your relationship with your service provider should be a long one. Short-term or immediate benefits often cost you more. There are no definite rules about what you should pay for a link. The best way is to find out which of the services and options offered are most important to you. Get quotes or price lists, and compare against various providers. Be sure that you know exactly what you are getting before you decide. Choose the one that gives you most for your money.

Take extra precautions against hidden charges such as PNET license fees, peak hours surcharges, and storage charges. Make sure you do an "apples to apples" comparison. Comparing a "basic" account from one provider with a full-featured package from another provider may get you into trouble. Make sure you know what benefits and features you are getting. What the provider thinks is the best deal for you may really be something with many features you'll find useless.

INTERNET SERVICE PROVIDERS

Go ahead and ask for customer references. Talk to them and ask for their experience with the provider. See what they like about the provider and what they don't. Ask them if they feel that the provider is working in their best interest. If possible, ascertain that the references don't have any sort of insider relationship with the provider such as being the relative of a member of the board of directors. Find out where the ISP's new customers come from. The most interesting statistic is how many of their customers have switched from other providers!

When choosing an Internet service provider, you should also find out where their offices are located. Some may be located in homes, while others may be found in shopping malls. The problems? An up-to-standard office for ISPs should have 24-hour access, 24-hour air-conditioning, site security, and phone-line expandability. The lack of any one of these characteristics could mean serious trouble. Computer systems and equipment generate a lot of heat, and without round-the-clock air-conditioning everything is in jeopardy. ISPs located inside malls could face a long system down time in the event of a system failure, due to lack of access to their premises. Home-based offices impose another type of danger: The number of phone lines that can be installed into a residential building is very limited. Furthermore, it's not likely that many supporting staff will be able to fit into a tiny home office; it's possible such an ISP has no full-time support staff at all. Your best bet is to visit the providers on site, or at least get their addresses to see where they are located.

21 INTERNET PRESENCE PROVIDERS

AS THE INTERNET EXPLODES in popularity, new service industries are emerging with thousands of entrepreneurs looking to cash in by catering to the needs of new users. The *Internet presence provider* (IPP) is one of these new services. Individuals and companies are becoming aware of the marketing, promotional, and customer-service benefits that can be gained from having a presence on the Web. But many people would rather hire someone to build their Web pages than try and figure out HTML themselves. Enter the Internet presence provider.

INTERNET PRESENCE PROVIDERS

AN IPP IS A PERSON OR SERVICE that develops a business's or individual's Internet presence (for a listing of IPPs, see Appendix U). For all practical purposes, this means someone who creates Web sites. The term "Web developer" has also emerged to describe people who provide this service. The distinction between a Web developer and an IPP is that the IPP may also develop other Internet presence vehicles such as FTP or Gopher sites while the Web developer focuses exclusively on the Web. But such a precise definition of terms is rarely recognized, and the two titles are generally used interchangeably both inside and outside the industry.

There is also plenty of cross-pollination occurring among other new Internet-related services. Some Internet service providers (ISPs) offer custom Web page creation in addition to their normal Web-hosting and dial-up access services. And many IPPs offer at least temporary if not full Web-hosting services and dial-up access along with their normal Web page creation services.

Such inexact terminology can cause confusion, so for this chapter, the term IPP will refer to any company or individual who does Web page creation, regardless of the other services they may provide.

Creating a Web Site

The process of creating a Web site requires a variety of different skills. Often an IPP will need to be adept at marketing and communications, artistic interpretation and design, basic data entry, and code-crunching programming all at the same time.

Because the Web is so new, the marketing aspect comes into play when interpreting the intentions of those clients who want a Web site or single Web page, but don't have the foggiest notion of what to put on it, what is possible to put on it, or why they should have a Web site in the first place. All they know is that everyone else is doing it and they don't want to be left behind. This requires the IPP to help the client define their communications goals and show the client how the Web can fit into their overall public relations, sales, and customer service plan. In fact, some Internet consultants do not do any actual Web page creation themselves, but focus entirely on helping clients with their Web marketing efforts. See Chapter 23 and Appendix W for a more detailed discussion and listing of Internet consultants.

Functions of the IPP

Once the IPP knows what the customer wants to do with their Web site, production of the site is divided into the following four broad categories of tasks:

- *Artwork*—Development of image-based content such as illustrations, photos, or graphics and assembling it with effective graphic layout and design

INTERNET PRESENCE PROVIDERS

- *Copy-writing*—Development of text content

- *HTML markup*—Construction of the Web pages in hypertext

- *Programming*—Development of additional functionality for the Web site with CGI, PERL, Java, or other non-HTML coding

Because the Web has become such a visual medium, it is often design, the desired look and feel of Web pages, that determines how content is presented. Many IPPs start with a discussion of the overall design and images to be used before any actual HTML coding begins.

Sometimes a client will have worked with their own design agency, which has already helped define the creative approach to the customer's current marketing effort. As with Web consultants, the niche of the Web-based design agency has seen phenomenal growth recently. Many design firms that started in other mediums (such as production for print or video) have quickly branched out to include graphic production for Web projects as well. See Chapter 22 and Appendix V for more information and a listing of Web design agencies.

Regardless of how the Web page looks, however, the most useful part of a Web page for the viewer is the content. This can come in digital form such as a library of informational files, images, or software that can be downloaded from the Web site. But in most cases, it is the written content on the pages themselves which brings the viewer to the site, causes them to linger, and makes them bookmark the site to return to at a later time. This content can come from anywhere—the client's advertising or public relations agency, previously published materials, outside resources, or from copy written by the customers themselves. It is the IPP's job to determine the best way to present this information on the Web page. This must be judged from a design/layout point of view—how the words will flow in relation to the graphic elements on the Web page—and also from a readership point of view—the copy must be clear, succinct, and at a level appropriate for the intended audience.

Too often IPPs dispense with the second part of this function, basically just putting whatever copy the customer provides on the Web page without any sort of editing, feedback, or review cycle. The experienced IPP, however, knows that what is said on the Web page is just as important as how it is displayed. A good IPP will assist the client in making intelligent choices about Web content development.

The third piece of the Web page development puzzle is the overall site layout or flow, and the actual HTML markup or construction of the Web pages. In some cases, an IPP won't start with the markup until all decisions about graphics and content are finalized. Other IPPs jump right into the HTML phase and solve problems or address site flow issues as they go. In most cases, it helps to have a master plan for how the site will

INTERNET PRESENCE PROVIDERS

be laid out before proceeding with the markup itself. This means drawing up an organizational chart to visualize which primary pages will be linked from the home page (often based on general categories that the material will naturally fall into); which pages will be sub-pages off the primary pages; and how many levels deep these links and pages will go within the organizational structure.

Given a customer's overall marketing goals, artwork, and content development, a good IPP should be able to suggest a Web site structure to serve the client's needs. Once issues of goals and development are addressed and answered, the HTML becomes a matter of executing the proper programming syntax to achieve the desired, pre-determined effect.

Achieving Cross-Platform Compatibility   Once the desired content and design has been decided on, another part of the HTML process then becomes important. This has to do with achieving compatibility with the various Web browsers on the market. Ideally, the pages on the site will look good across all browser formats and computer operating system platforms (Windows 95, Windows 3.11, Macintosh OS, and Unix). A good IPP will be aware of the various emerging standards and which proprietary browser functions can be supported without making the site too narrowly focused for multiplatform or multibrowser use.

An IPP should also be able to present various options for specific programming beyond the essential HTML markup. Things to consider are feedback functionality, order processing, or the inclusion of multimedia or animated elements. When considering such programming options, however, it is important to take into account the level of computer savvy of the intended viewer. Certain programming functions may do more harm than good if they require the user to have computer programming skills in order to set up their computer or Web browser to view the page as intended. Another factor is the compatibility of the programming elements across multiple platforms and browsers. The overriding concern should always be whether the programming elements are necessary or useful in the first place, whether they enhance or detract from the overall presentation of the Web site.

From IPP to ISP

When the site is complete and the IPP has taken the customer through final edits and last-minute changes, the last task is to get the site up on the Web. This is usually a fairly straightforward process, but knowing the relationship of your IPP to the ISP hosting the site is certainly important. If the IPP will be sending the completed site to an ISP, a good presence provider will know what questions to ask of the ISP, and will have already paved the way for a smooth transfer of the site.

INTERNET PRESENCE PROVIDERS

In some cases the IPP will create the site in demo form on the ISP's server, so no site transfer will need to take place at all—the house gets built on the lot, so to speak. The advantage of this is that all the scripting and programming can be tested and modified if necessary to conform to the server's specifications during the production phase. In other cases, the completed site will need to be uploaded to the host ISP from the computer where it was created. Either way, the presence provider needs to ensure that the host ISP has a space ready to host the site, that all the appropriate parties have access to the site, that the site functions properly once it is moved to its final home, and that the intended address or URL of the site actually works. Some of these are actually ISP responsibilities, but a good IPP will understand what is happening and why, and will help keep the process on schedule.

The Bottom Line

Of course one question everyone always asks is how much a Web page costs. This question is nearly impossible to answer without first having more information from the client. It is like estimating the cost of a house—you need to know first the preferences of the homebuyer or client. To estimate the cost of a Web site, you need to know how much the ISP will charge to host the Web site (the lot to build the house on); how many Web pages will make up the entire site (the square footage, number of rooms); and what it will take to develop the content of the site, that is, will high-end graphics or more affordable clip art be used (the quality of the building materials).

Even with all this information, the quotes or bids a customer may receive for a Web project will probably range wildly depending on the level of experience and skill of the various IPPs and the prices they command for their services. There is no such thing as an average price—some firms can ask for and commonly receive tens or hundreds of thousands of dollars for high-profile, complicated, or large Web projects. On the other end of the scale, college students and eager entrepreneurs may be willing to create single Web pages or whole Web sites for next to nothing just to gain experience and build a reputation.

Generally, the old adage "you get what you pay for" has never been so true as it is in this emerging service industry. But there are a few questions a client should make sure to ask during the bidding process to help gauge the IPP's ability and expertise.

Evaluating Your IPP

The first thing is to see the IPP's portfolio: Make sure to ask for a list of URLs to Web sites the IPP has worked on previously. Check them out on a browser—*not* on the IPP's own computer—so you can see how they look in a "real world" setting. Sometimes, the IPP will only be able

INTERNET PRESENCE PROVIDERS

to claim partial credit for the site—maybe the HTML markup, or the design and creative concept. When you see a Web site that impresses you, make sure to clarify with the IPP which elements of the site were their responsibility.

You may also find it worthwhile to ask the IPP for names and phone numbers of previous clients as references. It is important to get a quality product at a good price, but you should also measure the "hassle factor" to determine how easy or difficult it will be to work with a selected IPP. Your presence provider should be easy to reach by e-mail or phone and be able to easily accommodate your content—either images or text that you provide, or images or text files provided to you by design, public relations, advertising, or other agencies. It is the IPP's job to translate files appropriately. Regardless of their preferred platform, an IPP should be able to accept files from Macintosh, Unix, or PC systems.

And, of course, you can check references to see if your selected IPP has a track record of delivering on time and on budget. With a few common-sense questions, a little time spent on the Web, and a few short phone calls you can save yourself a lot of grief and frustration down the road. Especially when putting serious money into a project about which few people can truly call themselves experts, it makes sense to maintain a healthy level of skepticism and add a little investigative work to make sure the IPP you select will do the right job at the right price for you.

22 WEB DESIGNERS

WITH THE RECENT EXPLOSION of commercial Web sites, many design and illustration agencies (or individual artists or design professionals) have been quick to add Web design to their repertoire of services. Some have been forced into the production of graphics for Web pages by image-conscious clients who want to keep a consistent look across all their promotional materials and don't trust computer programmers to capture the desired look.

WEB DESIGNERS

MANY WEB DESIGNERS come from a background in graphic design for print, such as production of brochures, print ads, or other collateral promotional or informational materials. A few have a background in design for electronic media such as video production or television advertising. Fortunately, there are relatively few aspects of graphic production that are unique to the Web or that these designers haven't already encountered in creating images for other purposes. In fact, the most important aspects of Web design are the same requirements that apply to all visual media. These include the need to balance form with function and an understanding of how image balance, color, shading, and light can be manipulated to achieve a desired effect.

But because the Web is an electronic medium, it helps if the artist is able to skillfully handle the latest tools of digital production. Graphics applications such as Adobe's Photoshop and Illustrator have become the norm for many graphic artists. Those familiar with these applications will have an easier time either creating new images or modifying existing images for use on the Web. Finally, the ability of the graphic designer to envision the entire Web site is crucial to the development of a successful Web site. The way the information will flow and the placement of the images on the pages are important factors in the aesthetic effect of the page. These factors have an impact not only on how much enjoyment users will have when viewing the page, but also on how easy it will be for them to explore the site as a whole and find the information they need.

Web-Specific Design Considerations

Because the Web is an electronic medium, it has one important requirement not found in other media—the need for conservation of image size. This is due to the limitations imposed by the basic hardware and communications software tools needed to connect to the Web in the first place.

A few lucky people have high-speed Internet connections, but most of the world still connects to the Web through a standard phone line connected to a 14.4- or 28.8-kbps modem. This creates a bottleneck for the digital information traveling through various communications lines (such as the viewer's own phone line), from the site where it originated to the computer sitting on the viewer's desktop.

With printed images, there are no constraints on the number of colors in, the complexity of, or the size of the piece being produced except those imposed by the size of the paper being used and the project's budget. But when a Web page displays images that are rich with color and large in size, the page takes much longer to appear on the viewer's browser than a page filled with plain, black text. This means that on the Internet, file size becomes a limiting criterion comparable to that of budget (or paper size) on printed pieces.

WEB DESIGNERS

This is because the images on the page are in digital form, and all the information in those digital files must first pass through the viewer's phone line, modem, and computer processor before it appears in the viewer's browser window. Computers with high-speed Internet connections usually have no trouble receiving the information as fast as it can be sent by the host computer serving up the Web page. But those using standard dial-up Internet connections must wait for all that digital information to squeeze through their phone lines and modems. On top of this, the standard home computer usually isn't capable of processing the digital information coming in as fast as the high-powered Internet host computers (servers) and the high-speed communications lines they connect to are capable of sending it.

As a result, anyone who has spent much time browsing will tell you that some Web pages can take a long time to appear in the browser window. In fact, many don't make it all the way through to completion on the first pass and need to be reloaded or have the screen refreshed before you can view all the elements on the page. This is what happens when a Web page is bloated with lots of large image files.

Producing Digital Images

Each element of a Web page, whether it is a word, a photo, or an illustration, must be in digital form. For words, this is easy—they are typed into a word processor. For photos, graphics, or other images, the process is a little trickier. Print images must be scanned using a process similar to that used by fax machines, which take visual information and turn it into digital information that can then be transmitted over the phone lines. Another option is for the images to be created in digital form in the first place, such as with a graphics or illustration application. Most images for print or broadcast production are actually produced on computers now, and must go through a translation process to take them from the computer where they originated to the printed advertisement or video tape where they end up. The world of photography is also now becoming digitized, with more and more cameras on the market that save images to a computer disk instead of film.

Image Size Optimization

For Web designers, getting the image into digital form is only the beginning of the process. Once the desired image is either created on the computer or converted to computerized form, the big job is to "optimize" that image for the Web. This means manipulating it in such a way as to make it as small a computer file as possible while still maintaining the integrity of the image. The smaller the computer file, the faster and more reliably it will travel across the phone lines, through the various computers on the Web, through the viewer's modem and on to their computer screen.

WEB DESIGNERS

This is perhaps the greatest challenge that Web designers face when creating images for the Web. To make this process go smoothly, there are a few things that Web designers can do from the start. The first has to do with the use of color—the more colors in an image, the larger the digital image file will be. A good designer knows how to achieve a desired graphic effect while at the same time keeping the number of colors required to create the image to a minimum. By developing a color palette first, and then building all the images off that palette, a designer can not only create a look and feel that is consistent throughout the Web site, but can also ensure that the images take up as little disk space as possible.

Second, a Web designer can limit the size of the image in terms of purely physical dimensions. An 8"×10" photo will make a much larger digital image file once it is scanned than a similar photo that is 5"×7" in size. A good designer will be able to determine the best size for an image to balance the other elements on the page and will understand the costs and benefits of using large versus small images.

Third, final file size is influenced by the type of image being used or created. Typically, a color photograph will create a much larger digital image file than an illustration with the same dimensions due to the amount of complexity and subtlety of colors often found in a photo image. A good designer will know how to balance the use of photos versus illustrations on a Web page and will be able to create images or illustrations that can carry the same graphic impact as a photograph, if necessary.

Finding a Web Designer

It is actually rather hard to find a Web design firm that sticks exclusively to design. This is because the design and production of Web pages are so closely related. Often a Web design firm is also an Internet presence provider (IPP). Some full-service agencies are staffed with skilled professionals who can develop the overall creative approach, execute the illustrations and the graphic layout, as well as implement the HTML production and other services that IPPs provide. For a geographical directory of IPPs, see Appendix U.

The variety of services offered by the different companies providing Web design makes it hard to pinpoint what a "reasonable" cost may be for the development of Web page graphics. If you hire a firm that does all the services mentioned above under one roof, there will be the obvious overhead costs associated with keeping a staff that large. On the other hand, having everything provided by one company can save you the time and hassle of having to shop around to get the best price for the various pieces and then hoping that you can make them all—designers, HTML coders, ISP, and any other consultants you may need—work together smoothly.

WEB DESIGNERS

Another factor that makes it nearly impossible to establish a standard rate for Web graphics is the different levels of skill and experience designers may possess. As with IPPs, you usually get exactly what you pay for—highly skilled graphics people are finding themselves more and more in demand, and in these days of image-conscious corporate identity, it is not unusual to find top graphics people getting paid several thousand dollars for a single logo or the creation of a few stylized icons. On the other hand, there are lots of people in the industry who call themselves professionals or "artists" without having much of a track record or many professional pieces in their portfolio to back up their claims. These folks will often have more affordable rates as they try to build their portfolio and clientele.

For a geographical listing of all types of Web designers, from full-service agencies to freelance solo artists, see Appendix V.

Assessing Designers

To help ease the process of selecting a graphic artist, there are a few standard elements that are emerging as common touchstone pieces on Web pages. You can use samples of these elements to compare apples with apples. This requires asking for a per-piece bid as opposed to a time-based bid or an overall package bid, but most graphic artists, if they are serious about bidding on your project, will be able to accommodate this request.

The basic graphic pieces of a Web page are the following:

- The *splash screen* or home page graphic. This is often a complete graphic image that offers clickable hotspots within the image that will take the user to various hyperlinks within the Web site. Many Web sites use a complete splash screen image map to fill the home page or the top section of the home page (usually sized to fit a standard 14-inch computer monitor window).

- The *page header* and *page footer*. These are often navigational aids that appear at the top and bottom of each page on a Web site to establish a consistent look and feel throughout the site and to provide easy-to-find buttons for moving forward, backward, and laterally through a Web site.

- Graphical elements of the Web site, including navigational buttons or icons that depict the general concept of the intended destination as a graphical representation (a mailbox to depict an e-mail hyperlink, for instance); stylized logos or logo modifications; and educational or explanatory images that depict a process or product in operation.

Comparing these specific design elements individually as done by different designers is easier and more revealing than simply looking over each designer's body of work. This practice will also alert you to the number of considerations at issue in the design process, and therefore to the likely expense of realizing these ideas.

WEB DESIGNERS

Not only will it cost money to have an illustrator create the images, there is usually an additional charge to have a designer put all the images together on the Web page in such a way that they complement each other and serve their intended function. You need someone with an eye for page layout and overall graphic impact to pull everything together into a cohesive unit.

Having some idea of how many and what type of images you would like to have in your Web site will give a graphic designer a better handle on how to bid the project. Another way to handle this, if you don't feel comfortable providing detailed information to the designer, is to have the designer suggest an overall design complete with illustrations to you. This makes it hard to compare bids, however, because two different designers will rarely arrive at the same page count, illustration count, and overall graphic presentation. In these instances, you can only go by your preference among the designs they submit, by the bottom line, and of course by a comparison of the competing designers' portfolios and references as well.

Of course, it is not absolutely necessary that you have a graphic designer work on your Web page at all. If your intended audience is just there for the facts, all you may need is an IPP to simply translate your content into HTML and put it on the page without regard for the "look and feel" of the Web site. But remember that even if you do that, you are still choosing a graphic look—it is just that you have chosen a generic look which may or may not appeal to the viewers who will be visiting your Web site.

Conclusion

The right graphics can make a Web site look professional, make it easier to navigate and assist the viewer in quickly finding the content they are seeking, and make the site a fun place to visit—a quality that can in turn lead to repeat traffic and word-of-mouth advertising. But the wrong graphics can slow down the presentation of your Web pages, turn off viewers who don't like or approve of the graphic direction you have chosen, and confuse or mislead viewers who can't accurately interpret the messages you intend your images to portray. In short, making the right choices with regard to your Web page graphics will make all the difference in the world to the success of your Web site.

23 WEB CONSULTANTS

BECAUSE THE WEB is such a relatively new phenomenon compared with other forms of mass communication, Web consultants are sometimes deemed "experts in the field" (usually self-appointed) with as little as one year's (or even less) experience with the Web. Of course, there are many factors involved in becoming a true Web expert other than time clocked in front of a computer screen, but this is certainly one of the most important factors. And, frankly, given the rate of growth and metamorphosis of the Web, certain "rules" about how the Web worked even six months ago may not be relevant today. The most important factor, then, may

WEB CONSULTANTS

be the amount of Web contact a consultant has on an ongoing basis, and his or her ability to interpret current changes in light of previous, sometimes similar events. But more than this, a true Web expert should be able to apply the lessons of experience in such a way as to arrive at useful, educated guesses for the future.

The Role of the Web Consultant

Now no one, not even Bill Gates, really knows how the Web will continue to evolve and where it will be in even as short a time as a year from now. But short-term assessments concerning the rate of growth, demographics of users, computer platforms of choice, and the next "killer app" on the horizon, should be possible for those steeped in this information on a daily basis. Good Web consultants may not be right 100 percent of the time, but they should be right most of the time and should have some defined method by which they arrive at their educated guesses.

Sometimes the role of the Web or Internet consultant is wrapped up in a larger package that includes other Internet-related services such as Web page development or Web design (see Chapters 21 and 22). Because the development of a client's Web site should include assessments about the end-user's Web habits, abilities, and browsing tools, a certain amount of consulting will be required to bring such relevant background information to light. You, the client, can then make choices about the structure and design of the Web site with this information in mind.

Sometimes the Web designer or HTML programmer has enough information to act as the consultant, but the best arrangement is often to bring together a team of people with expertise in each separate discipline—art creation, programming, and project management. In some cases a client starts with a selected consultant who then assembles the other players as necessary on behalf of the client, much as a general contractor assembles subcontractors for a client's construction project. Sometimes the client starts with an Internet service provider (often asked to perform consulting services by default) who will assemble the team either from in-house staff or from outside contractors, or the ISP may suggest an outside consultant to the client. These are some of the logical permutations by which a design and consultancy team may be assembled.

But a Web consultant's contribution is rarely limited to Web advice alone. Most are more appropriately called "Internet consultants," since they provide information to clients regarding a whole host of communications possibilities available through the Internet. For starters, any consultant worth their salt will be able to help a client start from scratch and get connected to the Internet in the first place. Many have business relationships or partnerships with Internet service providers (ISPs), and some can even provide clients with discount rates at particular ISPs in exchange for repeated referrals.

WEB CONSULTANTS

Consultants should also be able to provide clients with a range of options, prices, and a "best match" suggestion for choosing the right ISP to meet their needs. Some consultants purposely avoid close business relationships with any one ISP so that they can appear more objective in their ISP recommendations.

Optimizing ISP Use

Once an ISP is selected for a client, a consultant may bring to the client's attention some of the less obvious variables and timing issues involved with tasks that the ISP can perform. Among these are reserving a location on the ISP's server for the client's Web site, requesting a file transfer (FTP) space also on the ISP server, requesting additional e-mail functionality (such as multiple mailboxes or customized e-mail routing) from the ISP, and requesting a virtual server and custom domain name registration.

Custom domain names are offered by more and more ISPs as companies become aware of the possibility of having their Web address shortened to "www.companyname.com" as opposed to longer Web addresses (URLs) beginning with the service provider's name, followed by a name chosen by the client (www.serviceprovider.com/companyname, for example). Of course, the longer the URL, the harder it is to remember, the more chance for error by a user typing it into their browser, and the harder it is to convey to others—especially over the phone or face-to-face. Having to say, "http://..." is difficult enough for many people, and the format of URLs is still working its way into the collective vernacular of our society.

A *virtual server* is a server space actually hosted by an ISP but that appears to be located with the client alone, giving no visible indication in either the URL or in e-mail addresses of the ISP's name or location. This is a preferred Internet address option for many businesses because it allows them the advantage of having a shorter, custom Internet identity without having to set up an entire Internet server within their own office.

Other Consultancy Services

This leads to another function of many Internet consultants—helping clients who *do* wish to set up and maintain dedicated Internet server hardware, software, and staffing within their own office or home location. Because this process can be costly, complicated, and time consuming, some consultants focus on this service alone, offering themselves as general contractors who either do the work themselves or subcontract with technical specialists to set up and maintain the necessary hardware, software, and communications lines. Some computer companies, such as IBM, or software companies, such as Netscape, also provide overall consultation services to clients who buy the company's Internet server-specific products en route to establishing dedicated Internet server connections.

WEB CONSULTANTS

Once a client is connected, good consultants will offer solutions that fit the Internet's unique capabilities into the larger context of the client's overall communications goals, be they marketing-related, sales-driven, or related to internal communications and the establishment of intranets. Intranets are proprietary, often password-protected networks made available to selected individuals connected to a particular project or company. They can run through the greater infrastructure of the Internet and take advantage of all the Internet tools such as FTP, the Web, and e-mail.

Some consultants who specialize in this arena come from a background in marketing, sales, or communications and have learned to apply time-tested principles of effective communications to the new medium of the Internet. Though there are many new Internet-specific applications and variations to learn, good consultants should also bring basic communications principles and skills to the Internet—concepts such as clear and concise writing, developing a user-friendly interface, and applying need-driven technologies rather than bells and whistles.

Interpreting the Hype

Because the Internet and especially the Web are so new and provocative, they are also often subject to a certain amount of hype—some justified, most not—which consultants, above all others, should be aware of and able to evaluate carefully. Of course companies selling Internet-related goods and services will paint their latest contribution as the widget you can't live without. It is the consultant's job to weigh the manufacturer's information and promotional "spin" against the reality of the consultant's own hands-on experience with the product, as well as the objective reviews of other consultants, information resources, and Internet luminaries.

In this way, the consultant becomes a first line of defense for clients who lack the information needed to make important buying decisions about Internet-related goods and services. The consultant can also act as a filter who knows which questions to ask of a particular vendor and can size up the potential down side of a Web development option. For example, a good consultant can find out what the vendors won't tell you or don't want you to know about the shortcomings of their latest offerings, and can tell you how a product compares to its competition.

The Cost of a Consultant

Based on the consultant's own level of experience and the size of the budgetary decisions they influence on behalf of their clients, a consultant's fee can range just as dramatically as that of a Web developer or designer. Some consultants also double as presenters, trainers, and speakers at conventions and conferences. Some are also authors whose availability and pricing will fluctuate depending on the current level of their notoriety.

WEB CONSULTANTS

Combined with these variables is the nearly impossible chore of trying to compare apples with apples among consultants. In this text we have already shown how Web consultants may provide advice on any of several specialized tasks, including site organization, technical communications, and marketing. Assuming you have determined what kind of consultant you need, the following five tips may help in selecting an Internet consultant:

- Ask for empirical evidence that the person has more experience than you do on the Internet. Although the Web has only been on the scene since 1993, the best consultants have at least a couple of years' experience working with clients on Internet-related projects.

- Ask to see published material. A good consultant gains recognition through publication of their works or "white papers," either on the Internet or in some known periodical.

- Like all good businesspeople, ask for references. A minimum of three successful clients should be presented for your inquiry.

- Look for projects or books that the consultant has worked on in the last year.

- Inquire about a feasibility study. All good Internet consultants should be willing to conduct a feasibilty study (paid for by the client) on other similar businesses on the Internet, or to collect evidence that an Internet population exists for the client's service or product.

Nearly all consultants will be able to point to some experience or specialty that sets them apart from the rest, but with some careful questions like these, you should be able find one that is a good match for you. A consultant can become a long-term partner providing you with tangible savings in time and money. They can also provide you with the intangible savings of peace of mind and the knowledge that you have a guide who can help you blaze a trail into the new communications frontier.

24 ISDN SERVICES

MOST HOME INTERNET USERS are satisfied with the connection speed they are able to attain through a standard 14.4-kbps or 28.8-kbps modem. Or if not satisfied, they are at least resigned to the fact that this is the lowest-cost, least-hassle option for connecting to the Internet and the Web. The speed of standard modem connections is at least adequate for enjoying 99 percent of the Web material available.

ISDN SERVICES

When 28.8 Is Not Enough

But for Web professionals, time truly is money, and the option of connecting to the Web through a high-speed line makes sense even if equipment and installation prices are much higher in comparison to regular modem connections, and even though 100-percent compatibility is never guaranteed.

The most popular of the high-speed options is called *Integrated Services Digital Network* (ISDN). With ISDN it is not necessary to establish a dedicated communications line to gain the benefit of higher speed and digital connectivity. ISDN is a digital telephone communications architecture that provides an integrated voice and data capability that runs through standard telephone lines. In most cases, the same copper wires used today for plain old telephone service can be used successfully for ISDN. This means many homes and offices are already ISDN-ready. Most of the world's existing telephone network is already digital. The only part that typically isn't digital is the section that runs from the local exchange to your house or office. ISDN makes that final leg of the network digital.

ISDN distributes voice, data, video, image, and fax at speeds up to four times faster than standard telephone connections. It can attain speeds of up to 128 kbps before compression. With compression, users in many applications today can achieve throughput speeds of from 256 kbps to more than 1,024 kbps—more than a megabit per second.

In addition, digital lines are almost totally error-free, which means that the slowdowns and errors typically encountered in standard modern transmissions are no longer a problem. Another advantage is that a single ISDN line can serve as many as eight devices—digital telephones, fax machines, desktop computers, video units, and more. Each device, in turn, can be assigned its own telephone number, so that incoming calls can be routed directly to the appropriate device. Any two of these devices can be in use at the same time for voice or data transmissions, and the lines can also be combined for higher data speeds. ISDN can also be used for lower-speed data transmissions, such as for e-mail or credit card authorization, which can occur simultaneously with higher-speed transmissions.

Basic-rate ISDN does this by dividing the telephone line into three digital channels: two B channels and one D channel, each of which can be used simultaneously. The B channels are used to transmit data, at rates of 64 kbps or 56 kbps (depending on your telephone company). The D channel does the administrative work, such as setting up and tearing down the call and communicating with the telephone network. With two B channels, you can make two calls simultaneously.

Even though, technically, your home or office may be ISDN-ready, ISDN service is not yet available in all locations. Your telephone company must have installed the necessary equipment in the central office that serves you. One requirement is that you must be within a given

ISDN SERVICES

distance of the telephone company equipment that serves you (typically 18,000 feet). Further complications arising from the way your home or office is wired may interfere with ISDN transmission. As a result, even if the equipment is installed at the central office, it is possible you will not be able to get ISDN due to line interference or your distance from the central office.

To determine whether your particular wiring will support ISDN, your telephone company can perform a *line qualification* test. Some telephone companies offer what is called "ISDN Anywhere," which means that if you order ISDN, they will find a way to get it to you. In cases where the telephone company does not have the right equipment in the local central office that serves you, they can use line extension technology to serve you. However, the use of line extension technology may significantly increase the cost of your ISDN service. Generally, ISDN has better availability in urban and suburban areas but is hard to get in rural areas.

Once you have determined the availability of ISDN, the next issue is cost. ISDN rates are known as *tariffs,* and they vary by phone company. Generally, ISDN pricing is broken into three distinct elements:

- **Installation charge.** This is a one-time charge for installation. In some cases, part or all of this charge may be waived if you commit to keeping your ISDN line for a specified period of time. However, this charge may also include the installation of a new telephone line to your home—an option recommended by most service providers.

- **Monthly charge.** In addition to your basic telephone service, your phone company will charge you by the month for ISDN service.

- **Usage charges.** This is a per-minute, per-call charge associated with use of the ISDN line. Usually a monthly charge will include a base number of hours of usage each month, with the usage charge kicking in after the base amount is exceeded. Some packages have no usage charges at all, or may waive usage charges during evenings and weekends.

In general, ISDN service prices have been dropping as more and more phone companies have recognized its growth potential, and business as well as home users have become aware of its advantages for speed and reliability. Microsoft offers an excellent Web resource that can provide specific information about ISDN service, pricing, and availability in your area. To view this Web resource, direct your browser to http://www .microsoft.com/windows/getisdn/order.htm.

To connect your computer to an ISDN line you will need an *adapter,* also called an *ISDN modem* by some manufacturers. These adapters come in two flavors: internal and external. Internal ISDN adapters are cards that you put inside your PC. External adapters connect through a port on the back of your PC.

ISDN SERVICES

Internal adapters are expansion cards that are installed inside your PC. Of course, you will need an open slot in your PC that supports the same type of bus (ISA, EISA, and PCI are the most common) as the card you want to install. If you are running Windows 95, you should look for compatible adapters so that your Windows 95 operating system can automatically detect and configure the adapter for you. Some of the manufacturers that offer Windows 95-compatible adapters are:

- Diamond Multimedia (Diamond Supra NetCommander ISDN)

- Digi International (DataFire-U, DataFire-S/T, DataFire/4-S/T, PC IMAC)

- Eicon Technology/G.Diehl ISDN (DIVA ISA, DIVA PCMCIA)

- Elmic Systems (Surf-2-Surf ISDN Adapter)

- U.S. Robotics (U.S. Robotics Sportster 128k ISDN Internal Adapter or ISDN Network Adapter)

External ISDN adapters can be easier to install and often do not require any special software, but they usually do not provide the same level of performance as their internal cousins. External ISDN adapters often look just like modems. Communication programs control external ISDN modems just as they control analog modems, through standard AT commands.

One reason why external ISDN adapters do not perform as well as internal models is that external adapters plug into a PC's serial or parallel port. But most PC serial ports will not transmit information faster than 115 kbps, which is less than ISDN's maximum data speed of 128 kbps. In addition, external ISDN modems can impact the performance of your system by requiring a lot of computing power from your CPU. At a minimum, a 486/33 is required, but a faster PC is recommended for using an external ISDN adapter.

In order to use your ISDN service, you need to know which interface your equipment expects. There are two ISDN interfaces:

- *U-Interface* uses a single pair of wires between your location and the central office. It is designed for ISDN use over long distances and is the appropriate interface if you only have one device hooked up to ISDN.

- *Subscriber/Termination (S/T) Interface* uses two pairs of wires to communicate between your wall jack and your ISDN equipment. This is the interface you need if you plan to use the multiline capabilities of ISDN and split the signal out to several devices.

ISDN SERVICES

Some ISDN adapters connect directly to a U-Interface. If the PC is the only piece of equipment to be connected to an ISDN line, this type of adapter is the easiest to install. Manufacturers may describe this feature as a "built-in NT-1" or simply as a U-Interface ISDN adapter.

The phone company's ISDN wiring officially ends at what is called the *demarcation point* or *demarc*, usually just inside the building. You are responsible for the "inside wiring" from the demarc to your ISDN equipment, including the wall jacks. The telephone company or an electrical contractor will install and maintain the inside wiring for an additional charge. If you are just connecting your PC to the ISDN line, the wiring requirements may be very simple. Many homes and offices are wired with extra sets of telephone wires, and one of those sets can be used for your ISDN line.

There are a few wiring issues that can occur that may affect your service and can necessitate the extra charge of having the phone company work on your inside wiring. These include the following:

- Extra wires are already in use for analog line(s).

- Extra wires are used to power lighted phone buttons.

- Extra wires are not connected directly to the demarc.

- Wiring is structured as a daisy-chain rather than the recommended single direct connection between the ISDN wall jack and the demarc (also known as a *home run*).

If you plan to connect more than just your PC to your ISDN modem connection, you will need further instruction and information about compatible products. Your phone company should be able to help you arrive at the appropriate solutions based on the size of your company and your anticipated communications needs. There are also a number of private consultants (see Chapter 23, "Web Consultants") who specialize in helping businesses establish ISDN connections and in resolving compatibility and connectivity issues.

In terms of alternative high-speed connections, there really aren't many other options if you want more bandwidth at home or at a small business. The other, faster network choices tend to be priced beyond the reach of most individuals or small companies. If you are looking for a continuous connection, such as connecting a Web server to the Internet, a dedicated frame-relay or T-1 line may make more sense. ISDN is a circuit-switched service, which means it is only connected when it is being used. Leaving your ISDN connection on all the time can be more expensive than a dedicated line or leased line, which has a flat monthly price.

ISDN SERVICES

In coming years, the bandwidth bottleneck currently haunting residential and small business users will be alleviated with new technologies such as the Asymmetric Digital Subscriber Line (ADSL), which works over regular telephone wires, and cable modems, which work over coaxial cable television wiring. Both of these services will offer multiple megabits per second, but it will take time before these options become viable alternatives and are available in more than just a few "test" regions.

There are seven different ISDN service providers (based on telephone company service areas) in the continental U.S. See the listing in Appendix X for a provider in your region.

COMPARISON CHARTS

WEB SERVERS

A.1 Turnkey Web Servers ■

(Products listed in alphabetical order by company name.)	Apple Computer Corp. Apple Internet Server Solution 6150/66	BBN Systems & Technologies BBN Internet Server	Digital Equipment Corp. Easy Web Server	Intergraph Computer SystemsWeb Server 10	Silicon Graphics WebForce Indy
Price	$3,314	$9,895	$6,495	$6,940	$17,495
Software configuration					
Operating system	Mac OS System 7.5.1	Berkeley Software Design (Unix) BSD/OS 1.1	Windows NT Work-station 3.51	Windows NT Work-station 3.51	Silicon Graphics Irix 5.3
Web server	StarNine Technolo-gies WebStar 1.2.1	BBN Internet Server 1.2 (includes NCSA HTTPd 1.4.1)	Netscape Communi-cations Server 1.1	Netscape Communi-cations Server 1.1	Netscape Communi-cations Server 1.1
Non-Web services	AppleSearch 1.5	e-mail, FTP, Gopher, News, Telnet	FTP, WINS (Windows Internet Name Server)	FTP, WINS (Windows Internet Name Server)	e-mail, FTP, Telnet
Primary DNS support	N	Y	N	N	Y
Multinode addressing	N	N	N	N	N
Supports Common Log Format	N	Y	Y	Y	Y
CGI scripting languages sup-ported	All that support Apple events	C, C++, Bourne Shell, C Shell, Perl	C, C++	C, C++	C, C++, C Shell, Bourne Shell, Perl
System performance monitor	Y	N	Y	Y	Y
Management client	WebStar Admin 1.0	FrontDoor for Macin-tosh 1.2	Netscape Navigator 1.1	Netscape Navigator 1.1	Netscape Navigator 1.1
Web browser	Netscape Navigator 1.1	Netscape Navigator 1.1	Netscape Navigator 1.1	Netscape Navigator 1.1	Netscape Navigator 1.1
HTML editor	Bare Bones Software BBEdit 3.1.1	None	Shareware included with Internet Road-map CD	Internet Assistant for Microsoft Word for Windows 6.0	Silicon Graphics WebMagic Pro 2.01
Other applications	ACME Script Wid-gets 2.0, AppleShare 4.0.2 for Windows, Adobe Acrobat Pro 2.0, Butler, Link/Web, Claris Filemaker Pro, User 2.1v2 (runtime), HyperCard 2.2.1, Web Map 1.0.1, MacTCP Ping 2.04, TCP/IP OSAX 1.2, Apple RAID Software 1.1	Chameleon Sampler (Eudora 1.4, WinVN news reader, Archie client, Cello Web browser, Finger client, WinTalk client, WS IRC client)	Internet Roadmap CD (numerous share-ware programs)	Windows 6.0, Intergraph CD (information about the vendor)	Adobe Photoshop 3.0, Adobe Illustrator 5.5, Iris Impressa-rio, Silicon Graphics Enhanced Digital Media Tools, MovieMaster, MovieConvert
Backups	Apple Internet Server Solution and System 7.5.1 on CD-ROM	None	NT 3.51 on CD-ROM, Netscape server on CD-ROM and floppies	NT 3.51 on Netscape server CD-ROM	All software on CD-ROM
Books included	*HTML Manual of Style* (ZD Press, 1995)	*Internet Starter Kit* (Hayden Books, 1994)	None	*Web Publishing with Word for Windows "(Que, 1995)"*	None
Hardware configuration					
Processor	PowerPC 601/66MHz	Intel Pen-tium/75MHz	DEC Alpha/166MHz	Intel Pen-tium/75MHz	MIPS R4600SC/133MHz
Case	Desktop	Tower	Mini-desktop	Desktop	Desktop
Empty socket for second CPU	N	N	N	Y	Y
Total slots/empty slots	1/1 Nubus	5 ISA, 3 PCI/2 ISA, 3 PCI	None	3 PCI, 3 ISA/2 PCI, 3 ISA	2 proprietary
External cache installed/maxi-mum	128K/256K	128K/256K	256K/256K	512K/512K	512K/512K
RAM installed/maximum	16MB/72MB	16MB/256MB	32MB/256MB	24MB/256MB	32MB/256MB
I/O ports	2 serial, SCSI-1, Ethernet (10BASE-T, AUI), microphone, speaker	2 serial, parallel, Ethernet (10BASE-T, AUI, BNC), SCSI-2	Fast SCSI-2, bidirec-tional parallel port, Ethernet (AUI, BNC, 10BASE-T), line in/out, microphone, headphones	2 serial, parallel, joy-stick, line in/out, microphone, Ether-net (AUI and 10BASE-T)	2 serial, parallel, Ethernet (AUI, 10BASE-T), ISDN, Fast SCSI-2, micro-phone, stereo line in/out, S-Video/Com-posite line in, digital video in
Hard drive	Quantum Empire 1080S	Quantum Empire 540S	Quantum Empire 1080S	Quantum Lightning 540S	Seagate Technology Hawk 2LP ST31200N
Size and type of bus	1.08GB Fast Wide SCSI-3/Nubus	540MB Fast Wide SCSI-3/PCI	1.08GB Fast Wide SCSI-2/PCI	540MB Fast SCSI-2/PCI	1.05GB Fast SCSI-2/GIO
CD-ROM drive	Sony	None	None	Sony CDU-76S	None

Y—Yes N—No N/A—Not applicable INA—Information not available

Table Continues →

■ Turnkey Web Servers

(Products listed in alphabetical order by company name.)	Apple Computer Corp. Apple Internet Server Solution 6150/66	BBN Systems & Technologies BBN Internet Server	Digital Equipment Corp. Easy Web Server	Intergraph Computer SystemsWeb Server 10	Silicon Graphics WebForce Indy
Speed and type	Quad-speed SCSI	N/A	N/A	Quad-speed SCSI-2	N/A
Backup device	N/A	Hewlett-Packard 35470A (2GB)	N/A	N/A	N/A
Video-capture device	N/A	N/A	N/A	N/A	IndyCam
Monitor	Apple 14-Inch	Philips Consumer Electronics Magnavox 14-inch	None	Intergraph 21-inch	Silicon Graphics GDM17E11 17-inch
Network card/bus	Integrated/Nubus	SMC Ethercard Elite 16C Ultra/ISA	Integrated/PCI	Integrated/PCI	Integrated/GIO
SERVICE AND SUPPORT					
Warranty (parts and labor)	1 year for hardware; 90 days for software (for defects only)	90 days for hardware; 30 days for software	3 years, first year on site for hardware; 90 days toll-free phone support	3 years, first on site for system; 1 year for monitor, keyboard; 90 days for pre-loaded software, 30 days for shrink-wrapped	1 year (phone support limited to diagnosis of problem and parts replacement)
Extended warranties/ service contracts	AppleCare: $372 (est.)/year on site; $336 (est.)/year for parts shipping	$750/year for software support; $400 first year for hardware on site, $150/year for each additional year or $800 for 5 years; $100/year for system status reporting; $50/year for DNS administration	$345 for 3 years on site with next-day turnaround; $519 for 3 years on site with 4-hour turnaround; $240/year for software support; $312/year for software support with updates	$17/month for on site for years 1-3; $37/month continues on site service after year 4	$1,120/year for hardware and software; $1,420/year onsite
Toll-free tech support	Y	With service contract	With service contract	With service contract	With service contract
Hours (Eastern time)	24 hours, 7 days	M-F 9 a.m. to 8 p.m.	M-F 8 a.m. to 8 p.m.	M-F 7 a.m. to 9 p.m.	24 hours, 7 days
Online help	Web	Internet e-mail	None	Internet e-mail, BBS	Internet e-mail

Y—Yes   N—No   N/A—Not applicable   INA—Information not available

End ■

A.2 150MHz Pentium-based Potential Web Servers ■

(Products listed in alphabetical order by company name.)	Caliber Voyager III 150	Compaq DeskPro XL 6150	DTK QUIN-54M/P150	Dell Dimension XPS Pro150	Digital Celebris XL 6150
Price	$3,899	$8,999	$3,449	$7,029	$8,316
Processor	Pentium/150	Pentium Pro/150	Pentium/150	Pentium Pro/150	Pentium Pro/150
Installed RAM	16MB EDO	64MB	16MB EDO	64MB	64MB
Hard disk manufacturer and model	Seagate ST32430W	IBM DPES-31080	Seagate ST32140A	Seagate ST32140A	Seagate ST31230N
Drive capacity and interface	2GB Fast/Wide SCSI-2	1GB Fast SCSI-2	2.1GB Fast ATA-2	2GB Fast ATA-2	1GB SCSI-2
Monitor manufacturer and model	Sceptre CC-615GL	Compaq QVision 172	Tatung CM15VDS	Dell D1726S-HS	Digital FR-PCXCV-AC
Screen dimension (diagonal, inches)	15, 14	17, 16	15, 13.5	17, 15.5	15, 14.2
Graphics adapter	Diamond Stealth64 Video 3240	Matrox MGA Millennium	Diamond Stealth64 Video 3240	Number Nine Imagine 128	Matrox MGA Millennium
Memory	2MB VRAM	4MB WRAM	2MB VRAM	4MB VRAM	2MB WRAM
CD-ROM drive	Plextor PX-4XCS	Sanyo CRD-254SH	TEAC CD-56E	TEAC CD-56E	Toshiba XM-5302B
Drive speed and interface	4X SCSI	4X SCSI-2	6X ATAPI	6X ATAPI	4X ATAPI
MOTHERBOARD COMPONENTS					
Motherboard manufacturer	ASUStek	Compaq	DTK	Intel	Digital
Chip set manufacturer	Intel Triton	Intel 82450GX	Intel Triton	Intel 82450KX	Intel 82450GX
BIOS manufacturer and version	Award 4.50PG	Compaq	Award 4.50PG	AMI X03	Phoenix 4.05
EXPANDABILITY					
Maximium RAM	128MB	512MB	128MB	128MB	512MB
Expansion-bus slots	2 ISA, 2 PCI, 1 PCI/ISA	3 EISA, 1 PCI, 1 PCI/EISA	4 ISA, 2 PCI, 1 PCI/ISA	2 ISA, 3 PCI, 1 PCI/ISA	3 ISA, 2 PCI, 1 PCI/ISA
Accessible drive bays (5.25", 3.5")	4, 1	3, 0	4, 1	3, 1	3, 1
Internal drive bays (5.25", 3.5")	0, 2	0, 2	0, 4	0, 2	0, 1
Power-supply wattage	230W	240W	250W	200W	300W
Parallel, serial, mouse ports	1, 2, 1	1, 2, 1	1, 2, 0	1, 2, 1	1, 2, 1
SERVICE AND SUPPORT					
7-day, 24-hour live technical support	N	Y	N	Y	Y
Standard warranty on parts/labor	2 years/1 year	3 years/3 years	2 years/2 years	3 years/1 year	3 years/3 years
On-site service charge (first year)	Included	Included	$50	Included	Included

Y—Yes N—No N/A—Not applicable INA—Information not available

Table Continues →

■ 150MHz Pentium-based Potential Web Servers

	DirectWave Blue Thunder PO150	HP Vectra XU 6/150	IBM PC 330 with Pentium Pro Processor	Micron P150 Millennia	Micron Pro 150 Magnum Plus
Price	$7,499	$8,600	$7,649	$3,047	$8,497
Processor	Pentium Pro/150	Pentium Pro/150	Pentium Pro/150	Pentium/150	Pentium Pro/150
Installed RAM	64MB	64MB ECC	64MB	16MB EDO	64MB
Hard disk manufacturer and model	Seagate ST32550W	Seagate ST32550N	Quantum Fireball 1080A	Quantum Fireball 1280A	Quantum Grand Prix XP32151S
Drive capacity and interface	2GB Fast/Wide SCSI-2	2GB Fast SCSI-2	1GB Fast ATA-2	1.2GB Fast ATA-2	2GB SCSI-3
Monitor manufacturer and model	MAG InnoVision DX17F	HP D2817A	IBM P70	ADI ADI4V	Hitachi Accuvue XU
Screen dimensions (diagonal, inches)	17, 16	17, 15.5	17, 16	15, 14	21, 20.5
Graphics adapter	Matrox MGA Millennium	Matrox MGA Millennium	Matrox MGA Millennium	Diamond Stealth64 Video 3240	Number Nine Video 3240 Pro
Memory	2MB WRAM	2MB WRAM	4MB WRAM	2MB VRAM	8MB VRAM
CD-ROM drive	TEAC CD-56E	Sony CDU-76S	TEAC CD-56E	TEAC CD-56E	Plextor PX-63CS
Drive speed and interface	6X ATAPI	4X SCSI-2	6X ATAPI	6X ATAPI	6X SCSI
MOTHERBOARD COMPONENTS					
Motherboard manufacturer	ASUStek	HP	Intel	Micronics	Micronics
Chip set manufacturer	Intel 82450KX	Intel 82450KX	Intel 82450KX	Intel Triton	Intel 82450KX
BIOS manufacturer and version	AMI (10/10/94)	Phoenix	IBM (9/20/95)	Phoenix 4.04	Phoenix 4.50
Expandability					
Maximum RAM	512MB	256MB	128MB	128MB	256MB
Expansion-bus slots	2 ISA, 3 PCI, 1 PCI/ISA	2 ISA, 3 PCI, 1 PCI/ISA	2 ISA, 3 PCI, 1 PCI/ISA	4 ISA, 4 PCI, 1 PCI/ISA	3 ISA, 2 PCI, 1 PCI/ISA
Accessible drive bays (5.25", 3.5")	4, 1	3, 2	3, 1	3, 1	3, 1
Internal drive bays (5.25", 3.5")	0, 4	0, 2	0, 2	0, 2	0, 2
Power-supply wattage	300W	200W	200W	230W	200W
Parallel, serial, mouse ports	1, 2, 0	1, 2, 1	1, 2, 1	1, 2, 1	1, 2, 1
SERVICE AND SUPPORT					
7-day, 24-hour live technical support	N	N	Y	Y	Y
Standard warranty on parts/labor	1 year/lifetime	3 years/3 years	3 years/3 years	3 years/1 year	3 years/1 year
On-site service charge (first year)	$45	Included	Included	Included	Included

Y—Yes   N—No   N/A—Not applicable   INA—Information not available

150MHz Pentium-based Potential Web Servers ■

	MiTAC Performance Pro-32	NEC PowerMate Pro150	Reason Square 5 LX-TR/1E-150	SAG STF 150	Sys Performance Pro 150
Price	$5,999	$7,969	$2,695	$3,900	$7,894
Processor	Pentium Pro/150	Pentium Pro/150	Pentium/150	Pentium/150	Pentium Pro/150
Installed RAM	64MB	64MB	16MB EDO	16MB EDO	64MB
Hard disk manufacturer and model	Seagate ST32550N	Western Digital Caviar 31600	Quantum Fireball 1080A	Seagate ST32550W	Quantum Atlas XP34300W
Drive capacity and interface	2GB Fast SCSI-2	1.5GB EIDE	1GB Fast ATA-2	2GB Fast/Wide SCSI-2	Two 4.1GB Fast/Wide
Monitor manufacturer and model	Mitac L1564-PDM	NEC MultiSync XV 17	Pacom 5FS	ViewSonic 17EA	MAG InnoVision DX17F
Screen dimensions (diagonal, inches)	15, 13.8	17, 15.3	15, 14	17, 16	17, 16
Graphics adapter	Diamond Stealth64 Video 3240	Matrox MGA Millennium	Diamond Stealth64 Video 2201	Number Nine Imagine 128	Diamond Stealth64 Video 3240
Memory	2MB VRAM	4MB WRAM	2MB DRAM	4MB VRAM	2MB VRAM
CD-ROM drive	Plextor PX-63CS	TEAC CD-56E	TEAC CD-56E	Sony CDU-76S	TEAC CD-56E
Drive speed and interface	6X SCSI	6X ATAPI	6X ATAPI	4X SCSI-2	6X ATAPI
MOTHERBOARD COMPONENTS					
Motherboard manufacturer	ASUStek	Intel	Intel	SAG Electronics	ASUStek
Chip set manufacturer	Intel 82450KX	Intel 82450KX	Intel Triton	Intel Triton	Intel 82450KX
BIOS manufacturer and version	AMI (10/10/94)	AMI 1.06	AMI 1.00.03CB0	Award 2.0	AMI (10/10/94)
EXPANDABILITY					
Maximium RAM	512MB	128MB	128MB	512MB	512MB
Expansion-bus slots	2 ISA, 3 PCI, 1 PCI/ISA	2 ISA, 3 PCI, 1 PCI/ISA	2 ISA, 3 PCI, 1 PCI/ISA	4 ISA, 3 PCI, 1 PCI/ISA	2 ISA, 3 PCI, 1 PCI/ISA
Accessible drive bays (5.25", 3.5")	4, 1	3, 1		5, 2	6, 1
Internal drive bays (5.25", 3.5")	2, 0	0, 2	3, 1	1, 2	0, 3
Power-supply wattage	250W	200W	0, 2	300W	250W
Parallel, serial, mouse ports	1, 2, 0	1, 2, 1	200W	1, 2, 0	1, 2, 0
SERVICE AND SUPPORT			1, 2, 0		
7-day, 24-hour live technical support	N	Y	N	N	N
Standard warranty on parts/labor	1 year/1 year	3 years/3 years	3 years/6 years	2 years/1 year	Varies/1 year
On-site service charge (first year)	$99	Included	$49	$75	$95

Y—Yes   N—No   N/A—Not applicable   INA—Information not available

Table Continues →

■ 150MHz Pentium-based Potential Web Servers

	Vektron Home Office Pro-P150	Zenon Dream Media P-150	ZDS Z-Station GT	ZDS Z-Station GT Pentium Pro
Price	$2,895	$2,499	$3,463	$7,234
Processor	Pentium/150	Pentium/150	Pentium/150	Pentium Pro/150
Installed RAM	16MB EDO	16MB EDO	16MB	64MB
Hard disk manufacturer and model	Western Digital Caviar AC31600	Quantum Fireball 1080A	Western Digital Caviar AC31600	Western Digital Caviar 31600
Drive capacity and interface	1.5GB EIDE	1GB Fast ATA-2	1.5GB EIDE	1.5GB EIDE
Monitor manufacturer and model	MAG InnoVvision DX15F	MAG InnoVision DX15F	ZDS ZCM-1540	Nokia ZCM-1740
Screen dimensions (diagonal, inches)	15, 14	15, 14	15, 13	"17, 16"
Graphics adapter	Diamond Stealth64 Video 3240	Diamond Stealth64 Video 3240	Diamond Stealth64 Video 2201	Diamond Stealth64 Video 2201
Memory	2MB VRAM	2MB VRAM	2MB VRAM	2MB DRAM
CD-ROM drive	TEAC CD-56E	Goldstar GCD-R542B	Sanyo CDR-S1G	Toshiba XM-5302B
Drive speed and interface	6X ATAPI	4X ATAPI	4X ATAPI	4X ATAPI
MOTHERBOARD COMPONENTS				
Motherboard manufacturer	SuperMicro	ASUStek	ZDS	ZDS
Chip set manufacturer	Intel Triton	Intel Triton	OPTi Viper	Intel 82450KX
BIOS manufacturer and version	AMI (10/10/94)	Award 4.50PG	Phoenix 4.05.019	AMI 1.06
EXPANDABILITY				
Maximium RAM	128MB	128MB	144MB	128MB
Expansion-bus slots	4 ISA, 4 PCI	2 ISA, 3 PCI, 1 PCI/ISA	2 ISA, 1 PCI, 1 PCI/ISA	2 ISA, 3 PCI, 1 PCI/ISA
Accessible drive bays (5.25", 3.5")	3, 2	2, 2	2, 1	3, 1
Internal drive bays (5.25", 3.5")	0, 1	0, 2	0, 0	0, 2
Power-supply wattage	200W	240W	150W	200W
Parallel, serial, mouse ports	1, 2, 0	1, 2, 0	1, 2, 1	1, 2, 1
SERVICE AND SUPPORT				
7-day, 24-hour live technical support	N	N	Y	Y
Standard warranty on parts/labor	1 year/lifetime	1 year/1 year	3 years/3 years	3 years/3 years
On-site service charge (first year)	$50	$50	Included	Included

Y—Yes   N—No   N/A—Not applicable   INA—Information not available

End ■

A.3   166MHz Pentium-based Potential Web Servers ∎

(Products listed in alphabetical order by company name.)	AcerPower P166	Comtrade 3D Game Station 8X	Dell Dimension XPS P166c	Digital Celebris GL 5166ST	DTK QUIN-54M/P166
Price	$3,895	$3,375	$3,899	$5,218	$3,849
Processor	Pentium/166	Pentium/166	Pentium/166	Pentium/166	Pentium/166
Installed RAM	16MB	16MB EDO	16MB EDO	16MB EDO	16MB EDO
Hard disk manufacturer and model	Western Digital Caviar AC31600	Quantum Fireball 1280A	Quantum Fireball 1080A	Western Digital Caviar AC31600	Seagate ST32140A
Drive capacity and interface	1.5GB EIDE	1.2GB Fast ATA-2	1GB Fast ATA-2	1.5GB EIDE	2.1GB Fast ATA-2
Monitor manufacturer and model	Acer 7176i72	MAG InnoVision DX-17F	Dell D1726S-HS	Digital PCXBV-KA	ADI MicroScan 5EP
Screen dimensions (diagonal, inches)	17, 16	17, 16	17, 15.5	17, 16	17, 15.5
Graphics adapter	Diamond Stealth64 Video 3240	Diamond Edge 3D 3240	Number Nine Imagine 128	Matrox MGA Millennium	Diamond Stealth64 Video 3240
Memory	2MB VRAM	2MB VRAM	4MB VRAM	2MB WRAM	2MB VRAM
CD-ROM drive	Mitsumi CRMC-FX400D	Diamond 8422-IDE	TEAC CD-56E	Toshiba XM-530TA	TEAC CD-56E
Drive speed and interface	4X ATAPI	8X ATAPI	6X ATAPI	4X ATAPI	6X ATAPI
MOTHERBOARD COMPONENTS					
Motherboard manufacturer	Acer	Tyan	Dell	Digital	DTK
Chip set manufacturer	Intel Triton	Intel Triton	Intel Triton	Intel Triton	Intel Triton
BIOS manufacturer and version	Acer R01-N5	Award 4.50PG	AMI/Dell X22	Phoenix (7/25/95)	Award 4.50PG
EXPANDABILITY					
Maximum RAM	128MB	128MB	128MB	128MB	128MB
Expansion-bus slots	4 ISA, 4 PCI, 1 PCI/ISA	4 ISA, 3 PCI, 1 PCI/ISA	3 ISA, 3 PCI, 1 PCI/ISA	2 ISA, 2 PCI/ISA	4 ISA, 2 PCI, 1 PCI/ISA
Accessible drive bays (5.25", 3.5")	3, 2	3, 2	3, 1	3, 1	4, 1
Internal drive bays (5.25", 3.5")	0, 2	0, 3	0, 2	0, 2	0, 3
Power-supply wattage	240W	210W	230W	200W	250W
Parallel, serial, mouse ports	1, 2, 1	1, 2, 0	1, 2, 1	1, 2, 1	1, 2, 0
SERVICE AND SUPPORT					
7-day, 24-hour live technical support	Y	N	Y	Y	N
Standard warranty on parts/labor	3 years/1 year	1 year/1 year	3 years/1 year	3 years/3 years	2 years/2 years
On-site service charge (first year)	Included	$25	Included	Included	$50

Y—Yes   N—No   N/A—Not applicable   INA—Information not available

Table Continues →

166MHz Pentium-based Potential Web Servers

	EPS Evolution P-166	Gateway P5-166 XL	IBM PC 350-P166	Micron P166 Millennia Plus	Mitsuba Premier System 166
Price	$2,795	$3,789	$4,400	$4,446	$3,900
Processor	Pentium/166	Pentium/166	Pentium/166	Pentium/166	Pentium/166
Installed RAM	16MB EDO	16MB EDO	16MB EDO	16MB EDO	16MB EDO
Hard disk manufacturer and model	Quantum Fireball 1280A	Western Digital Caviar AC31600	Quantum Fireball 1080A	Quantum Grand Prix XP32151S	Quantum Fireball 1080S
Drive capacity and interface	1.2GB Fast ATA-2	1.5GB EIDE	1GB Fast ATA-2	2GB SCSI-3	1GB SCSI-3
Monitor manufacturer and model	CTX 1565D	Gateway Crystal-Scan 17	IBM G70	ADI ADI4V	Mitsuba P766DU
Screen dimensions (diagonal, inches)	15, 14	17, 16	17, 16	15, 14	17, 16.5
Graphics adapter	Number Nine 9FX Motion 771	Matrox MGA Millennium	Matrox MGA Millennium	Diamond Stealth64 Video 3240	Diamond Stealth64 Video 3240
Memory	2MB VRAM	4MB WRAM	4MB WRAM	2MB VRAM	2MB VRAM
CD-ROM drive	TEAC CD-56E	Wearnes CDD-620	TEAC CD-56E	Plextor PX-63CS	Sony CDU-76S
Drive speed and interface	6X ATAPI	6X ATAPI	6X ATAPI	6X SCSI	4X SCSI-2
MOTHERBOARD COMPONENTS					
Motherboard manufacturer	EPS	Intel	Intel	Micronics	Intel
Chip set manufacturer	Intel Triton	Intel Triton	Intel Triton	Intel Triton	Intel Triton
BIOS manufacturer and version	Award 4.50PG	AMI 1.00.01CN0	AMI 0.05.03.CC0M	Phoenix 4.04	AMI 1.0
EXPANDABILITY					
Maximum RAM	128MB	128MB	128MB	128MB	128MB
Expansion-bus slots	4 ISA, 4 PCI, 1 PCI/ISA	2 ISA, 3 PCI, 1 PCI/ISA	3 ISA, 2 PCI/ISA	4 ISA, 4 PCI, 1 PCI/ISA	3 ISA, 4 PCI, 1 PCI/ISA
Accessible drive bays (5.25", 3.5")	3, 2	3, 1	2, 1	3, 1	4, 1
Internal drive bays (5.25", 3.5")	0, 2	0, 3	0, 2	0, 2	0, 4
Power-supply wattage	230W	200W	200W	200W	250W
Parallel, serial, mouse ports	1, 2, 0	1, 2, 1	1, 2, 1	1, 2, 1	1, 2, 0
SERVICE AND SUPPORT					
7-day, 24-hour live technical support	N	Y	Y	Y	Y
Standard warranty on parts/labor	3 years/1 year	3 years/1 year	3 years/3 years	3 years/1 year	2 years/2 years
On-site service charge (first year)	Included	Included	Included	Included	Included (2 years)

Y—Yes   N—No   N/A—Not applicable   INA—Information not available

166MHz Pentium-based Potential Web Servers ■

	NEC PowerMate P166	PerComp P166 Professional	PowerSpec*PC Reference Series P166	Quantex QP5/166 SM-2	Reason Square 5 LX-TR/1E-166
Price	$4,169	$3,449	$3,878	$3,299	$3,495
Processor	Pentium/166	Pentium/166	Pentium/166	Pentium/166	Pentium/166
Installed RAM	16MB EDO	16MB EDO	16MB EDO	16MB EDO	16MB EDO
Hard disk manufacturer and model	Western Digital Caviar AC31600	Western Digital Caviar AC31600	Western Digital Caviar AC31600	Western Digital Caviar AC31600	Quantum Fireball 1080A
Drive capacity and interface	1.5GB EIDE	1.5GB EIDE	1.5GB EIDE	1.5GB EIDE	1GB Fast ATA-2
Monitor manufacturer and model	NEC MultiSync XV 17	Delta/PerComp DA-1765 VAF	Micro Electronics P766DU	MAG InnoVision DX17F	Samsung 17GLSi
Screen dimensions (diagonal, inches)	17, 15	17, 16	17, 16.5	17, 16	17, 16
Graphics adapter	Matrox MGA Millennium	Matrox MGA Millennium	Diamond Edge 3D 2220	STB PowerGraph 64 Video	Diamond Stealth64 Video 3240
Memory	2MB WRAM	2MB WRAM	2MB DRAM	2MB EDO DRAM	4MB VRAM
CD-ROM drive	TEAC CD-56E	TEAC CD-56E	Aztech CDA 668-01I	Aztech CDA 668-01I	TEAC CD-56E
Drive speed and interface	6X ATAPI	6X ATAPI	6X ATAPI	6X ATAPI	6X ATAPI
MOTHERBOARD COMPONENTS					
Motherboard manufacturer	NEC	PerComp	Acer	Intel	Intel
Chip set manufacturer	Intel Triton	Intel Triton	Intel Triton	Intel Triton	Intel Triton
BIOS manufacturer and version	Phoenix 4.05.C	Award 4.50PG	Phoenix 4.04	AMI 1.00CBO v.2.0	AMI 1.00.03.CBO
Expandability					
Maximum RAM	128MB	128MB	128MB	128MB	128MB
Expansion-bus slots	3 ISA, 1 PCI, 1 PCI/ISA	4 ISA, 3 PCI	4 ISA, 4 PCI, 1 PCI/ISA	4 ISA, 3 PCI	2 ISA, 3 PCI, 1 PCI/ISA
Accessible drive bays (5.25", 3.5")	3, 1	2, 2	3, 2	4, 1	3, 1
Internal drive bays (5.25", 3.5")	0, 1	0, 1	0, 4	0, 2	0, 2
Power-supply wattage	200W	230W	200W	250W	200W
Parallel, serial, mouse ports	1, 2, 1	1, 2, 0	1, 2, 0	1, 2, 0	1, 2, 0
SERVICE AND SUPPORT					
7-day, 24-hour live technical support	Y	Y	N	N	N
Standard warranty on parts/labor	3 years/3 years	1 year/1 year	3 years/3 years	1 year/1year	3 years/6 years
On-site service charge (first year)	Included	Included	N/A	Included	$49

Y—Yes   N—No   N/A—Not applicable   INA—Information not available

Table Continues →

ZIFF-DAVIS PRESS

■ 166MHz Pentium-based Potential Web Servers

	Robotech Cobra XLT P166	Royal Ultra Media-15	SAG STF 166	Sys Performance P166T	USA Flex PT-166 Ultimate Multimedia Tower
Price	$3,399	$2,945	$4,590	$3,495	$4,395
Processor	Pentium/166	Pentium/166	Pentium/166	Pentium/166	Pentium/166
Installed RAM	16MB EDO	16MB	16MB EDO	16MB EDO	16MB EDO
Hard disk manufacturer and model	Quantum Fireball 1080A	Quantum Fireball 1280AT	Seagate ST15150W	Quantum Fireball 1280A	Western Digital Caviar AC31600
Drive capacity and interface	1GB Fast ATA-2	1.2GB Fast ATA-2	4GB Fast/Wide SCSI-2	Two 1.2GB Fast ATA-2	1.5GB EIDE
Monitor manufacturer and model	Cobra NZ17	MAG InnoVision DX15FG	ViewSonic 17EA	MAG InnoVision DX17F	MAG InnoVision DX17F
Screen dimensions (diagonal, inches)	17, 16	15, 14	17, 16	17, 16	17, 16
Graphics adapter	Diamond Stealth64 Video 3240	Diamond Stealth64 Video 3240	Number Nine Imagine 128	Diamond Stealth64 Video 3240	Number Nine Vision 330
Memory	2MB VRAM	2MB VRAM	4MB VRAM	2MB VRAM	2MB VRAM
CD-ROM drive	TEAC CD-56E	Aztech CDA 668-01I	Sony CDU-76S	NEC CDR-512	Acer CD-665A-002
Drive speed and interface	6X ATAPI	6X ATAPI	4X SCSI-2	6X SCSI-2	5X ATAPI
MOTHERBOARD COMPONENTS					
Motherboard manufacturer	Robotech	Royal	SAG Electronics	ASUStek	Intel
Chip set manufacturer	Intel Triton	Intel Triton	Intel Triton	Intel Triton	Intel Triton
BIOS manufacturer and version	Award 4.50PG	Award 4.50PG	Award 4.50PG	Award 4.50PG	AMI 1.00.01CL0
EXPANDABILITY					
Maximum RAM	128MB	128MB	512MB	128MB	128MB
Expansion-bus slots	4 ISA, 3 PCI, 1 PCI/ISA	3 ISA, 3 PCI, 1 PCI/ISA	4 ISA, 3 PCI, 1 PCI/ISA	2 ISA, 3 PCI, 1 PCI/ISA	2 ISA, 3 PCI, 1 PCI/ISA
Accessible drive bays (5.25", 3.5")	4, 1	3, 2	5, 2	3, 2	6, 1
Internal drive bays (5.25", 3.5")	0, 4	0, 3	1, 2	0, 2	0, 5
Power-supply wattage	230W	230W	300W	230W	230W
Parallel, serial, mouse ports	1, 2, 0	1, 2, 0	1, 2, 0	1, 2, 0	1, 2, 0
SERVICE AND SUPPORT					
7-day, 24-hour live technical support	N	N	N	N	Y
Standard warranty on parts/labor	2 years/lifetime	1 year/lifetime	2 years/1 year	Varies/1 year	3 years/lifetime
On-site service charge (first year)	Included	N/A	$75	$95	Included

Y—Yes   N—No   N/A—Not applicable   INA—Information not available

166MHz Pentium-based Potential Web Servers ■

	US Computer Patriot LX 166	Zenon Dream Media P-166
Price	$3,499	$2,829
Processor	Pentium/166	Pentium/166
Installed RAM	16MB EDO	16MB EDO
Hard disk manufacturer and model	Quantum Fireball 1280A	Western Digital Caviar AC31600
Drive capacity and interface	1.2GB Fast ATA-2	1.5GB EIDE
Monitor manufacturer and model	Wyse WY-15E	MAG InnoVision DX17F
Screen dimensions (diagonal, inches)	15, 14	15, 14
Graphics adapter	Diamond Stealth64 Video 3240	Diamond Stealth64 Video 3240
Memory	2MB DRAM	2MB VRAM
CD-ROM drive	TEAC CD-56E	Goldstar GCD-R542B
Drive speed and interface	6X ATAPI	4X ATAPI
MOTHERBOARD COMPONENTS		
Motherboard manufacturer	C Point Corp.	ASUStek
Chip set manufacturer	Intel Triton	Intel Triton
BIOS manufacturer and version	Phoenix 4.04	Award 4.50PG
EXPANDABILITY		
Maximium RAM	128MB	128MB
Expansion-bus slots	3 ISA, 3 PCI, 1 PCI/ISA	2 ISA, 3 PCI, 1 PCI/ISA
Accessible drive bays (5.25", 3.5")	3, 1	2, 2
Internal drive bays (5.25", 3.5")	1, 4	0, 2
Power-supply wattage	250W	240W
Parallel, serial, mouse ports	1, 2, 0	1, 2, 0
SERVICE AND SUPPORT		
7-day, 24-hour live technical support	N	N
Standard warranty on parts/labor	2 years/lifetime	1 year/1 year
On-site service charge (first year)	$35	$50

Y—Yes N—No N/A—Not applicable INA—Information not available

End ■

ACCESS
TECHNOLOGIES

B.1 V.34 Fast Modems ∎

(Products listed in alphabetical ordedr by company name.)	Archtek America SmartLink 2834A V.34	AT&T Paradyne Comsphere 3800Plus	Best Data Best Data Smart One 2834FX	Boca Research V.34 28,000bps External BocaModem	Cardinal Technologies Cardinal 28.8
Price (external modem)	$231	$796	$212	$229	$189
CONFIGURATION					
Maximum data speed/transmission rate	28.8 Kbps/ 115.2 Kbps	33.6 Kbps/ 134.4 Kbps	28.8 Kbps/ 115.2 Kbps	28.8 Kbps/ 115.2 Kbps	28.8 Kbps/ 115.2 Kbps
Signal converter	AT&T Microelectronics 1633 F08 AB	AT&T Microelectronics DSP 16A	Rockwell International R6682-21	Rockwell International RC288DPi	Rockwell International R6682
Controller	AT&T Microelectronics C882-29Q-5	Motorola 68302FC25C	Rockwell International L3902-57	Rockwell International L39/U	Rockwell L3902
Transmission type	Asynchronous/ Synchronous	Asynchronous/ Synchronous	Asynchronous	Asynchronous	Asynchronous
Display	LED	LED/LCD	LED	LED	LED
Security features	N/A	Password verification	N/A	N/A	N/A
Leased-line features	N/A	Four-wire	N/A	N/A	N/A
COMPATIBILITY					
Data standards	Bell 103, Bell 212A, Bell 201C, Bell 208A, V.21, V.22, V.22bis, V.23, V.25bis, V.29, V.32, V.32bis, V.34	Bell 103, Bell 212A, V.21, V.22, V.22bis, V.23, V.25bis, V.29, V.32, V.32bis, V.34	Bell 103, Bell 212A, V.21, V.22, V.22bis, V.23, V.32, V.32bis, V.34	Bell 103, Bell 212A, V.21, V.22, V.22bis, V.29, V.32, V.32bis, V.34	Bell 103, Bell 212A, V.21, V.22, V.22bis, V.23, V.29, V.32, V.32bis, V.34
Compression standards	V.42bis, MNP 5	V.42bis, MNP 5	V.42bis, MNP 5	V.42bis, MNP 5	V.42bis, MNP 5
V.fast-class compatible	N	N	Y	Y	Y
Alternate I/O hardware	N/A	N/A	N/A	Boca 16550 serial card	N/A
Bundled/optional	N/A	N/A	N/A	Bundled	N/A
Port type	N/A	N/A	N/A	Serial	N/A
Maximum data speed	N/A	N/A	N/A	115.2 Kbps	N/A
UPGRADE OPTIONS					
Method (from V.fc to V.34)	Flash ROM	Flash ROM	Chip	Chip	Flash ROM
SUPPORT					
Warranty (parts and labor)	Five years parts, two years labor	Two years	Two years	Five years	Lifetime
Toll-free tech support	N	Y	N	N (1-900 number)	N

Y—Yes N—No N/A—Not applicable INA—Information not available

Table Continues →

V.34 Fast Modems

	E-Tech Research Bullet 100E	Hayes Microcomputer Products Hayes Optima 288 V.34/V.FC+Fax	Logicode Technology Quicktel 2814XV	Motorola Information Systems V.3400	Multi-Tech Systems MT2834ZDX
Price (external modem)	$398	$419	$199	$665	$229
CONFIGURATION					
Maximum data speed/ transmission rate	28.8 Kbps/ 115.2 Kbps	28.8 Kbps/ 230.4 Kbps	28.8 Kbps/ 115.2 Kbps	28.8 Kbps/ 115.2 Kbps	28.8 Kbps/ 115.2 Kbps
Signal converter	AT&T Microelectronics V.34	Rockwell International R6682DPi	Rockwell International RC288DPi	Motorola 56002	AT&T Microelectronics DSP 33x
Controller	Motorola 68702	Hayes code on Motorola 68302	Rockwell International L3902-57	Motorola 68302	Zilog 182
Transmission type	Asynchronous/ synchronous	Asynchronous/ synchronous	Asynchronous/ synchronous	Asynchronous/ synchronous	Asynchronous
Display	LED/LCD	LED	LED	LCD	LED
Security features	Callback	N/A	N/A	Password verification, callback	N/A
Leased-line features	Two-wire	N/A	Two-wire	Two-/Four-wire	N/A
COMPATIBILITY					
Data standards	Bell 103, Bell 212A, V.21, V.22, V.22bis, V.23, V.25bis, V.32, V.32bis, V.34	Bell 103, Bell 212A, V.22, V.22bis, V.25bis, V.32, V.32bis, V.34	Bell 103, Bell 212A, V.21, V.22, V.22bis, V.23, V.29, V.32, V.32bis, V.34	Bell 103, Bell 212A, V.21, V.22, V.22bis, V.25bis, V.32, V.32bis, V.34	Bell 103, Bell 212A, V.22, V.22bis, V.29bis, V.32, V.32bis, V.34
Compression standards	V.42bis, MNP 5	V.42bis, MNP 5	V.42bis, MNP 5	V.42bis, MNP 5	V.42bis, MNP 5
V.fast-class compatible	N	Y	Y	Y	N
Alternate I/O hardware	N/A	Hayes ESP-2	Logicode 16550 serial card	N/A	Multi-Tech serial board
Bundled/Optional	N/A	$77 (Average mail order)	$99 (Direct)	N/A	$99 (Direct)
Port type	N/A	Serial	Serial	N/A	Serial
Maximum data speed	N/A	921.6 Kbps	115.2 Kbps	N/A	115.2 Kbps
UPGRADE OPTIONS					
Method (from V.fc to V.34)	Flash ROM	Chip	Chip	Chip	Flash ROM
SUPPORT					
Warranty (parts and labor)	Two years	Five years registered owners, two years otherwise	Lifetime	Two years	10 years
Toll-free tech support	N	N	N	Y	Y

Y—Yes   N—No   N/A—Not applicable   INA—Information not available

V.34 Fast Modems ■

	Practical Peripherals ProClass 288MT V.34	Supra SupraFAXModem 288	U.S. Robotics Sportster 28800 Data/Fax	Zoom Telephonics Zoom/Fax-Modem V.34X
Price (external modem)	$266	$220	$234	$224
CONFIGURATION				
Maximum data speed/ transmission rate	28.8 Kbps/ 230.4 Kbps	28.8 Kbps/ 115.2 Kbps	28.8 Kbps/ 115.2 Kbps	28.8 Kbps/ 115.2 Kbps
Signal converter	Rockwell International R6682-21/RC288DPi	Rockwell International RC288DPi	Texas Instruments C51	Rockwell International RC 288DPi
Controller	Intel MSH S-80C32U-44/Intel Proprietary	Rockwell International L390	Intel 80186	Rockwell International L390
Transmission type	Asynchronous/ synchronous	Asynchronous/synchronous	Asynchronous	Asynchronous
Display	LED	2-digit LED numeric display	LED	LED
Security features	N/A	N/A	N/A	N/A
Leased-line features	Two-wire	N/A	N/A	N/A
COMPATIBILITY				
Data standards	Bell 103, Bell 212A, V.21, V.22, V.22bis, V.23, V.32, V.32bis, V.34	Bell 103, Bell 212A, V.21, V.22, V.22bis, V.23, V.29, V.32, V.32bis, V.34	Bell 103, Bell 212A, V.21, V.22, V.22bis, V.23, V.29, V.32, V.32bis, V.34	Bell 103, Bell 212A, V.21, V.22, V.22bis, V.23, V.29, V.32, V.32bis, V.34
Compression standards	V.42bis, MNP 5	V.42bis, MNP 5	V.42bis, MNP 5	V.42bis, MNP 5
V.fast-class compatible	Y	Y	Y	Y
Alternate I/O hardware	Hayes ESP-2	N/A	N/A	N/A
Bundled/Optional	$77 (Average mail order)	N/A	N/A	N/A
Port type	Serial	N/A	N/A	N/A
Maximum data speed	230.4 Kbps	N/A	N/A	N/A
UPGRADE OPTIONS				
Method (from V.fc to V.34)	Chip	Flash ROM	Chip	Chip
SUPPORT				
Warranty (parts and labor)	Lifetime	Five years	Five years	Seven years
Toll-free tech support	N	N	N	N

Y—Yes   N—No   N/A—Not applicable   INA—Information not available   **End** ■

■ B.2 Modems

Company	Model	Price	Max. Data/Fax Transmission (kbps)	Error Correction/ Data Compression
ActionTec	DataLink 28.8	$369	28.8/14.4	MNP5, V.42b
ActionTec	ComNet 28.8	$589	28.8/14.4	MNP5, V.42b
Amagic Technologies	1428VQH	$130	28.8/14.4	MNP5, V.42b
Amagic Technologies	1428VQE	$145	28.8/14.4	MNP5, V.42b
Amquest	AM2814IHY	$330	28.8/14.4	MNP5/10/10EC, V.42b
Amquest	AM2814IV	$330	28.8/14.4	MNP5/10/10EC, V.42b
Angia Communications	SJ288C SafeJack	$349	28.8/14.4	MNP5, ETC, V.42b
Angia Communications	V.34 Ethernet Combo Card	$549	28.8/14.4	MNP2-5, V.42b
Apex Data	Mobile Plus Cellular V.32	$224	14.4/14.4	MNP5/10, LAPM, V.42b, TX-CEL
Apex Data	Mobile Plus Cellular V.34	$352	28.8/14.4	MNP5/10, LAPM, V.42b, TX-CEL
Archtek America	2834A	$289	28.8/14.4	MNP5, LAPB/N, V.42b
Archtek America	2834BRV	$289	28.8/14.4	MNP5, LAPB/N, V.42b
Aspen Technologies	28.8VFXSPDSVD	$310	28.8/14.4	V.42b
Aspen Technologies	28.8PC	$345	28.8/14.4	V.42b
AT&T Paradyne	Comsphere 3825 Plus	$695	33.6/14.4	MNP5, ETC, V.42b
ATI Technologies	14400 ETC-E	$129	14.4/14.4	MNP5, V.42b
ATI Technologies	19200 ETC-E	$139	19.2/14.4	MNP5, LAPM, V.42b
Best Data Products	Smart One 2834FLX	$299	28.8/14.4	MNP5/10/10EC, LAPM, V.42b
Best Data Products	Smart One 2834VLX	$319	28.8/14.4	MNP5/10/10EC, LAPM, V.42b
Black Box	32192 turbo MD840A	$895	19.2/14.4	MNP5, V.42b
Black Box	3400 MD880A	$895	28.8/14.4	MNP5,V.42b
Boca Research	SoundExpression 28.8SRS	$369	28.8/14.4	MNP5, LAPM, V.42b
Boca Research	SoundExpression 28.8SI/D	$449	28.8/14.4	MNP5, LAPM, V.42b
Cardinal Technologies	MVP288XV External	$209	28.8/14.4	MNP4-5, V.42b, T.30
Cardinal Technologies	MVP288C2 PC Card	$299	28.8/14.4	MNP4-5/10EC, V.42b
Creative Labs	Modem Blaster 14.4	$100	14.4/14.4	MNP5, V.42b
Creative Labs	Modem Blaster 28.8	$220	28.8/14.4	MNP5, V.42b
Creative Labs	PhoneBlaster	$299	14.4/14.4	MNP5, V.42b
CXR Telecom	1945-FLI V.32ter	$845	19.2/9.6	MNP5, LAPM, ETC, V.42b
CXR Telecom	2845-FLI V.34	$895	28.8/9.6	MNP5, LAPM, ETC, V.42b
D-Link Systems	DME-650T	$299	19.2/14.4	MNP2-5, V.42
D-Link Systems	DM-144FC	$299	14.4/14.4	MNP2-4/10, LAPM, V.42
Dayna Communications	PC2144 CommuniCard	$329	14.4/14.4	MNP5/10/10EC, LAPM, V.42b, TX-CEL
Dayna Communications	PC2288 CommuniCard	$499	28.8/14.4	MNP5/10/10EC, LAPM, V.42b, TX-CEL
Diamond Multimedia Systems	TeleCommander 3500XL	$299	28.8/14.4	MNP5/10, LAPM, V.42b
Digicom Systems	PCMCIA 14.4 Data/Fax	$239	14.4/14.4	MNP5, V.42b
Digicom Systems	Scout 288V34i	$259	28.8/14.4	MNP5, V.42b

Y—Yes   N—No   N/A—Not applicable   INA—Information not available

Modems ∎

Company	Model	Price	Max. Data/Fax Transmission (kbps)	Error Correction/ Data Compression
E-Tech Research	E288MX	$289	28.8/14.4	MNP5, V.42b
E-Tech Research	100E	$449	28.8/14.4	MNP5, V.42b
Epson America	EFM144FP	$199	14.4/14.4	MNP2-5/10, LAPM, V.42b
Epson America	EFM144C	$269	14.4/14.4	MNP2-5, LAPM, V.42b
EXP Computer	ThinFax 288i	$449	28.8/14.4	MNP5, LAPM, V.42b
Explorer Communications	FM-288EX	$349	28.8/14.4	MNP5, LAPM, V.42b
Explorer Communications	FM-288R	$350	28.8/14.4	LAPM, MNP10EC, V.42b
Global Village Communications	TelePort Gold II	$155	14.4/14.4	MNP5, LAPM, V.42b
Global Village Communications	TelePort/Platinum for Mac	$279	28.8/14.4	MNP5, LAPM, V.42b
GVC/MaxTech	PCM288R	$299	28.8/14.4	MNP2-5, V.42b
GVC/MaxTech	XSVD288I	$299	28.8/14.4	MNP2-5, V.42b
Hayes	Optima 144 Business	$519	14.4/14.4	MNP5, LAPM, V.42b
Hayes	Optima 288 Business	$579	28.8/14.4	MNP5, LAPM, V.42b
I/O Magic	Lightning 14.4	$169	14.4/14.4	MNP5, V.42b
I/O Magic	Lightning 28.8	$349	28.8/14.4	MNP5/10, V.42b
IBM	WaveRunner 04H7686	$545	28.8/14.4	MNP5/10, LAPM, V.42b
IBM	PCMCIA 04H7122	$1,095	14.4/14.4	MNP5/10, LAPM, V.42b, TX-CEL
J-Mark Computer	A1428VQH34V	$225	28.8/14.4	MNP5
J-Mark Computer	A1428VQC34	$285	14.4/14.4	MNP5
Kingston Technology	DataRex PC Card	$215	14.4/14.4	MNP5/10, V.42
LeeMah DataCom	SafeConnect 28.8 V.34	$199	28.8/14.4	MNP5, LAPM, V.42b
LeeMah DataCom	Fastraq 28.8 V.34 HC	$299	28.8/14.4	MNP5, LAPM, V.42b
LeeMah DataCom	Fastraq 28.8 V.34 E	$399	28.8/14.4	MNP5, LAPM, V.42b
Logicode Technology	28V14XV	INA	28.8/14.4	MNP5, V.42b
Logicode Technology	28V14HV	INA	28.8/14.4	MNP5, V.42b
MagicRAM	933414	$125	14.4/14.4	MNP5, LAPM, V.42b
MagicRAM	933288	$225	28.8/14.4	MNP5/10, LAPM, V.42b
Megahertz	XJ3288	$349	28.8/14.4	MNP5/10/10EC, LAPM, ETC, V.42b
Megahertz	CC6288	$349	28.8/14.4	MNP5/10EC, LAPM, ETC, V.42b
Microcom	TravelCard 28.8P	$449	28.8/14.4	MNP5/10, LAPM, V.42b
Microcom	DeskPorte Fast	$579	28.8/14.4	MNP5/10, LAPM, V.42b
MidWest Micro	Infotel 28.8 (005249)	$199	28.8/14.4	MNP2-5, V.42b
MidWest Micro	Infotel 28.8 V.34 (005993)	$219	28.8/14.4	MNP2-5, V.42b
miro Computer Products	miroConnect 34 wave	$349	28.8/14.4	MNP5, V.42b
Motorola ISG	326X	$745 (min.)	14.4/N/A	MNP5, LAPM, V.42b
Motorola ISG	326X Fast	$825 (min.)	28.8/N/A	MNP5, LAPM, V.42b
MultiTech Systems	MT2834ZDX	$349	28.8/14.4	MNP5, LAPM, V.42b
MultiTech Systems	MT2834LT	$399	28.8/14.4	MNP5, LAPM, V.42b

Y—Yes　N—No　N/A—Not applicable　INA—Information not available

Table Continues →

■ Modems

Company	Model	Price	Max. Data/Fax Transmission (kbps)	Error Correction/ Data Compression
New Media	28.8 NetSurfer	$400	28.8/14.4	MNP5, LAPM, ETC, V.42b
New Media	28.8 NetSurfer International	$550	28.8/14.4	MNP5/10, LAPM, V.42b
NovaLink Technologies	NovaModem 144	$199	14.4/14.4	MNP2-5/10/10EC, LAPM, V.42b
NovaLink Technologies	NovaModem 288	$399	28.8/14.4	MNP2-5/10, LAPM, V.42b
Ositech Communications	Queen of Diamonds 14.4	$649	14.4/14.4	MNP5/10/10EC, LAPM, V.42b
Ositech Communications	Queen of Diamonds 28.8	$849	28.8/14.4	MNP5/10/10EC, LAPM, V.42b
Pearl America	Pearl V.34 Internal	$125	28.8/14.4	MNP5, V.42b
Pearl America	Pearl V.34 External	$135	28.8/14.4	MNP5, V.42b
Penril Datability	ALX V.32/19.2	$845	19.2/14.4	MNP2-5, LAPM, V.42b
Penril Datability	ALX V.34	$895	33.6/14.4	MNP2-5, LAPM, V.42b
Powercom America	DM-2814VH	$189	28.8/14.4	MNP5, LAPM, V.42b
Powercom America	DM-2814V	$239	28.8/14.4	MNP5, LAPM, V.42b
Practical Peripherals	ProClass 288LCD V.34	$459	28.8/14.4	MNP5, V.42b
Practical Peripherals	MacClass 288LCD V.34	$459	28.8/14.4	MNP5, V.42b
Prometheus Products	CyberPort Pro PC288ev	$239	28.8/14.4	MNP5, LAPM, V.42b
Prometheus Products	CyberPhone PC288evsp	$239	28.8/14.4	MNP5, LAPM, V.42b
Supra	Express F/MAC	$159	28.8/14.4	MNP5, V.42b
US Robotics	Sporster External for PC	$119	14.4/14.4	MNP 2-4, MNP 5, V 42b
US Robotics	Sporster External for Macintosh	$119	14.4/14.4	MNP 2-4, MNP 5, V 42b
US Robotics	Courier	$479	28.8/14.4	MNP 2-4, MNP 5, V42b
Zoom	VFX (Mac and PC)	$160	14.4/14.4	MNP5, V.42b
Zoom	V-34I Model 275	$140	28.8/14.4	MNP5, V.42b

Y—Yes   N—No   N/A—Not applicable   INA—Information not available

End ■

B.3 Cable Modems ■

(Products listed in alphabetical order by company name.)	Alexon Cable Master (CM-1)	Com21/3Com ComPort	Digital Equipment Corp. LCB	First Pacific Networks FPN 3000
Estimated Price	$350	$370	$425	$440
Speed	Assymetrical; 64 kbps up; 2.016 Mbps down	Symmetrical; 1.9 Mbps up; 30 Mbps down	Symmetrical; 10 Mbps	Straight Ethernet: 10 Mbps up and 10 Mbps down
Modulation	FSK up; 64QAM down	QPSK up; QAM down	QPSK up; 64QAM down	SQPSK up; AMPSK down
Frequency	10–57 MHz up; 72–800 MHz down	5–40 MHz up; 88–800 MHz down	5-42 Mhz up 54-550 MHz down	48–72 MHz up; 240–264 MHz down

	General Instrument/Fore Systems SURFboard ATM	Hewlett Packard QuickBurst	Hybrid Networks Remote Link Adapter 211	IBM Name unknown
Price	$390	$475	$400	$500
Speed	Symmetrical; 1.7 Mbps up; 27 Mbps down	Symmetrical; 15 Mbps up; 30 Mbps down	Symmetrical; 512 kbps up; 30 Mps down	ATM transport protocol
Modulation	QPSK up; 64QAM down	QPSK up; 64QAM down	2,4, & 8 VSB up; 64QAM down	QPSK up; 64QAM down
Frequency	5–20 MHz up; 50–860 MHz down	10–32 MHz up; 88–806 MHz down	5–40 MHz up; 50–750 MHz down	5–40 MHz up; 54–750 MHz down

	LANcity LCP	Motorola CyberSurfr	Pioneer Speed Station	Scientific Atlanta Not yet named
Price	$375	$450	$475	INA
Speed	Symmetrical; 10 Mbps	Symmetrical; 768 kbps up; 10 Mbps down	Symmetrical; 2.5 Mbps up; 28.5 Mbps down	INA
Modulation	QPSK	4-DQPSK up; 64QAM down	4 DQPSK up; 64QAM down	QPSK up; 64QAM down
Frequency	5–42 Mhz up; 54–550MHz down.	5–42 MHz up; 50–750 MHz down	1.3 MHz	5–40 MHz up; 50–750 MHz down

	Terayon TeraPro	Toshiba PCX	Zenith HomeWorks
Price	$400	$375	$395
Speed	Symmetrical; 10 Mbps up and down	Assymetrical; 2.048 Mbps up; 8.192 Mbps down	Symmetrical; depending on model, 500 kbps or 4 Mbps
Modulation	S-CDMA	QPSK	BPSK
Frequency	5–42 MHz up; 54–750 MHz down	Agile	12–108 MHz up; 50–750 MHz down

Y—Yes　N—No　N/A—Not applicable　INA—Information not available　　　　**End ■**

C

GRAPHICS CARDS, VIDEO CAPTURE CARDS, SCANNERS

C. 1   Graphics Cards ■

(Products listed in alphabetical order by company name.)	Actix Systems Picasso 64 Plus AVC	Actix Systems GraphicsEngine Ultra 64 AV	Alaris Matinee	Amquest SpeedQuest 64
Price	$249	$299	$260	$149
Interface	PCI	PCI	PCI	PCI or VLB
Standard/maximum RAM	2MB/2MB DRAM	2MB/4MB DRAM	2MB/2MB DRAM	2MB/2MB EDO
Graphics chip (video accelerator)	IGS IGA1602	S3 86C968	Alliance ProMotion 6410	S3 Trio64
Maximum colors/refresh rate at 640×480	16 million/75Hz	16 million/105Hz	16 million/75Hz	16 million/120Hz
Maximum colors/refresh rate at 800×600	16 million/75Hz	16 million/105Hz	16 million/75Hz	16 million/INA
Maximum colors/refresh rate at 1,024×768	65,000/75Hz	65,000/100Hz	65,000/75Hz	INA
Maximum colors/refresh rate at 1,280×1,024	256/75Hz	256/85Hz	256/75Hz	256/INA
Maximum colors/refresh rate at 1,600×1,200	256/75Hz	256/80Hz	INA	INA
Internal/Chip-RAM data path (bits)	64/INA	64/32	64/64	64/64
RAMDAC speed (MHz)	160	75	135	135
Connectors*	VGA	VGA, VAFC	VGA, VAFC	VGA, VFC
Video playback	Hardware, software	Software	Hardware	Hardware, software
Resolution/colors at maximum frame rate	1,024×768/256 (37 fps)	1,024×768/65,000 (25 fps)	INA	INA

Y—Yes   N—No   N/A—Not applicable   INA—Information not available   *PMC = proprietary media connector;
VAFC = VESA advanced feature connector; VFC = VESA feature connector;

Table Continues →

■ Graphics Cards

	Artist Graphics Artist 2000	ATI Technologies Video Xpression	ATI Technologies Xclaim GA	AverMedia Firestorm 192	AVM Technology AV Media
Price	$395	$239	$649	$749	$399
Interface	PCI	PCI	PCI	PCI	PCI
Standard/maximum RAM	2MB/2MB VRAM	2MB/2MB EDO	4MB/4MB VRAM	6MB/6MB DRAM	2MB/4MB DRAM
Graphics chip (video accelerator)	Artist Graphics 3GA	ATI 264VT	ATI mach64	S3 Vision864 x3	INA
Maximum colors/refresh rate at 640×480	16 million/85Hz	16 million/120Hz	16 million/100Hz	16 million/120Hz	16 million/75Hz
Maximum colors/refresh rate at 800×600	16 million/85Hz	16 million/120Hz	16 million/100Hz	16 million/120Hz	16 million/75Hz
Maximum colors/refresh rate at 1,024×768	65,000/85Hz	65,000/120Hz	16 million/100Hz	16 million/120Hz	64,000/75Hz
Maximum colors/refresh rate at 1,280×1,024	256/15Hz	256/85Hz	32,000/75HZ	16 million/85Hz	64,000/75Hz
Maximum colors/refresh rate at 1,600×1,200	INA	INA	32,000/75HZ	16 million/66Hz	INA
Internal/Chip-RAM data path (bits)	64/64	64/64	64/64	192/192	64/64
RAMDAC speed (MHz)	135	INA	135	INA	170
Connectors	VGA	VGA, proprietary	VGA, DB-15	PMC	VAFC
Video playback	INA	Hardware, software	Hardware, software	INA	Hardware, software
Resolution/colors at maximum frame rate	INA	640×480/65,000 (30 fps)	INA	INA	1,280×1,024/64,000 (30 fps)

Y—Yes   N—No   N/A—Not applicable   INA—Information not available

Graphics Cards ■

	Boca Research Voyager 64	Boca Research Voyager Movie Player	Cardexpert Technologies Cardex Thunder	Cardexpert Technologies Genesis/V Pro	Colorgraphic Communications Pro Lightning PCI
Price	$199	$399	$149	$289	$995
Interface	PCI	PCI	PCI	PCI	PCI
Standard/maximum RAM	2MB/2MB DRAM	2MB/2MB DRAM	2MB/2MB DRAM	2MB/4MB VRAM	2MB DRAM/INA
Graphics chip (video accelerator)	S3 Trio64	S3 Trio64V+ (S3 Scenic/MX2)	Cirrus Logic 54M30	S3 Vision968	S3 Trio64V+
Maximum colors/refresh rate at 640×480	16 million/75Hz	16 million/75Hz	16 million/75Hz	16 million/85Hz	16 million/75Hz
Maximum colors/refresh rate at 800×600	16 million/75Hz	16 million/75Hz	16 million/75Hz	16 million/85Hz	16 million/75Hz
Maximum colors/refresh rate at 1,024×768	65,000/75Hz	65,000/75Hz	64,000/75Hz	64,000/85Hz	64,000/75Hz
Maximum colors/refresh rate at 1,280×1,024	256/75Hz	256/75Hz	256/75Hz	256/75Hz	256/75Hz
Maximum colors/refresh rate at 1,600×1,200	256/48Hz	256/48Hz	INA	256/60Hz	256/49Hz
Internal/Chip-RAM data path (bits)	64/64	64/64	32/32	64/64	64/64
RAMDAC speed (MHz)	135	135	86	170	135
Connectors	VGA	VGA	VGA	VGA	VGA, VAFC
Video playback	INA	Hardware	INA	Software	INA
Resolution/colors at maximum frame rate	INA	800×600/256 (30 fps)	INA	1,024×768/256 (36 fps)	INA

Table Continues →

Graphics Cards

	Colorgraphic Communications Mega Lightning	CompuVid School Board Pro	Creative Labs 3D Blaster	DFI WG3120P2	DFI WG9140P
Price	$1,495	$999	$349	$224	$499
Interface	PCI	ISA	VLB	PCI	PCI
Standard/maximum RAM	4MB VRAM/INA	2MB/2MB VRAM	1MB DRAM/1MB VRAM	2MB/2MB DRAM	4MB/4MB VRAM
Graphics chip (video accelerator)	S3 Vision968	Cirrus Logic GD5428	3D Labs Glint	S3 Trio64	Weitek Power 9100 (9130)
Maximum colors/refresh rate at 640×480	16 million/85Hz	16 million/60Hz	16 million/75Hz	16 million/75Hz	16 million/120Hz
Maximum colors/refresh rate at 800×600	16 million/85Hz	64,000/72Hz	65,000/75Hz	16 million/75Hz	16 million/120Hz
Maximum colors/refresh rate at 1,024×768	16 million/85Hz	64,000/87Hz	256/75Hz	64,000/75Hz	16 million/120Hz
Maximum colors/refresh rate at 1,280×1,024	16 million/75Hz	256/87Hz	INA	256/75Hz	16 million/100Hz
Maximum colors/refresh rate at 1,600×1,200	64,000/60Hz	INA	INA	256/37.5Hz	64,000/70Hz
Internal/Chip-RAM data path (bits)	64/64	32/32	128/128	64/64	64/64
RAMDAC speed (MHz)	175	80	135	INA	135
Connectors	VGA	VGA	VGA	VGA	VGA, VMC
Video playback	INA	INA	Hardware, software	INA	INA
Resolution/colors at maximum frame rate	INA	INA	CPU-dependent	INA	1,280×1,024/16.7 million (30 fps)

Y—Yes N—No N/A—Not applicable INA—Information not available

Graphics Cards ■

	Diamond Multimedia Stealth SE 2MB	Diamond Multimedia Edge 3D 3400XL	Elitegroup Computer Systems VI-640 2MB	Elitegroup Computer Systems VI-940B	Elsa Winner 1000 AVI
Price	$169	$649	$299	$330	$219
Interface	PCI	PCI	PCI	PCI	PCI
Standard/maximum RAM	2MB/2MB DRAM	4MB/4MB VRAM	2MB/4MB	2MB/2MB	2MB DRAM/INA
Graphics chip (video accelerator)	S3 Trio732	Nvidia NV1 (provides 3-D support)	ATI mach64	S3 Trio64	S3 868
Maximum colors/refresh rate at 640×480	16 million/60Hz	1 billion/120Hz	16 million/INA	16 million/INA	16 million/133Hz
Maximum colors/refresh rate at 800×600	65,000/72Hz	1 billion/120Hz	16 million/INA	INA	16 million/85Hz
Maximum colors/refresh rate at 1,024×768	65,000/43Hz	1 billion/100Hz	INA	INA	64,000/104Hz
Maximum colors/refresh rate at 1,280×1,024	256/43Hz (I)	32,000/85Hz	256/INA	INA	256/76Hz
Maximum colors/refresh rate at 1,600×1,200	INA	32,000/60Hz	INA	256/INA	256/52Hz
Internal/Chip-RAM data path (bits)	32/32	32/64	INA	INA	64/64
RAMDAC speed (MHz)	135	170	INA	INA	135
Connectors	VFC	VGA, line-in, external microphone	VGA, DB-15	VGA, DB-15	VGA
Video playback	INA	Hardware	Software	Software	Hardware
Resolution/colors at maximum frame rate	INA	640×480/32,000 (30 fps)	INA	INA	INA

Table Continues →

■ Graphics Cards

	Elsa Gloria-8	Focus Information Systems Premier 2000	Focus Information Systems RoadRunner 64V	Fujitsu Microelectronics Sapphire 3D Designer	Fujitsu Microelectronics Sapphire 25X
Price	$2,799	$205	$229	$995	$1,989
Interface	PCI	PCI	PCI	PCI	PCI
Standard/maximum RAM	8MB VRAM/8MB DRAM	2MB/2MB DRAM	2MB/2MB DRAM	4MB DRAM/2MB VRAM	4MB DRAM/4MB VRAM
Graphics chip (video accelerator)	S3 968 (with Glint 300SX for 3-D support)	Ark Logic ARK2000DV	S3 Trio64V+/765	3D Labs Glint 300SX (provides 3-D support)	3D Labs Glint 300SX (provides 3-D support)
Maximum colors/refresh rate at 640×480	16 million/200Hz	16 million/90Hz	16 million/75Hz	16 million/140Hz	16 million/140Hz
Maximum colors/refresh rate at 800×600	16 million/200Hz	16 million/90Hz	16 million/75Hz	16 million/140Hz	16 million/140Hz
Maximum colors/refresh rate at 1,024×768	16 million/200Hz	64,000/75Hz	64,000/75Hz	65,000/140Hz	16 million/140Hz
Maximum colors/refresh rate at 1,280×1,024	16 million/124Hz	256/75Hz	256/75Hz	256/90Hz	65,000/90Hz
Maximum colors/refresh rate at 1,600×1,200	16 million/85Hz	256/60Hz	256/56Hz	256/65Hz	65,000/65Hz
Internal/Chip-RAM data path (bits)	64/64	64/64	64/64	32/64	32/64
RAMDAC speed (MHz)	220	135	135	170	170
Connectors	VGA	VGA	VGA	VGA	VGA
Video playback	Hardware	INA	Hardware	INA	INA
Resolution/colors at maximum frame rate	INA	INA	1,024×768/256 (30 fps)	INA	INA

Y—Yes   N—No   N/A—Not applicable   INA—Information not available

Graphics Cards ■

	Genoa Systems Phantom 64 V2001	Genoa Systems VideoBlitz IIIAV/Phantom Pro	Hercules Computer Technologies Terminator 64/DRAM	Hercules Computer Technologies Terminator Professional	InnoMicro PBB1100 Action Media II
Price	$229	$399	$239	$559	$750
Interface	PCI	PCI	PCI	VLB	ISA
Standard/maximum RAM	2MB/2MB DRAM	2MB/4MB VRAM	2MB/2MB DRAM	4MB/4MB VRAM	4MB/4MB DRAM
Graphics chip (video accelerator)	S3 Trio64V+	S3 Vision968	S3 Trio64	S3 Vision968	Intel I750
Maximum colors/refresh rate at 640×480	16 million/106Hz	16 million/200Hz	65,000/120Hz	16 million/150Hz	12 million/72Hz
Maximum colors/refresh rate at 800×600	16 million/90Hz	16 million/160Hz	256/120Hz	16 million/120Hz	12 million/72Hz
Maximum colors/refresh rate at 1,024×768	64,000/84Hz	64,000/125Hz	256/90Hz	16 million/75Hz	256/44Hz
Maximum colors/refresh rate at 1,280×1,024	256/75Hz	256/95Hz	256/75Hz	16 million/100Hz	INA
Maximum colors/refresh rate at 1,600×1,200	256/60Hz	256/72Hz	INA	65,000/72Hz	INA
Internal/Chip-RAM data path (bits)	64/64	64/64	64/64	64/64	32/32
RAMDAC speed (MHz)	135	185	135	220	33
Connectors	VGA, VAFC	VGA, VAFC	VFC	VFC	VGA, VAFC
Video playback	Hardware, software	Software	INA	Hardware, software	Hardware
Resolution/colors at maximum frame rate	1,024×768/256 (30 fps)	1,024×768/64,000 (30 fps)	INA	INA	320×240/12 million (30 fps)

Table Continues →

Graphics Cards

	InSync Technologies VGA Image I/O 734	InSync Technologies VGA Image I/O 722	Integrated Micro Solutions Twin Turbo-128S	Integrated Micro Solutions Twin Turbo-128P4	Jazz Multimedia Jakarta
Price	$595	$959	$319	$599	INA
Interface	PCI	PCI	PCI	PCI	PCI
Standard/maximum RAM	2MB/2MB DRAM	2MB/4MB DRAM	2MB/2MB VRAM	4MB/4MB VRAM	2MB/INA VRAM
Graphics chip (video accelerator)	Tseng Labs W32P	Tseng Labs W32P	IMS TwinTurbo 128	IMS	Tseng Labs ET4000 W32P (Viper)
Maximum colors/refresh rate at 640×480	16 million/60Hz	16 million/60Hz	16 million/90Hz	16 million/90Hz	16 million/75Hz
Maximum colors/refresh rate at 800×600	65,000/72Hz	65,000/72Hz	16 million/90Hz	16 million/90Hz	16 million/75Hz
Maximum colors/refresh rate at 1,024×768	65,000/72Hz	65,000/72Hz	65,000/80Hz	16 million/80Hz	INA
Maximum colors/refresh rate at 1,280×1,024	256/87Hz	256/87Hz	256/75Hz	16 million/75Hz	256/75Hz
Maximum colors/refresh rate at 1,600×1,200	INA	INA	256/60Hz	65,000/60Hz	INA
Internal/Chip-RAM data path (bits)	32/32	32/32	64/64	128/128	32/INA
RAMDAC speed (MHz)	135	135	135	175	INA
Connectors	VGA	VGA, RCA	VGA, VFC	VGA	INA
Video playback	INA	INA	Hardware, software	Software	(Hardware), Software
Resolution/colors at maximum frame rate	INA	INA	704×480/32,000 (30 fps)	704×480/32,000 (30 fps)	INA

Y—Yes   N—No   N/A—Not applicable   INA—Information not available

Graphics Cards ■

	Jazz Multimedia 3-D Magic	Matrox Graphics Millenium	Matrox Graphics Millenium	Micro-Labs Ultimate TrueColor/XL2	Micro-Labs Ultimate WinVideo
Price	$489	$379	$977	$199	$299
Interface	PCI	PCI	PCI	ISA	PCI
Standard/maximum RAM	4MB/4MB VRAM	2MB/8MB WRAM	4MB/8MB WRAM	2MB/2MB DRAM	2MB/4MB DRAM
Graphics chip (video accelerator)	Nvidia NV1 [3DS]	Matrox 2064W [3DS]	Matrox 2064W (IBM ViP905) [3DS]	Tseng Labs ET4000/W32I	Tseng Labs ET6000
Maximum colors/refresh rate at 640×480	INA	16 million/200Hz	16 million/200Hz	16 million/90Hz	16 million/90Hz
Maximum colors/refresh rate at 800×600	INA	16 million/200Hz	16 million/200Hz	65,000/90Hz	16 million/90Hz
Maximum colors/refresh rate at 1,024×768	INA	16 million/120Hz	16 million/120Hz	256/75Hz	16 million/90Hz
Maximum colors/refresh rate at 1,280×1,024	INA	16 million/110Hz	16 million/110Hz	256/43.5Hz	16 million/75Hz
Maximum colors/refresh rate at 1,600×1,200	INA	16 million/80Hz	16 million/80Hz	INA	INA
Internal/Chip-RAM data path (bits)	INA	64/64	64/64	64/64	128/128
RAMDAC speed (MHz)	INA	220	220	80	135
Connectors	VGA	VGA	VGA	VGA	VGA
Video playback	Hardware, software	Software	Software	INA	Hardware
Resolution/colors at maximum frame rate	INA	1,024×768/65,000 (30 fps)	1,024×768/65,000 (30 fps)	INA	1,024×768/16.8 million (30 fps)

Table Continues →

Graphics Cards

	miro Computer Products miroCrystal 12SD	miro Computer Products miroVideo 40SV	Number Nine Visual Technologies 9FX Vision 330	Number Nine Visual Technologies Imagine 128 Series 2	Ocean Information Systems Octek Speed 64
Price	$189	$599	$199	INA	$149
Interface	PCI	VLB	PCI	PCI	PCI
Standard/maximum RAM	2MB/2MB DRAM	4MB/4MB VRAM	2MB/2MB DRAM	4MB/4MB VRAM	2MB/2MB DRAM
Graphics chip (video accelerator)	S3 Trio32	S3 Vision968	S3 Trio64	Number Nine Imagine 128 S2 (provides 3-D support)	Ark Logic 2000
Maximum colors/refresh rate at 640×480	16 million/70Hz	16 million/100Hz	16 million/100Hz	16 million/200Hz	16 million/90Hz
Maximum colors/refresh rate at 800×600	16 million/70Hz	16 million/100Hz	16 million/100Hz	16 million/200Hz	16 million/90Hz
Maximum colors/refresh rate at 1,024×768	65,000/70Hz	16 million/100Hz	65,000/80Hz	16 million/150Hz	64,000/75Hz
Maximum colors/refresh rate at 1,280×1,024	256/70Hz	65,000/100Hz	256/72Hz	65,000/100Hz	256/60Hz
Maximum colors/refresh rate at 1,600×1,200	INA	65,000/75Hz	INA	65,000/85Hz	256/86Hz (I)
Internal/Chip-RAM data path (bits)	32/64	64/64	64/64	128/128	64/64
RAMDAC speed (MHz)	135	220	135	220	135
Connectors	VGA	VGA	VGA	VGA	VGA, VAFC
Video playback	Sotware	Hardware, software	Software	Hardware	INA
Resolution/colors at maximum frame rate	240×160/65,000 (30 fps)	1,024×768/65,000 (30 fps)	INA	INA	INA

Y—Yes   N—No   N/A—Not applicable   INA—Information not available

Graphics Cards ■

	Omnicomp Graphics 3Demon SX44	Omnicomp Graphics 3Demon SX88	Orchid Technology Kelvin Video 64	Personal Computer Graphics Photon Torpedo 864 PCI	Power Pixel Technologies PixelMaker
Price	$1,995	$2,935	$239	$237	INA
Interface	PCI	PCI	PCI	PCI	VLB
Standard/maximum RAM	4MB VRAM/4MB DRAM	8MB VRAM/8MB DRAM	2MB/2MB DRAM	2MB/4MB DRAM	2MB/2MB
Graphics chip (video accelerator)	3D Labs Glint 300SX (provides 3-D support)	3D Labs Glint 300SX (provides 3-D support)	Alliance 6410	S3 Vision864	Tseng Labs ET4000 W32P
Maximum colors/refresh rate at 640×480	16 million/INA	16 million/INA	16 million/90Hz	16 million/INA	16 million/INA
Maximum colors/refresh rate at 800×600	16 million/INA	16 million/INA	16 million/90Hz	INA	INA
Maximum colors/refresh rate at 1,024×768	16 million/INA	16 million/INA	65,000/75Hz	65,000/INA	INA
Maximum colors/refresh rate at 1,280×1,024	INA	16 million/INA	256/72Hz	INA	16/INA
Maximum colors/refresh rate at 1,600×1,200	INA	16 million/INA	256/60Hz	256/INA	INA
Internal/Chip-RAM data path (bits)	INA	INA	64/64	64/64	INA
RAMDAC speed (MHz)	INA	INA	150	INA	INA
Connectors	VGA	VGA	VGA	INA	VGA, VAFC, DB-15
Video playback	INA	INA	Hardware, software	INA	INA
Resolution/colors at maximum frame rate	INA	INA	1,024×768/256 (30 fps)	INA	INA

Table Continues →

Graphics Cards

	Prolink Computer PCI32-T9440	Prolink Computer PCI64-CL5446	Radius Precision Color 8/1600 v.2	Radius ThunderColor 30/1600	Reveal Computer Products Speedcat Jaguar
Price	$95	$229	$599	$2,499	$199
Interface	PCI	PCI	PCI	PCI	PCI
Standard/maximum RAM	2MB/2MB DRAM	2MB/2MB DRAM	2MB/2MB VRAM	6MB/6MB VRAM	2MB/2MB DRAM
Graphics chip (video accelerator)	Trident T9440	Cirrus Logic GD5446	S3 968	Radius proprietary	Cirrus Logic GD5436
Maximum colors/refresh rate at 640×480	16 million/75Hz	16 million/75Hz	16 million/75Hz	16 million/75Hz	16 million/75Hz
Maximum colors/refresh rate at 800×600	16 million/60Hz	16 million/60Hz	16 million/71Hz	16 million/71Hz	16 million/75Hz
Maximum colors/refresh rate at 1,024×768	64,000/87Hz	64,000/75Hz	65,000/71Hz	16 million/71Hz	65,000/75Hz
Maximum colors/refresh rate at 1,280×1,024	256/87Hz	256/87Hz	65,000/71Hz	16 million/71Hz	256/75Hz
Maximum colors/refresh rate at 1,600×1,200	INA	INA	65,000/71Hz	16 million/69Hz	INA
Internal/Chip-RAM data path (bits)	32/32	64/64	128/128	96/96	64/64
RAMDAC speed (MHz)	INA	INA	220	220	135
Connectors	VGA	VGA	DB-15	DB-15	VGA, DB-15
Video playback	INA	Software	Hardware/software)	INA	INA
Resolution/colors at maximum frame rate	INA	320×200/256 (30 fps)	1,024×768/256 (31 fps)	INA	INA

Y—Yes   N—No   N/A—Not applicable   INA—Information not available

Graphics Cards ■

	Reveal Computer Products Speedcat Cougar	SIIG Aurora 4000	Spider Graphics Tarantula 64	Spider Graphics Tarantula Lite	STB Systems Powergraph 64 Video
Price	$199	$295	$359	INA	$229
Interface	PCI	PCI	PCI	VLB	PCI
Standard/maximum RAM	2MB/2MB DRAM	2MB/4MB EDO	2MB/4MB VRAM	2MB/2MB VRAM	2MB/2MB DRAM
Graphics chip (video accelerator)	Cirrus Logic GD5440	S3 Trio 64V+	S3 Vision 964	S3 Trio32	S3 Trio64V+
Maximum colors/refresh rate at 640×480	16 million/60Hz	16 million/85Hz	16 million/INA	65,000/INA	16 million/160Hz
Maximum colors/refresh rate at 800×600	65,000/60Hz	16 million/85Hz	INA	INA	16 million/140Hz
Maximum colors/refresh rate at 1,024×768	256/75Hz	64,000/85Hz	INA	INA	65,000/120Hz
Maximum colors/refresh rate at 1,280×1,024	256/87Hz	256/75Hz	INA	INA	256/75Hz
Maximum colors/refresh rate at 1,600×1,200	INA	256/98Hz (I)	INA	INA	256/75Hz
Internal/Chip-RAM data path (bits)	32/32	64/64	INA	INA	64/64
RAMDAC speed (MHz)	86	135	INA	INA	135
Connectors	VGA, DB-15	VGA	INA	VGA	INA
Video playback	(Hardware), software	(Hardware), software	INA	INA	Hardware, software
Resolution/colors at maximum frame rate	1,024×768/64,000 (30 fps)	1,024×768/256 (31 fps)	INA	INA	1,024×768/256 (30 fps)

Table Continues →

Graphics Cards

	TeleVideo Systems AllMedia	VIC Hi-Tec Video Packer Turbo	VideoLogic GrafixStar 300	VideoLogic GrafixStar 700	Visionetics International VIGA+64
Price	INA	$449	$189	$449	$1,595
Interface	PCI	PCI	PCI	VLB	ISA
Standard/maximum RAM	2MB/VRAM	2MB/2MB DRAM	2MB/2MB EDO	4MB/4MB VRAM	2MB/2MB VRAM
Graphics chip (video accelerator)	Brooktree BtV Media Stream (provides 3-D support)	INA	S3 Trio64	S3 Vision968	Trident
Maximum colors/refresh rate at 640×480	16 million/76Hz	16 million/72Hz	16 million/120Hz	16 million/120Hz	16 million/72Hz
Maximum colors/refresh rate at 800×600	16 million/76Hz	16 million/60Hz	16 million/120Hz	16 million/120Hz	16 million/72Hz
Maximum colors/refresh rate at 1,024×768	16 million/75Hz	64,000/75Hz	65,000/100Hz	16 million/100Hz	16 million/72Hz
Maximum colors/refresh rate at 1,280×1,024	65,000/75Hz	256/75Hz	256/75Hz	16 million/90Hz	INA
Maximum colors/refresh rate at 1,600×1,200	256/45Hz (I)	INA	INA	65,000/60Hz	INA
Internal/Chip-RAM data path (bits)	64/64	32/32	64/64	64/64	32/32
RAMDAC speed (MHz)	INA	INA	INA	170	135
Connectors	VGA, 2 phone	VGA, VAFC	VGA, VFC, VMC	VGA, VFC, VMC	VGA
Video playback	(Hardware), software	Hardware	(Hardware)	(Hardware)	Hardware
Resolution/colors at maximum frame rate	1,024×768/256 (31 fps)	160×120/16 million (15 fps)	1,152×864/65,000 (30 fps)	1,600×1,200/65,000 (30 fps)	320×240/256 (30 fps)

Y—Yes   N—No   N/A—Not applicable   INA—Information not available

End ■

C. 2   Video Capture Cards

(Products listed in alphabetical order by company name.)	Alpha Systems Lab MegaMotion	ATI Technologies Video-It	Cardinal Technologies SNAPplus-VL	Creative Labs Video Blaster RT300	Diamond Multimedia Systems VideoStar Pro
Price	$995	$332	$594	$333	$469
CONFIGURATION					
Bus versions available	ISA	ISA, VL-Bus	VL-Bus	ISA	ISA
Minimum system requirements	486SX, 8MB RAM	486/25, 4MB RAM	486DX, 4MB RAM	386DX, 4MB RAM	486SX/25, 8MB RAM
Overlay	Y	N	Y	N	Y
VESA feature connector	Y	N	N	N	Y
Graphics accelerator/RAM included	N	N	Cirrus Logic CL-GD5434/1MB DRAM	N	N
Simultaneous preview function	Y	N	N	N	N
I/O requirements	One IRQ, one I/O port	One I/O port	One IRQ, three I/O ports, and a memory address range excluded from expanded memory	One IRQ, one I/O port	Two IRQs, two I/O ports, and a memory address range excluded from expanded memory
Maximum number of colors for graphics at 640x480	256	Same as graphics card	16.8 million	Same as graphics card	256 colors
Windows driver used in testing	ASL MM Video 1.0.6	VIDEO iT 1.0	SNAPplus-VL	VideoBlaster 1.1.0.0	VideoStar 1.02
VIDEO CAPTURE					
Bundled video capture/editing software	Adobe Premiere 1.1a	ATI Media Capture 1.0 (capture) and Media Merge 1.1 (editing)	Cardinal Sentfactor Multimedia Tools	Adobe Premiere 1.1a	Adobe Premiere 1.1a
Basic MS VidEdit features	Y	N	N	Y	Y
Incoming color controls	Hue, saturation, contrast, brightness, RGB	Hue, saturation, contrast, brightness	Hue, saturation, contrast, brightness	Hue, saturation, contrast, brightness	Hue, saturation, contrast, brightness
Video for Windows Runtime	Y	Y	N	Y	Y
Video inputs	One proprietary connector (S-Video or composite)	One S-Video, two composite	One S-Video, one composite	One S-Video, three composite	One S-Video, two composite
Video standards	NTSC, PAL, PAL-N	NTSC, PAL	NTSC, PAL, SECAM	NTSC, PAL	NTSC, PAL
Audio inputs	N	N	N	N	N
Audio chip	INA	INA	NA	NA	INA
Analog/digital converter	Brooktree/t855KPF	Philips TDA 8708/8709	Philips 7110	Philips 7191	Philips 9051
Compression chip	C-Cube CL550	Intel 82750PD	AuraVision VXP500	Intel 82750PE	Zoran ZR36045 PQC
Codecs supported	Motion JPEG	Indeo 3.1	AuraVision	Indeo 3.2	Motion JPEG
Video formats supported	YUV 4:4:4, 4:2:2, 4:1:1; RGB 15-, 16-, and 24-bit; RGB 5:5:5	YUV 9 and 12; RGB 8-, 16-, and 24-bit	YUV 4:2:2, 4:1:1, RGB 24-bit	YUV 9	YUV 4:1:1, RGB 8-, 16-, 24-bit
File formats supported	AVI, MOV	AVI	AVI	AVI, MOV	AVI, MOV
Maximum capture rate at 320×240	30 fps	15 fps	15 fps	30 fps	30 fps
Resolutions supported	Adjustable to 640×480	160×120, 240×180, 320×240	Adjustable to 320×240	160×120, 240×180, 320×240	40×30, 160×120, 320×240, 640×480
VIDEO PLAYBACK					
Video scaling chip	Cirrus Logic Px2070	INA	AuraVision VXP500	INA	AuraVision VXP500
Codecs supported	Motion JPEG, Indeo, Cinepak, Video 1, QuickTime	INA	AuraVision, Cinepak, Indeo, Motion JPEG, QuickTime, Video 1, Xing MPEG	INA	AuraVision, Cinepak, Indeo, Motion JPEG, QuickTime, Video 1, Xing MPEG
Native playback frame rate at 320×240	30 fps	INA	15 fps	INA	30 fps
Video encoding	NTSC or PAL	N	N	N	N
WARRANTY **(PARTS AND LABOR)**	Two years	Five years	One year	One year	One year

Y—Yes   N—No   N/A—Not applicable   INA—Information not available

Table Continues →

■ Video Capture Cards

	Hauppauge Computer Works Win/TV Cinema N	Intel Smart Video Recorder Pro	miro Computer Products miroVIDEO DC-1	Orchid Technology Vidiola Premium	Umax Technologies Maxmedia MR
Price	$289	$409	$650	$657	$359
CONFIGURATION					
Bus versions available	ISA	ISA	ISA	ISA	ISA
Minimum system requirements	386	486SX/25, 4MB RAM	486, 8MB RAM	386, 4MB RAM	386, 8MB RAM
Overlay	Y	N	N	Y	Y
VESA feature connector	Y	N	N	Y	Y
Graphics accelerator/RAM included	N	N	N	N	N
Simultaneous preview function	Y	N	N	Y	Y
I/O requirements	One IRQ, one I/O port, and a memory address range excluded from expanded memory	One IRQ, one I/O port	One IRQ, one I/O port, one DMA channel, and a memory address range excluded from expanded memory	One IRQ, two I/O ports	One IRQ, one I/O port, and a memory address range excluded from expanded memory
Maximum number of colors for graphics at 640×480	16.8 million colors	Same as graphics card	Same as graphics card	65,536	65,536
Windows driver used in testing	Win/TV Capture 3.67	ISVR Pro 1.1	miro 1.13	Vidiola Capture Driver 1.0a	Maxmedia MR 2.4
VIDEO CAPTURE					
Bundled video capture/editing software	ULead Systems MediaStudio	Asymetrix Digital Video Producer	Adobe Premiere 1.1a	Adobe Premiere 1.1a	Prolab Technology VideoWork
Basic MS VidEdit features	Y	Y	Y	Y	Y
Incoming color controls	Tint, saturation, contrast, brightness	Hue, saturation, contrast, brightness	Hue, saturation, contrast, brightness	Hue, saturation, contrast, brightness	Hue, saturation, contrast, brightness
Video for Windows Runtime	Y	Y	Y	Y	Y
Video inputs	One composite	One S-Video, one composite	One S-Video, one composite	One S-Video, one composite	One S-Video, two composite
Video standards	NTSC, PAL	NTSC, PAL	NTSC, PAL, SECAM	NTSC, PAL	NTSC, PAL, SECAM
Audio inputs	N	N	N	N	N
Audio chip	INA	INA	INA	INA	INA
Analog/digital converter	Philips 9051	Philips 7196	Philips 7196	Philips 7191b	Philips 7191
Compression chip	AuraVision VXP500	Intel 82750PE	LSI Logic L64702QC-33	C-Cube CL 550	AuraVision VXP500
Codecs supported	AuraVision	Indeo 3.2	Motion JPEG	Motion JPEG	AuraVision
Video formats supported	YUV 4:1:1 and 4:2:2	YUV 9	YUV 4:1:1	YUV 4:1:1, 4:2:2, RGB 8-, 16-, 24-bit	YUV 4:1:1, 4:2:2; RGB 8-, 16-, 24-bit
File formats supported	AVI	AVI	AVI, MOV	AVI, MOV	AVI
Maximum capture rate at 320×240	15 fps	30 fps	30 fps	30 fps	15 fps
Resolutions supported	Adjustable up to 320×240	160×120, 240×180, 320×240	80×120, 160×120, 320×240	160×120, 240×180, 320×240	Adjustable up to 320×240
VIDEO PLAYBACK					
Video scaling chip	AuraVision VxP500	INA	INA	AuraVision VxP500	AuraVision VxP500
Codecs supported	AuraVision, Cinepak, Indeo, Motion JPEG, QuickTime, Video 1, Xing MPEG	INA	INA	AuraVision, Cinepak, Indeo, Motion JPEG, QuickTime, Video 1, Xing MPEG	AuraVision, Cinepak, Indeo, Motion JPEG, QuickTime, Video 1, Xing MPEG
Native playback frame rate at 320×240	15 fps	INA	INA	30 fps	15 fps
Video encoding	N	N	NTSC	NTSC	N
WARRANTY (PARTS AND LABOR)	One year	One year	Two years	One year	One year

Y—Yes   N—No   N/A—Not applicable   INA—Information not available

Video Capture Cards ■

	VIC Hi-Tech VideoPacker Plus	VideoLogic DVA-4000/ MediaSpace
Price	$375	$1,995
CONFIGURATION		
Bus versions available	ISA	Two ISA cards, one daughtercard
Minimum system requirements	386, 4MB RAM	386
Overlay	Y	Y
VESA feature connector	Y	Y
Graphics accelerator/RAM included	N	N
Simultaneous preview function	Y	Y
I/O requirements	One IRQ, one I/O port, and a memory address range excluded from expanded memory	One IRQ, two I/O ports
Maximum number of colors for graphics at 640×480	256	256
Windows driver used in testing	Video Packer 1.0	MediaSpace 2.2.1
VIDEO CAPTURE		
Bundled video capture/editing software	ULead Systems Vid-eoStudio	Adobe Premiere 1.1a
Basic MS VidEdit features	N	Y
Incoming color controls	Hue, saturation, contrast, brightness	Hue, saturation, contrast, brightness
Video for Windows Runtime	Y	Y
Video inputs	One S-Video, two composite	One proprietary (S-Video or composite)
Video standards	NTSC, PAL	NTSC, PAL
Audio inputs	Y	Y
Audio chip	ESS/ES4AA-F	AOSP 2105
Analog/digital converter	Philips 9051	AOSP 2105
Compression chip	AuraVision VXP500	C-Cube CL-550
Codecs supported	AuraVision	Motion JPEG, MSP
Video formats supported	YUV 4:1:1, 4:2:2; RGB 8-, 16-, 24-bit	(proprietary) YUV 4:1:1
File formats supported	AVI	AVI, MSP (proprietary)
Maximum capture rate at 320×240	15 fps	30 fps
Resolutions supported	80×60, 160×120, 320×240, 640×480	Adjustable up to 640×480
VIDEO PLAYBACK		
Video scaling chip	AuraVision VxP500	VideoLogic M2B
Codecs supported	AuraVision, Cinepak, Indeo, Motion JPEG, QuickTime, Video 1, Xing MPEG	Motion JPEG
Native playback frame rate at 320×240	15 fps	30 fps
Video encoding	N	N
WARRANTY	One year	One year
(PARTS AND LABOR)		

Y—Yes   N—No   N/A—Not applicable   INA—Information not available   **End** ■

■ C. 3 Scanners

(Products listed in alphabetical order by company name.)	A4 Tech USA WinScan Pro 800	Agfa Graphic Systems Arcus II	Apple Computer Color OneScanner	Behavior Tech Computer 6700 ScanFlex	Canon Computer Systems IX-3010
Price	$179	$3,495	$859	$599	$569
Form factor	Handheld, imaging/OCR	Flatbed, imaging/OCR	Flatbed, imaging	Flatbed, imaging/OCR	Flatbed, imaging/OCR
Scanner type	Color, grayscale, black and white	Color, grayscale, black and white	Color	Grayscale, black and white	Grayscale, black and white
Scan area (in inches)	4.1 (wide)	8.5×14	8.5×14	8.5×14	8.5×14
Maximum optical resolution	800×800	600×1,200	300×300	400×400	300×1,200
Interface(s)	PRO	SCSI-2	SCSI	Bus	SCSI-2
Output file formats	BMP, EPS, GIF, PCX, TIF	Photoshop native	EPS, PICT, TIF	BMP, EPS, JPG, PCX, TGA, TIF	BMP, PCX, TIF

	Canon Computer Systems IX-4015	Corex Technologies CardScan	DPI Electronic Imaging Systems ArtGetter II/30	Epson America Personal Document Station	Epson America ES-1000C-LE Mac
Price	$799	$299	$1,199	$599	$849
Form factor	Flatbed, imaging/OCR	Handheld, imaging/OCR	Flatbed, imaging/OCR	Flatbed, imaging/OCR	Flatbed, imaging/OCR
Scanner type	Color, grayscale, black and white	Grayscale, black and white	Color, grayscale, black and white	Grayscale, black and white	Color, grayscale, black and white
Scan area (in inches)	8.5×14	8.5×14	8.5×14	8.5 (wide)	8.5×11.7
Maximum optical resolution	400×1,200	400×400	1,600×400	300×300	400×800
Interface(s)	SCSI-2	Bus, Parallel	SCSI	Parallel	Parallel, SCSI
Output file formats	BMP, PCX, TIF	ASCII	BMP, EPS, GIF, JPG, PCX, TIF	BMP, EPS, GIF, PCX, TGA, TIF	BMP, EPS, GIF, PCX, TGA, TIF

	Epson America ES-1000C-LE PC	Epson America ES-1200C Pro PC	Hewlett-Packard ScanJet 3C	Hewlett-Packard ScanJet 3P	Logitech ScanMan 256
Price	$849	$1,499	$1,179	$399	$99
Form factor	Flatbed, imaging/OCR	Flatbed, imaging/OCR	Flatbed, imaging/OCR	Flatbed, imaging/OCR	Handheld, imaging/OCR
Scanner type	Color, grayscale, black and white	Color, grayscale, black and white	Color, grayscale, black and white	Grayscale, black and white	Grayscale, black and white
Scan area (in inches)	8.5×11.7	8.5×11.7	8.5×13.65	8.5×11	4.1 (wide)
Maximum optical resolution	400×800	600×600	600×1,200	300×600	100×400
Interface(s)	P, SCSI	P, SCSI	SCSI	SCSI	P
Output file formats	BMP, EPS, GIF, PCX, TGA, TIF	BMP, EPS, GIF, PCX, TGA, TIF	BMP, EPS, MacPaint, PCX, PICT, TIF	PCX, PICT, MacPaint, TIF	BMP, EPS, JPG, PCX, TIF

	Logitech ScanMan EasyTouch	Logitech ScanMan Color	Logitech ScanMan PowerPage	Microtek Lab ScanMaker III 36-bit	Microtek Lab ScanMaker 45t
Price	$249	$299	$399	$2,500	$7,995
Form factor	Handheld, imaging/OCR	Handheld, imaging/OCR	Flatbed, imaging/OCR	Flatbed, imaging/OCR	Flatbed, imaging
Scanner type	Grayscale, black and white	Color, grayscale, black and white	Grayscale, black and white	Color, grayscale, black and white	Color, black and white
Scan area (in inches)	4.1 (wide)	4.1 (wide)	8.5 (wide)	8.5×13	5×5
Maximum optical resolution	100-400	400×400	25-400	600×1,200	1,000×1,000
Interface(s)	P	Bus	P	PRO, SCSI	PRO, SCSI
Output file formats	BMP, EPS, JPG, PCX, TIF	BMP, EPS, JPG, PCX, TIF	BMP, EPS. JPG, PCX, TIF	EPS, PICT, PCX, TIF	EPS, PICT, PCX, TIF

Y—Yes   N—No   N/A—Not applicable   INA—Information not available

Scanners ■

	Mustek TwainScan Color 24	Mustek ScanMagic Color II	Mustek Plug and Scan 256	Mustek Color Artist Pro	PixelCraft ProImager 4000
Price	$159	$159	$199	$199	$2,995
Form factor	Handheld, imaging/OCR	Handheld, imaging/OCR	Handheld, imaging/OCR	Handheld, imaging/OCR	Flatbed, imaging
Scanner type	Color, grayscale, black and white	Color, grayscale, black and white	Grayscale, black and white	Color, grayscale, black and white	Color, grayscale, black and white
Scan area (in inches)	4.13 (wide)	4.13 (wide)	4.13 (wide)	4.13 (wide)	8.5×11.7
Maximum optical resolution	400¥400	400×400	400×400	400×800	600×2,400
Interface(s)	Bus	Bus	PCMCIA Type II	Bus	SCSI
Output file formats	BMP, GIF, JPG, PCX, TIF	BMP, GIF, JPG, PCX, TIF	BMP, GIF, JPG, PCX, TIF	BMP, GIF, JPG, PCX, TIF	Software native

	PixelCraft ProImager 7000	PixelCraft ProImager 8000	Plustek USA PageReader 800	Polaroid SprintScan 35	Primax Electronics ColorMobile Office
Price	$9,995	$12,995	$199	$2,495	$289
Form factor	Flatbed, imaging	Flatbed, imaging	Flatbed, imaging/OCR	Flatbed, imaging	Handheld, imaging/OCR
Scanner type	Color, grayscale, black and white	Color, grayscale, black and white	Grayscale, black and white	Color, grayscale	Color, grayscale, black and white
Scan area (in inches)	11.7×17	11.7×17	8.5×14	INA	4.1 (wide)
Maximum optical resolution	400×2,400	400×4,000	400×200	2,700×2,700	400×133
Interface(s)	SCSI	SCSI	PRO, P	SCSI-2	P
Output file formats	Software native	Software native	BMP, JPG, PCX, TIF	Photoshop native	BMP, CGM, EPS, GIF, JPG, PCX, TIF, WMF

	Primax Electronics DataPen	Relisys Avec 2400	Umax Technologies PowerLook	Umax Technologies Mirage D-16L	Umax Technologies Gemini D-16
Price	$299	$399	$3,495	$6,999	$1,895
Form factor	Handheld, OCR	Flatbed, imaging/OCR	Flatbed, imaging/OCR	Flatbed, imaging/OCR	Flatbed, imaging/OCR
Scanner type	Black and white	Color, grayscale, black and white	Color, grayscale, black and white	Color, grayscale, black and white	Color, grayscale, black and white
Scan area (in inches)	INA	8.5×14	8.5×11.7	12×17	8.5×11.7
Maximum optical resolution	300×300	600×300	600×1,200	800×1,600	800×1,600
Interface(s)	P	SCSI	SCSI	SCSI	SCSI
Output file formats	ASCII	BMP, EPS, PCX, PSD, TIF	BMP, JPG, PCX, PCD, TGA, TIF	BMP, JPG, PCX, PCD, TIF	BMP, JPG, PCX, PCD, TIF

	VisionShape B1000 Check Scanner
Price	$6,500
Form factor	Flatbed, imaging/OCR
Scanner type	Grayscale, black and white
Scan area (in inches)	5 (wide)
Maximum optical resolution	200×200
Interface(s)	SCSI
Output file formats	TIF

Y—Yes   N—No   N/A—Not applicable   INA—Information not available   **End ■**

SOUND CARDS

D.1: Sound Cards ■

(Products listed in alphabetical order by company name)	Advanced Gravis UltraSound Plug & Play Pro	Amquest Commando	Antex Electronics Z1E	WaveRider Pro 32-3D	Creative Labs Sound Blaster AWE32 PnP
Price	$199	$249	$595	$119	$250
Interface	ISA/16	ISA/16	ISA/16	ISA/16	ISA/16
Sample/playback size (bits)	16/16	16/16	16/16	16/16	16/16
Stereo sampling/playback (KHz)	48/48	44.1/44.1	48/48	4-48/4-48	44.1/44.1
Mono sampling/playback (KHz)	48/48	44.1/44.1	48/48	NA/NA	NA/NA
Synthesizer type	Wave-table	Wave-table, frequency modulator	Frequency modulator	Wave-table, frequency modulator	Wave-table, frequency modulator
Onboard ROM	1MB	INA	INA	1MB	1MB

Y—Yes   N—No   N/A—Not applicable   INA—Information not available

Table Continues →

■ Sound Cards

	Crystal Computer Crystalizer TidalWave 32 PnP	Ensoniq Soundscape Elite	Everex Systems 3D Sound Express Plus	Focus Infomation Systems MusicMaker Pro	Focus Infomation Systems MusicMaker PnP
Price	$300	$169	$169	$79	$95
Interface	ISA/16	ISA/16	ISA/16	ISA/16	ISA/16
Sample/playback size (bits)	16/16	16/16	16/16	16/16	16/16
Stereo sampling/playback (KHz)	48/48	48/48	48/48	44.1/44.1	48/48
Mono sampling/playback (KHz)	96/96	INA	48/48	INA	INA
Synthesizer type	Wave-table, frequency modulator	Wave-table, frequency modulator	Wave-table, frequency modulator	Frequency modulator	Frequency modulator
Onboard ROM	2MB	2MB	1MB	INA	INA

Y—Yes N—No N/A—Not applicable INA—Information not available

Sound Cards ■

	Focus Infomation Systems MusicMaker Wave	Formosa USA Sound Conductor SC1670	Formosa USA Sound Conductor SC1630	Formosa USA Sound Conductor SC1650	Formosa USA Sound Conductor SCFOTO24
Price	$149	$49	$49	$54	$54
Interface	ISA/16	ISA/16	ISA/16	ISA/16	ISA/16
Sample/playback size (bits)	16/16	16/16	16/16	16/16	16/16
Stereo sampling/playback (KHz)	48/48	44.1/44.1	44.1/44.1	44.1/44.1	44.1/44.1
Mono sampling/playback (KHz)	INA	44.1/44.1	44.1/44.1	44.1/44.1	44.1/44.1
Synthesizer type	Wave-table, frequency modulator	Frequency modulator	Frequency modulator	Frequency modulator	Frequency modulator
Onboard ROM	INA	INA	INA	INA	INA

Y—Yes   N—No   N/A—Not applicable   INA—Information not available

Table Continues →

■ Sound Cards

	Formosa USA Sound Conductor SCFEWOO2	IBM DSP Wavetable Sound Card	IBM Multimedia Modem Plus	IBM 3D PCMCIA Sound card	Kye International Genius SoundMaker 16 PnP/3D
Price	$89	$199	$299	$299	NA
Interface	ISA/16	ISA/16	ISA/16	P/II	ISA/16
Sample/playback size (bits)	16/16	16/16	16/16	16/16	16/16
Stereo sampling/playback (KHz)	44.1/44.1	44.1/44.1	44.1/44.1	44.1/44.1	4-44.1/4-44.1
Mono sampling/playback (KHz)	44.1/44.1	44.1/44.1	44.1/44.1	44.1/44.1	INA
Synthesizer type	Wave-table, frequency modulator	Wave-table	Wave-table, frequency modulator	Wave-table	Frequency modulator
Onboard ROM	1MB	4MB	4MB	6MB	INA

Y—Yes   N—No   N/A—Not applicable   INA—Information not available

Sound Cards ■

	Kye International Genius SoundMaker 16 IE	MediaTrix Peripherals AudioTrix Pro	Multiwave Innovation Audiowave 16 PnP	Multiwave Innovation Audiowave 32 PnP	New Media Gamejammer
Price	$140	$295	$69	$119	$250
Interface	ISA/16	ISA/16	ISA/16	ISA/16	P/II
Sample/playback size (bits)	16/16	16/16	16/16	16/16	16/16
Stereo sampling/playback (KHz)	4-44.1/4-44.1	48/48	44.1/44.1	44.1/44.1	NA
Mono sampling/playback (KHz)	INA	48/48	44.1/44.1	44.1/44.1	44.1/44.1
Synthesizer type	Frequency modulator	Wave-table, frequency modulator	Frequency modulator	Wave-table, frequency modulator	Frequency modulator
Onboard ROM	INA	2MB	INA	1MB	INA

Y—Yes   N—No   N/A—Not applicable   INA—Information not available   **Table Continues** →

Sound Cards

	New Media Wavjammer	New Media Toast 'n' Jam	NewCom HiFi 16i Sound Card	Orchid Technology Nusound PnP 32	Prolink Computer Sound 16-ES1688
Price	$300	$600	$59	$199	$45
Interface	P/I	P/II	ISA/16	ISA/16	ISA/16
Sample/playback size (bits)	16/16	16/16	16/16	16/16	16/16
Stereo sampling/playback (KHz)	44.1/44.1	44.1/44.1	48/48	48/48	44.1/44.1
Mono sampling/playback (KHz)	44.1/44.1	44.1/44.1	48/48	48/48	44.1/44.1
Synthesizer type	Frequency modulator	Frequency modulator	Frequency modulator	Wave-table, frequency modulator	Frequency modulator
Onboard ROM	INA	INA	INA	1MB	INA

Y—Yes   N—No   N/A—Not applicable   INA—Information not available

Sound Cards ■

	Prolink Computer TV-VGA-Combo	Reveal Computer Products Wave Extreme 32 SC800	Roland Sound Canvas GS SCP-55B	Spectrum Signal Processing V.34 OfficeF/X	TeleVideo Multimedia TeleSound
Price	$195	$99	$130	$299	$88
Interface	PCI	ISA/16	P/II	ISA/16	ISA/16
Sample/playback size (bits)	16/16	16/16	16/16	16/16	16/16
Stereo sampling/playback (KHz)	INA/44.1	44/44	44.1/44.1	44.1/44.1	48/48
Mono sampling/playback (KHz)	INA/44.1	44/44	44.1/44.1	INA	48/48
Synthesizer type	Frequency modulator	Wave-table	Wave-table	Wave-table, frequency modulator	Frequency modulator
Onboard ROM	INA	1MB	6MB	INA	INA

Y—Yes N—No N/A—Not applicable INA—Information not available   **Table Continues →**

■ Sound Cards

	TeleVideo Multimedia TeleWave Q32/SRS	Turtle Beach Systems TBS-2000	Turtle Beach Systems Tropez Plus
Price	$92	$199	$249
Interface	ISA/16	ISA/16	ISA/16
Sample/playback size (bits)	16/16	16/16	16/16
Stereo sampling/playback (KHz)	48/48	4-48/4-48	4-48/4-48
Mono sampling/playback (KHz)	48/48	4-48/4-48	4-48/4-48
Synthesizer type	Wave-table, frequency modulator	Wave-table, frequency modulator	Wave-table, frequency modulator
Onboard ROM	2MB	2MB	4MB

Y—Yes N—No N/A—Not applicable INA—Information not available   End ■

D.2: Audio Players ■

(Products listed in alphabetical order by company name)	DSP Group TrueSpeech Internet	Progressive Networks RealAudio	VocalTec Internet Wave	Xing Technologies StreamWorks
Price (encoder/decoder)	Free/free	Free/free	Free/free	$2,500—Audio only; $25,000 (to 400 Mbps); $50,000 (to 1.6 GBps)/free
Address (for downloading)	www.dpsg.com	www.realaudio.com	www.vocaltec.com	www.xingtech.com
Media	Audio	Audio	Audio	Audio/Video
Underlying technology	DSP TrueSpeech	Proprietary	Proprietary	MPEG-1, MPEG-2
Bandwidth	8.5 kbps	10 kbps	Scalable 9.6 kbps (5.5KHz); 14.4 kbps (8KHz); 28.8 kbps (16KHz or music)	8.5 kbps to 128 kbps
ENCODER				
Environments	Windows	Windows, Macintosh	Windows	Dedicated hardware platform
Real-time encoding	Y	Y	Y	Y
DECODER (PLAYER)				
Playback environments	Windows, Macintosh	Windows, Macintosh	Windows, Macintosh	Windows, Macintosh, Power Macintosh, XWindows
Browser integration	MIME	MIME	MIME	MIME
Minimum modem speed	14.4 kbps	14.4 kbps	9.6 kbps	9.6 kbps
Decoder download size	273K	312K	1.2MB (includes Internet Phone)	563K
PLAYER FEATURES				
Status bar	Y	Y	Y	Y
Start at random points?	Y	Y	N	Y
Stop and resume	No, stop and start over	Y	Y	Y
Volume control	N	Y	Y	No for MIME player; yes for stand-alone player

Y—Yes N—No N/A—Not applicable INA—Information not available   End ■

WEB BROWSERS

Web Browsers ■

(Products listed in alphabetical order by company name.)	Aimnet Internet Ranger	Compuserve/Spry Spry Internet in a Box	Delrina CyberJack	Frontier Technologies Super-Highway Access	FTP Software Explore Anywhere 2.0
Price	$70	$10	$129	$89+	$199
Supported platforms	Windows 95, Windows 3.1	Windows 95, Windows 3.1, Macintosh	Windows 95	Windows 95, Windows 3.1	Windows 95, Windows 3.1
Connection	SLIP/PPP, TCP/IP network	SLIP/PPP, TCP/IP network	SLIP/PPP, TCP/IP network	SLIP/PPP, TCP/IP network	SLIP/PPP, TCP/IP network
Security protocols	None	S-HTTP	None	None	None
HTML					
SGML	N	Y	N	N	N
HTML 2.0	Y	Y	Y	Y	Y
HTML 3.0	Y	Y	Y	Y	N
Tables	N	N	Y	N	N
Backgrounds	N	Y	Y	Y	N
Colors	Y	Y	Y	Y	N
Fonts	N	N	Y	N	N
HTML+	N	N	N	N	N
Frames	N	N	N	N	N
FEATURES					
Supported image formats	Regular GIF, JPEG	Regular GIF, JPEG, progressive JPEG	Regular GIF, JPEG	Regular GIF, JPEG, progressive JPEG	Regular GIF, JPEG, client-side image map
Bookmarks	Y	Y	Y	Y	Static
Viewing history	N	N	Y	Y	N
Memory cache	Y	Y	Y	Y	Y
Source-file viewing	Y	Y	Y	Y	Y
Customizable toolbar	N	N	N	N	N
Multi-threaded connection	Y	Y	Y	Y	N
HTML authoring tools	N	N	N	N	N
EXTENSIONS					
Plug-ins	N	N	N	N	N
Helper applications	Y	Y	Y	Y	Y
Acrobat	Y	N	N	N	N
Digital Paper	N	N	N	N	N
VRML	N	N	N	N	N
Decoding capability	None	None	PKZIP	None	None
Scripting languages supported	None	None	None	None	None
E-mail	Y, Supports MIME and POP3	Y, Supports MIME	Y, Supports MIME	Y, Supports MIME and POP3	Y, Supports MIME, POP3, and MAPI
NNTP	Y	Y	Y, Supports multi-threaded news	Y	Y
Telnet	Y	Y	Y	Y	Y

Y—Yes N—No N/A—Not applicable INA—Information not available

Table Continues →

■ Web Browsers

	Hummingbird Hummingbird Columbus 1.0	IBM Web Explorer 2.1	Ipswitch CyberSuite	Microsoft Internet Explorer 2.0	NCSA NCSA Mosaic
Price	INA	$39	$95	Free	Free
Supported platforms	Windows 95, Windows NT, Windows 3.1	Windows 3.1	Windows 95, Windows NT, Windows 3.1	Windows 95, Windows NT, Windows 3.1, Unix, Macintosh	Windows 95, Windows NT, Windows 3.1, Unix, Macintosh
Connection	SLIP/PPP, TCP/IP network	SLIP/PPP, TCP/IP network	SLIP/PPP, TCP/IP network	SLIP/PPP, TCP/IP network	SLIP/PPP, TCP/IP network
Security protocols	None	SSL, S-HTTP	None	SSL, PCT, RSA	None
HTML					
SGML	N	N	N	N	Y
HTML 2.0	Y	Y	Y	Y	Y
HTML 3.0	N	Y	Y	Y	Y
Tables	N	Y	Y	Y	Y
Backgrounds	N	Y	Y	Y	Y
Colors	N	Y	Y	Y	N
Fonts	N	N	N	Y	N
HTML+	N	N	N	Y	N
Frames	N	N	N	Y	N
FEATURES					
Supported image formats	Regular GIF, JPEG	Regular GIF, JPEG	Regular GIF, JPEG	Regular and transparent GIF, JPEG, progressive JPEG, client-side image map	Regular GIF, JPEG
Bookmarks	Y	Y	Y	Y	Y
Viewing history	N	Y	Y	Y	Y
Memory cache	Y	Y	Y	Y	Y
Source-file viewing	Y	Y	Y	Y	Y
Customizable toolbar	N	Y	N	Y	N
Multi-threaded connection	N	Y	N	Y	N
HTML authoring tools	Y	N	N	N	N
EXTENSIONS					
Plug-ins	N	N	Y	Y	N
Helper applications	Y	Y	Y	Y	N
Acrobat	N	N	N	N	N
Digital Paper	Y	N	N	N	N
VRML	N	N	N	Y	N
Decoding capability	None	None	None	None	None
Scripting languages supported	None	Java available	None	JavaScript, VB Script, Java	None
E-mail	Y, Supports MIME, POP3, and MAPI	Y, Supports MIME, POP3, and MAPI	Y, Supports MIME and POP3	Y, Supports MIME, POP3, and MAPI	N
NNTP	Y	Y, Supports multi-threaded news	Y	Y	Y
Telnet	Y	Y	Y	N	Y

Y—Yes N—No N/A—Not applicable INA—Information not available

Web Browsers ■

	NCSA Secure NCSA Mosaic	Netscape Netscape 1.2 Personal Edition	Netscape Netscape Navigator 2.0	Netscape Netscape 2.0 for Unix	Netscape Netscape Navigator 2.0 Gold
Price	Free	$45	$49	$49	$79
Supported platforms	Windows 3.1, Unix, Solaris, SunOS, SGI, HP-UI, OSFI	Windows 95, Windows NT, Windows 3.1, Unix, Macintosh	Windows 95, Windows NT, Windows 3.1, Macintosh	Unix, Solaris, SunOS, SGI, HP-UI, OSFI	Windows 95, Windows NT, Windows 3.1, Unix, Macintosh
Connection	TCP/IP network	SLIP/PPP, TCP/IP network	SLIP/PPP, TCP/IP network	TCP/IP network	SLIP/PPP, TCP/IP network
Security protocols	S-HTTP, RSA	SSL, RSA	SSL, RSA	SSL, RSA	SSL, RSA

HTML
SGML	Y	N	N	N	N
HTML 2.0	Y	Y	Y	Y	Y
HTML 3.0	Y	Y	Y	Y	Y
Tables	Y	Y	Y	Y	Y
Backgrounds	Y	Y	Y	Y	Y
Colors	N	Y	Y	Y	Y
Fonts	N	Y	Y	Y	Y
HTML+	N	Y	Y	Y	Y
Frames	N	N	Y	Y	Y

FEATURES
Supported image formats	Regular GIF, JPEG	Regular and transparent GIF, JPEG, progressive JPEG	Regular, transparent, and animated GIF, JPEG, progressive JPEG, client-side image map	Regular, transparent, and animated GIF, JPEG, progressive JPEG, client-side image map	Regular, transparent, and animated GIF, JPEG, progressive JPEG, client-side image map
Bookmarks	Y	Y	Y	Y	Y
Viewing history	Y	Y	Y	Y	Y
Memory cache	Y	Y	Y	Y	Y
Source-file viewing	Y	Y	Y	Y	Y
Customizable toolbar		N	N	N	N
Multi-threaded connection	N	Y	Y	Y	Y
HTML authoring tools	N	N	N	N	Y

EXTENSIONS
Plug-ins	N	Y	Y	Y	Y
Helper applications	N	Y	Y	Y	Y
Acrobat	N	Available	Available	Available	Available
Digital Paper	N	N	N	N	N
VRML	N	N	N	N	N
Decoding capability	None	None	None	None	None
Scripting languages supported	None	None	JavaScript, Java	JavaScript, Java	JavaScript, Java
E-mail	N	Y, Supports MIME and MAPI	Y, Supports MIME, POP3, and MAPI	Y, Supports MIME, POP3, and MAPI	Y, Supports MIME, POP3, and MAPI
NNTP	N	Y, Supports multi-threaded news	Y, Supports multi-threaded news	Y, Supports multi-threaded news	Y, Supports multi-threaded news
Telnet	Y	Y	Y	Y	Y

Y—Yes N—No N/A—Not applicable INA—Information not available

Table Continues →

■ Web Browsers

	OmniGroup OmniWeb 2.0	Oracle Oracle Power Browser 1.5	Peter Brooks SlipKnot 1.5	Quarterdeck Quarterdeck Internet Suite	Softronics Softerm Plus
Price	INA	INA	$30	$79	INA
Supported platforms	Unix	Windows 95, Windows NT, Windows 3.1	Windows 95, Windows NT, Windows 3.1	Windows 3.1	Windows 95, Windows 3.1
Connection	TCP/IP network	SLIP/PPP, TCP/IP network	Serial	SLIP/PPP, TCP/IP network	SLIP/PPP, TCP/IP network
Security protocols	None	SSL	None	SSL	None
HTML					
SGML	N	N	N	N	Y
HTML 2.0	Y	Y	Y	Y	Y
HTML 3.0	Y	Y	N	Y	N
Tables	Y	Y	N	N	N
Backgrounds	Y	Y	N	N	N
Colors	Y	Y	N	Y	N
Fonts	Y	Y	N	Y	N
HTML+	Y	Y	N	N	N
Frames	Y	Y	N	N	N
FEATURES					
Supported image formats	Regular GIF, transparent GIF, JPEG, progressive JPEG	Regular, transparent, and animated GIF, JPEG, client-side image map	Regular GIF, JPEG	Regular GIF, JPEG, progressive JPEG	Regular GIF, transparent GIF, JPEG, client-side image map
Bookmarks	Y	Y	Y	Y	Y
Viewing history	Y	Y	Y	N	N
Memory cache	Y	Y	N	Y	Y
Source-file viewing	Y	Y	Y	Y	Y
Customizable toolbar	Y	N	N	N	N
Multi-threaded connection	Y	Y	N	Y	Y
HTML authoring tools	N	Y	N	N	N
EXTENSIONS					
Plug-ins	Y	Y	N	N	N
Helper applications	Y	Y	N	Y	Y
Acrobat	Y	N	N	Y	N
Digital Paper	N	N	N	N	N
VRML	N	N	N	N	N
Decoding capability	None	None	None	None	None
Scripting languages supported	None	VB Script, Java	None	None	None
E-mail	N	Y, Supports POP3	N	Y, Supports MIME	Y, Supports MIME, POP3, and MAPI
NNTP	N	N	N	Y	Y
Telnet	Y	Y	N	Y	Y

Y—Yes   N—No   N/A—Not applicable   INA—Information not available

Web Browsers ■

	Spyglass Spyglass Enhanced	Sun Microsystems HotJava 1.0b	SunSoft Web Scout	Tradewave Tradewave Mac- Web	Tradewave Tradewave Win- Web
Price	Varies	Free	$145	INA	INA
Supported platforms	Windows 95, Windows NT, Windows 3.1, Unix, Macintosh, Solaris, SunOS, SGI	Windows 95, Windows NT, Unix, Solaris	Solaris, SunOS	Macintosh	Windows 3.1
Connection	SLIP/PPP, TCP/IP network	SLIP/PPP, TCP/IP network	TCP/IP network	SLIP/PPP, TCP/IP network	SLIP/PPP, TCP/IP network
Security protocols	None	None	S-HTTP, RSA	None	None
HTML					
SGML	N	N	N	N	N
HTML 2.0	Y	Y	Y	Y	Y
HTML 3.0	Y	N	Y	Y	Y
Tables	Y	N	N	Y	Y
Backgrounds	Y	N	Y	Y	Y
Colors	Y	N	Y	Y	Y
Fonts	N	N	N	N	N
HTML+	N	N	N	N	N
Frames	N	N	N	N	N
FEATURES					
Supported image formats	Regular GIF, JPEG, client-side image maps	Regular GIF, JPEG	Regular GIF, JPEG, progressive JPEG	Regular GIF, JPEG, progressive JPEG	Regular GIF, JPEG, progressive JPEG
Bookmarks	Y	Y	Y	Y	Y
Viewing history	Y	N	Y	Y	Y
Memory cache	Y	N	Y	Y	Y
Source-file viewing	Y	Y	Y	Y	Y
Customizable toolbar	Y	N	N	N	N
Multi-threaded connection	Y	Y	Y	Y	Y
HTML authoring tools	N	N	N	N	N
EXTENSIONS					
Plug-ins	Y	N	N	N	N
Helper applications	Y	N	Y	Y	Y
Acrobat	N	N	N	N	N
Digital Paper	N	N	N	N	N
VRML	N	N	N	N	N
Decoding capability	None	None	None	None	None
Scripting languages supported	None	Java	None	None	None
E-mail	Y, Supports MIME	N	Y, Supports MIME and MAPI	N	N
NNTP	Y	N	Y, Supports multi-threaded news	Y, Supports multi-threaded news	Y, Supports multi-threaded news
Telnet	Y	N	Y	Y	Y

Y—Yes   N—No   N/A—Not applicable   INA—Information not available

Table Continues →

■ Web Browsers

	University of Kansas Lynx	William Perry Emacs W3	Wollongang Emissary	W30 Arena
Price	Free	Free	$99	Free
Supported platforms	Unix	Windows 95, Windows NT, Windows 3.1, Unix, Macintosh	Windows 95, Windows NT, Windows 3.1	Unix, Solaris, SunOS, SGI
Connection	Serial, TCP/IP network	SLIP/PPP, TCP/IP network	SLIP/PPP, TCP/IP network	SLIP/PPP, TCP/IP network
Security protocols	None	SSL available	SSL, S-HTTP. RSA	none
HTML				
SGML	N	N	N	N
HTML 2.0	Y	Y	Y	Y
HTML 3.0	N	Y	Y	Y
Tables	N	Y	N	Y
Backgrounds	N	Y	Y	Y
Colors	N	Y	Y	Y
Fonts	N	Y	N	N
HTML+	N	Y	N	N
Frames	N	N	N	N
FEATURES				
Supported image formats	None	Regular GIF, transparent GIF, JPEG	Regular GIF, JPEG, progressive JPEG	None
Bookmarks	Y	Y	Y	N
Viewing history	N	Y	Y	N
Memory cache	N	Y	Y	N
Source-file viewing	Y	Y	Y	Y
Customizable toolbar	N	N	N	N
Multi-threaded connection	N	N	Y	N
HTML authoring tools	N	N	N	N
EXTENSIONS				
Plug-ins	N	N	Y	N
Helper applications	N	Y	Y	Y
Acrobat	N	INA	N	N
Digital Paper	N	N	N	N
VRML	N	N	N	N
Decoding capability	None	None	None	None
Scripting languages supported	None	None	None	None
E-mail	N	Y, Supports MIME	Y, Supports MIME	N
NNTP	N	N	Y, Supports multi-threaded news	N
Telnet	Y	N	Y	N

Y—Yes   N—No   N/A—Not applicable   INA—Information not available

End ■

PLUG-INS

F.1   Document-Handling Plug-ins ■

(Products listed in alphabetical order by company name)	Adobe Acrobat 3.0b	BrainTech Groupscape	Inso Word Viewer 1.02	Net-Scene PointPlus 1.0b3	Tumbleweed Software Envoy
Price	Free	Free	Free	Free	Free
Address	http://www .adobe.com	http://www .braintech.com/ grpdemo.htm	http://www .inso.com/plug.htm	http://www .net-scene.com/	http://www.twcorp .com/plugin.htm
PLATFORM COMPATIBILITY					
Windows 95	Y	Y	Y	Y	Y
Windows 3.1	Y	Y	Y	Y	Y
Unix	Y	N	N	N	N
Macintosh PPC	Y	N	In progress	N	Y
Macintosh 68X	Y	N	In progress	N	Y
Supported formats	Portable Document Format (PDF)	Lotus Notes	Microsoft Word 6.0, 7.0	Microsoft PowerPoint	Envoy documents
Description	PDF files are dynamic, platform-independent, and easy to create. They allow for design control, print-ready documents, and a wide variety of authoring applications.				

Y—Yes   N—No   N/A—Not applicable   INA—Information not available

Table Continues →

ZIFF-DAVIS PRESS

■ Document-Handling Plug-ins

	Visual Components Formula One/Net
Price	Free
Address	http://www .visualcomp.com/ f1net/download.htm
PLATFORM COMPATIBILITY	
Windows 95	Y
Windows 3.1	Y
Unix	N
Macintosh PPC	N
Macintosh 68X	N
Supported formats	Spreadsheets
Description	

Y—Yes   N—No   N/A—Not applicable   INA—Information not available

End ■

F.2   Multimedia and 3-D Plug-ins ■

(Products listed in alphabetical order by company name)	Apple Computer Apple QuickTime Plug-in 1.0b10	Brad Anderson ExpressVR 1.0b2	Chaco Communications VR Scout 1.22	Chaco VR Scout	Digigami CineWeb
Price	Free	Free	Free	Free	Free
Address	http:// quicktime.apple.com	http://www.cis .upenn.edu/~brada/ VRML/ExpressVR .html	http://www .chaco.com	http://www .chaco.com	http://www .digigami.com
PLATFORM COMPATIBILITY					
Windows 95	Y	N	Y	Y	Y
Windows 3.1	Y	N	In progress	N	Y
Unix	N	N	N	N	N
Macintosh PPC	Y	Y	In progress	N	N
Macintosh 68X	Y	Y	In progress	N	N
Supported multimedia formats	QuickTime				QuickTime, AVI, MPEG, FLC, ISMAP, WAV
Supported 3-D formats	QTVR	VRML	VRML	VRML	
Description	Multiple platforms beyond Macintosh are supported.			Chaco is a provider of advanced multiuser Internet software. VR Scout is a VRML viewer with fast and complete VRML 1.0 implementation.	Digigami develops high-performance Internet and intranet multimedia tools using industry standard, open Web technologies. CineWeb is a multimedia plug-in.

Y—Yes   N—No   N/A—Not applicable   INA—Information not available

Table Continues →

■ Multimedia and 3-D Plug-ins

	Dimension X Liquid Reality 0.96b	FutureWave FutureSplash1.0b	GEO Interactive Media Group Emblaze 1.5b	Gold Disk Astound Web Player 1.0	ICB ViewMovie 1.0a10
Price	Free trial	Free	Free	Free	Free
Address	http://www .dimensionx.com/ products/lr/ index.html	http://www .futurewave.com/	http://www.Geo .inter.net/ technology/ emblaze/ downloads.html	http://www .golddisk.com	http://www.well .com/user/ivanski/ download.html
PLATFORM COMPATIBILITY					
Windows 95	Y	Y	In progress	Y	In progress
Windows 3.1	In progress	Y	Y	Y	N
Unix	N	N	N	N	N
Macintosh PPC	In progress	Y	Y	In progress	Y
Macintosh 68X	In progress	Y	Y	In progress	Y
Supported multimedia formats		Streamed animation	Real-time animation	Astound, Studio N	QuickTime
Supported 3-D formats	VRML				
Description		Also supports MIDI sound files		Allows for streaming playback of high-impact multimedia content over the Web	

Y—Yes   N—No   N/A—Not applicable   INA—Information not available

Multimedia and 3-D Plug-ins ■

	Integrated Data Systems VRealm 1.0	Intelligence at Large MovieStar 1.0b8	InternetConsult Animated Widgets	InterVU Inc. InterVU 0.92b	Iterated Systems CoolFusion 1.1
Price	Free trial	Free	Free	Free	Free
Address	http://www .ids-net.com	http://www .beingthere.com/ moviestar/ index.html	http://www .InternetConsult .com/animplug.html	http://www.intervu .com/prevu.html	http://webber .iterated.com
PLATFORM COMPATIBILITY					
Windows 95	Y	Y	Y	Y	Y
Windows 3.1	In progress	Y	N	N	N
Unix	N	N	N	N	N
Macintosh PPC	In progress	Y	N	Y	In progress
Macintosh 68X	In progress	Y	N	Y	In progress
Supported multimedia formats	VRML	QuickTime, Streamed input	Animation Widgets	MPEG	Streaming AVI
Supported 3-D formats		QTVR			
Description	Offers users full VRML compliance with extensions for behaviors and an intuitive interface.		This plug-in offers true animation in a client-server environ- ment.		Plays stream video, allowing for nearly instantaneous playback. There's no need to wait until the entire file is loaded— it plays video as it is received.

Y—Yes   N—No   N/A—Not applicable   INA—Information not available   **Table Continues** →

Multimedia and 3-D Plug-ins

	John Louch Whurlplug 1.0d6	Kevin McMurtrie KM's Multimedia Plug 0.3.2.	Kinetix Topper 1.0b	Macromedia ShockWave/Direct or 4.0	mBED mBED 1.0b1
Price	Free	Free	Free	Free	Free
Address	http://product.info .apple.com/qd3d/ viewer.html	ftp://ftp.wco.com/ users/mcmurtri/ MySoftware/	http://www.ktx.com	http://www .macromedia.com	http://www .mbed.com/
PLATFORM COMPATABILITY					
Windows 95	N	N	Y	Y	Y
Windows 3.1	N	N	N	Y	Y
Unix	N	N	N	N	N
Macintosh PPC	Y	Y	N	Y	Y
Macintosh 68X	N	Y	N	Y	Y
Supported multimedia formats		QuickTime		Director Multimedia	mbedlets
Supported 3-D formats	QD3D		VRML		
Description				Shockwave for Director allows for high-impact, interactive multimedia on the Internet. This is a very popular multimedia tool.	

Y—Yes   N—No   N/A—Not applicable   INA—Information not available

Multimedia and 3-D Plug-ins

	Netscape Live3D 1.0b1	Open2u Action 1.0b	Power Soft Media Splash	Silicon Graphics Cosmo Player 1.0b	Software Publishing Corporation ASAP WebShow 1.0b8
Price	Free trial	Free	Free (alpha version)	Free	Free
Address	http://home .netscape.com/ comprod/products/ navigator/live3d/ download_live3d.html	http://www.open2u .com/action/	http://www .powersoft.com/ media.splash/ product/index.html	http://webspace .sgi.com/ cosmoplayer/	http://www .spco.com
PLATFORM COMPATIBILITY					
Windows 95	Y	Y	Y	Y	Y
Windows 3.1	Y	In progress	In progress	N	Y
Unix	N	N	N	N	N
Macintosh PPC	In progress	N	N	N	N
Macintosh 68X	Y	N	N	N	N
Supported multimedia formats		MPEG	media.splash		ASAP WordPower
Supported 3-D formats	VRML			VRML	
Description		Allows Web clients to view MPEG movies with synchronized sound over the Inter- net. ActionStudio supports generation of MPEG movies for use in Web pages.			Supports any document created by the ASAP WordPower software package.

Y—Yes   N—No   N/A—Not applicable   INA—Information not available

Table Continues →

Multimedia and 3-D Plug-ins

	TEC Solutions Tech Player 1.0.3	Totally Hip Software Sizzler
Price	Free	Free
Address	http://www .tecs.com/ TECPlayer_docs	http://www .totallyhip.com/ sizzler/6_sizz.html
PLATFORM COMPATIBILITY		
Windows 95	In progress	Y
Windows 3.1	In progress	Y
Unix	N	N
Macintosh PPC	Y	Y
Macintosh 68X	Y	Y
Supported multimedia formats	QuickTime	Sizzler Multimedia files
Supported 3-D formats		
Description		

Y—Yes   N—No   N/A—Not applicable   INA—Information not available

End ■

F.3   Sound Plug-ins ■

(Products listed in alphabetical order by company name)	Arnaud Masson MIDIPlugin 1.2.1b	DSP Group TrueSpeech	Echo Speech Corp. EchoSpeech	FastMan RapidTransit 1.0b	FutureWave FutureSplash 1.0b
Price	Free	Free	Free ($99 for commercial use)	Free	Free
Address	http://planete.net/ ~amasson/	http://www .dspg.com	http://www .echospeech.com/ plugin.htm	http:// monsterbit.com/ rapidtransit/ RTHome.html	http://www .futurewave.com/
PLATFORM COMPATIBILITY					
Windows 95	N	Y	Y	Y	Y
Windows 3.1	N	Y	Y	Y	Y
Unix	N	N	N	N	N
Macintosh PPC	Y	N	In progress	N	Y
Macintosh 68X	Y	N	In progress	N	Y
Supported sound formats	MIDI	TrueSpeech	Compressed speech	RT sound compression	MIDI
Description		DSP Group's TrueSpeech Player enables high-quality audio to be transmitted over the Internet without the need for special server software.			Also supports streamed animation multimedia files

Y—Yes   N—No   N/A—Not applicable   INA—Information not available

Table Continues →

■ Sound Plug-ins

	Live Update Crescendo 2.0	Live Update Crescendo Plus 2.0	Progressive Networks RealAudio 2.0.2	Sseyo Koan 1.0	Voxware ToolVox 1.1b2
Price	$10	$20	Free	Free	Free
Address	http://www .liveupdate.com	http://www .liveupdate.com	http://www .realaudio.com	http://www .sseyo.com/	http://www .voxware.com
PLATFORM COMPATIBILITY					
Windows 95	Y	Y	Y	Y	Y
Windows 3.1	Y	Y	In progress	Y	Y
Unix	N	N	Y	N	N
Macintosh PPC	Y	Y	Y	N	Y
Macintosh 68X	Y	Y	Y	N	In progress
Supported sound formats	MIDI	MIDI, Streaming enable	RealAudio stream	MIDI, Koan Pro	Speech
Description	With Crescendo, you can add music to your Web site or just listen to music as you surf the sites.	Crescendo PLUS offers some bonuses, such as the streaming of MIDI files and a full-featured control panel with a volume slider.	Provides live and on-demand real-time audio with 14.4Kbps or faster connections to the Internet. RealAudio Version 2.0 allows Web masters a custom-ized environment for delivering audio from Web sites.		Voxware's Toolvox allows Web masters and clients to com-press, stream, and play high-quality voice files at up to 53:1 compression ratios. Toolvox includes both an authoring tool and player software. It offers real-time voice delivery even at the slow speed of 2400 Kbps.

Y—Yes   N—No   N/A—Not applicable   INA—Information not available

Sound Plug-ins ■

	William H. Tudor Speech Plug-In 1.0	Yamaha MIDIPlug 1.0b1E
Price	Free	Free
Address	http://www.albany.net/~wtudor/	http://www.yamaha.co.jp/english/xg/html/midhm.html
PLATFORM COMPATIBILITY		
Windows 95	N	Y
Windows 3.1	N	Y
Unix	N	N
Macintosh PPC	Y	Y
Macintosh 68X	Y	N
Supported sound formats	Apple Text to Speech Software	MIDI, SMF 0/1
Description		

■ F.4   Graphics Plug-ins

(Products listed in alphabetical order by company name)	AutoDesk Whip 1.0b	Carberry Technology FIGleaf Inline 1.0	Corel Corporation CMX Viewer	Data Views Corporation WebXpresso	Infinop Lightning Strike 1.6
Price	Free trial	$20	Free	Free	Free
Address	http://www .autodesk.com/ products/autocad/ whip/whip.htm	http://www .ct.ebt.com	http://www .corel.com	http://www .dvcorp.com	http://www .infinop.com
PLATFORM COMPATIBILITY					
Windows 95	Y	Y	Y	Y	Y
Windows 3.1	N	Y	N	Y	Y
Unix	N	N	N	N	Y
Macintosh PPC	N	In progress	N	N	Y
Macintosh 68X	N	In progress	N	N	Y
Supported graphics formats	DWG, DFX, AutoCAD	TIFF, CGM, EPS, BMP, WMF, PNG, PPM, GIF, JPEG, others	CMX	XPM	wavelet compression
Description		Allows users to view scalable, dynamic, vector, and raster images on the Web	Allows users to integrate smooth, scalable vector graphics in their Web page designs	DVC produces dynamic user-interface software development tools. DVC products include the X-Designer, DV-GIPSY, DataViews, DV-Xpresso, DV-Centro, and WebXpresso.	Infinop works in the field of data compression. Lightning Strike is no exception, providing a unique image-compression system based on wavelets.

Y—Yes   N—No   N/A—Not applicable   INA—Information not available

Graphics Plug-ins ■

	InterCAP Graphics Systems InterCAP InLine 1.0b	Iterated Systems Fractal Viewer 1.1	Lari Software LightningDraw GX 1.0b	Macromedia ShockWave/ FreeHand 5.0b1	MDL Information Systems Chemscape Chime 0.9a
Price	Free	Free	Free	Free	Free for academic, personal, and home use
Address	http://www .intercap.com/ about/ DownloadNow.html	http://www .iterated.com/ fracview/fv_home .htm	http://www .larisoftware.com/ Products/ WebPlugin.html	http://www .macromedia.com	http://www .mdli.com
PLATFORM COMPATIBILITY					
Windows 95	Y	Y	N	Y	Y
Windows 3.1	N	Y	N	Y	Y
Unix	N	N	N	N	N
Macintosh PPC	N	In progress	Y	Y	Y
Macintosh 68X	N	In progress	In progress	Y	Y
Supported graphics formats	CGM, Zooming enabled	FIF	GX	FreeHand Graphic files	PDB, MDL Molfile, CSMLF, RSF, TGF, MDL-Rxn, IEMBL
Description		This plug-in supports the Fractal Image Format (FIF).			This is a chemical viewer, rendering chemical informa- tion in 2-D and 3-D formats within an HTML page or table.

Y—Yes   N—No   N/A—Not applicable   INA—Information not available

Table Continues →

■ Graphics Plug-ins

	Micrografx QuickSilver 1.0b2	Pegasus RapidVue 1.0	SoftSource DWG/DFX Viewer 1.2	SoftSource SVF Viewer 1.2	TMS TMS ViewDirector
Price	Free	Free	$50	$50	Free
Address	http://www .micrografx.com	http://www.jpg.com/ snapshots.html	http://www .softsource.com/ softsource/	http://www .softsource.com/ softsource/ plugins/ svf-plugin.html	http://www .tmsinc.com
PLATFORM COMPATIBILITY					
Windows 95	Y	Y	Y	Y	Y
Windows 3.1	Y	Y	N	N	Y
Unix	N	N	N	N	N
Macintosh PPC	N	In progress	N	N	In progress
Macintosh 68X	N	In progress	N	N	In progress
Supported graphics formats	ABC QuickSilver, ABC Graphics Suite	Pegasus Imaging Snapshots	DWG, DFX, SVF	SVF	TIFF, CALS, JPEG, PCX/DCX, BMP, others
Description	Extends the ABC Graphics Suite, allowing placement, viewing, and interaction with object graphics inside Web pages.		Supports viewing AutoCAD and DXF drawings. Also supported is the SVF (Simple Vector Format), a file format developed jointly by SoftSource and NCSA. These products include scalable vector graphics that allow for zoom, pan, and layer visibility controls.		Not only displays graphic file formats like TIFFs and others, but allows for zooming in or out. Also supported is an image-enhancement feature to improve the display.

Y—Yes   N—No   N/A—Not applicable   INA—Information not available

End ■

F.5 Miscellaneous Plug-ins

(Products listed in alphabetical order by company name)	Alpha Software Concerto 1.0b2	Argus Technologies Argus Map Viewer 1.0b4	Bill Noon ListenUp	Citrix System WinFrame	Digital Dreams ShockTalk 1.1.3N
Price	Free	Free	Free	Free	Free
Address	http://www .alphasoftware.com	http://www .argusmap.com/	http://snow.cit .cornell.edu/noon/ ListenUp.html	http://www .citrix.com	http://www .surftalk.com/ shocktalk/index.html
PLATFORM COMPATIBILITY					
Windows 95	Y	Y	N	Y	N
Windows 3.1	In progress	Y	N	Y	N
Unix	N	N	N	N	N
Macintosh PPC	N	N	Y	N	Y
Macintosh 68X	N	N	N	N	Y
Function	Form Support for CGI	Geographic Viewer	Apple Plain Talk speech recognition	Windows application Web interface	Speech recognition for ShockWave
Description	Alpha Software Corporation is a software developer focusing on productivity for businesses and consumers, most especially in the PC database marketplace. Alpha Four was the first product to offer the power of a relational database with an easy-to-use menu-driven interface.			Citrix System's WinFrame supports the execution of Windows applications over the Internet. This includes direct access from a Web page. Also supported is Web site development using standard Windows utilities and tools.	

Y—Yes   N—No   N/A—Not applicable   INA—Information not available

Table Continues →

Miscellaneous Plug-ins

	Farallon Look@Me	FTP Software KEYView 4.2	Galacticomm Galacticomm Worldgroup 2.0	IChat IChat 1.10 (1.13)	Inso CyberSpell 2.0
Price	Free	Free trial	Free	Free	$25
Address	http://www .farallon.com	http://www.ftp.com/ mkt_info/evals/ kv_dl.html	http://www .gcomm.com/show/ plugin.html	http://www.ichat .com/	http://www.inso .com/consumer/ cyberspell/ democybr.htm
PLATFORM COMPATIBILITY					
Windows 95	Y	Y	Y	Y	Y
Windows 3.1	N	N	Y	N	Y
Unix	N	N	N	N	N
Macintosh PPC	Y	N	N	Y	N
Macintosh 68X	Y	N	N	Y	N
Function	Timbuktu Web interface	File format conversion	Galacticomm BBS connection	Web IRC agent	E-mail Spell Checker
Description	Farallon is a developer of networking and Internet products for productivity. Farallon's Look@Me offers real-time person-to-person communication over the Internet. Farallon's Timbuktu Pro is a real-time Internet collaboration software.			Provides communication over the Web, in real time, without learning new applications. IChat can make a Web page into a chatroom—basically an in-line IRC agent.	

Y—Yes   N—No   N/A—Not applicable   INA—Information not available

Miscellaneous Plug-ins

	ISYS/Odyssey Development ISYS Hindsite	MVP Solutions Talker 2.0	Microcom Carbon Copy/Net 1.0b	OneWave OpenScape	PenOp PenOp 1.0
Price	$40	Free	Free	Free	Free
Address	http://www .rmii.com/isys_dev/ hindsite.html	http://www .mvpsolutions.com/ PlugInSite/ Talker.html	http://www .microcom.com/cc/ ccdnload.htm	http://www .busweb.com	http://www.penop .com/download.htm
PLATFORM COMPATIBILITY					
Windows 95	Y	N	Y	Y	Y
Windows 3.1	Y	N	Y	Y	N
Unix	N	N	N	N	N
Macintosh PPC	In progress	Y	N	In progress	N
Macintosh 68X	In progress	Y	N	In progress	N
Function	Viewing history	Apple Text to speech software	Remote PC control	Component-based development	Encrypted transmission
Description	Provides Web clients the ability to perform full-text searches on the contents of previously accessed Web pages. ISYS acts like a personal Internet assistant, remembering each site that is visited.			Provides security and efficiency when moving an existing client-server application onto the Internet. Also includes the ability for customers to create new Internet and intranet applications. OpenScape is based on the idea of reusable software components.	

Y—Yes N—No N/A—Not applicable INA—Information not available   **Table Continues** →

■ Miscellaneous Plug-ins

	PointCast Pointcast 1.0	SmartBrowser HistoryTree 1.0a1	Starfish Software EarthTime
Price	Free	Free	$20
Address	http://www .pointcast.com	http://www .smartbrowser.com/	http://www .starfishsoftware .com/getearth.html
PLATFORM COMPATIBILITY			
Windows 95	Y	Y	Y
Windows 3.1	Y	Y	N
Unix	N	N	N
Macintosh PPC	In progress	N	N
Macintosh 68X	in progress	N	N
Function	Personalized news, weather, etc.	Special viewing history display	Global TimeZone locator
Description	Provides current news and informa- tion to anyone via the Internet. The PointCast Network offers a free service, providing up-to-the- minute news and information.		

Y—Yes   N—No   N/A—Not applicable   INA—Information not available

End ■

E-MAIL
APPLICATIONS

E-mail Applications ∎

(Products listed in alphabetical order by product name.)	Elm (Electronic Mail for Unix) 2.4 USENET Community Trust	Email Connection 2.5 ConnectSoft	EMBLA ICL Prosystems	EMBLA Lite ICL Prosystems	Eudora Lite Qualcomm
Price	Free	Free	Free	Free	Free
Supported platforms	Unix	Windows 95, Windows 3.1	Windows 95, Windows 3.1	Windows 95, Windows 3.1	Windows 95, Windows 3.1, DOS, Macintosh, Unix
Supported protocols	SMTP, MIME	SMTP, POP, MAPI, MIME	SMTP, IMAP, MIME	SMTP, POP, MIME	SMTP, POP, MIME
TYPE OF CONNECTION					
Direct	Y	N	N	N	Y
Remote					
Online	N	N	Y	N	Y
Offline	N	Y	Y	Y	Y
Disconnected	N	N	N	N	N
Serial	Y	N	N	N	Y
TCP/IP	Y	Y	Y	Y	Y
FEATURES					
Word wrap	Not directly supported	Y	Y	Y	Y
Sorting	Y	Y	Y	Y	Y
Folders	Y	Y	Y	Y	Y
Address book	Y	Y	Y	Y	Y
Attaching files	Y	Y	Y	Y	Y
Signatures	Y	Y	Y	Y	Y
Configurable header	Y	Y	Y	Y	Y
Importing files	Y	Y	Y	Y	Y
Return receipts	N	N	N	N	N
Printer support	Y	Y	Y	Y	Y
Search folders	N	Y	N	N	Y
Toolbar	N	Y	Y	Y	Y
Spellchecker	N	Y	N	N	N
Drag-and-drop	N	Y	Y	Y	N
Audio	N	N	N	N	N
EXTRAS					
HTTP	N	N	N	N	N
NNTP	N	N	N	N	N
Fax	N	N	N	N	N

Y—Yes N—No N/A—Not applicable INA—Information not available

Table Continues →

■ E-mail Applications

	Eudora Pro Qualcomm	ExpressIT Infinite Technologies	Messenger RUA Infonet Software Solutions	ML Mike Macgirvin	MS Exchange Microsoft Corporation
Price	$89.00	Free	INA	Free	Free (with Windows 95)
Supported platforms	Windows 95, Windows 3.1, DOS, Macintosh, Unix	Windows 3.1, DOS	Windows 95, Windows 3.1	Unix	Windows 95
Supported protocols	SMTP, POP, MAPI, MIME	SMTP	X.400, POP	SMTP, POP, IMAP, MIME	SMTP, MAPI
TYPE OF CONNECTION					
Direct	Y	Y	Y	Y	N
Remote					
Online	Y	N	N	Y	N
Offline	Y	N	N	Y	Y
Disconnected	N	N	N	N	N
Serial	Y	Y	N	Y	N
TCP/IP	Y	Y	Y	Y	Y
FEATURES					
Word wrap	Y	Y	Y	Y	Y
Sorting	Y	Y	Y	Y	Y
Folders	Y	Y	Y	Y	Y
Address book	Y	Y	Y	Y	Y
Attaching files	Y	Y	Y	Y	Y
Signatures	Y	Y	Y	Y	Y
Configurable header	Y	Y	Y	Y	Y
Importing files	Y	Y	Y	Y	Y
Return receipts	Y	N	Y	N	N
Printer support	Y	Y	Y	Y	Y
Search folders	Y	N	N	Y	N
Toolbar	Y	Y	Y	Y	Y
Spellchecker	Y	Y	N	Y	N
Drag-and-drop	N	N	N	N	N
Audio	N	N	N	N	N
EXTRAS					
HTTP	N	N	N	N	N
NNTP	Y	N	N	Y	N
Fax	N	N	N	N	N

Y—Yes N—No N/A—Not applicable INA—Information not available

E-mail Applications ◼

	Pegasus Mail v3.0 David Harris	Pine 3.94 University of Washington	PinePC University of Washington	POPMail 3.2 University of Minnesota	Pronto Mail 2.0 Commtouch
Price	Free	Free	Free	Free	$69
Supported platforms	Windows 95, Windows 3.1, DOS, Macintosh	Unix	Windows 3.1	Windows 3.1	Windows 95, Windows 3.1
Supported protocols	SMTP, POP, MIME	SMTP, MIME	SMTP, MIME	SMTP, POP, MIME	SMTP, MAPI, MIME
TYPE OF CONNECTION					
Direct	N	Y	Y	N	N
Remote					
Online	N	Y	Y	N	Y
Offline	Y	N	N	Y	Y
Disconnected	N	N	N	N	Y
Serial	N	Y	Y	N	N
TCP/IP	Y	Y	Y	Y	Y
FEATURES					
Word wrap	Y	Y	Y	Y	Y
Sorting	Y	Y	Y	Y	Y
Folders	Y	Y	Y	Y	Y
Address book	Y	Y	Y	Y	Y
Attaching files	Y	Y	Y	Y	Y
Signatures	Y	Y	Y	Y	Y
Configurable header	Y	Y	Y	Y	Y
Importing files	Y	Y	Y	Y	Y
Return receipts	N	N	N	N	N
Printer support	Y	Y	Y	Y	Y
Search folders	N	N	N	N	N
Toolbar	Y	N	N	Y	Y
Spellchecker	N	N	N	N	N
Drag-and-drop	Y	N	N	N	Y
Audio	N	N	N	N	N
EXTRAS					
HTTP	N	N	N	N	N
NNTP	N	Y	Y	N	N
Fax	N	N	N	N	N

Y—Yes N—No N/A—Not applicable INA—Information not available   **Table Continues →**

■ E-mail Applications

	Simeon ESYS Corporation	Siren Mail Siren Software	TkMail v2.0 Paul Raines	Z-Mail 4.0 Network Computing Devices	Z-Mail Lite Network Computing Devices
Price	$95.00	INA	Free	Free trial	Free trial
Supported platforms	Windows 95, Windows 3.1, DOS, Macintosh, Unix	Windows 95, Windows 3.1, DOS	Unix	Windows 95, Windows 3.1	Unix
Supported protocols	SMTP, IMAP, IMSP, MIME	SMTP, MAPI, MIME	SMTP, MIME	SMTP, POP, MAPI, MIME	SMTP, POP, MIME
TYPE OF CONNECTION					
Direct	N	N	Y	Y	Y
Remote					
Online	Y	N	N	Y	Y
Offline	Y	Y	N	Y	Y
Disconnected	N	N	N	N	N
Serial	N	N	Y	Y	Y
TCP/IP	Y	Y	Y	Y	Y
FEATURES					
Word wrap	Y	Y	Not directly supported	Y	Y
Sorting	Y	Y	Y	Y	Y
Folders	Y	Y	Y	Y	Y
Address book	Y	Y	Y	Y	Y
Attaching files	Y	Y	Y	Y	Y
Signatures	Y	Y	Y	Y	Y
Configurable header	Y	Y	Y	Y	Y
Importing files	Y	Y	Y	Y	Y
Return receipts	Y	N	N	N	N
Printer support	Y	Y	Y	Y	Y
Search folders	N	N	N	Y	Y
Toolbar	Y	Y	Y	Y	N
Spellchecker	N	N	Not directly supported	Y	Y
Drag-and-drop	N	Y	N	N	N
Audio	N	Y	N	N	N
EXTRAS					
HTTP	N	N	N	N	N
NNTP	Y	Y	N	N	N
Fax	N	Y	N	N	N

Y—Yes N—No N/A—Not applicable INA—Information not available

E-mail Applications

	Z-Mail for Macintosh Network Computing Devices
Price	Free trial
Supported platforms	Macintosh
Supported protocols	SMTP, POP, MIME
TYPE OF CONNECTION	
Direct	Y
Remote	
Online	Y
Offline	Y
Disconnected	N
Serial	N
TCP/IP	Y
FEATURES	
Word wrap	Y
Sorting	Y
Folders	Y
Address book	Y
Attaching files	Y
Signatures	Y
Configurable header	Y
Importing files	Y
Return receipts	N
Printer support	Y
Search folders	Y
Toolbar	Y
Spellchecker	Y
Drag-and-drop	N
Audio	N
EXTRAS	
HTTP	N
NNTP	N
Fax	N

Y—Yes   N—No   N/A—Not applicable   INA—Information not available

End ∎

GRAPHICS
SOFTWARE

Graphics Software ■

(Products listed in alphabetical order by company name.)	ACD Systems ACDSee 1.0b6	ACD Systems PicaView	Adobe Dimensions 2.0	Adobe Illustrator 4.1	Adobe Illustrator 5.5
Price	$18	INA	INA	$495	$995
Address	http://www.acdvictoria.com/acd/	http://www.acdvictoria.com/acd/picaview.htm	http://www.adobe.com/prodindex/dimensions/	http://www.adobe.com/prodindex/illustrator/	http://www.adobe.com/prodindex/illustrator/
Supported platforms	Windows 95, Windows 3.1	Windows 95	Macintosh	Windows 95, Windows 3.1, Macintosh, Unix	Macintosh, Unix
File conversion support	BMP, GIF, JPEG, PCX, PNG, TGA, TIFF	BMP, GIF, JPEG, PCX, PNG, TGA, TIFF	EPS	EPS, GIF (with plug-in), IFF, JPEG, PCX, PICT, TGA, TIFF	EPS, GIF (with plug-in), IFF, JPEG, PCX, PICT, TGA, TIFF
MANIPULATION FEATURES AND TOOLS					
Color/grayscale conversion	N	N	Y	Y	Y
File size/DPI control	N	N	Y	Y	Y
Drawing capabilities	N	N	Y	Y	Y
Advanced manipulation features and tools	N	N	Y	Y	Y
Filters	N	N	N	N	N
Plug-ins	N	N	N	N	N
Extras	N	File Manager add-on	3-D imaging	Acrobat File Reader	Acrobat File Reader

Y—Yes   N—No   N/A—Not applicable   INA—Information not available

Table Continues →

■ Graphics Software

	Adobe Illustrator 6.0	Adobe Photoshop 3.0.5	Adobe Photoshop 3.0.1	Alchemy Mindworks GIF Construction	Alchemy Mindworks Graphic Workshop 1.1w
Price	$595	$895	$995	INA	$40
Address	http://www.adobe .com/prodindex/ illustrator/	http://www.adobe .com/prodindex/ photoshop/	http://www.adobe .com/prodindex/ photoshop/	http://www .mindwork- shop.com/alchemy/ gifcon.html	http://www .mindworkshop .com/alchemy/ gww.html
Supported platforms	Macintosh	Windows 95, Win- dows 3.1 Macintosh	Unix	Windows 95, Windows 3.1	Windows 95, Windows 3.1
File conversion support	EPS, GIF (with plug- in), IFF, JPEG, PCX, PICT, TGA, TIFF	BMP, EPS, GIF, GIF89a (with plug-in), IFF, JPEG, progres- sive JPEG (with plug- in), PCX, PICT, SUN, TGA, TIFF	BMP, EPS, GIF, GIF89a (with plug-in), IFF, JPEG, progres- sive JPEG (with plug- in), PCX, PICT, SUN, TGA, TIFF	GIF, GIF89a	BMP, CDR, CGM, CLP, DIB, FITS, FLI/FLC, GIF, GIF89a, ICO, IFF, JPEG, MSP, PCX, PNG, RAS, RLE, SUN, TGA, TIFF, WMF, WPG, XBM
MANIPULATION FEATURES AND TOOLS					
Color/grayscale conversion	Y	Y	Y	Y	Y
File size/DPI control	Y	Y	Y	Y	Y
Drawing capabilities	Y	Y	Y	N	Y
Advanced manipulation features and tools	Y	Y	Y	N	Y
Filters	N	Y	Y	N	N
Plug-ins	N	Y	Y	N	N
Extras	Acrobat File Reader	N	N	N	Lots of extras

Y—Yes   N—No   N/A—Not applicable   INA—Information not available

Graphics Software ■

	Matthew Battey Matt Paint 1.9.4	Cerious Software Thumbs Plus 3.0	EarthWare Image Viewer 95	Image Eye 3.0a8 FMJ Software	FoxTrot Software Picture Viewer 2.96
Price	$25	$65	$30	Free	Free
Address	http://hyperarchive .lcs.mit.edu/ HyperArchive/ Archive/gst/grf/	http://www .cerious.com/	http://www.ewl.com /	http://www.nada .kth.se/~f93-maj/ fmsoft.html	http://www .mingspring.com/ ~jock/foxtrot/
Supported platforms	Macintosh	Windows 95, Win- dows 3.1	Windows 95	Windows 95, Win- dows 3.1, DOS	Windows 95
File conversion support	EPS, GIF, PICT, TIFF	BMP, CDR, DXF, GIF, GIF89a, ICO, JPEG, progressive JPEG, PNG, TGA, TIFF	BMP, GIF, JPEG, PCX, PNG, TIFF	BMP, DIB, FIG, ICO, IFF, JPEG, PCS, PIC, RAS, RLE, SUN, TGA, TIFF	BMP, DIB, ICO, RLE, WMF
MANIPULATION FEATURES AND TOOLS					
Color/grayscale conversion	Y	N	N	N	N
File size/DPI control	Y	N	N	N	N
Drawing capabilities	Y	N	N	N	N
Advanced manipulation features and tools	Y	N	N	N	N
Filters	N	N	N	N	N
Plug-ins	N	N	N	N	N
Extras	N	Thumbnail viewer	N	N	N

Y—Yes   N—No   N/A—Not applicable   INA—Information not available   **Table Continues →**

■ Graphics Software

	Aaron Giles JPEGView 3.3.1	Aaron Giles Transparency 1.0	Group 42 GraphX Viewer 1.51	Group 42 Web Image	Hamrick Software VuePrint 4.6
Price	Free	Free	Free	$39.95	$40
Address	INA	INA	http://www.group42 .com/	http://www.group42 .com/	http://www .hamrick.com/
Supported platforms	Macintosh	Macintosh	Windows 3.1	Windows 95, Windows 3.1	Windows 3.1
File conversion support	BMP, GIF, JPEG, PICT, TIFF	GIF, GIF89a,	BMP, GIF, JPEG, PCX, PNG, RAS, SUN, TGA, TIFF	BMP, GIF, GIF89a, JPEG, progressive JPEG, PCX, PNG, RAS, SUN, TGA, TIFF	BMP, DIB, FLI/FLC, GIF, GIF89a, JPEG, PCX, RLC, TGA, TIFF
MANIPULATION FEATURES AND TOOLS					
Color/grayscale conversion	Y	N	Y	Y	N
File size/DPI control	Y	N	Y	Y	N
Drawing capabilities	N	N	Y	Y	N
Advanced manipulation features and tools	N	N	Y	Y	N
Filters	N	N	N	N	N
Plug-ins	N	N	N	N	N
Extras	N	N	UU Encode/Decode	Web Effects	MPEG and ZIP files

Y—Yes   N—No   N/A—Not applicable   INA—Information not available

Graphics Software ■

	JASC Paint Shop Pro 3.12	Thorsten Lemke GraphicConverter 2.4.3	Leonard Loureiro LView Pro	Macromedia FreeHand 5.0	MetaTools Kai's Power Tools
Price	$69	$30	$30	INA	INA
Address	http://www.jasc .com/psp.html	INA	http://world.std .com/~mmedia/ lviewp.html	http://www .macromedia.com/	http://www .metatools.com/
Supported platforms	Windows 95, Windows 3.1	Macintosh	Windows 95, Windows 3.1	Windows 95, Windows 3.1 Macintosh	Windows 95, Macintosh
File conversion support	BMP, CDR, CGM, CLP, DIB, DXF, GIF, GIF89a, IFF, JPEG, MSP, PBM, PCX, PIC, RAS, RLE, TGA, TIFF, WMF, WPG	BMP, CGM, CLP, FIF, FITS, FLI/FLC, GIF, GIF89a, ICO, IFF, JPEG, MSP, PBM, PCX, PIC, PICT, RIFF, RLE, SUN, TGA, TIFF, WMF, WPG, XBM	BMP, DIB, GIF, GIF89a, JPEG, PBM, PCX, TGA, TIFF	BMP, CDR, DGM, DXF, EPS, TIFF, WMF	
MANIPULATION FEATURES AND TOOLS					
Color/grayscale conversion	Y	Y	Y	Y	N
File size/DPI control	Y	Y	Y	Y	N
Drawing capabilities	Y	Y	Y	Y	N
Advanced manipulation features and tools	Y	N	Y	Y	Y
Filters	N	N	Y	N	Y
Plug-ins	N	N	N	N	Y
Extras	N	Slideshow	Screen shot	N	Plug-ins for Adobe Photoshop

---

Y—Yes   N—No   N/A—Not applicable   INA—Information not available

Table Continues →

■ Graphics Software

	Kevin Mitchell GIF Converter 2.3.7	Pedagoguery Software Gif*gIf*giF	Yves Piguet GIF Builder 0.3.2	Polybytes PolyView 2.5.2	Eric Shieh Jade 1.0.3
Price	$30	$28	Free	$20	Free
Address	INA	http://espresso.cafe.net/peda/ggg/	http://piazza.com/free/gifbuild.html	http://198.207.242.3/authors/polybytes/default.html	INA
Supported platforms	Macintosh	Windows 95, Windows 3.1, Macintosh	Macintosh	Windows 95	Macintosh
File conversion support	GIF, GIF89a, PICT, RIFF, RLE, TIFF	GIF, GIF89a	GIF, GIF89a	BMP, GIF, ICO, JPEG, PCX, PNG, TIFF, WMF	JPEG, progressive JPEG
MANIPULATION FEATURES AND TOOLS					
Color/grayscale conversion	Y	N	N	Y	N
File size/DPI control	Y	N	N	Y	N
Drawing capabilities	Y	N	N	Y	N
Advanced manipulation features and tools	N	N	N	Y	N
Filters	N	N	N	Y	N
Plug-ins	N	N	N	N	N
Extras	N	N	N	Slideshow	N

Y—Yes   N—No   N/A—Not applicable   INA—Information not available

End ■

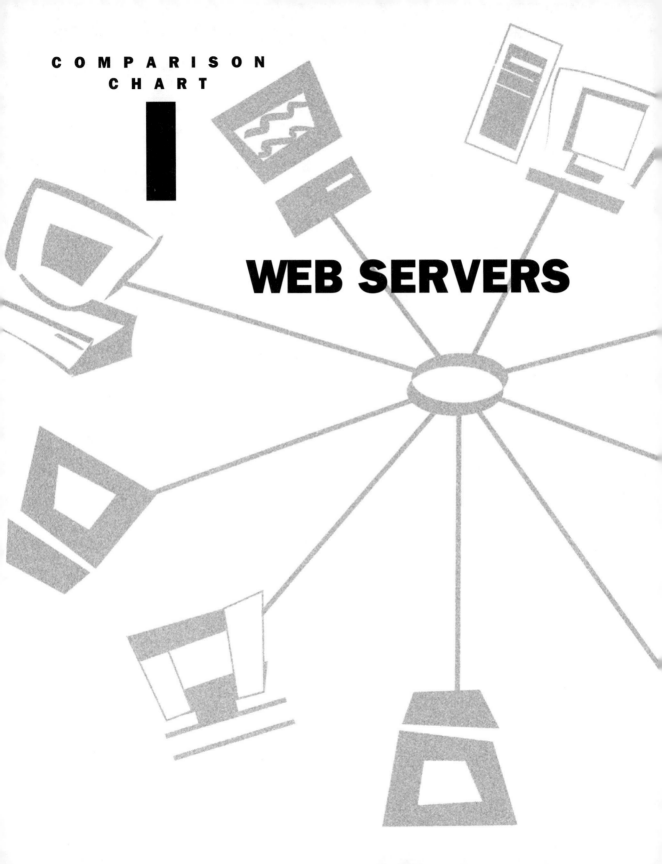

WEB SERVERS

Web Servers ▪

(Products listed in alphabetical order by company name.)	Apache HTTP Server Project Apache	Community ConneXion Apache SSL-US	Computer Software Manufaktur Alibaba	EMWAC EMWAC Freeware HTTPS	John Franks GN
Version	1.02	1.0.3 & 1.1	2.0	0.99	2.24
Price	Free	$495	$99	Free	Free
Web site	http://www .apache.org/	http://apachessl .c2.org/	http://www.csm .co.at/csm/	http://emwac.ed .ac.uk/html/ internet_toolchest/ https/contents.htm	http://hopf.math .nwu.edu:70/
Supported operating systems	OS/2, most versions of UNIX	Most versions of UNIX	Windows NT (Intel), Windows 95	Windows NT (Intel, MIPS, Alpha, PowerPC)	Most versions of UNIX
LOGGING OPTIONS					
Common log format	Y	Y	Y	N	N
Customization of standard log	Y	Y	Y	N	N
Supports multiple logs	Y	Y	Y	N	N
CGI scripts can make log entries	N	N	Y	N	Y
Generate referrer logs	Y	Y	Y	N	N
Generate browser logs	Y	Y	Y	N	N
User tracking	Y	Y	Y	N	N
SECURITY					
Protocols supported	None	SSL v. 2	SSL v. 2	None	None
User authentication	Y	Y	Y	N	N
Restrict by domain name	Y	Y	Y	N	Y
Restrict by IP address	Y	Y	Y	N	Y
OTHER FEATURES					
GUI-based setup	N	N	Y	N	N
GUI-based maintenance	N	N	Y	Y	N
Remote maintenance	Y	Y	Y	N	N
Different directory roots for different IP addresses	Y	Y	Y	N	N
Built-in scripting language	None	Apache Server API	ISAPI, CGIDLL	N	N
Built-in image map handling	Y	Y	Y	Y	N
Client uploads	N	N	N	N	N
Windows CGI	N/A	N/A	Y	N	N/A
Search engine	N	N	Y	WAIS Toolkit for Windows NT	Y
Native (non-CGI) link to a DBMS	N	N	N	N	N
Can be an HTTP proxy server	N	N	Y	N	N
Source code for server	Included	Included	Not available	Not available	Included

Y—Yes   N—No   N/A—Not applicable   INA—Information not available

Table Continues →

■ Web Servers

	FTP Software Esplanade	FTP Software Esplanade Secure Edition	GNN GNNserver	IBM GoServe for OS/2	IBM IBM Internet Connection Server
Version	1.2	1.2	2.03	2.48	4.0
Price	$399	$399	Free, but subscip-tions for support	Free	Free
Web site	http://www.ftp.com/esplanade	http://www.ftp.com/esplanade	http://www.tools.gnn.com/	http://www2.hursley.ibm.com/goserve/	http://www.ics.raleigh.ibm.com/
Supported operating systems	Windows NT (Intel)	Windows NT (Intel)	Windows NT (Intel, Alpha), most versions of UNIX	OS/2	Windows NT (Intel), OS/2, UNIX (AIX)
LOGGING OPTIONS					
Common log format	Y	Y	Y	Y	Y
Customization of standard log	N	N	N	Y	N
Supports multiple logs	Y	Y	Y	Y	Y
CGI scripts can make log entries	Y	Y	N	Y	Y
Generate referrer logs	Y	Y	Y	Y	N
Generate browser logs	Y	Y	Y	Y	N
User tracking	N	N	N	Y	Y
SECURITY					
Protocols supported	None	SSL v.2	SSL v.2	None	None
User authentication	Y	Y	Y	Y	Y
Restrict by domain name	Y	Y	Y	Y	Y
Restrict by IP address	Y	Y	Y	Y	Y
OTHER FEATURES					
GUI-based setup	Y	Y	Y	Y	Y
GUI-based maintenance	Y	Y	Y	Y	Y
Remote maintenance	N	N	Y	Y	Y
Different directory roots for different IP addresses	Y	Y	Y	Y	N
Built-in scripting language	N	N	TCL and C API	Rexx	N
Built-in image map handling	Y	Y	Y	Y	Y
Client uploads	N	N	N	N	N
Windows CGI	Y	Y	Y	N/A	N/A
Search engine	N	N	Illustra text blade index	N	N
Native (non-CGI) link to a DBMS	N	N	Y	Y	N
Can be an HTTP proxy server	N	N	N	N	Y
Source code for server	Not available	Not available	Not available	Not available	Not available

Y—Yes   N—No   N/A—Not applicable   INA—Information not available

Web Servers ■

	IBM IBM Internet Connection Secure Server	ILAR Concepts FolkWeb	Internet Factory Commerce Builder	Microsoft Microsoft Internet Information Server	Brian Morin Fnord Server
Version	4.0	1.01	1.5	1.0	0.6.0.23
Price	Free	$120	$795	Free, but fee for support	Free
Web site	http://www.ics .raleigh.ibm.com/	http://www.ilar.com/	http://www.ifact .com/ifact/inet.htm	http://www.microsoft. com/infoserv	http://www.wpi.edu/ ~bmorin/fnord/
Supported operating systems	Windows NT (Intel), OS/2, UNIX (AIX)	Windows NT (Intel), Windows 95	Windows NT (Alpha, PowerPC), Windows 95	Windows NT (Intel, MIPS, Alpha, PowerPC)	Windows NT (Intel), Windows 95
LOGGING OPTIONS					
Common log format	Y	Y	Y	N	Y
Customization of standard log	N	N	Y	Y	N
Supports multiple logs	Y	Y	Y	N	N
CGI scripts can make log entries	Y	Y	N	Y	N
Generate referrer logs	N	N	Y	N	Y
Generate browser logs	N	N	Y	N	N
User tracking	Y	Y	Y	N	N
SECURITY					
Protocols supported	SSL v.2, S-HTTP	None	SSL v. 2	SSL v.2, PCT	None
User authentication	Y	Y	Y	Y	Y
Restrict by domain name	Y	Y	Y	N	N
Restrict by IP address	Y	Y	Y	Y	Y
OTHER FEATURES					
GUI-based setup	Y	Y	Y	Y	Y
GUI-based maintenance	Y	Y	Y	Y	Y
Remote maintenance	Y	N	Y	Y	N
Different directory roots for different IP addresses	N	N	Y	Y	N
Built-in scripting language	N	N	SM, Y	Y	N
Built-in image map handling	Y	Y	Y	Y	N
Client uploads	N	N	N	N	N
Windows CGI	N/A	Y	Y	Y	N
Search engine	N	N	N	N	N
Native (non-CGI) link to a DBMS	N	Y	Y	N	N
Can be an HTTP proxy server	Y	N	Y	N	N
Source code for server	Not available	Not available	Not available	Not available	Included

Y—Yes N—No N/A—Not applicable INA—Information not available

Table Continues →

■ Web Servers

	NCSA NCSA HTTPd	Netscape Netscape Enterprise Server	Netscape Netscape FastTrack Server	Open Market Open Market Secure WebServer	Open Market Open Market WebServer
Version	1.5a	2.0	2.0	1.1	1.1
Price	Free	$995	$295	$450 and up	$450 and up
Web site	http://hoohoo .ncsa.uiuc.edu/	http://www .netscape.com/	http://www .netscape.com/	http://www .openmarket.com	http://www .openmarket.com
Supported operating systems	Most versions of UNIX	Windows NT (Intel, MIPS, Alpha), most versions of UNIX	Windows NT (Intel, MIPS, Alpha), most versions of UNIX	Most versions of UNIX	Most versions of UNIX
LOGGING OPTIONS					
Common log format	Y	Y	Y	Y	Y
Customization of standard log	N	Y	Y		
Supports multiple logs	Y	Y	Y	Y	Y
CGI scripts can make log entries	Y	Y	Y	Y	Y
Generate referrer logs	Y	Y	Y	Y	Y
Generate browser logs	Y	Y	Y	Y	Y
User tracking	N	Y	Y	Y	Y
SECURITY					
Protocols supported	None	SSL v.2, SSL v.3	SSL v.2, SSL v.3	SSL v.2, S-HTTP, PCT	PCT
User authentication	Y	Y	Y	Y	Y
Restrict by domain name	Y	Y	Y	Y	Y
Restrict by IP address	Y	Y	Y	Y	Y
OTHER FEATURES					
GUI-based setup	Y	Y	Y	Y	Y
GUI-based maintenance	N	Y	Y	Y	Y
Remote maintenance	N	Y	Y	Y	Y
Different directory roots for different IP addresses	Y	Y	Y	Y	Y
Built-in scripting language	N	NSAPI and Java applet API	NSAPI and Java applet API	TCL, WSAPI, and FastCGI	TCL, WSAPI, and FastCGI
Built-in image map handling	Y	Y	Y	Y	Y
Client uploads	N	Y	Y	N	N
Windows CGI	N/A	Y	Y	N/A	N/A
Search engine	Internal search engine as well as freeWAIS support	Y	N	PLWeb Intro from PLS, Excite from Architext, and Open Text Index	PLWeb Intro from PLS, Excite from Architext, and Open Text Index
Native (non-CGI) link to a DBMS	N	Y	Y	N	N
Can be an HTTP proxy server	N	N	N	N	N
Source code for server	Included	Not available	Not available	Not available	Not available

Y—Yes   N—No   N/A—Not applicable   INA—Information not available

Web Servers ■

	Oracle Oracle WebServer	O'Reilly & Associates O'Reilly & Associates WebSite	Peak Technologies ExpressO HTTP Server	Process Software Purveyor WebServer	Quarterdeck Quarterdeck MacHTTP
Version	2.0	1.1E	B1.8	1.2	2.2
Price	$2495	$499	$195	$295	$95
Web site	http://www .oracle.com	http://website .ora.com/	http://www .capitalcity.com:4321/	http://www .process.com/	http://www .starnine.com/
Supported operating systems	Windows NT (Intel, MIPS), Sun SPARC Solaris 2.4	Windows NT (Intel), Windows 95	Windows NT (Intel, MIPS, Alpha, PowerPC), Windows 95, UNIX, Macintosh OS. All require Java Runtime	Windows NT (Intel, Alpha), Windows 95, Novell NetWare	Macintosh
LOGGING OPTIONS					
Common log format	Y	Y	Y	Y	N
Customization of standard log	Y	N	Y	Y	N
Supports multiple logs	INA	Y	Y	Y	N
CGI scripts can make log entries	INA	N	Y	Y	N
Generate referrer logs	INA	Y	Y	Y	N
Generate browser logs	INA	Y	Y	Y	N
User tracking	INA	N	N	Y	N
SECURITY					
Protocols supported	SSL v.2, PCT	None	None	SSL v.2	None
User authentication	Y	Y	Y	Y	Y
Restrict by domain name	Y	Y	Y	Y	Y
Restrict by IP address	Y	Y	Y	Y	Y
OTHER FEATURES					
GUI-based setup	Y	Y	Y	Y	N
GUI-based maintenance	Y	Y	Y	Y	N
Remote maintenance	Y	Y	Y	Y	N
Different directory roots for different IP addresses	Y	Y	Y	Y	N
Built-in scripting language	N	N	N	ISAPI	Y
Built-in image map handling	Y	Y	Y	Y	N
Client uploads	N	N	Y	N	N
Windows CGI	N	Y	N	N	N/A
Search engine	N	Built-in indexer and search engine	N	WAIS	AppleSearch
Native (non-CGI) link to a DBMS	Y	N	N	N	N
Can be an HTTP proxy server	Y	N	Y	Y	N
Source code for server	Not available	Not available	Included with extra fee	Included with extra fee	Not available

Y—Yes N—No N/A—Not applicable INA—Information not available

Table Continues →

■ Web Servers

	Quarterdeck Quarterdeck WebServer	Quarterdeck Quarterdeck WebSTAR 95/NT	Quarterdeck Quarterdeck WebSTAR Mac	R.I.S. Technologies COSMOS Web Server	SPRY SPRY SafetyWeb Server
Version	1.0	2.0	1.2.4	1.0	1.1
Price	$49	$99	$499	$2,000 to $20,000	$245
Web site	http://www .quarterdeck.com/	http://www .quarterdeck.com/	http://www .quarterdeck.com/	http://www.ris.fr/	http://server.spry .com/
Supported operating systems	Windows NT (Intel), Windows 95, Windows 3.1	Windows NT (Intel), Windows 95	Macintosh	Most versions of UNIX	Windows NT (Intel)
LOGGING OPTIONS					
Common log format	Y	N	N	Y	Y
Customization of standard log	N	N	Y	N	Y
Supports multiple logs	N	Y	N	N	Y
CGI scripts can make log entries	N	N	Y	Y	N
Generate referrer logs	N	Y	Y	Y	Y
Generate browser logs	N	N	Y	Y	Y
User tracking	N	N	N	Y	N
SECURITY					
Protocols supported	None	None	SSL v.2	SSL v.2	SSL v.2
User authentication	Y	Y	Y	N	Y
Restrict by domain name	Y	Y	Y	N	Y
Restrict by IP address	Y	Y	Y	N	Y
OTHER FEATURES					
GUI-based setup	Y	Y	Y	Y	Y
GUI-based maintenance	Y	Y	Y	Y	Y
Remote maintenance	N	N	Y	Y	Y
Different directory roots for different IP addresses	N	Y	N	Y	Y
Built-in scripting language	N	Y	Y	CosmosAPI	BGI
Built-in image map handling	N	Y	N		Y
Client uploads	N	N	N	N	N
Windows CGI	N	Y	N/A	N/A	N
Search engine	N	N	AppleSearch	Keyword	Architext
Native (non-CGI) link to a DBMS	N	N	N	N	Y
Can be an HTTP proxy server	N	N	N	N	Y
Source code for server	Not available	Not available	Not available	Not available	Not available

Y—Yes   N—No   N/A—Not applicable   INA—Information not available

Web Servers ■

	SPRY SPRY Web Server	Stairways Software NetPresenz
Version	1.1	4.0.1
Price	$245	$10 to $2,000
Web site	http://server.spry.com/	http://www.share.com/stairways/
Supported operating systems	Windows NT (Intel)	Macintosh OS
LOGGING OPTIONS		
Common log format	Y	N
Customization of standard log	Y	N
Supports multiple logs	Y	N
CGI scripts can make log entries	N	N
Generate referrer logs	Y	Y
Generate browser logs	Y	N
User tracking	N	N
SECURITY		
Protocols supported	None	None
User authentication	Y	N
Restrict by domain name	Y	N
Restrict by IP address	Y	Y
OTHER FEATURES		
GUI-based setup	Y	Y
GUI-based maintenance	Y	Y
Remote maintenance	Y	Y
Different directory roots for different IP addresses	Y	N
Built-in scripting language	BGI	N
Built-in image map handling	Y	N
Client uploads	N	N
Windows CGI	N	N/A
Search engine	N	N
Native (non-CGI) link to a DBMS	Y	N
Can be an HTTP proxy server	Y	N
Source code for server	Not available	Not available

Y—Yes   N—No   N/A—Not applicable   INA—Information not available

End ■

WEB
MANAGEMENT
TOOLS

Web Management Tools ■

(Products listed in alphabetical order by company name.)	Adobe SiteMill1.0	Dave Winer (Author) Clay Basket 1.0b7	DeltaPoint QuickSite 1.0.2	GNN GNNpress 1.1	HeyerTech Webmaster Pro 1.0
Price	199	Free	$100	Free	99
Address	http://www.adobe .com/prodindex/ sitemill/	http://www .hotwired.com/ staff/userland/ yabbadabba/	http://delta. deltapoint.com/qs/	http://www.tools .gnn.com/press/	http://www .heyertech.com/
Operating systems	Macintosh	Macintosh	Windows 95, Windows/Windows for Workgroups 3.1	Windows 95, Windows NT, Windows/Windows for Workgroups 3.1, Sun OS, Macintosh	Macintosh
HYPERLINK FEATURES					
Automatic update of links	Y	Y	Y	N	N
Verification of all links	Y	N	N	Y	N
Automatic creation of links	N	Y	Y	Y	N
BUILT-IN AUTHORING TOOLS					
HTML editing	Y	Y	Y	Y	Y
WYSIWYG	Y	N	Y	Y	N
Direct HTML editing	N	Y	Y	Y	Y
Image conversion to GIF and JPEG	Y	N	N	N	Y
Image map creation	Y	N	Y	Y	Y
Automated wizards and standard templates	N	Y	Y	Y	Y
OTHER FEATURES					
List of all files on your site	Y	Y	Y	Y	Y
Graphical representation of your site	Y	N	N	Y	N
Hierarchical representation of your site	N	Y	N	Y	N
Real-time monitoring	N	N	N	N	N
To-do list	N	N	N	N	N
Database integration management	N	N	Y	Y	N
Firewall support	N	N	N	Y	N

Y—Yes   N—No   N/A—Not applicable   INA—Information not available

Table Continues →

■ Web Management Tools

	InContext WebAnalyzer 1.1	Microsoft FrontPage 1.1	NetCarta WebMapper 1.0	Luckman Interactive Web Commander	Blue Sky Software Web Office
Price	$80	$149	$499	$129 (Windows 95) $249 (Windows NT)	$499
Address	http://www .incontext.com/ products/ analyze.html	http://www .microsoft.com/ msoffice/frontpage/	http://www .netcarta.com/ prod/webmapper/	http://www .luckman.com/ wc/wcnew.html	http://www .bluesky.com/ infowbo.htm
Operating systems	Windows 95, Windows/Windows for Workgroups 3.1	Windows 95, Windows NT	Windows 95, Windows NT	Windows 95, Windows NT	Windows 95, Windows NT
HYPERLINK FEATURES					
Automatic update of links	N	Y	N	N	N
Verification of all links	Y	Y	Y	N	Y
Automatic creation of links	N	N	N	N	N
BUILT-IN AUTHORING TOOLS					
HTML editing	N	Y	N	Y	Y
WYSIWYG	N	Y	N	Y	Y
Direct HTML editing	N	N	N	N	Y
Image conversion to GIF and JPEG	N	Y	N	N	Y
Image map creation	N	Y	N	Y	Y
Automated wizards and standard templates	N	Y	N	Y	N
OTHER FEATURES					
List of all files on your site	Y	Y	Y	Y	Y
Graphical representation of your site	Y	Y	N	Y	N
Hierarchical representation of your site	N	Y	Y	Y	N
Real-time monitoring	N	N	N	Y	N
To-do list	N	Y	N	N	N
Database integration management	N	N	N	Y	N
Firewall support	N	N	N	N	N

Y—Yes   N—No   N/A—Not applicable   INA—Information not available

Web Management Tools ■

	O'Reilly & Associates WebSite 1.1
Price	$249
Address	http://website .ora.com/
Operating systems	Windows 95, Windows NT
HYPERLINK FEATURES	
Automatic update of links	N
Verification of all links	Y
Automatic creation of links	N
BUILT-IN AUTHORING TOOLS	
HTML editing	Y
WYSIWYG	N
Direct HTML editing	Y
Image conversion to GIF and JPEG	N
Image map creation	Y
Automated wizards and standard templates	Y
OTHER FEATURES	
List of all files on your site	Y
Graphical representation of your site	Y
Hierarchical representation of your site	N
Real-time monitoring	N
To-do list	N
Database integration management	Y
Firewall support	N

Y—Yes   N—No   N/A—Not applicable   INA—Information not available   End ■

COMPARISON
CHART

K

E-MAIL
SERVERS

E-mail Servers ■

(Products listed in alphabetical order by company name.)	Consensys InterWare Mail Server 3.1	Hayes Computer Systems Krypton Internet Mail Server 1.0b	Internet Shopper Ltd NTMail 3.02	Ipswitch IMail Server 3.0	MetaInfo Sendmail with POP3 1.0
Address	http://www .consensys.com/ interware/mail/ mailadm.htm	http://www.hcsys .com	http://www .net-shopper.co.uk/ software/ntmail/ index.htm	http://www.ipswitch .com/pd_imailserver .html	http://www.metainfo .com/MetaInfo/ Sendmail/Homepage .htp
Price	$695	$500–1000	$60–500	$495	$495
Operating systems	Windows NT	Windows NT (Intel, MIPS)	Windows NT (Intel, Alpha)	Windows NT (Intel, Alpha, PowerPC)	Windows NT (Intel, Alpha, MIPS)
CONFIGURATION AND MANAGEMENT					
Configuration by HTML forms	N	N	Y	Y	N
Configuration by e-mail	N	Y	Y	N	N
User-managed accounts	N	Y	Y	Y	N
AUTOMATIC REPLY SETTINGS					
Vacation	N	N	N	Y	N
Reply	N	Y	Y	Y	N
Echo	N	N	N	N	N
SECURITY					
Password protections	Y	Y	Y	Y	Y
Does not run as a privileged user	N	N	N	Y	N
Allows limiting access by domain	N	N	N	N	N
Limited forms for configuration	N	N	Y	N	N
Login account not required for e-mail users	N	N	Y	Y	Y
Supports encryption	N	Y	N	N	N
STANDARD PROTOCOLS					
HTTP	N	N	Y	Y	N
SMTP	Y	Y	Y	Y	Y
MIME	Y	Y	Y	Y	Y
IMAP4	N	N	N	N	N
POP3	Y	Y	Y	Y	Y
MISCELLANEOUS					
Modular design	Y	Y	Y	Y	Y
Compatibility with legacy e-mail systems	Y	N	N	Y	N
Ability to handle multiple domains	Y	Y	Y	Y	Y
Support for nicknames	Y	Y	Y	Y	Y
Support for mailing lists	Y	N	Y	Y	Y
Easy forwarding of messages	Y	Y	Y	Y	Y

Y—Yes N—No N/A—Not applicable INA—Information not available

■ E-mail Servers

	Netscape Netscape Mail Server 2.0	On Technology DaVinci SMTP eMAIL 4.1	Seattle Lab SLmail 2.0	Software.com Post.Office 1.9.3b	University of California at Berkeley Sendmail 8.7.5
Address	http://home .netscape.com/ comprod/ server_central/ product/mail/ index.html	http://www.on.com/ on/onprods/dvsmtp. html/tig7908	http://www .seattlelab.com/ prodsmtp.html	http://www.software .com/prod/po/ po.html	ftp://ftp.cs.berkeley .edu/pub/sendmail/
Price	$995	$995 (client packs sold separately)	$100–325	$495	Free
Operating systems	Windows NT (Intel, Alpha), OSF/1 2.0; HP-UX 9.04, 10.0; AIX 3.2.5, 4.1; IRIX 5.2, 5.3, 6.2; Solaris 2.3, 2.4, 2.5	Novell Netware	Windows NT (Intel), Windows 95, Windows/Windows for Workgroups 3.1	Windows NT (Intel, MIPS), Solaris 1.x/2.x, SGI IRIX 5.3	Most versions of Unix
CONFIGURATION AND MANAGEMENT					
Configuration by HTML forms	Y	N	N	Y	N
Configuration by e-mail	Y	N	N	Y	N
User-managed Accounts	Y	N	N	Y	N
AUTOMATIC REPLY SETTINGS					
Vacation	Y	N	Y	Y	N
Reply	Y	N	Y	Y	N
Echo	Y	N	Y	Y	N
SECURITY					
Password protections	Y	N	Y	Y	Y
Does not run as a privileged user	Y	N	N	Y	N
Allows limiting access by domain	Y	N	N	Y	N
Limited forms for configuration	Y	N	N	Y	N
Login account not required for e-mail users	Y	N	N	Y	N
Supports encryption	Y	N	N	N	N
STANDARD PROTOCOLS					
HTTP	Y	N	N	Y	N
SMTP	Y	Y	Y	Y	Y
MIME	Y	Y	Y	Y	Y
IMAP4	Y	N	N	N	N
POP3	Y	Y	Y	Y	N
MISCELLANEOUS					
Modular design	Y	N	Y	Y	Y
Compatibility with legacy e-mail systems	Y	N	N	N	N
Ability to handle multiple domains	Y	N	Y	Y	N
Support for nicknames	Y	N	Y	Y	Y
Support for mailing lists	Y	N	Y	Y	Y
Easy forwarding of messages	Y	N	Y	Y	Y

Y—Yes   N—No   N/A—Not applicable   INA—Information not available

End ■

COMPARISON
CHART

L

FTP SERVERS

FTP Servers ■

(Products listed in alphabetical order by company or author name.)	Arcane Software Vermillion FTPD 1.12	Cat Soft Serv-U 2.0c	Alun Jones (author) WFTPD 2.2	Jgaa's Freeware War-ftpd 1.20b
Price	$30 and up	$25 and up	$20	Free
Address	http://jhunix.hcf.jhu .edu/~mbk/	http://catsoft.dorm .duke.edu/ features.htm	http://www.eden .com/~alun	http://home.sol.no/ jgaa/tftpd.htm
Supported platforms	Windows 95, Windows NT (Intel)	Windows 95, Windows NT (Intel), Windows/Windows for Workgroups 3.1	Windows 95, Windows NT (Intel), Windows/Windows for Workgroups 3.1	Windows 95, Windows NT
SECURITY				
Passwords	Y	Y	Y	Y
Individually configurable read/write/modify privileges	Y	Y	N	Y
IP address/domain name restrictions	Y	Y	Y	Y
Directory mapping	Y	Y	Y	Y
Virtual path names	Y	N	N	Y
Disable account in response to bad passwords	N	N	N	N
OTHER FEATURES				
Duplicate file name checker	N	N	N	Y
Not-wanted files list	N	N	N	Y
Allows multiple simultaneous users and transfers	Y	Y	Y	Y
Allows groups and classes of users	Y	Y	N	Y
Resume option	Y	Y	Y	Y
Configurable messages	Y	Y	Y	Y
Timeout feature	Y	Y	Y	Y
Multihoming	Y	Y	Y	Y

Y—Yes N—No N/A—Not applicable INA—Information not available

Table Continues →

■ FTP Servers

	Larry Nezar (author) FreeWay	Stairways Software NetPresenz 4.0.1	Washington University wu-ftpd 2.4	WonLoo Technologies LanFTPD 3.1
Price	Free	$10 and up	Free	$495
Address	http://www.agric.za/freeway	http://www.share.com/stairways/netpresenz/netpresenzdocs.html	ftp://wuarchive.wustl.edu/packages/wuarchive-ftpd/	http://wonloo.com/wonloo/lanftpd.htm
Supported platforms	Windows 95	Macintosh	Most versions of Unix	NetWare
SECURITY				
Passwords	Y	Y	Y	Y
Individually configurable read/write/modify privileges	Y	Y	Y	Y
IP address/domain name restrictions	Y	Y	Y	Y
Directory mapping	Y	N	Y	Y
Virtual path names	Y	N	N	N
Disable account in response to bad passwords	N	N	Y	Y
OTHER FEATURES				
Duplicate file name checker	N	N	N	N
Not-wanted files list	N	N	N	N
Allows multiple simultaneous users and transfers	Y	Y	Y	Y
Allows groups and classes of users	N	Y	Y	Y
Resume option	N	Y	Y	Y
Configurable messages	Y	Y	Y	Y
Timeout feature	Y	Y	Y	Y
Multihoming	N	N	N	N

Y—Yes   N—No   N/A—Not applicable   INA—Information not available

End ■

NEWS SERVERS

News Servers ■

(Products listed in alphabetical order by company name.)	Consensys InterWare News Server	NetManage NNS News Server 2.07a	NetManage IntraNet Forum Server	Netscape Netscape News Server 2.0	NetWin Ltd Dnews
Address	http://www.consensys.com/interware/news/newsadm.htm	http://www.netmanage.com/netmanage/nns/index.html	http://www.netmanage.com/netmanage/intra_server/index.html	http://home.netscape.com/comprod/server_central/product/news/	http://world.std.com/~netwin/dnews.htm
Price	$795	Free	$995	$995	$485-2950
Operating systems	Windows NT (Intel)	Windows NT (Intel)	Windows NT (Intel)	Windows NT (Intel, Alpha), OSF, HP-UX, AIX, IRIX, SunOS, Solaris	Windows NT, Windows 95, Novell Netware, Linux, Solaris, AIX, Irix, BSDI, SunOS, OSF
SECURITY					
Encryption	N	N	N	Y	N
Username/password for private newsgroups	Y	N	Y	Y	Y
SERVER ADMINISTRATION					
Remote server recovery	N	N	N	Y	N
Configuration via HTML forms	N	N	N	Y	N
Configurations for individual users, groups of users, and newsgroups	Y	N	Y	Y	Y
NEWS ITEM STORAGE					
Files	Y	N	Y	N	N
Database blocks	N	N	N	N	Y
MISCELLANEOUS					
Allows incoming and outgoing newsfeeds	Y	Y	Y	Y	Y
Capable of smart newsfeeds	N	N	N	Y	Y
Rich content postings for news articles	Y	N	N	Y	Y
Smart expiration of news articles	N	N	N	N	Y
Private and public newsgroup settings	Y	N	Y	Y	Y
Transparent multiplatform support	N	N	N	Y	N

Y—Yes N—No N/A—Not applicable INA—Information not available

Table Continues →

■ News Servers

	Rich Salz INN 1.4sec
Address	ftp://ftp.uu.net/ networking/ news/nntp/inn/
Price	Free
Operating systems	Most versions of Unix
SECURITY	
Encryption	N
Username/password for private newsgroups	N
SERVER ADMINISTRATION	
Remote server recovery	N
Configuration via HTML forms	N
Configurations for individual users, groups of users, and newsgroups	N
NEWS ITEM STORAGE	
Files	Y
Database blocks	N
MISCELLANEOUS	
Allows incoming and outgoing newsfeeds	Y
Capable of smart newsfeeds	N
Rich content postings for news articles	N
Smart expiration of news articles	N
Private and public newsgroup settings	Y
Transparent multiplatform support	N

Y—Yes   N—No   N/A—Not applicable   INA—Information not available

End ■

COMPARISON
CHART

N

ADMINISTRATIVE
TOOL PRODUCTS

N.1   Basic Tools

	Netcarta WebMapper	Coretex SiteTrack	Apache HTTP Server Project	Pukka Domain Admin Tool 2.0	Transarc ENCINA
Price	$499	$3495	Free	$110	$8,000
Address	www.netcarta.com	www.coretex.com/ sitetrack/	www.apache.org	www.dynamic-web .com/software/ pukka/	www.transarc.com
Telephone	(408) 461-8920	(215) 854-0646	INA	INA	(412) 338-4400
Supported platforms	Windows 95, Windows NT	IRIX 5.2, 5.3, SunOS 4.1.3, Solaris 2.3, 2.4	SunOS, Solaris, HP-UX, IRIX, AIX, OSF/1, OS/2	Windows NT	Windows 95, Windows NT, SunOS, Solaris, HP-UX, AIX
FEATURES					
User/group/directory management	N	N	Y	Y	Y
Batch editing	N	N	Y	Y	Y
Script editor	N	N	N	Y	N
Status reporting	N	N	Y	Y	Y
User disk space usage report	N	N	Y	Y	N
Audit trail	N	N	Y	Y	N
Security threat detection	N	N	N	Y	N
Import/export user IDs passwords	N	N	N	Y	N
Multiple domain addressing	N	N	Y	N	N
Site visitation reports	N	Y	Y	Y	N
Graphical report by domain	Y	Y	N	N	N
Repair broken links	Y	N	N	N	N
Other tools	Remote status reporting, diagnostic and performance tuning utilities, automated configuration				

Y—Yes   N—No   N/A—Not applicable   INA—Information not available

Table Continues →

■ Basic Tools

	Neoglyphics **NeoStats**
Price	n/a
Address	www.neog.com
Telephone	(800) 406-5033
Supported platforms	Windows NT, Unix

FEATURES	
User/group/directory management	N
Batch editing	N
Script editor	N
Status reporting	N
User disk space usage report	N
Audit trail	N
Security threat detection	N
Import/export user IDs passwords	N
Multiple domain addressing	N
Site visitation reports	Y
Graphical report by domain	Y
Repair broken links	N
Other tools	

Y—Yes   N—No   N/A—Not applicable   INA—Information not available

End ■

N.2   Remote Resource Management

	Apache HTTP Server Project	Pukka Domain Admin Tool 2.0	Chisolm Technologies DCE Cell ManagerLite	Transarc ENCINA	Digital Clusters
Price	Free	$110	$5,750	$8,000	$3,499 (hardware and software)
Address	www.apache.org	www.dynamic-web .com/software/ pukka/	www.chistech.com	www.transarc.com	www.digital.com
Telephone	INA	INA	(800) 762-0253	(412) 338-4400	(800) 344-4825
Supported platforms	SunOS, Solaris, HP-UX, IRIX, AIX, OSF/1, OS/2	Windows NT	Windows NT, SunOS, Solaris, HP-UX, AIX, OSF/1	Windows 95, Windows NT, SunOS, Solaris, HP-UX, AIX	Windows NT
Network computer status	Y	Y	Y	Y	Y
Network printer status	N	Y	Y	Y	Y
Printer queue updates	N	N	Y	N	N
Distributed file system support	N	N	Y	Y	N
Workloads partitioning	N	N	Y	Y	Y
Shared resource management	N	N	Y	Y	Y
Load balancing	N	N	Y	Y	Y
Pager alert	N	N	Y	Y	N
Client workstation alert	N	N	Y	Y	Y

Y—Yes   N—No   N/A—Not applicable   INA—Information not available   End ■

■ N.3   IP Addressing and Access Restriction Tools

	Apache HTTP Server Project	Deerfield Communications Wingate	Harvest Glimpse 3.6	Harvest WebGlimpse 3.5
Price	Free	Free	Free	Free
Telephone	INA	(517) 732-8856	INA	INA
Supported platforms	SunOS, Solaris, HP-UX, IRIX, AIX, OSF/1, OS/2	Windows 95, Windows NT	OSF/1 DEC Alpha; Solaris 5.3, 5.5; Sun OS 4.1.1, 4.1.3; LINUX, freeBSD	AIX 3.2.5, 4.1; IRIX 6.1, SGI IRIX 5.3, HP-UX, DEC Ultrix, NeXT, Mach 3.1
Address	www.apache.org	www.otsego.com/ wingate	www.mordor. transarc.com	www.mordor. transarc.com
IP ADDRESS TOOLS				
Many users per IP address	N	Y	Y	N
IP and domain address management	Y	Y	N	N
Non-IP intensive virtual host support	Y	Y	N	N
Listen to multiple IP addresses	Y	Y	N	N
ACCESS RESTRICTION				
By time of day	N	N	Y	N
By application	N	N	Y	N
By IP address/URL	Y	N	Y	N
By domain	N	N	Y	N
By incoming filter	N	N	Y	N
OTHER FEATURES				
Indexing and querying tools	N	N	Y	N
HTML search engine	N	N	N	Y
Automated configuration	Y	N	N	N

Y—Yes   N—No   N/A—Not applicable   INA—Information not available

End ■

N.4   Commerce Tools ■

	Netscape Merchant	Microsoft Merchant	ICAT Electronic Commerce Suite™
Price	INA	INA	INA
Telephone	(415) 937-2555	(206) 635-7123	(800) 558-4228
Supported platforms	Solaris 2.4, 2.5; IRIX 5.3; IBM RS/6000; AIX 4.1; HP-UX	Windows NT	Windows NT, Digital Alpha NT, Macintosh Sun Solaris, SunOS, SGI IRIX
Address	cgi.netscape.com/ comprod/products/ iapps/capps/mersys _data_sheet.html	www.microsoft.com/ ecommerce/	www.icat.com
SET compliant	Y	Y	N
SSL compliant	Y	Y	Y
PCT (Private Communications Technology) compliant	Y	Y	N
Automatic credit verification	Y	Y	Y
Automatic credit authorization	Y	Y	Y
Storefront setup supported	Y	Y	N

Y—Yes   N—No   N/A—Not applicable   INA—Information not available

End ■

HTML EDITORS

HTML Editors ■

(Products listed in alphabetical order by company name.)	Adobe Systems PageMill 2.0	Bare Bones Software BBEdit 4.0.1	Corel CorelWeb Designer	Microsoft FrontPage 1.1	Netscape Navigator Gold 3.0
Price	$100	$110	$100	$150–$700	Free or $100
Supported platforms	Macintosh/(Windows due Fall 1996)	Macintosh	Windows	Windows95, Windows NT	Windows, Macintosh, Unix
Quality and type of documentation	Excellent	Excellent; help on CD	Average; built-in help	Good; built-in and online help	On line
Expertise level	Novice to expert	Intermediate to expert	Novice to advanced	Novice to expert	Novice to advanced
WYSIWYG	Y	N	Y	Y	Y
Supports drag-and-drop	Y	HTML floating palette with drag-and-drop HTML coding	N	Y	Y
Quality of find and replace function	Average	Very sophisticated	Not very sophisticated	Average	Good
Multiple browser preview	N	Y	N	Y	N
Graphics conversion	GIF/JPEG	N	N	Y	N
Supports image mapping	Y	N	Y	Y	Supports third-party applications
Supports tables/frames	Y	Supports tables only	Y	Y	Y
Supports Netscape extensions	Y/QuickTime	N	Y	Y	Y
Templates included?	Y	N	Y	Y/Also supplies wizards	Y/Online templates and tutorials for working with HTML
Special features		Has a Fix PageMill extension	Handles formatted text	Allows you to designate your multimedia editors	

Y—Yes   N—No   N/A—Not applicable   INA—Information not available

Table Continues →

■ HTML Editors

	SoftQuad HoTMetaL PRO 3.0
Price	$150
Supported platforms	Windows, Macintosh, Unix
Quality and type of documentation	Average; built-in help
Expertise level	Intermediate
WYSIWYG	N
Supports drag-and-drop	N
Quality of find and replace function	Good
Multiple browser preview	N
Graphics conversion	Does not support JPEG
Supports image mapping	N
Supports tables/frames	Y
Supports Netscape extensions	Y
Templates included?	Y
Special features	

Y—Yes   N—No   N/A—Not applicable   INA—Information not available

P

SITE
AUTHORING
TOOLS

Site Authoring Tools ■

(Products listed in alphabetical order by company name.)	Adobe Systems SiteMill 1.0	Microsoft FrontPage 1.1	NetObjects NetObjects Fusion 1.0	Netscape Communications LiveWire 1.0/Pro
Supported platforms	Macintosh (PC due fall 1996)	Windows 95, Windows NT	Windows 95, Windows NT	Windows 95, Windows NT, Unix
Price	$299	$150 to $700	$650	$110
Documentation	Excellent	Poor	Unavailable	Online
Expertise level	Novice to expert	Novice to expert	Intermediate to expert	Intermediate to expert
Flow chart	N	Y	Y	Y
WYSIWYG	Y	Y	Y	Y
Drag-and-drop	Y	Y	Y	Y
Find and replace	Y	Y	Y	Y
Link management	Y	Y	Y	Y
Multiple browser preview	N	Y	Y	Y
Graphics conversion	N	N	N	N
Image mapping	Y	Y	Y	N
Support for tables/frames	N/N	Y/Y	Y/N	Y/Y
Extensions	Some Netscape	Some Netscape	Netscape and Microsoft extensions	All Netscape
Templates and wizards	N	Y	Y	Y
CGI/Java script support	N/N	Y/N	Y/Y	Y/Y (includes JavaScript compiler)
Support for third-party technology	N	Y	Y	Y
Special features		Allows designation of mulitmedia editors		

Y—Yes   N—No   N/A—Not applicable   INA—Information not available

End ■

Q

JAVA TOOLS

Java Tools ■

	Aimtech Jamba (beta)	Applicom Software RadJa 2.0	Borland C++ 5.0 with Java Enhancement	Borland C++ 5.0 Development Suite	BulletProof JDesignerPro/JAGG
Price	$495	Free	$249	$349	$495
Supported platforms	Windows 95, Windows 3.1	Windows 95	Windows 95, Windows NT	Windows 95, Windows NT	Windows NT
THE BASICS					
Compiler	N	With javac	Native	Native	N
Just-in-time compilation	N	N	N	Y	N
Other language compilers	N	N	C++ and C	C++ and C	N
Editor	Y	N	Y	Y	N
Debugger	N	N	Y	Y	N
Source-level debugger	N	N	Y	Y	N
DEVELOPMENT ENVIRONMENT					
Visual tools	Y	Y	Y	Y	Y
GUI tools	Y	Y	Y	Y	Y
Toolbar	Y	Y	Y	Y	Y
Drag-and-drop editing	Y	Y	Y	Y	Y
Graphic class browser	N	N	Y	Y	N
Class tree	N	N	Y	Y	N
Project manager	N	N	Y	Y	Y
Templates	N	N	N	N	Y
ADDITIONAL TOOLS					
Applet builder	Y	Y	N	N	N
Scriptless code generation	Y	Y	Y	Y	Y
HTML tools	Y	Y	Y	Y	Y
Database connectivity	N	N	N	N	ODBC, JDBC
Prototype testing	Y	Y	Y	Y	N
Native method support	N	N	Y	Y	N
TECHNICAL SUPPORT					
Tutorials	N	N	N	N	N
Online help	N	N	Y	Y	N

Y—Yes   N—No   N/A—Not applicable   INA—Information not available   **Table Continues →**

■ Java Tools

	Effective Edge, Tim Wilkenson, and others Jolt (Java Open Language Toolkit)	Kinetix Hyperwire	Metrowerks Codewarrior 9 Discover Programming	Metrowerks Codewarrior 9 Gold	Microsoft J++
Price	Free	INA (free beta)	$99	$399	INA
Supported platforms	Windows 95, Solaris, SunOS	Windows 95, Windows NT	Power PC, Macintosh 68K	Power PC, Macintosh 68K	Windows 95, Windows NT
THE BASICS					
Compiler	Native	N	Javac	Javac	Native
Just-in-time compilation	Kaffe interpreter	N	N	N	Y
Other language compilers	N	N	N	C++, C, and Perl	N
Editor	N	N	Y	Y	Y
Debugger	N	N	Y	Y	Y
Source-level debugger	N	N	Y	Y	Y
DEVELOPMENT ENVIRONMENT					
Visual tools	N	Y	Y	Y	Y
GUI tools	N	Y	Y	Y	Y
Toolbar	N	Y	Y	Y	Y
Drag-and-drop editing	N	Y	Y	Y	Y
Graphic class browser	N	N	Y	Y	Y
Class tree	N	N	N	N	Y
Project manager	N	N	Y	Y	Y
Templates	N	N	N	N	Y
ADDITIONAL TOOLS					
Applet builder	N	Y	N	N	Y
Scriptless code generation	N	Y	Y	Y	Y
HTML tools	N	Y	N	N	Y
Database connectivity	N	N	N	N	N
Prototype testing	N	Y	N	N	Y
Native method support	N	N	N	N	Y
TECHNICAL SUPPORT					
Tutorials	N	N	Y	Y	N
Online help	N	N	Y	Y	Y

Y—Yes   N—No   N/A—Not applicable   INA—Information not available

Java Tools ■

	Natural Intelligence Roaster	Penumbra Software Mojo 1.0f	Penumbra Software Mojo 1.0 Enterprise Edition	Power Production WebBurst	Quintessential Diva 1.0b
Price	$299 ($99 academic)	$109	$495	$299	Free
Supported platforms	Power PC, Macintosh 68K	Windows 95, Windows NT	Windows 95, Windows NT	Windows 3.1, Power PC, Macintosh 68K	Windows 95, Windows NT
THE BASICS					
Compiler	Native	N	N	N	Javac
Just-in-time compilation	N	N	N	N	N
Other language compilers	N	N	N	N	Perl
Editor	Y	Y	Y	Y	Y
Debugger	Y	N	N	N	N
Source-level debugger	N	N	N	N	N
DEVELOPMENT ENVIRONMENT	Y	N	N	N	Y
Visual tools	Y	Y	Y	Y	N
GUI tools	Y	Y	Y	Y	N
Toolbar	Y	Y	Y	Y	N
Drag-and-drop editing	Y	Y	Y	Y	N
Graphic class browser	Y	Y	Y	N	N
Class tree	Y	Y	Y	N	N
Project manager	Y	Y	Y	N	N
Templates	Y	N	N	N	N
ADDITIONAL TOOLS					
Applet builder	Y	Y	Y	Y	Y
Scriptless code generation	Y	Y	Y	Y	N
HTML tools	Y	Y	Y	Y	Y
Database connectivity	JDBC	N	ODBC, JDBC	N	N
Prototype testing	N	Y	Y	Y	N
Native method support	N	N	N	N	N
TECHNICAL SUPPORT					
Tutorials	Y	N	N	N	N
Online help	Y	N	N	N	Y

Y—Yes   N—No   N/A—Not applicable   INA—Information not available

Table Continues →

■ Java Tools

	Rogue Wave Software JFactory	Silicon Graphics Cosmo Code	Spider Technologies NetDynamics	SunSoft JDK 1.0 (Java Development Kit)	SunSoft Java Workshop
Price	$195	$495	INA	Free	$295
Supported platforms	Windows 3.1, Solaris, OS/2, HP-UX	IRIX	Windows 95, Windows NT	Windows 95, Windows NT, Unix, Power PC, Macintosh 68K	Windows 95, Windows NT, Solaris
THE BASICS					
Compiler	With JDK	With JDK	With JDK	Javac	With JDK
Just-in-time compilation	N	N	N	N	Y
Other language compilers	N	N	N	N	N
Editor	Y	Y	Y	N	Y
Debugger	N	Y	N	N	Y
Source-level debugger	N	Y	N	N	Y
DEVELOPMENT ENVIRONMENT					
Visual tools	Y	Y	Y	N	Y
GUI tools	Y	Y	Y	N	Y
Toolbar	Y	Y	Y	N	Y
Drag-and-drop editing	Y	Y	Y	N	Y
Graphic class browser	Y	Y	Y	N	Y
Class tree	Y	Y	Y	N	Y
Project manager	Y	Y	Y	N	Y
Templates	N	N	Y	N	Y
ADDITIONAL TOOLS					
Applet builder	Y	N	N	N	Y
Scriptless code generation	Y	Y	N	N	Y
HTML tools	Y	N	N	N	Y
Database connectivity	N	N	ODBC, others	N	N
Prototype testing	Y	Y	Y	N	Y
Native method support	N	N	N	N	Y
TECHNICAL SUPPORT					
Tutorials	N	N	N	N	N
Online help	N	N	N	N	N

Y—Yes   N—No   N/A—Not applicable   INA—Information not available

Java Tools ■

	Symantec Café	Thought Nutmeg 1.0
Price	$99	$495 ($49 students)
Supported platforms	Windows 95, Windows NT, Power PC	NA
THE BASICS		
Compiler	Native	N
Just-in-time compilation	Power PC only	N
Other language compilers	N	N
Editor	Y	N
Debugger	Y	N
Source-level debugger	Y	N
DEVELOPMENT ENVIRONMENT		
Visual tools	Y	N
GUI tools	Y	N
Toolbar	N	N
Drag-and-drop editing	Y	N
Graphic class browser	Y	N
Class tree	Y	N
Project manager	Y	N
Templates	N	Smalltalk-style collection class library
ADDITIONAL TOOLS		
Applet builder	Y	N
Scriptless code generation	Y	N
HTML tools	Y	N
Database connectivity	N	N
Prototype testing	N	N
Native method support	N	N
TECHNICAL SUPPORT		
Tutorials	N	N
Online help	N	N

Y—Yes   N—No   N/A—Not applicable   INA—Information not available   **End** ■

R

COMPILERS, INTERPRETERS, AND CGI PROGRAMS

R.1 Compilers and Interpreters ■

(Products listed in alphabetical order by company name)	Borland C++ 4.5	Borland C++ 4.5 with Database Toolkit	Borland C++ 5.0	Borland C++ 5.0 Development Suite	Borland Delphi 2.0 Desktop
Price	$329	$529	$339	$439	$400
Product type	Compiler	Compiler	Compiler	Compiler	Compiler
Supported platforms	Windows 95, Windows 3.1, DOS	Windows 95, Windows 3.1, DOS	Windows 95, Windows 3.1	Windows 95, Windows 3.1, DOS	Windows 95, Windows 3.1
LANGUAGE					
C	Y	Y	Y	Y	N
C++	Y	Y	Y	Y	N
Perl	N	N	N	N	N
TCL	N	N	N	N	N
Visual Basic	N	N	N	N	N
Other	N	N	N	Java	Object Pascal
UTILITIES					
GUI	Y	Y	Y	Y	Y
Debugger	Y	Y	Y	Y	Y
Other	N	Database Toolkit	N	VBX, CodeGuard, PVCS Version Manager, Install Shield Express, Owl 5.0	N

Y—Yes   N—No   N/A—Not applicable   INA—Information not available

Table Continues →

■ Compilers and Interpreters

	Borland Delphi 2.0 Developer	Borland Turbo C++ 4.5	Borland Visual Solutions Pack 1.1	Tim Bunce Perl5 Modules	Liant Software Corp C++/Views
Price	$650	$82	$109	free	$749
Product type	Compiler	Compiler	Extension	Extension	Compiler
Supported platforms	Windows 95, Windows 3.1	Windows 95, Windows 3.1	Windows 95, Windows 3.1	Windows 95, Windows 3.1, DOS, Macintosh, Unix	Windows 95, Windows 3.1
LANGUAGE					
C	N	Y	Y	N	Y
C++	N	Y	Y	N	Y
Perl	N	N	N	Y	N
TCL	N	N	N	N	N
Visual Basic	N	N	N	N	N
Other	Object Pascal	N	N	N	N
UTILITIES					
GUI	Y	Y	Y	N	Y
Debugger	Y	Y	Y	N	Y
Other	Interbase, ReportSmith, Install Shield Express, Visual Component Library	N	GUI Utility extensions for C++ compilers	CGI-related libraries	N

Y—Yes   N—No   N/A—Not applicable   INA—Information not available

Compilers and Interpreters ■

	Microsoft Visual Basic 4.0	Microsoft Visual C++ 1.52 Professional	Microsoft Visual C++ 4.0 Cross-Development Edition	Microsoft Visual C++ 4.0 Professional	Microsoft Visual C++ 4.0 Standard Edition
Price	$100	$121	$1999	$499	$99
Product type	Compiler	Compiler	Compiler	Compiler	Compiler
Supported platforms	Windows 95, Windows 3.1	Windows 95, Windows 3.1	Macintosh	Windows 95, Windows 3.1, DOS	Windows 95, Windows 3.1, DOS
LANGUAGE					
C	N	Y	Y	Y	Y
C++	N	Y	Y	Y	Y
Perl	N	N	N	N	N
TCL	N	N	N	N	N
Visual Basic	Y	N	N	N	N
Other	N	N	N	N	N
UTILITIES					
GUI	Y	Y	Y	Y	Y
Debugger	Y	Y	Y	Y	Y
Other	N	N	Fortran extension	Fortran extension, Microsoft Profiler	N

Y—Yes   N—No   N/A—Not applicable   INA—Information not available

Table Continues →

■ Compilers and Interpreters

	Powersoft Watcom C/C++ 10.6	John Ousterhout Tcl 7.5	John Ousterhout TK 4.1	Richard Stallman GNU CC	Tsuka Systems Cool C
Price	$269	free	free	free	$145
Product type	Compiler	Interpreter	Extension	Compiler	Interpreter
Supported platforms	Windows 95, Windows 3.1	Windows 95, Windows 3.1, DOS, Unix	Windows 95, Windows 3.1, DOS, Unix	Unix	Windows 95, Windows 3.1
LANGUAGE					
C	Y	N	N	Y	Y
C++	Y	N	N	Y	N
Perl	N	N	N	N	N
TCL	N	Y	Y	N	N
Visual Basic	N	N	N	N	N
Other	N	N	N	Objective C	N
UTILITIES					
GUI	Y	N	Y	N	Y
Debugger	Y	Y	N	Y	Y
Other	N	N	N	N	N

Y—Yes   N—No   N/A—Not applicable   INA—Information not available

Compilers and Interpreters ■

	Larry Wall Perl 5.0
Price	free
Product type	Interpreter
Supported Platforms	DOS, Unix
LANGUAGE	
C	N
C++	N
Perl	Y
TCL	N
Visual Basic	N
Other	N
UTILITIES	
GUI	N
Debugger	Y
Other	N

■ R.2 CGI Programs

(Products listed in alphabetical order by company or author name)	Dan Austin W3OClock	George Burgyan Counter 4.0	Rod Clark Logger.cgi	Clickable Software Database Search Engine	Clickable Software Page Launcher
Price	free	free	free	$135	$25
Location	http://www.wolfenet .com/~rniles/files/	http://www .webtools.org/ counter/	http://www.wolfenet .com/~rniles/files/	http://www .clickables.com/	http://www .clickables.com/
LANGUAGE					
C/C++	Y	N	N	N	N
Perl	N	Y	Y	Y	Y
TCL	N	N	N	N	N
Visual Basic	N	N	N	N	N
Other	N	N	N	N	N
DESCRIPTION	A clock program that displays the time or date.	This is the ultimate access counter. It comes equipped with all the gizmos you'd expect from a counter program.	Records information about who has accessed your page into a log file; can identify user name, domain name and IP addresses.	A very nice search engine that supports boolean logic terms (and, or); the HTML output is fully config-urable.	Creates a list of HTML hotlinks within a pull-down list box.

Y—Yes   N—No   N/A—Not applicable   INA—Information not available

CGI Programs ■

	Clickable Software Turnstiles	Clickable Software Webkey Password Security	ClickShop GoldPaint	Frank Cremer Scintilla's WWW Access Counter	Haese Web Products Chat 2.0
Price	$85	$45	$990	free	$25
Location	http://www .clickables.com/	http://www .clickables.com/	http:// clickshop.com/	http://www .scintilla.utwente .nl/~frank/ counter.html	http://www.rzuser .uni-heidelberg.de/ ~dhaese/index.html
LANGUAGE					
C/C++	N	N	INA	Y	N
Perl	Y	Y		N	Y
TCL	N	N		N	N
Visual Basic	N	N		N	N
Other	N	N		N	N
DESCRIPTION	Analyzes your standard access or stats log, producing a graphical report of accesses and domain names.	Acts as a security guard, protecting all or any portion of your site from unauthorized access; a name-password pair is required to gain access.	An excellent shopping cart script that even includes PGP encryption for credit card information; will run on Unix, Windows 95, and Windows NT.	An access counter for Web pages that records hits and returns an image to the page.	Creates an IRC-like chat room from your Web pages.

Y—Yes N—No N/A—Not applicable INA—Information not available

Table Continues →

■ CGI Programs

	ITM Services Register.pl 1.2	LIFE.com Classifieds	LIFE.com Download Recorder	LIFE.com Go! Button	LIFE.com Public Service Announcements
Price	free	$149 ($299 source code)	$99 ($299 source code)	free ($99 source code)	$99 ($249 source code)
Location	http://www.selah .net/files/register.txt	http://www .lifecom.com/ osisgi0.htm	http://www .lifecom.com/ osisgi0.htm	http://www .lifecom.com/ osisgi0.htm	http://www .lifecom.com/ osisgi0.htm
LANGUAGE					
C/C++	N	N	N	Y	N
Perl	Y	N	N	N	N
TCL	N	N	N	N	N
Visual Basic	N	Y	Y	Y	Y
Other	N	N	N	N	N
DESCRIPTION	A nifty script that allows you to password protect files within directories to restrict access to certain Web pages.	A great program for creating classified ads on your Web page; sections can be defined and users can enter information directly.	Records the date, time, file name, and IP address of users who download a file from your site.	Places all your favorite URLs into a drop-down menu that users can select from.	Provides an easy way for users to display PSAs; automatically deletes entries after a specified time.

Y—Yes   N—No   N/A—Not applicable   INA—Information not available

CGI Programs ▮

	LIFE.com Virtual Yellow Pages	O'Reilly and Associates PolyForm 2.0	Pelicore Media Group FrameChat 1.0	Lincoln Stein Mailmerge 1.2	Sunshine Electronics Interactive Messager 1.0
Price	$149 ($499 source code)	$149	free	free	$50
Location	http://www .lifecom.com/ osisgi0.htm	http://wgg.com/ wgg/best/ polyhome.html	http://www.muzik .com/framechat/ framechat.tar	http:// www-genome .wi.mit.edu/ftp/pub/ software/WWW/ mailmerge/	http://www .rockmall.com/ scripts.htm
LANGUAGE					
C/C++	N	N	N	N	N
Perl	N	N	Y	Y	Y
TCL	N	N	N	N	N
Visual Basic	Y	N	N	N	N
Other	N	Executable	N	N	N
DESCRIPTION	A do-all program that provides for multiple searches, direct user input, and a random advertising ticker.	An all-in-one product for forms and e-mail that requires no programming since it is template- based; also contains its own SMTP client for automatically e-mailing the user.	An IRC-like chat script for incorporation into your Web pages; a disadvantage is that scripts like this can be a major burden on your server.	A Perl script for handling simple HTML forms without the need to write scripts; uses user-defined templates to establish variables.	A guestbook and a graffiti wall wrapped into one; allows users to post messages to a board that others can reply to.

Y—Yes　N—No　N/A—Not applicable　INA—Information not available　　　　　**Table Continues →**

■ CGI Programs

	Sunshine Electronics Interactive Poll Script 2.0	Sunshine Electronics Interactive Trivia Challenge 1.0	WebGenie Software CGI*Star	Andrew Wilcox Vend 0.2.1	Matt Wright Animation 1.2
Price	$79	$79	$35-$50	free	free
Location	http://www .rockmall.com/ scripts.htm	http://www .rockmall.com/ scripts.htm	http://www .webgenie.com/ software/ cgistar.html	http://www .maine.com/ awilcox/vend/	http:// worldwidemart .com/scripts/
LANGUAGE					
C/C++	N	N	N	N	N
Perl	Y	Y	Y	Y	Y
TCL	N	N	N	N	N
Visual Basic	N	N	N	N	N
Other	N	N	Executable	N	N
DESCRIPTION	A polling script that can be configured with any questions and answers you set up; comes with lots of additional features.	Creates a trivia test with multiple choice and true/false questions. and autoscores the test for you.	An application that will create Perl scripts for forms; runs on Unix or Windows NT.	A shopping cart program, allowing users to select items to buy from a catalog and tracking products and quantities selected.	Animates a sequence of GIFs for you.

Y—Yes   N—No   N/A—Not applicable   INA—Information not available

CGI Programs ■

	Matt Wright Free for All Link Page 2.1	Matt Wright Guestbook.cgi	Matt Wright Random Image Displayer 1.2	Matt Wright Random Link Generator 1.0	Matt Wright Simple Search 1.0
Price	free	free	free	free	free
Location	http:// worldwidemart .com/scripts/	http:// worldwidemart .com/scripts/	http:// worldwidemart .com/scripts/	http:// worldwidemart .com/scripts/	http:// worldwidemart .com/scripts/
LANGUAGE					
C/C++	N	N	N	N	N
Perl	Y	Y	Y	Y	Y
TCL	N	N	N	N	N
Visual Basic	N	N	N	N	N
Other	N	N	N	N	N
DESCRIPTION	Allows users to add their favorite URL to a displayable list file thereby letting your users do the work of maintaining links.	A customizable guestbook script, the contents of which can be e-mailed to any destination.	Randomly selects (from a list you define) images to display as graphics or background for your Web page.	Chooses links from a list that you config-ure, allowing users to go to your favorite sites randomly.	A great search engine for your site if it contains less than a few hundred files.

Y—Yes   N—No   N/A—Not applicable   INA—Information not available   **End** ■

S

VRML TOOLS

S.1   VRML Tools ■

(Products listed in alphabetical order by company name.)	Black Sun CyberLife	DimensionX Liquid Reality	Intervista WorldView	Netscape Live3D	Onlive Tecnology Onlive
Supported platforms	Windows 95, Windows NT, Unix (Macintosh winter 1996)	Windows 95, Windows NT (Macintosh and Unix spring 1997)	Windows 95, Windows NT, Windows 3.1 (Macintosh and Unix spring 1997)	Windows 95, Windows NT, Windows 3.1, Macintosh, Unix	Windows 95, Windows NT, Windows 3.1
BROWSER TYPE					
Netscape plug-in	Y	Y	Y	Y	N
Internet Explorer plug-in	Y	Y	Y	Y	N
Stand-alone	N	N	Y	N	Y
ActiveX Control	Y	Y	Coming	INA	INA
TECHNOLOGY					
VRML 1.0	Y	Y	Y	Y	Y
VRML 2.0	Y	Winter 1996	Y	Y	INA
Proprietary technology	N	N	N	N	Y
FEATURES					
Ease of navigation	Good	Fair	Good	Good	Good
Interface design	Good	Good	Good	Fair	Good
Interface functionality	Good	Fair	Good	Fair	Fair
Rendering speed	Good	Fair	Good	Good	Excellent
Sound	Y	Y	Y	Y	Y
3-D sound	Y	Y	INA	Y	Y
Voice chat	Spring 1997	INA	INA	Spring 1997	Y
Built-in avatar editing	Y	Y	Spring 1997	INA	Y

Y—Yes   N—No   N/A—Not applicable   INA—Information not available

Table Continues →

■ VRML Tools

	OZ Inc. Play3D	OZ Inc. OZ Virtual	Silicon Graphics Cosmo Player	Superscape VisNet	Virtus Voyager
Supported platforms	Windows 95, Windows 3.1	Windows 95, Windows NT (Unix spring 1997)	Windows 95, Windows NT, Unix (Macintosh spring 1997)	Windows 95, Windows NT, Windows 3.1 (Macin- tosh summer 1997)	Windows 95, Windows NT, Windows 3.1, Macintosh, Unix
BROWSER TYPE					
Netscape plug-in	N	N	Y	Y	Y
Internet Explorer plug-in	N	N	N	Y	N/A
Stand-alone	Y	Y	N	Y	Y
ActiveX Control	INA	N/A	INA	Y	N/A
TECHNOLOGY					
VRML 1.0	Y	Y	Y	Y	Y
VRML 2.0	Y	Winter 1996	Y	Winter 1996	Winter 1996
Proprietary technology	Y	Y	N	Y	N
FEATURES					
Ease of navigation	Good	Good	Good	Excellent	Fair
Interface design	Excellent	Excellent	Good	Good	Good
Interface functionality	Excellent	Good	Good	Good	Good
Rendering speed	Good	Fair	Fair	Excellent	Good
Sound	Y	Y	Y	Y	Y
3-D sound	Y	Y	INA	N	N
Voice chat	INA	Winter 1996	INA	INA	INA
Built-in avatar editing	INA	INA	Y	INA	INA

Y—Yes N—No N/A—Not applicable INA—Information not available

ZIFF-DAVIS PRESS

VRML Tools ■

	VReam WIRL	Worlds Inc. Worlds Gold
Supported platforms	Windows 95, Windows NT, Windows 3.1	Windows 95, Windows NT, Windows 3.1
BROWSER TYPE		
Netscape plug-in	Y	N
Internet Explorer plug-in	Y	N
Stand-alone	Y	Y
ActiveX Control	Y	N/A
TECHNOLOGY		
VRML 1.0	Y	N
VRML 2.0	Winter 1996	N
Proprietary technology	N	N
FEATURES		
Ease of navigation	Fair	Good
Interface design	Fair	Good
Interface functionality	Good	Good
Rendering speed	Good	Excellent
Sound	Y	Y
3-D sound	INA	Y
Voice chat	INA	Winter 1996
Built-in avatar editing	INA	Y

Y—Yes   N—No   N/A—Not applicable   INA—Information not available   **End ■**

■ S.2   VRML Authoring Tools

(Products listed in alphabetical order by company name.)	Black Sun CyberKit	DimensionX Liquid Reality	Paragraph Home Space Builder	Silicon Graphics Cosmo WORLDS
Supported platforms	(Windows 95 and Unix spring 1997, Macintosh summer 1997)	Windows 95, Windows NT, Windows 3.1 (Macintosh spring 1997)	Windows 95, Windows NT, Windows 3.1 (Macintosh spring 1997)	Unix (Windows 95 spring 1997)
HARDWARE REQUIREMENTS				
RAM	12MB (16MB preferred)	8MB (16MB preferred)	8MB (16MB preferred)	16MB (24MB preferred)
Hard-disk space	16MB	10MB	10MB	20MB
Other	SVGA		CD-ROM drive	
FEATURES				
Modeling	N	Y (limited)	N	Y (limited)
Animation	Y	Y	Y	Y
Behaviors	Y	Y	Y	Y
Avatar creation/editing	Y	Spring 1997	Spring 1997	Y
Avatar motion	Y	Spring 1997	Spring 1997	Y
USER LEVEL				
Beginner	Y	N	Y	N
Intermediate	Y	Y	Y	Y
Advanced	Y	Y	N	Y
TECHNOLOGY				
VRML 1.0	Y	Y	Y	Y
VRML 2.0	Y	Winter 1996	Y	Y
Proprietary	N	N	N	N

Y—Yes   N—No   N/A—Not applicable   INA—Information not available

VRML Authoring Tools ■

	Superscape VRT 4.0	Virtus 3D Website Builder	VReam VRCreator	Worlds Inc. Gamma
Supported platforms	Windows 95, Windows NT, Windows 3.1, DOS	Windows 95, Windows NT, Macintosh	Windows 95, Windows NT, Windows 3.1 (Macintosh spring 1997)	(Windows 95 spring 1997, Unix summer 1997)
HARDWARE REQUIREMENTS				
RAM	16MB (24MB preferred)	8MB (16MB preferred)	8MB (16MB preferred)	16MB (24MB preferred)
Hard-disk space	20MB	10MB	10MB	20MB
Other	CD-ROM drive	CD-ROM drive	CD-ROM drive	VGA graphics adaptor for PC
FEATURES				
Modeling	Y	N	N	Y (limited)
Animation	INA	INA	Spring 1997	Y
Behaviors	Y	Y	Y	Y
Avatar creation/editing	INA	INA	INA	Y
Avatar motion	INA	INA	INA	Y
USER LEVEL				
Beginner	N	Y	Y	Y, if using libraries
Intermediate	Y	Y	Y	Y
Advanced	Y	Y	Y	Y
TECHNOLOGY				
VRML 1.0	Y	Y	Y	Y
VRML 2.0	Winter 1996	Coming	Winter 1996	Coming
Proprietary	Y	N	N	N

Y—Yes   N—No   N/A—Not applicable   INA—Information not available   E n d ■

DIRECTORY OF NATIONAL AND INTERNATIONAL INTERNET SERVICE PROVIDERS

International Internet Service Providers ■

THIS DIRECTORY CONTAINS addresses and phone numbers for large Internet service providers serving the entire United States and the world. There are currently almost 2,500 Internet service providers in the United States. Since these providers are constantly changing, the best way to find a local ISP is to look in your phone book under Computers, or to use one of the search services, such as Yahoo, and enter "Internet Service Providers" as the search topic. The following URL also will provide a list of service providers by state:
http://www.yahoo.com/Business_and_Economy/Companies/Internet_Services/
Internet_Access_Providers/Regional/U_S__States/

International Providers

Channel One Internet Services
getwired@sonetis.com
280-55 Metcalfe St.
Ottawa, Ontario, K1P 6L5
Canada
Tel: (613) 236-8601
Fax: (613) 236-8764

Demon Internet Limited
internet@demon.net
Gateway House
322 Regents Park Rd.
London N3 2QQ
United Kingdom
Tel: (44 181) 371-1000
Fax: (44 181) 371-1150

EUnet Communications Services BV
info@EU.net
Singel 540
1017 AZ Amsterdam
Netherlands
Tel: (31 20) 623-3803
Fax: (31 20) 622-4657

International Internet Service Providers

Institute for Global Communications
support@igc.apc.org
PeaceNet/EcoNet/ConflictNet/LaborNet
18 deBoom St.
San Francisco, CA 94107
Tel: (415) 442-0220
Fax: (415) 546-1794

JVNCnet
market@jvnc.net
Global Enterprise Services
3 Independence Way
Princeton, NJ 08540
Tel: (609) 897-7300

UUNET
info@uunet.uu.net
3110 Fairview Park Dr., Suite 570
Falls Church, VA 22042
Tel: (703) 204-8000

Performance Systems International, Inc.
info@psi.com
510 Huntmar Park Dr.
Herndon, VA 22070
Tel: (800) 827-7482

National Internet Service Providers ■

National Providers

Colorado Supernet
info@csn.org
Colorado School of Mines
1500 Illinois St.
Golden, CO 80401
Tel: (303) 296-8202

DATABANK, Inc.
info@databank.com
1473 Hwy 40
Lawrence, KS 66044
Tel: (913) 842-6699
Fax: (913) 842-8518

NetCom On-Line Communication Services
info@netcom.com
4000 Moorpark Ave., Suite 209
San Jose, CA 95117
Tel: (408) 983-5950

The Portal Information Network
info@portal.com
20863 Stevens Creek Blvd., Suite 200
Cupertino, CA 95014
Tel: (408) 973-9111
Fax: (408) 725-1580

U

DIRECTORY OF INTERNET PRESENCE PROVIDERS

This directory provides a partial listing by country or state of companies providing Internet presence services. The services offered can include anything from specialized Web page design and marketing to full-service graphic design, software consulting, and animation services. Use the Internet addresses supplied to investigate which company in your area offers the type of service most suitable for your needs.

Directory of Internet Presence Providers ■

International

Canada

Building 29 Design Group Inc.
http://www.bldg29.com/

Optimization Systems Associates
http://www.osacad.com/

South Africa

Bumper Productions
http://www.bumper.co.za/index.htm

United Kingdom

Mountcomp
http://www.mountcomp.co.uk/

New Media Factory
http://www.mediafactory.co.uk/

■ Directory of Internet Presence Providers

United States

Alabama

Advantage Services Goto Communication
http://www.us-goto.com/

Internet Gadsden
http://www.gadsden.net/

Internet Solutions
http://www.insol.net/

Alaska

Alaska Internet Marketing, Inc.
http://www.interax.com/~huntfishalaska/aim.shtml

AngelWorks
http://www.alaska.net/~angelwrk/index.html

Cyberice
http://www.cyberice.com/

Impact Web Design
http://www.alaskana.com/

Multimakers
http://www2.polarnet.com/~multim/

Netmode
http://www.netmode.com/

Directory of Internet Presence Providers ■

Arizona

Access Plus+—Internet Marketing Packages
http://www.resultsdirect.com/rd/accessp.htm

Arastar Internet
http://www.arastar.net/

Arizona Web Products, Inc.
http://www.webcom.com/~jcbell/

Bamboo Publishing and Advertising
http://bamboo.silicon.com

Community Media Services
http://emol.org/emol/

DataMax OnLine, Inc.
http://www.data-max.com/

E2 Internet Services
http://www.e2internet.com/

Future Unlimited
http://www.futureunltd.com/

Global Internet Attitude Co.
http://www.giaco.com

Home in Arizona
http://www.dbqinc.com/

Infoplus
http://www.infop.com/

Peddler's Plaza
http://www.peddler.com/

◼ Directory of Internet Presence Providers

Primenet
http://www.primenet.com/

TeleSys Development Systems (TNET)
http://www.tnet.com/

The River Internet Access Co.
http://www.theriver.com/

TRCWeb Communications
http://www.trcone.com/

Web Services
http://www.tucsonbiz.com/

Arkansas

AlphaNet Internet Marketing Solutions, Inc.
http://www.alphanet1.com/

Aristotle Internet Access
http://www.aristotle.net/

ArkansasUSA
http://ArkansasUSA.com/Index.html

Compnet Web Services
http://www.compnetar.com/cws/

Futura
http://www.futura.net/

KG2 Web Design
http://www.axs.net/~kgriffin/

Net M Communications
http://www.netm.com/mall/infoprod/netm/netmhome.htm

Snider Telecom/TCE WWW Services
http://www.snider.net/fulldex.html

Directory of Internet Presence Providers ■

California

Addnet
http://www.addnet.com/

Antelope Internet Systems
http://www.antelope.com/

Bay Area Art Source
http://www.foggy.com/baas.html

BayScenes
http://www.bayscenes.com/

BEEP
http://turnpike.net/emporium/B/beep/index.html

Big Bear Online
http://www.bigbear.com/

Blue Racer Web Design
http://www.sirius.com/~bluracer/

Cyber World
http://www.cyber-world.com/

Elan GMK
http://elan-gmk.com/int_mk.htm

Encore Creation—Digital Imaging
http://www.ec-di.com/

Ernest & Allen
http://www.ernestallen.com/

Fountainhead Internet Systems
http://www.fountainhead.com/

■ Directory of Internet Presence Providers

Fractal Images Company
http://www.fractals.com/tfic/html/tfic_intro.html

FullDigital.com
http://urban1.fulldigital.com/

GeneralNET
http://www.generalnet.com/gnhome/

GetWWW'ed
http://www.GetWWWed.com/index.html

Idyll Mountain Internet
http://www.idyllmtn.com/

InReach Internet Communications
http://www.inreach.com/

Intergear Interactive
http://www.intergear.com/

Key Connections
http://www.keyconnect.com/

Kinetic Cybersystems
http://kcyb.com/

KnowledgeSet Corporation
http://www.kset.com/

Magic Windows
http://www.magicwindows.com/~mwinfo/webpages.html

ManyMedia
http://www.manymedia.com/

MultiMedia Hype Productions
http://mediahype.com/

Directory of Internet Presence Providers ▪

My P. C. Man Computer Consulting
http://www.my-pc-man.com/

Net.Trade
http://www.nettrade-usa.com/

Netcetera Digital Media
http://www.netcetera.net/

Oceanus Technologies
http://www.oceanus.com/

Pacific Blue Micro
http://www.ocnet.net/pbm/

Pacific Building Industry
http://www.pacificbuilding.com/

Pacific Coast Software
http://www.pacific-coast.com/

PC Services
http://206.72.148.228/

Praxis Online Campaigns
http://www.nextpolitics.com/praxis/

Prism Communications
http://www.prism.com/

Right Angle Design
http://www.rightangle.com

SD Professionals Network
http://www.sdpros.com/sdpros/

Softelligence
http://www.softelligence.com/

■ Directory of Internet Presence Providers

Spiderweb Communications
http://www.spiderweb.com/

Team Solutions
http://www.teamsolution.com/

True World Access, Inc.
http://www.trueworld.com/

Tsunami-2000
http://www.Tsunami-2000.com/

World One Telecommunications
http://www.worldone.com/

Colorado

Advanced Solutions Group
http://www.asgusa.com/

AmericaNet.Com—Internet Publications of America
http://www.americanet.com/AMERICANET/ipoa.html

Labyrinth Computer Services
http://labyrinth.com/

Mktplace.net
http://www.mktplace.net/

Mountain States Internet
http://www.mstates.com/

NetGrafx Internet Web Services
http://www.netgrafx.com/

Osborn Designs
http://www.osnet.com

Directory of Internet Presence Providers

The Vail Valley
http://vail.net/

Connecticut

Alphabet Systems
http://www.alphabet.com/
Comments: Specializes in multilingual sites, including those using non-Latin writing systems

Atlantic Computing Technology
http://www.atlantic.com/

Communications Unlimited—Online Marketing
http://www.comunlimited.com/

ConnMart, Inc.
http://www.connmart.com/

Downtown Hybrid City
http://gs1.com/HomePages/dir.html

e-Media
http://www.e1.com/

Hickory Hill
http://hickoryhill.com/index.htm

High Ridge Associates
http://www.highridge.com/

Innovative Internet Marketing Solutions
http://www.virtuallyeverything.com/iims/index.htm

Internet NewMedia
http://www.netsavvy.com/

■ Directory of Internet Presence Providers

Internet Publishing Services
http://www.interpublish.com/

J Zimmerman Consulting
http://www.jznet.com/

LexiConn Internet Services, Inc.
http://www.lexiconn.com/

Nutmeg Information Services
http://www.nutmegis.com/

Nutmeg Solutions
http://www.thenutmeg.com/

Online Marketing International Inc.
http://olm.net/

Pequot Group
http://www.pequot.com/

Planet Earth Inc.
http://www.planetearthinc.com/

Quality Graphics & Marketing
http://www.qgm.com/

Website Designs
http://corpcenter.com/cummings/home.html

Westwater Communications
http://www.westwater.com/

Delaware

Delaware Valley Business Net
http://www.dvbiznet.com/

Directory of Internet Presence Providers ■

First State Network
http://www.firststate.com/

InterNet Delaware
http://www.del.net/

Florida

Access/Website/Design
http://www.netrunner.net/access/website/design/

AdverNet
http://www.advernet.com/

AKUA Interactive Media, Inc
http://www.safari.net/~akua/

All World Network, Inc.
http://www.allworld.com/

Allen-Watson Inter@ctive
http://www.awint.com/

Applied Computing Solutions, Inc.
http://www.acs.supernet.net/

Camelot Web Services, Inc.
http://www.camelot-wsi.net/

CanTek USA
http://www.cantek.com

Capstone Studio
http://www.capstudio.com/

Citicom Online Communication Services, Inc.
http://www.citicom.com/

■ Directory of Internet Presence Providers

Computer Clinic
http://www.supernet.net/~pvignola/

Coral Technologies Inc.
http://www3.islands.com/coral/home.html

CyberGate
http://www.gate.net/start.html

Cyberscapes Inc.
http://www.cyberscapes.com/

Data Movers
http://Palms.america.com/dm_pro.htm

Dyna-Net Web Services
http://www.dyna-net.com/

EnterWeb Inc.
http://www.enterwebinc.com/

Florida Network Solutions, Inc.
http://www.fns.net/

GDI Communications
http://www.gdic.com/

Glimmer
http://glimmer.com/

Greyhawkes Cyberservices
http://www.greyhawkes.com/

Health Quest
http://www.health-quest.com/

Interactive Marketspace, Inc.
http://bizport.com/im/

Directory of Internet Presence Providers ■

Internet Gateway, Inc.
http://www.inetgate.com

J Weber Thompson
http://www.jwtco.com/

Loiodice Dot Com
http://loiodice.com/

MainStreet MarketPlace
http://www.mainstusa.com/

Mims Mall
http://www.mims.com/mimsmall/

MJA Technologies
http://www.mja.net/

Nature Coast Inc.
http://naturecoast.com/

NetSide
http://www.netside.net/

OneWeb Designs
http://fdt.net/~oneweb/

Online Development
http://www.ondev.com/spmi/ondev/

OpenNet Technologies, Inc.
http://www2.opennet.com/

Photo Design Group, Inc.
http://www.photodesigngroup.com

Pirates Cove Bazaar
http://www.privateers.com/

■ Directory of Internet Presence Providers

Red Design
http://www.reddesign.com/

ROI Marketing Inc.
http://www.roimark.com

Scott Online Design
http://www.scott-design.com/

Space Coast Community Network
http://www.sccnweb.com/

spot grafix, inc
http://www.shadow.net/~tomp/

Tangled Webs, Inc.
http://www.twebs.com/

TECHNET Enterprises of Florida
http://emporium.turnpike.net/T/TECHNETEOF/index.html

Visible Light, Inc.
http://www.visiblelight.com/

Webtron
http://www.wunder.com/

WebXpress, Inc.
http://www.web-xpress.com/

WorldWide Marketing Headquarters, Inc.
http://www.netline.net/~wmh/

Directory of Internet Presence Providers ■

Georgia

MediumCool
http://www.mediumcool.com/

AADS Web Development
http://www.mindspring.com/~aarons/

B.F. Services, Inc.
http://www.bfservs.com/

bhl Enterprises, Inc.
http://www.bhl.com/

Bluemoon MultiMedia
http://www.gacoast.com/navigator/bluemoonpage.html

Boston Communications
http://boscomm.com

Data Design Systems
http://revsoft2.is.net/alpcinar/designs.html

The Georgia Link
http://www.galink.com/

Hopkins Communications
http://www.pmicro.net/

idealNet
http://www.idealnet.com/

Konz + Okrzesik, Inc.
http://www.infostarbase.com/ko.html

Kudzu Creations
http://atl1.america.net/com/kudzu/kudzu.html

■ Directory of Internet Presence Providers

The Mall in the Sky
http://www.mindspring.com/~mcafee/index.html

MultiMediums, Inc.
http://www.multimediums.com/

North Georgia Magazine
http://georgiamagazine.com/business/

Realm Development Group
http://www.realm.org/

Software Monster
http://www.swmonster.com/

World Class Connection
http://www.mindspring.com/~wcc/

Hawaii

BUILD*NET
http://www.hrcn.com/

Cyber Services, Inc.
http://www.cybersrv.com/

Cyber Services, Inc. Hawaii
http://www.hula.net/~cyber/

1st Source, Inc.
http://www.1source.com/

Graphic Communication—Advertising and Design
http://www.htmlmagic.com/~graphic/

H-4, Hawaii's Data SuperHighway
http://www.hotspots.hawaii.com/

Directory of Internet Presence Providers ■

Hawaii Internet Emporium Index
http://www.aloha.com/~petemart/info/index.html

Hawaii Online (HOL)
http://www.aloha.net/

HI-Way Multimedia
http://hisurf.aloha.com/hiway.html

Information Marketplace
http://www.infomarket.com/

InterLink Hawaii
http://www.ilhawaii.net/

InterNet Marketing Group
http://www.img-corp.com/

Ke'nalu—Surfside Internet Services
http://204.188.88.156/

MauiTech
http://www.maui-tech.com/

Megapage
http://www.mpin.com
Comments: Includes all major US and Japanese search engines, with multiple language support

Tropical Night Hawaii BBS
http://www.tnight.com/

■ Directory of Internet Presence Providers

Idaho

Northwest Voyager
http://www.caboose.com/lrc/

Regional Marketing Concepts
http://rmc.net/rmcmenu.html

Illinois

Access Illinois
http://www.accessil.com/

CyberSpace Solutions, Inc.
http://www.addressbook.com/csi/

DD&A Marketing & Promotions
http://www.marketpromo.com/

JapanLink
http://www.japanlink.com/
Comments: Provides multilingual Web site hosting

3WD: World Wide Web Design
http://www.3wd.com/

Indiana

B.C. Publishing
http://bcpub.com/phpl.cgi/bcpub.html

Clear Lake Communications
http://www.clearlake.com/

Hill-Luhring and Associates
http://www.hlanet.com/

Indiana Business Directory
http://www.astralite.com/index.html

Directory of Internet Presence Providers ■

LockHeed Guidance, Inc., WWW Strategic Business Consulting
http://www.iquest.net/guidance/ilinks.htm

Metropolitan Data Networks
http://www.mdn.com/

NetNITCO
http://www.nitco.com/

Quantum Web Solutions
http://www.qws.com/

Synergetic Resource Corporation
http://www.synernet-indy.com/src/

TGA
http://www.tgai.com/

Iowa

Captain Jack Communications
http://www.captainjack.com/

Internet Business Project
http://www.exclusive.com/bizproj/

Iowa Network Services
http://www.netins.net/

JEMM, Inc.
http://www.jemm.com/

Starri
http://www.starri.com/

Wen-Kor
http://www.netins.net/showcase/wenkor/

■ Directory of Internet Presence Providers

Kansas

Fast Lane Communications, Inc.
http://www.fastlane.com

Kentucky

April Group
http://www.bch.com/april.html

Clover.net
http://www.iglou.com/sheehy/clover/

Ivycom
http://www.win.net/ivycom/welcome.html

Pegasus Press, L.L.C.
http://www.pegasuspress.com/

Louisiana

Internet Impact
http://emporium.turnpike.net/~iimpact/index.html

Planet Symphony
http://www.planetsymphony.com/

ShopSWLA.com
http://www.shopswla.com

World Net of Louisiana
http://www.tradecompany.com/link2.html

Directory of Internet Presence Providers ■

Maine

Community Network
http://www.communitynetwork.com/

The Digital Scribe
http://www.agate.net/~psykiktv/dscribe.html

interactive marketing group
http://www.maineguide.com/img/

Maine OnLine
http://www.maineonline.com/

Maine Vacationland
http://www.mainevacation.com/

MegaLink Internet Services
http://www.megalink.net/

Moosehead OnLine
http://www.moosehead.net/

NetExpress Incorporated
http://www.nxi.com/

Phoenix Systems Internet Publishing
http://www.biddeford.com/phoenix/

Publishnet
http://www.publishnet.com/

Santa-Claws Online
http://santaclaws.com/us/maine

St. John Valley Communications
http://www.sjv.com/

■ Directory of Internet Presence Providers

Maryland

AccessAbility Internet Services, Inc.
http://www.ability.net/

Cove Software Systems
http://www.covesoft.com/

CyberShark Technologies
http://www.cybershark.com

Glows in the Dark Studios
http://www.glows.com/

Hibiscus Software, Inc.
http://www.motorcade.com/hibiscus.htm

Interactive Ads Inc.
http://interactiveads.com/

Kivex, Inc.
http://www.kivex.com/

Maryland Business Forum
http://www.intandem.com/

MetroDC Internet Specialists
http://shenwebworks.com:8001/mis

The NERDS Group
http://www.nerds.net/

Rockrose Web Services
http://www.rockroseweb.com

VirtualSprockets
http://www.spacely.com/

Directory of Internet Presence Providers

Web Direct Inc.
http://www.directweb.com/

WebTrek
http://www.webtrek.com/

Massachusetts

AB Software
http://www.ptown.com/abs/

BBG New Media
http://www.bbg.com/

CLC Marketing Inc.
http://www.clc-marketing.com/

Home Directions
http://homedirections.com

Lexi Communications, Inc.
http://www.iii.net/users/lexi/index.html

Media Concepts
http://www.tiac.net/users/joegold/medconc1.html

Spinners, Inc.
http://www.spinners.com/welcome.html

The Village Group
http://www.village.com/

Michigan

Brennan Communications
http://www.ljbrennan.com/

The Collective
http://www.thecollective.com/

■ Directory of Internet Presence Providers

Computer Magic
http://ic.net/~dennyvan/index.htm

Digital Expressions
http://public.navisoft.com/pub/digital/index.html

Green Lake Business Communications
http://www.greenlake.com

HTML Express, Ltd.
http://www.htmlexpress.com/

Internet Services
http://www.tcimet.net/isi/ishome.htm

The Krystal Web
http://www.profiles-net.com/krystal/

Michigan Mall
http://michmall.com/

Michigan Online Networks
http://molnet.com/

Netfinity Internet Services
http://www.netfinity.com/index.html

Q LTD.
http://www.qltd.com/

Serene Images
http://magic.netdtw.com/~serene/

Software Advantage Consulting Corporation
http://www.sacc.com/

Sycron Corporation
http://www.sycron.com/

Directory of Internet Presence Providers ■

Tiedemann Communications
http://www.tcomm.com/

Trident Electrical Systems
http://www.cris.com/~trident/

Virtual Server System
http://webcenter.net/virtual/server.html

Minnesota

Aquarius Realty
http://www.winternet.com/~aquarius/

Auguste Enterprises, Inc.
http://www.auguste.com/door.htm

Dan Gardner
http://www.umn.edu/nlhome/m093/gard0048/dan.html

Eye of the Mind Productions
http://www.eotm.com/

Hadden Web Studio
http://rrnet.com/~hwstudio/

Honeycomb World Wide Web Publishing
http://www.honeycomb.net/

Internet Broadcasting System
http://www.ibsys.com/

LiveWire Graphics
http://www.live-wire.com/

Midwestern Cybertising, Inc.
http://www.visi.com/~mci/index.html

■ Directory of Internet Presence Providers

mindframe.com
http://www.mindframe.com/

NetEngine Internet, Inc.
http://www.netengine.net/

Racoon.Com Internet Services
http://www.racoon.com/racoon.html

RE/SPEC Internet Services
http://www.respec.com/mpls.html

SpectorNet, Inc.
http://www.spectornet.com/

Str8line Productions
http://www.str8line.com/

Wirefeed Communications
http://www.wirefeed.com/

Mississippi

AccessNet
http://www.access-net.com/

Gulf Coast Internet Mall
http://www.gcnetmall.com/

Gulf Coast Online
http://www.mscoast.com/

Gulfcoast On-Line Development, Inc.
http://www.goldinc.com/

Mall of Cyberspace
http://WWW.Zmall.Com/

Directory of Internet Presence Providers ■

META3
http://www.meta3.com/

Southern Internet
http://www.southernnet.com

Missouri

C. M. Coffin Design
http://www.sound.net/~design/default.htm

Montana

DragonWare Software Inc.
http://dragonware.com/

The Montana Electronic Billboard
http://www.imt.net/~msm/msm1.htm

New Hampshire

Advanced Digital Research Labs
http://adrl.xtdl.com/adrl/

Creative
http://www.creative-hp.com/

Gran-Net Communications
http://www.gran-net.com/

NetRegister, Inc.
http://www.netregister.com/

Directory of Internet Presence Providers

New Jersey

Advanced Web Creations
http://www.webcreations.com/

Apollo Online
http://www.apollo-online.com/

Atlan System Corp
http://www.business1.com/atlan/

BATNET, Business & Trade Network
http://www.batnet1.com/

BillBoards in The Web
http://www.intheweb.com/billboards/

BZA Internet Marketing
http://www.bza.com

Connetix, Inc.
http://www.connetix.com/

DigiGraphics
http://www.digigrafix.com

DynamicWeb Transaction Systems
http://www.megamart.com/

ePresence.com
http://www.epresence.com/

Incore, Inc.
http://www.incore.com/

.indesign
http://www.indesign3.com/

Directory of Internet Presence Providers ■

Internet Graphic Design Inc.
http://www.webcom.com/igraphic/
Comments: Offers Web page design in English and Spanish

Internet Images Worldwide
http://www.inet-images.com

Jeff49er Productions
http://users.aol.com/jeff49ers/

JMarc Associates
http://www.jmarc.com/

Kabardine Associates
http://www.kabar.com/kabar/home.htm

MAK Communications
http://www.makcom.com/

Millennium Systems Group, Inc.
http://www.2000sys.com/

Mps Promotions
http://mpspromo.com/

Net Ventures Inc.
http://www.netvent.com/

New Jersey Internet Services (NJIS)
http://www.njservice.com/

NJ Community Organization
http://www.njcommunity.org/

raindance interactive
http://www.interactive.net/~unisyn/

■ Directory of Internet Presence Providers

Shalafi Website Development
http://www.shalafi.com

Think! Technology
http://www.thinktek.com/

Triemme Internet Marketing Group
http://www.triemme.com/

UniPress W3 Services
http://www.unipress.com/w3/

World Internet Resources
http://wir.com/world/

World Web Systems
http://yyy.algorithms.com/

World Wide Riches
http://www.wwriches.com/

New Mexico

Aquamarine
http://www.aquamarine.com/

GilaNet
http://www.gilanet.com/

TaosWebb Artists and Craftspeople
http://taoswebb.com/nmusa/arts/

Directory of Internet Presence Providers ■

New York

BusinessWORKS!
http://www.bworks.com

CyberAdvantage
http://CyberAdvantage.com/

CyberData Inc.
http://www.cyberdata.com/

Empire Web
http://www.infomall.org/empireweb/

Erin Edwards
http://www.webcom.com/~milcom/eehomepage.html

ExecNet
http://www.execnet.com/

Going Interactive
http://www.going.com/

Goodies
http://www.goodies.com/home.htm

GraFix.Com
http://GraFix.Com/

Innovative Systems of New York, Inc.
http://ison.com/

LinkDirect
http://www.linkdirect.com/

Matrix Online Media
http://www.mxol.com/

■ Directory of Internet Presence Providers

Net Technologies Inc.
http://www.nette.com/

New York Consulting Group
http://www.nycg.com/

NorthNet
http://www.northnet.org/

NYENET
http://www.nyenet.com/

Orlando World Services
http://www.rochester.ny.us/orlando/orlando.html

WiseLinks, Inc.
http://www.wiselinks.com/index.html

North Carolina

Carolina Online
http://www.nconline.com/

Crescendo Web Design, Inc.
http://crescendoweb.com/

Dynamic Web Solutions
http://www.dywebsol.com/

Kenetics, Inc.
http://www.kinetics.net/

Key Concepts Web Design
http://www.hway.net/keycon/indexb.html

Lost Province Multimedia
http://lostprovince.com/

Directory of Internet Presence Providers

NCNatural Web Services
http://www.ncnatural.com/

tysys.com
http://www.tysys.com/

Vcom1
http://www.vcom1.com/

North Dakota

Internet Marketplace
http://www.fargo-moorhead.com/

Ohio

A Net Success
http://www.2theweb.com/

Ad Marketing Internet Services
http://www.admarketing.com/

Advantage Communications
http://ourworld.compuserve.com/homepages/advgroup/

Boaters.Com
http://www.boaters.com/boaters/

CyberInk
http://www.erinet.com/wkurtz/index.html

desein haus
http://www.glasscity.net/~omoral/

EALnet
http://www.ealnet.com/

Firestar Networking Technologies
http://www.firestar.com/

Directory of Internet Presence Providers

Magnagraphics Inc.
http://www.magnainc.com/

Merchants of the Western Reserve
http://merchantmall.com/

NetForce Development, Inc.
http://www.nforce.com/

Rarey-Roth Inc.
http://rri.bright.net/rri/

sharkBYTES Internet Source
http://www.sharkbytes.com/

Sitemaster Services
http://www.sitemasters.com/sms/

Southwest Ohio Mall
http://www.southwestohiomall.com/

Teraform Communications
http://www.teraform.com/

The uNETverse
http://www.stjpub.com

Vantage One Communications
http://www.vantageone.com/v1/

The Webmasters Company
http://users1.ee.net/coldir/

WonderNet Digital Communications, Inc.
http://www.wondernet.com/

Zygaena Network Services
http://www.zygaena.com/

Directory of Internet Presence Providers ■

Oregon

AdNet
http://wwide.com/adnet.html

ALKhemic Design
http://www.opendoor.com/alkhemic/

Black Gothic Ltd.
http://www.blackgothic.com/

Creative Computer Concepts
http://www.chatlink.com/~ccubed/

Empire Net
http://www.empnet.com/

The KEEP Information Services
http://www.thekeep.net/

Multi-Net Communications
http://www.multinet.com/

Opinion Transfer Service
http://www.teleport.com/~repmail/

Oregon Marketplace Online
http://www.ormart.com/

PacInfo
http://www.pacinfo.com

PagOne Internet Advertising Services
http://www.pagone.com/

PDS Internet Services
http://www.pdss.com/

■ Directory of Internet Presence Providers

Specialized Web Ad Design
http://www.teleport.com/~celinec/design/

The Wave!—On The Oregon Coast
http://www.oregoncoast.com/

WaveNet Rogue Valley Guide
http://www.wave.net/guide/

Waystation Networking
http://www.waystation.com/

Web Trade
http://webtrade.com/index.html

Worldwide Advertising Inc.
http://wwide.com/

Pennsylvania

1USA.com
http://www.1usa.com/

Access Info-Net
http://www.poconomall.com/accessinfonet/

Allwilk Consulting
http://www.allwilk.com/

Art-Craft PA
http://www.art-craftpa.com/

CenPenn
http://www.cenpenn.com/

CHHYLnet
http://www.chhylnet.com/

Directory of Internet Presence Providers ∎

Commex International Co.
http://www.commex.com/

Compu-tek
http://www.compu-tek.com/

Data Hart
http://www.datahart.com/

Digital Wave Technologies, Inc.
http://www.digitalwave.com/

Dynamic Web Services
http://www.Dynamic-Web.com/

Electronic Solutions Professionals
http://www.elecsp.com/

Epimedia, Inc.
http://epimedia.com/

Future World Communications & Commerce, Inc.
http://www.fwcc.com/~fwccinc/

HellasNet
http://hellasnet.net/

Icon Services, Inc.
http://www.iconservices.com/

ICONN
http://www.iconn.com/

Imagination, Un-Ltd
http://iul.com/beardwww/1iuhome.htm

InfoTrends Group, Inc.
http://www.infotrends.com/

■ Directory of Internet Presence Providers

Innovative Desktop
http://www.capitalcity.com/Innovative/

Internet Expressions, Inc.
http://www.iexp.com/

Marple Info Services
http://www.marpleinfo.com/home.html

Nocturnal Images Multimedia Development Group
http://www.cybercitypa.com/NI/images.html

North East Web
http://www.northeastweb.com/index.html

PA-Downtown
http://pa-downtown.com/

Pocono Mall
http://www.poconomall.com/

WebWorks, Inc.
http://www.citipage.com/webworks/index.html

Western Pennsylvania Internet Connection
http://www.wpic.com/

World Anthem Technologies Inc.
http://www.worldanthem.com/

Rhode Island

College Hill Internet Consultants
http://www.collegehill.com/

DK Technologies
http://users.aol.com/dkwww/dk.htm

Directory of Internet Presence Providers ■

Rhode Island Internet
http://www.bitsandpcs.com/

Rhode Island Online Business Center (RIOBC)
http://www.riobc.com/

Spider Technology
http://www.spidertech.com/spidertech/spider.htm

South Carolina

Beachside
http://www.beachside.com/

Business Gateway
http://www.businessgateway.com/

Byte Concepts
http://abacus-mall.com/byteco/

CC Communications, Inc.
http://www.webcom.com/~cccomm/welcome.html

Conterra Communications, Inc.
http://www.conterra.com/

In Touch Technologies
http://www.awod.com/gallery/wgd/intouch/index.html

Innova.NET
http://www.innova.net/

InteliSys Technologica, Inc.
http://www.intelinet.net/

IQ World Wide Cat
http://www.iqcat.com/

■ Directory of Internet Presence Providers

Pride
http://www.pride-net.com/

Renaissance Interactive©, Inc.
http://www.ricommunity.com/renaissance/

South Carolina Systems and Services, Inc.
http://www.awod.com/gallery/wgd/scss/

Tennessee

Apex Internet Web Services
http://www.concentric.net/~ape47/index.htm

Check the Net
http://www.checkthenet.com/

DATANET
http://diint.datatek.com/datatek/sales/datatnet.htm

Eclipse
http://www.epmall.com/intro.html

Internet Services of West Tennessee
http://www.iswt.com/

Tennessee Web, Inc.
http://www.tennweb.com/twi

Tennessee.com
http://www.tennessee.com/

Texas

All Information Systems
http://allinfosys.com/

Directory of Internet Presence Providers ■

Anacom Merchant Services
http://www.anacom.com/

BestWeb
http://www.best-net.com/webspace

BizPro, Inc. Online Business Services
http://www.bizpro.com

CyberNet Marketing Group
http://www.eyemart.com/

data.net communications
http://www.data.net/

DFW Internet Services, Inc.
http://www.dfw.net/

Etex Intelenet
http://www.etex.net/

Ikebana Net, Inc.
http://www.ikebana.com/

Inter-Info
http://www.inter-info.com/

InterCity Services
http://www.icmall.com/icm_info.html

Internet Publishing Technologies
http://www.ipt.com/

Jerry McGhee & Associates
http://www.ccsi.com/yeeha/jma/jma.html

MarketBase Advertising & Marketing
http://numedia.tddc.net/MB/

◼ Directory of Internet Presence Providers

Network Communications International
http://www.n-c-i.com/

Powerline Resource Systems
http://plainview.com/

StarNet Online Services
http://www.1starnet.com/

Texas Hill Country
http://www.hconline.com/

WebNet Technologies, Inc.
http://webnet.pic.net/

WEBTex Technolgies
http://webtex.arn.net/

WebWize Internet Marketing Group
http://www.oneenterweb.com/

WebWright
http://www.wwwright.com/

White Hawk Productions
http://www.whitehawk.com/

Worldwide Business Systems
http://setexas.com/

Vermont

Vermont Internet
http://www.vermontinc.com/

A Very Vermont Store
http://www.veryvermont.com/store/

Viamar Internet Solutions
http://www.greenmtns.com/

Directory of Internet Presence Providers ■

Virginia

Bentoni Enterprises
http://www.bentoni.com/

Circa Industries
http://www.circa3k.com/

CurBet Communications
http://www.curbet.com/

First Avenue USA
http://www.firstaveusa.com/shop/

Genius, Inc.
http://www.genius-inc.com/

Irongate Networks, Inc.
http://www.irongate.com/

LiveNet
http://cappslivnet.com/

MEG Productions
http://www.megnet.com/

MohrWeb Creations
http://www.mohrweb.com/

OneEarth WWW Publishing
http://www.1earth.com/1e/

Panacea Consulting, Inc.
http://www.panatech.com/

SFS/Netready
http://www.netready.com/

■ Directory of Internet Presence Providers

Shenandoah Web Works
http://www.shenwebworks.com/

Sierra Multimedia Productions of Northern Virginia
http://www.sierramm.com/

SilverTree Internet Marketing
http://www.silvertree.com/

Summit Communications of Virginia
http://www.summit.net/

Virginia Net Corporation
http://www.va.net/

Washington

64k Internet Marketing
http://www.wolfe.net/~uujim/64k/64kpro.htm

Aslan Web Design
http://www.aa.net/~gregfam/aslan.htm

Carney, Hood, and Pancost, Inc.
http://www.accessnow.com/welcome.html

Imagine Web Design
http://www.olympus.net/biz/imagine/designf.htm

Info-Matic
http://www.info-matic.com/

LC Systems
http://www.lcsystems.com/index.htm

mcguire.com
http://www.mcguire.com/

Directory of Internet Presence Providers ■

Northwest Destinations
http://www.nwdestinations.com/

Northwest Internet Access, Inc.
http://www.nwinternet.com/

Northwest RAINet, Inc.
http://www.nwrain.net/

Pacific Northwest Region Virtual Village
http://www.tscnet.com/region.html

Palazzo deMix
http://www.palazzo.com/

QualData, Inc.
http://www.qualdata.com/

StratMan Associates, Inc.
http://www.stratman.com/

UltraPLEX Information Systems
http://www.uplex.net/

Washington World Wide Web
http://washweb.com/

Web Eye Technologies
http://www.wet.net/

Washington, D.C.

Buccaneer Systems
http://www.snm.com/

Clara Vista Corp.
http://www.fiesta.com/CVista/

■ Directory of Internet Presence Providers

CyberByte Electronic Storefronts
http://www.cyber-byte.com/stores/

DCWWW
http://dcwww.com/

En Route Information Highway
http://www.cais.com/eih/

I-Link, Inc.
http://i-linkcom.com/

Internet/WWW Consulting, Training, and Marketing
http://www.shore.net/~adfx/1690/1690.html

Interscape Systems Limited
http://www.charm.net/~iscape/

Millennium
http://www.milcom.com/

Next Generation
http://www.ngen.com/nextgen/home.html

NextWave Communications
http://www.next-wave.com/next-wave/

Offer Enterprises
http://www.offer-ent.com/

Our Internet Connection (OIC)
http://www.cais.com/oic/

Pixel Eyes, Inc.
http://www.pixeleyes.com

Proxima, Inc.
http://www.proxima.com/

Directory of Internet Presence Providers ■

TCCM Design
http://www.albany.net/~tricity/tccm.html

Warner Group
http://a092.sysplan.com/

Westlake Solutions Internet Training
http://www.westlake.com/

WizardNet
http://design.wizard.net/

West Virginia

Web by Areacode
http://www.areacode.com/

West Virginia Online
http://www.westvirginia.com/

Wisconsin

CyberSpace Mall
http://members.aol.com/ozmall/themall/index.html

Doyle Web Design
http://www.doyleweb.com/

FocalNet
http://www.focal.net/

Internet Presence Marketing, Inc.
http://www.ipmi.com/

On Line Design
http://www.genevaonline.com/~beaulieu/old.html

QCPRO.COM
http://qcpro.com/

■ Directory of Internet Presence Providers

Wyoming

Praxis Internet Services
http://www.pxs.com/index.html

Wyoming Cybermall
http://www.pxs.com/cybermall/

COMPARISON
CHART
V

DIRECTORY OF
WEB DESIGNERS

The following is a partial listing of Web designers compiled from various Internet sources.

Directory of Web Designers ■

Alabama

Web Design Publishing Company
http://www.webdzyne.com/

Arizona

Hundred Acre Woods Publishing
http://biz.rtd.com/hawp/

California

Com 4 Productions
http://victorvalley.com/rdws/

Epsilon
http://www.epsilon.net/

Ideaweb
http://www.ideaweb.com/

ISYS Global Internet Solutions
http://www.isys-web.com/

Netcetera Digital Media
http://www.netcetera.net/

The Noble Group
http://www.noblegroup.com/

Virtual Integrators, Inc.
http://www.integrators.com/

World Wide Network Marketing
http://wwnm.com/

■ Directory of Web Designers

Delaware

AdLynx of Delaware
http://www.adlynxcorp.com/

Summit Data Services, Inc.
http://www.summitdatasrv.com/

Florida

East Coast Networking
http://www.goldenknights.com/

World Class Ads by Muttnjef
http://www.muttnjef.com/

Illinois

Black Dog Design Co.
http://www.dogdesign.com/

Cybering Inc.
http://homepage.interaccess.com/~skatz/cybering.html

CyberShark, Inc.
http://www.sharkattack.com/

Virtual Naperville's CyberWave Development Team
http://www.vrnp.net/cyberwav.htm

Wombat Web Services
http://www.wombatweb.com/

Kansas

M. Design Business Consultants
http://www.tyrell.net/~mdesign/

NET fx Internet Marketing Group
http://www.netfxgroup.com/

Directory of Web Designers ■

Maine

JD Data Systems
http://brunswick.maine.com/people/jddata/

MDJ & Associates
http://www.mdjassoc.com/

StrayDog Publications
http://www.mint.net/straydog/index.html

Word Shop
http://www.agate.net/~wordshop/

Massachusetts

Achieva Software
http://www.achieva.com/

Data Prose
http://www.ultranet.com/~ksimmons/

priZm Image Center
http://www.prizm.com/

Michigan

BITS, Inc.
http://www.binweb.com/

Chase World Wide
http://ic.net/~kchase/cww.html

Digital Diamond Design
http://www.digitalDiamond.com/~saunders/

Eric's Computer Services
http://www.iserv.net/~ericscs/

■ Directory of Web Designers

Freelance Design
http://www.tir.com/~catss/design.htm

Net.Works, Inc.
http://www.rust.net/~network/

Online Marketing Company
http://www.online-marketing.com/

Paradigm Web Development
http://www.rust.net/~paradigm/web.htm

Web Corners
http://www.webcorners.com/

Minnesota

Bison Media
http://www.bisonweb.com/

Infinite Visions
http://www.infinitevisions.com

Mississippi

Hatfield Webpage Inc.
http://oscar.teclink.net/~hatfield/webpage.html

Missouri

Central Missouri Web Designs
http://www.compplus.net/map/

Directory of Web Designers ∎

New Hampshire

Tele-Media Communications
http://tele-media.com/

Web Strat
http://www.webstrat.com/

New Jersey

Advanced Web Creations
http://www.webcreations.com/

Broden Inc.
http://www.broden.com/

Internet Interactive, Inc.
http://www.iqubed.com/

New York

Central New York Home Page
http://www.cnyhomepage.com/

Century Designs
http://www.centurydesigns.com/

ComSite Web Service
http://www.com-site.com/

Jasmin Consulting Corporation
http://www.jasmin.com/

North Carolina

Duck Feet Productions
http://www.duckfeet.com/

Empire Systems Consultants
http://web.sunbelt.net/~esystems/es/es.html

■ Directory of Web Designers

Oklahoma

Internet Creative & Career Services of Oklahoma
http://www.icso.com/

Oregon

Digital Sunrise Web Design
http://www.teleport.com/~chrish

Koala Web Design
http://www.koalaweb.com

WebNW
http://www.webnw.com/

Web World
http://www.webwrld.com/

South Carolina

AnthoDawn Productions
http://www.netside.com/~anthdawn/

Hornet Software
http://www.rivertown.net/~hsoft/

Internet Technologies
http://www.globalvision.net/ITECH/

Tennessee

Home Page Construction & Development
http://www.telalink.net/~blane19/hpconstr.htm

Multi-Media Solutions, Inc.
http://m-media.com/

Directory of Web Designers ■

Texas

B&B Net Services
http://www.cyberramp.net/~cdb/

Bruce White's Web Page Designs
http://www.cyberstation.net/~bdwhite/bdwdes.html

Disk To Document
http://members.aol.com/Disk2d/Disk2Document.html

Hoppy's Webpage Makin'
http://www.geocities.com/SoHo/2893/

Utah

ICIS Web Design and Services
http://www.vii.com/~icis/home.htm

Mariner Enterprises
http://www.zmariner.com/

Utah Wired
http://comnet.com/

WebSetter
http://www.websetter.com/

Vermont

Northwood Industries
http://www.northwd.com/

RayWeb
http://together.net/~raylou/ray1.htm

WebWorks
http://www.together.net/~fatboy/promo.htm

■ Directory of Web Designers

Virginia

CMM—Corcoran Multimedia
http://www.cormedia.com/

The Computer Guy
http://www.erols.com/debic/tcg.html

FreedomNet Developement
http://www.freedomnet.com/home/webdev.htm

Lynch Consulting
http://members.aol.com/LynchCon3/

WebQuest Corporation
http://www.webq.com/

Washington

New Wave Computers
http://www.newwavecomputers.com/3.html

Unified Field Productions
http://www.wwmagic.com/ufp/

Washington Online
http://www.wa-online.com/

Washington, D.C.

AlphaBytes
http://www.paltech.com/alphabytes/

AtomicWeb
http://www.atomicweb.com/

Creative Web Solutions
http://www.erols.com/racich/CWS/

Directory of Web Designers ∎

Hilburn Communications
http://www.dmgi.com/hilburn.html

Image Communications
http://www.imagecomm.com/

Mark Wolinski Designs
http://www.nicom.com/~mrmark/

Palantir Systems, Inc.
http://www.digitaldc.com/

Route 66 Cyberspace East
http://www.info66.com

steveconley
http://www.steveconley.com/

Wordbiz.Net
http://www.wordbiz.com/

COMPARISON
CHART

W

DIRECTORY
OF WEB
CONSULTANTS

Directory of Web Consultants ■

United States

Alabama

Benton Newton & Partners Advertising
http://www.cre8ive.com
Comments: Benton Newton & Partners' CRE8IVE ONLINE is the new media division of the advertising firm. CRE8IVE services include new and traditional marketing and advertising services for corporate and retail clients worldwide.

Infomedia, Inc.
http://www.infomedia.net

Internet Training & Consulting Services
http://www.itcs.com/

Secure America, Inc.
http://www.secure-america.com
Comments: Specializes in consumer alarm consulting and alarm/service company operations development.

Traveller Information Services
http://www.traveller.com/

Arizona

Guerrilla Marketing Strategies
http://www.sedona.net/crubin

Internet Direct, Inc.
http://www.i-site.net

WEB SOLUTIONS
http://gray.cscwc.pima.edu/~smford/solutions.html

■ Directory of Web Consultants

California

A & Z Consulting
http://www.azc.com
Comments: Specializes in budget Web services.

Axis Consulting International, Inc.
http://www.axisus.com

BusinessWare, Inc.
http://www.ni.net/bizware.com

Cerberus Computer Consulting
http://www.cerb.com/

Config.Sys Consulting Group
http://users.aol.com/config/index.html
Comments: Caters to small businesses in San Diego and Los Angeles areas.

DISC (Digital Internet Systems Consultants)
http://www.dis.org/delux/

InTek Consulting Group/Integra, Inc.
http://www.intekinc.com

Internet Consulting Enterprises
http://www.pacificnet.net/~mprice/design.html
Comments: Specializes in interstate electronic commerce/electronic data interchange (EC/EDI) and high-compression full-duplex voice over the Internet.

Internet Literacy Consultants
http://www.matisse.net
Comments: In addition to consulting services, also produces a regular series of Internet seminars in the San Francisco Bay Area.

Internet Trainers and Consultants
http://www.internet-cafe.com/itc/itc.html

Directory of Web Consultants ■

InVision Consulting
http://www.iconsulting.com/

JDS Communications
http://www.jdscomm.com/index.html

Melnick Consulting Group
http://www.melnick.com

Michael Leonard Computer Consultant
http://www.electriciti.com/~mikeleo/index.html

Milligan Consulting Services
http://nmcs.clever.net

Mitra internet consultants
http://earth.path.net/mitra
Comments: Specializes in large complex systems with large numbers of users or information providers. Owner built America Online's gateway to Gopher and WAIS.

MKB Internet Consulting
http://www.ucsd.edu/mbreen

National Consultant Referrals, Inc.
http://www.cts.com/~kline/index.html
Comments: A consultant referral service that provides free referrals to prospective clients. Not solely concerned with Internet consultants.

Nutmeg Web Design and Consulting
http://www.unc.edu/~juliette/nutmeg_www.html

Paul Franklin Computer Consulting
http://www.well.com/www/pfrankli

Primus Consulting, Inc.
http://www.primus.com/

■ Directory of Web Consultants

RTN Computer Consultants Inc.
http://www.mind.net/rtn
Comments: Provides multilingual (Italian, French, Spanish, English) Web administration and development of Web servers/pages and marketing strateigies.

SystemGate Consulting
http://www.paclink.net/sysgate.htm
Comments: Provides consulting services in Southern California.

VirtualNet Consulting
http://www.virtual.net

Webdancers
http://www.mlode.com/~dancers/

Colorado

Banister Consulting
http://www.banister.com

On-Line Consulting
http://www.on-line.com/
Comments: Specializes in Windows NT Internet server systems designed specifically to meet your needs.

The Teahouse of Experience
http://www.csn.net/~grifftoe/
Comments: Helps clients create their own tools for working with the new information technologies; also offers consulting, design, development, implementation, and training services, specializing in hypermedia training.

Connecticut

Eldar Co.
http://eldarco.com

Imhotep Consulting
http://www.acsysweb.com/imhotep

Directory of Web Consultants ■

Mihelson & Co.
http://www.mihelson.com

Schroth Systems Consulting, Inc.
http://www.connix.com/~dschroth/
Comments: Provides custom applications in Access and FoxPro, PC and network support, Internet applications, and consulting.

Delaware

Dragon's Run Engineering & Research, Inc.
http://www.dragons.com
Comments: Provides technical consulting, software and hardware design services, and WWW services for the Macintosh environment. Offers 24-hour tech support.

iNet Communications
http://www.inet.net

Florida

ABV Computer Consulting
http://www.abv.com

AdverNet Internet Consultants
http://www.polaris.net/~advernet/

Dillon-Brew Consulting
http://www.polaris.net/~steved

Entertainment Consultants of Florida
http://www.accessorl.net/~shore/
Comments: Specializes in enhanced Web site development for complicated projects, including animations, music, databases (Oracle, Windows NT, Unix, custom/copyrightable), tables, and forms.

Gerald Green Consulting, Inc.
http://www.shadow.net/~grgreen

■ Directory of Web Consultants

Information Strategies
http://www.info-strategies.com
Comments: Facilitates the migration of small business cultures to the Internet culture by providing tutoring, education, referrals, consulting, Web page assistance, industry updates, and contract online research services.

International Consulting and Marketing Group, Inc.
http://www.bellnet.com/ICMG.htm
Comments: Provides Internet consulting and marketing, Web page preparation and design, and interactive business presentations. Their Web server is bilingual (English-German).

Internet Professionals, Inc.
http://www.nettally.com/Internet_Pros

Laser Consultants, Inc.
http://www.iu.net/lcijupiter/

021 Internet Consulting
http://www.worldpub.com/021

SPC Consultants
http://www.web2000.net

Georgia

Aaron Scott Internet Consultants
http://www.newsouth.com/014/asic.html

Compass Internet Consulting
http://www.nav.com/welcome/home.html

Integrated Consulting Group
http://www.icg-inc.com/~icg/

InTek Consulting Group, Inc./InTraWEB Communications
http://dev-com.com/~intekcg/icghome.htm

Directory of Web Consultants ■

Internet Connect
http://www.iccusa.com

Tech Direct, Inc.
http://www.techdirect.com

Hawaii

MLH Consulting
http://www.aloha.com/~mlh

Illinois

Adamson Consulting
http://www.adamson.com
Comments: Provides affordable Web site creation, maintenance, and hosting for small to medium-sized businesses.

net.WORTH consulting
http://www.misha.net/biz/net.WORTH

Superhighway Consulting
http://www.stpt.com/shc/
Comments: Specializes in utilizing the Internet for marketing or advertising purposes.

Synasoft Consulting Group
http://www.intelli.com/synasoft

Indiana

Data Communications Consulting, Inc.
http://www.dccinc.com
Comments: Offers full Internet services, including interface development to databases and other information retrieval systems, to corporate clients.

EZComm Consulting
http://www.ezcomm.com/

■ Directory of Web Consultants

Louisiana

Telemanagement Systems of America (TSA)
http://www.neworleans.com/
Comments: Specializes in Internet and WWW consulting for the hospitality, tourism, and special events industries.

Maryland

Genix Information Technologies
http://ubmail.ubalt.edu/~fgorton/genix.html

Porter Consulting Group
http://www.webtek.com/porter
Comments: Specializes in individual and small group training on the WWW, with special emphasis on government databases.

Triad Consulting, Inc.
http://www.corsair.com

Massachusetts

JNC Consulting & Design
http://www.tiac.net/users/jimt/jnc.html

Lara Consulting Group
http://www.lara.com/

Luminaire System Consulting
http://www.luminaire.com

North Sea Consulting
http://www.northsea.com

Shea Consulting
http://www.ultranet.com/~rshea/
Comments: Provides Internet connectivity consulting, Web page authoring, network design consulting, and marketing plan development for the Boston area.

Directory of Web Consultants ■

S.J.S. Consulting
http://www.sjs.com

Tucker Street Associates
http://www.tuckerstreet.com

Wagner Rios Communications Consultants
http://www.troubador.com/wrcc/welcome.htm
Comments: Specializes in Internet advertisement and sales.

Michigan

Johnson Consulting Network—JCN
http://www.jcn.com

Minnesota

5J's Computer Consulting Corporation
http://www.ties.k12.mn.us/~jensen/

Vitus Computer Consulting
http://www.winternet.com/~vitus/

Missouri

National Consulting Service
http://www.ncscorp.com/

Montana

CyberWorld Consulting
http://www.cw2.com

Nevada

Hundred Acre Consulting
http://www.pooh.com/
Comments: Specializes in real-time embedded systems, Unix, GNU software, networking, and Windows.

■ Directory of Web Consultants

New Jersey

Double Precision Publishing
http://www.doubleprecision.com

Gaw Information Systems
http://www.gaw.com/

Kevin Shea Internet Consulting
http://gramercy.ios.com/~telres/consult/consult.html

Sky Web Inc.
http://www.skyweb.net

Teamwork Internet Management
http://www.eclipse.net/~teamwork/

New Mexico

Computer Systems Consulting
http://www.spy.org/
Comments: Specializes in BSD Unix, Unix computer security, and Internet access and use. Also provides a public-access Internet site, the SPYBBS, located in Santa Fe, New Mexico.

NeuroMunch Internet Consultants
http://www.greatwhite.com

New York

AMMI World Wide Web Consultants
http://ammi.com

BBN Internetwork Consulting & Engineering
http://flippet.bbn.com

Design & Disaster Recovery Consulting
http://www.disaster.com

FS Consulting
http://wais.hs.jhu.edu:8000
Comments: Specializes in the development and installation of information retrieval systems based on WAIS (wide area information server), Z39.50, and HTTP protocol technology.

Ingress Consulting Group
http://www.ingres.com
Comments: Provides network security consulting and installation and support of the BorderWare firewall server.

Internet Consulting Corporation
http://www.icons.com/

Jasmin Consulting Corporation
http://www.jasmin.com/

Objective Consulting, Inc.
http://www.spiders.com/

Ohio

AAA My Mac To You Web Page Design
http://www.en.com/users/william/clients.html

New Age Consulting Services
http://www.nacs.net

Oklahoma

Phoenix Consulting, L.L.C.
http://www.phxcon.com
Comments: Specializes in electronic commerce, including EDI, offering both EC consulting services and systems integration (LAN, WAN, Internet).

■ Directory of Web Consultants

Oregon

Audio First
http://www.audiofirst.com/
Comments: Specializes in digital audio applications for the Web.

Gilchrist & Associates
http://www.gilchrist.com

Harvest Computer Consulting
http://www.chehalem.com/~bljoyce/harvest.shtml

Netogether.com
http://netogether.com/

The PC Consultant
http://www.lookup.com/Homepages/52668/home.html

RF Consulting
http://www.csos.orst.edu/~kenneke
Comments: Specializes in networking support for broadcasters (radio, television, and so on). Also provides a full range of engineering services for radio stations, including Digital Audio workstations, automation services, and others.

Wolfenstein Consulting
http://www.teleport.com/~wc
Comments: Provides significant discounts to nonprofit agencies.

Pennsylvania

Allwilk Consulting
http://www.allwilk.com/

Get Online!
http://www.lm.com/~lmann/online/online.html

Internet Mentoring & Research Services
http://www.libertynet.org/~IMRS
Comments: Specializes in teaching beginners how to navigate the Internet using advanced search techniques.

Directory of Web Consultants ■

Martin Consulting
http://www.nauticom.net/www/heather
Comments: Provides Internet documentation and training materials, both paper-based and electronic.

Rhode Island

O'Hara Consulting Services
http://ids.net/~ohara/home.html
Comments: Provides computer consulting services for Unix- and DOS/Windows-based networks; serves the southeastern New England area.

South Carolina

Computer Consultants Group
http://www.awod.com/gallery/wgd/ebnet/

Tennessee

Knox Consulting Group
http://www.cdc.net/~tknox

Texas

iNTernet Consulting & Marketing Services
http://www.cyberdom.com/ic&ms/ic&ms.htm

LWLutz WWWeb Design & Consultants
http://www.tripod.com/~lwlutz/

Gordon E. Peterson II
http://www.computek.net/public/gep2/

WebPageDesign & Consulting
http://www.webpagedesign.com

Zilker Internet Park
http://www.zilker.net
Comments: Offers Internet access in Austin, Texas, with local support staff.

■ Directory of Web Consultants

Utah

Yet Another Computer Consultant (Y.A.C.C.)
http://cybersphere.indirect.com/

Washington

CompuServe/SPRY, Inc. Consulting Group
http://www.dealernet.com

Fractal Internet Consulting
http://www.eskimo.com/~fractal

Ian Freed Consulting, Inc.
http://www.ifc.com/

ImageLinc Internet Design Consultants
http://imagelinc.com

Inter/Edit Consulting
http://www.iea.com/~jdavis/
Comments: Specializes in editorial, writing, and research services for Internet needs assessments, Internet business plans, online searches, analyses of Internet tools, and Web home pages.

Washington, D.C.

Datamax Corporation
http://www.dmax.com/

Ideal Computer Strategies
http://www.icstrategies.com

J.M. Young and Associates
http://www.xmission.com/~gastown/goldpages/training.htm

West Virginia

Twisted Pair Services
http://www.twisted.pair.com/

Directory of Web Consultants ∎

International

Australia

Tusra Internet Consultants
http://www.ocemail.com.au

WebArts
http://www.webarts.net.au

Canada

British Columbia
AIM Consulting
http://www.webcinc.com

Enternet Systems Consulting
http://entersys.net

G.F.Currie Consulting
http://www.netbistro.com/gfc/consult.html

Todd Logan Computer Consulting
http://matrix.infomatch.com/~todd/
Comments: Specializes in Internet software configuration and training for the Macintosh.

Nova Scotia
Cowper Computer Consultants
http://www.atcon.com

Sarge Computer Consultants
http://www.atcon.com/HPD/hpd.htm
Comments: Specializes in the development and implementation of Internet strategies for the law enforcement community.

■ Directory of Web Consultants

Ontario

Akedi Computer Consultants
http://ourworld.compuserve.com/homepages/Akedi

Datacalc Computer Consultants Corporation
http://www.valuenetwork.com/business/datacalc.html

Finite Systems Consulting (FSC)
http://www.finite-systems.com/fsc
Comments: Toronto-based firm provides a broad range of Internet and World Wide Web-related services to corporate and public-sector clients throughout Canada and the northeastern USA.

G.W. Loukes Consulting Services
http://www.sentex.net/~gloukes/

Quebec

A1 Web Page Promotion & Advertising Services
http://www.a1co.com/promo.html

France

Hervé Schauer Consultants (HSC)
http://www.freenix.fr/~schauer/hsc/
Comments: Specializes in Unix, TCP/IP, and Internet security issues.

Germany

Light Speed Consulting
http://www.cs.tu-berlin/~stefan/LSC2.htm

Hong Kong

WebZone Consultants Co.
http://www.hk.super.net/~webzone/webzone.html

Directory of Web Consultants

Ireland

Silmaril Consultants
http://www.ucc.ie/info/TeX/tug/people/pfcv.html

Israel

VR Systems & Consulting
http://www.atw.fullfeed.com:80/emporium/index.html

Japan

Web Japanese Assistance Consultant
http://web.kyoto-inet.or.jp/people/akazawa/
Comments: Primarily offers English/Japanese translation of your Web pages.

Malaysia

RAYMA Management Consultants, MALAYSIA
http://www.ibmpcug.co.uk/~ecs/business/rayma.htm

New Zealand

OaSIS Internet Services
http://www.oasis.co.nz

Singapore

JCMT Services
http://www.jcmt.com/jcmt
Comments: Provides authoring services for businesses targeting the Asian and Japanese markets. Provides translatation services and advertising copy for Web pages in Japanese, Korean, and Chinese.

McGallen & Bolden International Consulting Inc.
http://www.mcgallen.aus.net/
Comments: Web site provides Asian content and consulting programs.

■ Directory of Web Consultants

South Africa

Dragnet Internet Marketing Consultants
http://www.pix.za/dragnet/
Comments: Primarily serves the South African market, but also provides consulting for overseas clients.

Switzerland

InterPublish Consulting
http://www.geopages.com/SiliconValley/2127/

United Kingdom

Advanced Systems Consultants Ltd
http://www.advsys.co.uk

Herne Consultants Limited
http://dspace.dial.pipex.com/town/square/gc18/

Midnight Consultants
http://www.hhcl.com/rael/rael.html

COMPARISON CHART

X

ISDN PROVIDERS

X.1   ISDN Providers ■

Region	Primary ISDN Provider	Monthly Fee	Address/Phone
SOUTH:			
Alabama, Florida, Georgia, Kentucky, Louisiana, Mississippi, North Carolina, South Carolina, Tennessee	Bell South	$95 flat rate	http://www.bst.bls.com/ 1-800-858-9413
NORTHERN PLAINS & SOUTHWEST:			
Arizona, Colorado, Idaho, Iowa, Minnesota, Montana, Nebraska, New Mexico, North Dakota, Oregon, South Dakota, Utah, Washington, Wyoming	U.S. West	$70 per month plus usage fee after 30 hours	http://www.uswest.com/isdn/ (303) 965-7073
SOUTHERN PLAINS:			
Arkansas, Kansas, Missouri, Oklahoma, Texas	Southwestern Bell	$57.80 flat rate	http://www.sbcl.com 1-800-992-4736
FAR WEST:			
California, Nevada	Pacific Bell	$24.50 plus usage	http://www.pacbell.com/ 1-800-472-4736
NORTHEAST:			
Connecticut, Delaware, Maine, Massachusetts, New Hampshire, New York, Rhode Island, Vermont	NYNEX	$35 flat rate	http://www.nynex.com/ 1-800-438-4736
HAWAII:			
	GTE	$40–50 plus usage	http://www.gte.com/ 1-800-483-4926
GREAT LAKES:			
Illinois, Indiana, Michigan, Ohio, Wisconsin	Ameritech	$32–106 plus usage	http://www.ameritech.com/ 1-800-832-6328
MID-ATLANTIC:			
Maryland, New Jersey, Pennsylvania, Virginia, Washington, D.C., West Virginia	Bell Atlantic	$19.50 plus usage	http://www.ba.com/ 1-800-570-4736

Y—Yes   N—No   N/A—Not applicable   INA—Information not available

End ■

INDEX

INDEX

INDEX

INDEX

INDEX

INDEX

INDEX